ADVANCING U.S. LATINO ENTREPRENEURSHIP

ADVANCING U.S. LATINO ENTREPRENEURSHIP

A New National Economic Imperative

Edited by
Marlene Orozco, Alfonso Morales,
Michael J. Pisani, and Jerry I. Porras

Purdue University Press · West Lafayette, Indiana

Cataloging-in-Publication Data is on file with the Library of Congress.
Paper ISBN: 978-1-55753-937-3
epub ISBN: 978-1-55753-939-7
epdf ISBN: 978-1-55753-938-0

Cover photos
Maria Urena, copyright Alyson Aliano Photography
Tony Aguilar, copyright Julia Robinson
Jessica A. Acosta, copyright Stanford Graduate School of Business

To Jerry I. Porras for his vision on strengthening the U.S. economy by focusing on scaling Latino-owned businesses and his participation in creating both the Latino Business Action Network and the Stanford Latino Entrepreneurship Initiative.

Contents

Acknowledgments

We would like to thank the Stanford Latino Entrepreneurship Initiative (SLEI) and the current and former staff who lead the research program and the education scaling program as well as the Latino Business Action Network (LBAN) for its leadership in harnessing the power of business leaders across the country and for its financial support to SLEI's research efforts, alongside its principal partners, 21st Century Fox, Wells Fargo, John Arrillaga, Pitch Johnson, and the Chavez Family Foundation. We would also like to thank Purdue University Press for making this volume possible and all of the book contributors for engaging in thoughtful scholarship with SLEI for the past few years. SLEI has collected annual survey data made possible by the generosity of Latino business owners across the country who provide their time in completing our detailed surveys, including those who participate in the SLEI-Education Scaling program. Together we have formed a community of scholars and business leaders working to advance the study and knowledge of Latino-owned businesses.

As this book went to press, the SLEI family was saddened by the news of the untimely death of Dr. John Sargent, professor of international business and entrepreneurship at the University of Texas Rio Grande Valley (Edinburg, TX). John and wife, Linda Matthews, authored the chapter on "Mexican American Founder Narratives at High-Growth Firms on the South Texas–Mexican Border" contained in this volume. John was a lifetime student of business and economic phenomena in Mexico, Latin America, the Texas–Mexico borderlands, and of Latinos in the USA with publications in leading outlets (i.e., *Journal of World Business*, *World Development*, *Journal of Business Ethics*, and *Journal of Borderlands Studies*). John served as a mentor to many scores of students in Latino South Texas, sharing his deep knowledge of maquiladoras, supply chains, innovation, skill development, and more recently of business founders and Latino entrepreneurship. His scholarship, good nature, and friendship will be missed.   —The Editors

Latino Entrepreneurs: Challenges and Opportunities

Paul Oyer

The Mary and Rankine Van Anda Entrepreneurial Professor
Faculty Director, Stanford Latino Entrepreneurship Initiative
Stanford University, Graduate School of Business

The health and growth of the U.S. economy increasingly relies on the health and growth of the economic fortunes of the country's Latino population. Latinos are now the second fastest-growing ethnic group (after Asians) and the largest "minority" group in the United States. Latinos are likely to continue to grow in importance given immigration patterns (though these are increasingly unpredictable), the young average age of the Latino population, and the relatively high birth rate among Latinos. Historically, Latinos' role in the economy was heavily concentrated in certain areas such as southern Florida and southern California, but Latinos have become a sizable demographic group throughout most of the country.

So, simply due to its size and growth, the Latino population is a substantial part of our overall economy and is important to businesses, policy makers, and the entire country given the interconnections of the economy. It is worth noting that if American Latinos were their own separate country, they would be the seventh-largest economy in the world with a gross domestic product roughly equal to the 1.3 billion people in India (Schink and Hayes-Bautista 2017).

While Latinos are an important part of the U.S. economy, the group on balance is in a precarious position. At the entrepreneurship level, Latinos own businesses at a lower rate than the rest of the population. But the economic challenges to the Latino community go well beyond entrepreneurship, given that the average Latino household has less than one-fifth the wealth of a typical American household and earns about 46 cents on the dollar relative to the broader population (Dettling et al. 2017). These differences reflect underlying differences in education and other factors: as the labor market value of skill and education has increased in recent decades, the Latino population has had difficulty holding onto its relative standing in the U.S. economy.

The Stanford Latino Entrepreneurship Initiative (SLEI) and the contributors to this book are interested in understanding how entrepreneurship can play a role in developing the economic fortunes of American Latinos. In SLEI's 2017 State of Latino Entrepreneurship (SOLE) report, we published figures and statistics that highlight the current challenges of Latinos while also showing some signs of hope that Latino entrepreneurship is growing and is poised for future growth that will contribute to the economic development of Latinos.

Figure P.1, which is taken from the 2017 SOLE report, gives a graphical representation of some of the basic facts and shows causes for both concern and optimism. The top line on the graph reinforces the growth of the Latino population, which has more than doubled as a share of Americans in the last three decades. However, note that Latinos are significantly underrepresented as business owners. The share of businesses that are owned by Latinos is much lower than Latinos' share of the population, and the share of larger firms ("employer" firms, meaning firms that have employees beyond the owner) is about a third of the share of Latinos in the population. In other words, an important contributing factor to the

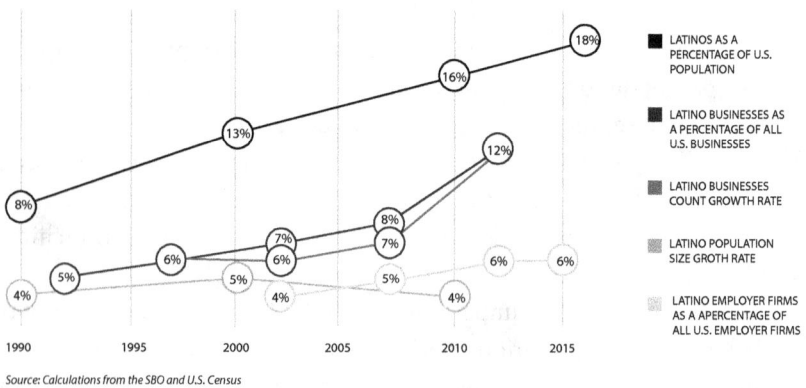

Source: Calculations from the SBO and U.S. Census

Figure P.1 Latino population and businesses in the U.S. (Source: Calculations from the SBO and U.S. Census.

difference in household wealth between Latino and non-Latino households appears to be that Latinos are much less likely to hold an ownership stake in a business.

The graph also suggests a hopeful side, as trends may be moving more in Latinos' favor. Latinos are clearly growing as a share of the population but are growing even faster as a share of business owners. So, the gap between the Latino population share and the share of businesses owned by Latinos appears to be closing in recent years. As the 2017 SOLE report details, the growth rate of Latino larger firms (those that employ workers beyond the founder) from 2007 to 2015 was robust and much faster than the growth rate for non-Latino firms with employees. In addition, the 2017 SOLE report provides optimistic statistics regarding success of Latino millennial entrepreneurs in starting businesses that are scaling successfully. Overall, as discussed in the SOLE report and in the chapter in this volume by SLEI researchers Marlene Orozco and Iliana Perez, there are as many as 5 million Latino-owned businesses in the United States. Thus, in terms of sheer numbers these businesses are a large economic force. While Latino business ownership and entrepreneurship lags the population as a whole, there is reason to think that the gap is closing.

So, why do Latinos lag in entrepreneurship and business ownership? And how do we help the Latino community continue to close the gap and become a more significant share of the ownership of businesses? This book provides some insight into those questions by looking at Latino entrepreneurship from many perspectives.

At a nationwide societal level, the differences we see between Latino and non-Latino ownership and assets reflect the fundamental differences in opportunity that exist for children (and adults, for that matter) based on where they are born and the circumstances in which they grow up. A lot of great work being done by social scientists shows that inequality has grown dramatically in the United States in recent decades and that socioeconomic upward mobility has slowed. Much of this is reinforced by differences in opportunity early in life. Addressing those concerns is beyond the scope of this book, as it requires a broad effort to ensure that Latino children, whether immigrant or native-born, have the tools they need to compete in the economy of the future.

But what can we do in the shorter term and more specifically focus on the entrepreneurship world? The SOLE report and the research in this volume show that there is a lack of preparedness for Latino entrepreneurs compared to other entrepreneurs. A substantial number of existing and potential Latino entrepreneurs are not properly equipped to open and grow businesses. They do not have proper business plans, procedures in place, and financial statements that are required to access capital, work with agencies such as the Small Business Administration, and grow a business. Latino entrepreneurs need to build and expand their networks to find more support and figure out how to better exploit the fact that they are, according to our SOLE report, more international than other businesses.

This book presents an excellent and detailed set of studies of both the big and the focused pictures of Latino entrepreneurship. The approaches taken by the authors are highly varied. As the Latino population is itself extremely heterogeneous, with important differences in country of origin, migration history and settlement patterns, and local/regional political and economic conditions, the wide range of chapters in the volume captures some of this diversity. The message of all the chapters in this volume and other analyses of Latino entrepreneurs is that Latino businesses face gaps in terms of being underrepresented overall, small, relatively unsophisticated, and underfinanced. They also face the additional challenges that as income inequality has increased dramatically in recent decades, many Latinos have been left behind, and Latino entrepreneurs, like all entrepreneurs, face the fact that business creation levels have slowed.

But the work in this book and elsewhere also paints a positive path in the future because some trends are in the right direction. The startup rate for Latinos is higher than for other groups (so they are catching up), and the younger generation of Latino entrepreneurs is making progress in starting businesses that will scale.

I hope this book will spark additional interest in the topic of entrepreneurship in the Latino community. I am hopeful that the research in this book and the research it spawns will influence policy discussions as policy makers try to help Latino entrepreneurs—and entrepreneurs of all types—create wealth and value in our economy. The findings have the potential to inform economic policy, giving policy makers an arsenal of data with which to critically assess existing policies and develop more effective policies. The chapters in the book can also contribute to scholarship by providing findings to assist scholars in arbitrating between competing theories about how and why specific conditions influence Latino entrepreneurship.

REFERENCES

Dettling, Lisa J., Joanne W. Hsu, Lindsay Jacobs, Kevin B. Moore, and Jeffrey P. Thompson. 2017. "Recent Trends in Wealth-Holding by Race and Ethnicity: Evidence from the Survey of Consumer Finances." *FEDS Notes.*

Schink, Werner, and David Hayes-Bautista. 2017. "Latino Gross Domestic Product (GDP) Report." *Latino Donor Collaborative.*

PART I

AN INTRODUCTION TO LATINO ENTREPRENEURSHIP—HISTORICAL PERSPECTIVES AND DATA SOURCES

CHAPTER 1

Introduction: Advancing U.S. Latino Entrepreneurship

Marlene Orozco, Alfonso Morales,
Michael J. Pisani, and Jerry I. Porras

What is entrepreneurship? As a fairly recent innovation in economic organization, it is the formation of an organization by way of multiple processes that minimize the risks associated with establishing a business. Shane (2003:4) defines entrepreneurship as "an activity that involves the discovery, evaluation and exploitation of opportunities to introduce new goods and services, ways of organizing, markets, processes, and raw materials through organizing efforts that previously had not existed." Entrepreneurship has also been conceived of as "the pursuit of opportunity beyond resources controlled" (Eisenmann 2013); as exploiting market opportunities, however large or small or at the margins of the economy (Kirzner 1973); as innovation in a dynamic environment that creates and destroys firms (Schumpeter 1912; Schumpeter 1942); and as opportunity or necessity-led self-employment (Williams 2007). Each of these definitions represents observations made of ideas and behaviors in particular social contexts. The definitions represent the interpretation of interaction, and likewise, the notion of *ethnic entrepreneurship* is not static and must conceptually be responsive to context. Let us first consider the entrepreneurship element of this notion.

Entrepreneurship has a long history of usage in describing the management of activities and indeed has only recently come to its particular economic usage. Likewise, the "economic" as independent of households or politics is also a fairly recent creation of modernity (Hirschman 1958). The Greeks consider the *oikos* a matter of managing household consumption, not the creation of goods and services, measured independently of households, politics, and religion (Booth 1993). Modernity complemented our original place-based notion of a market with abstract notions of capital, labor, and land markets as well as a variety of other ideas distinguishing the economy as a distinct institution. However we have measured economic activity, we have never fully separated it from other social institutions. In fact, households, politics, and religion all live in relatively reciprocal relationships with economic activity.

Still, it is this ability to measure that reifies economic activity and makes for analytic techniques to understand the economy and training techniques to hone success in economic activities. This reification allows us to say that generally speaking, capitalist economic organization allocates resources efficiently to clear markets—that is the theory anyway. However, for at least a century, scholars have uncovered two broad types of market distortions: collusion, which impedes efficiency, and discrimination, which impedes transactions that clear markets. Both have been labeled and described as "social constructions" that indicate how the economy is part of society. In fact, the constructivist perspective shows us that what the economist perspective labels "distortions" are, from other perspectives, the way people otherwise ignored by the dominant perspective express their economic ambitions and activities and the people practicing them—that is, how women, ethnic minorities, and their economic practices are structured in the shadow of the larger economy and society. Out of that shadow, we advance this volume.

Our interest is in entrepreneurship as practiced by Latino populations historically and with respect to distinct types of business and scales of analyses. Further, we are also describing organizational tools and analytic techniques for fostering that participation in the broader economy, and thus we are describing the work of the Latino Business Action Network (LBAN) and the creation of the Stanford Latino Entrepreneurship Initiative (SLEI). As an innovative aspect of this volume, we advance a dual-pronged objective of using research evidence to inform current and aspiring entrepreneurs as well as scholarship on ethnic entrepreneurship.

Figure 1.1 illustrates these various relationships by way of a mechanical gear metaphor, each part shifting and contributing to the whole of economic life. The specific opportunity we address is assembling research and tools of engagement that show the world how people of color, specifically Latinos, are the cornerstone of the emerging economy and, further, how programmatic activities are leveraging Latino assets and values across the economy as well as how the economy interfaces with society. The

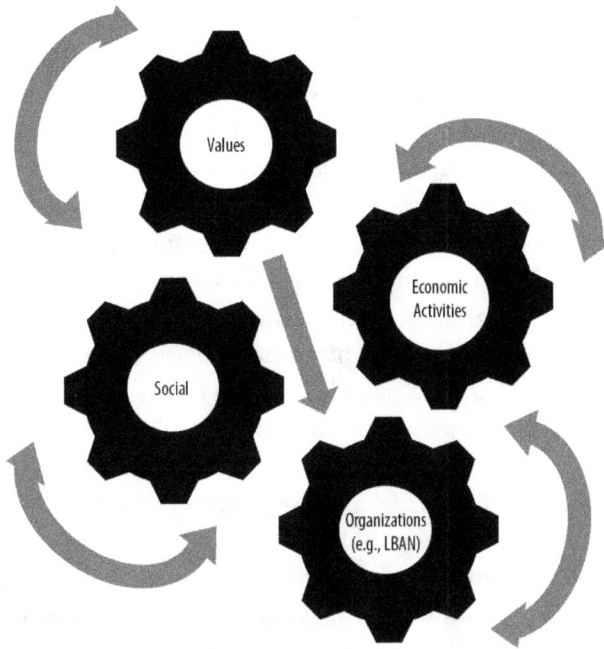

Figure 1.1 Latino entrepreneurship framework.

framework in Figure 1.1 shows that Latino (and broadly human) values are in a reciprocal relationship with economic practices. We purposefully chose what looks like integrated gears to show how values drive economic efforts. However, we must point out that like mechanical gears, there can be some slippage and incomplete meshing of the gears. Likewise, often—as in the case of persons passionately pursuing their business in the service of their family—those gears can be tightly fit, with the work driving entrepreneurs past exhaustion in pursuit of opportunities for their family. Irrespective of interpretation, readers should note that this framework is explicitly constructivist, initiated from broad social values that are refined or complemented by experience and training and implemented in economic activities, specifically businesses. Further, as readers will discover, authors in our collection attend to many questions of scale and scope of business activity and also exhibit a concern with business type and location while also expressing criticism of existing structures of support.

With this in mind, let us now consider the "ethnic" of ethnic entrepreneurship. Defining the ethnic is difficult, as the term's definition varies with historical context. While we might be frustrated by the lack of a stable definition of "Latino," such stability is afforded only to physical sciences and then is often questioned in liminal spaces of analyses as physicists, chemists, and other scientists wrestle with definitional questions. Hence, for us the absence of a stable definition is particularly pernicious, as it impedes policy, itself reliant—at least occasionally—on scientific understanding of social life. However, we are not dismayed, as contingency is the rule, and our effort here extends understanding even if we cannot provide final answers to the question of who is or is not a Latino. This volume does distinguish between race and ethnicity but also works with or combines the study of race and ethnicity. Furthermore, when possible authors consider both the meso-level group processes and the macro- or structural-level processes at play that condition life chances (Valdez and Golash-Boza 2017). It is not our position that the concepts of ethnicity and race are interchangeable, as these projects often come from distinct vantage points. As noted by Valdez and Golash Boza (2017), the ethnicity paradigm is often one of inclusion, whereas the racial paradigm is one of exclusion. What we do wish to make clear here is that authors are often confined to other scientists' definitions in the collection of data, and thus there are not only first-order questions of identity but also second-order questions of interpreting data collected in different sociohistorical circumstances and for uses that never mesh perfectly with the authors' problem.

Thus, readers will find in these chapters a creative variety of approaches to the presence or definition of "Latino." Some authors infer presence in one set of data from another (Robles, Morales, and Pisani, Chapter 4), others offer calculations of degree (Pisani and Guzman, Chapter 10), and still others suggest that conformity to existing definitions is sufficient to their chosen task. For us, "Latino" is in part a construction of power relationships and the imposition of categories and in part a self-construction of an "imagined community" (Anderson 1983). At the heart of each is interaction—interactions from which participants learn, impart learning to others, and change what is learned over time. Ultimately we offer no universally applicable definition, instead reminding readers that the appropriate definition will vary by the authors' purposes, the questions they seek to answer, or the arguments they wish to evince. As such, however important the imposition of a label, equally important can be the response. We acknowledge that the ambiguity of pan-ethnic labels such as "Hispanic" and "Latino" forge categorizations constructed by a variety of stakeholders to meet their strategic interests (Mora 2014). We are concerned here with entrepreneurship that pertains to a specific ethnic group: Latino entrepreneurs.

Clearly, in this sociohistoric moment, entrepreneurship is fundamentally economic. It is continuous with previous ways and forms of economic activity. While the economy is its own self-contained system of ideas and behaviors, it cannot be isolated from society by assumption or fiat. Instead, it is context—the relative power people have in the economy and the ongoing goals they discern—that compels them to draw on noneconomic resources from family, ethnicity, religion, or politics to help them realize goals. People bring these noneconomic foundations and tools into the relationship with their context and goals, and they experiment with options to achieve those goals. It is precisely this spirit of experimentation that enables those who are otherwise marginalized and powerless to seek opportunities for economic mobility through entrepreneurship—compare, for instance, how Spanish-language radio stations make program decisions (Morales 2002) and how Latino street vendors describe paying taxes on cash income (Morales 2012).

While entrepreneurship integrates multiple economic processes (accounting, supply chain management, logistics, etc.), for nonethnic entrepreneurs the choice and practice of these processes will mostly follow from the constraints given by other players in the economy. But for the ethnic and the otherwise "disadvantaged" entrepreneur, such constraints are only one type, another constraint being discrimination, overt or covert, in efforts to do business. The former is partly a question of skill, but the latter can be seen as a restriction or even control over behavior. Overcoming such limitations can hardly be accomplished with economic systems of ideas and behavior, and thus the ethnic entrepreneur must harness other powerful systems, such as kinship, coethnicity, politics, or religion, as resources to substitute for their inability to compete or even relate in more strictly economic playing fields.

This creativity, forced perhaps by power differentials and inequalities, has enabled ethnic experimentation with and participation in entrepreneurship. And for more than a century, scholarship on entrepreneurship has documented the creativity of the ethnic and the entrepreneurial. Strictly speaking, understanding ethnic business formation follows from the work of many scholars including W. E. B. Dubois, Louis Wirth, and Alejandro Portes. Proliferating in number since the 1980s, scholars have worked at the intersection of ethnicity and entrepreneurship. Certainly race has also been salient in this literature, and the needs of immigrants and women can be said to have influenced practical decision making about small business in cities (Morales 2009). More recently, our understanding of entrepreneurship has been amplified as we have established the many processes and points in the formation of ethnic enterprises. Yet, it is not only sheer demographic pressure and the growth of Latinos and their economic power that is compelling this work. Indeed, the movement of Latinos into previously little-known niches, the exploration of new policy opportunities, and the demonstration of the importance of new research collaboratives also motivate our effort.

Thus, when we consider *Latino* entrepreneurship, as a historically underserved group, Latino entrepreneurs experience the inevitability of resource constraints on an uneven and distorted playing field. For any business, access to capital is a major predictor of business growth, and consequently a lack of access can be a major barrier. Still, Latino entrepreneurship in the United States has been growing at the rate of about 1 million new Latino-owned businesses every five years since 2002. Even during the Great Recession of 2008–2009, the number of Latino-owned businesses continued to grow. According to the U.S. Census Bureau, the number of non-Latino-owned businesses declined during this period, and if we eliminated all of the new businesses created by Latinos, there would have been *fewer* businesses in 2012 than there were in 2007.

These trends captured our collective imaginations in the convening of scholars—those interested in and actively researching topics within Latino entrepreneurship—first brought together by the SLEI at Stanford University in 2016. The group represents scholars from a variety of disciplines including sociology, economics, policy, and geographical sciences. Over the past three years, this faculty research group has met annually with the desire to purposefully enlarge the scale and scope of research on Latino entrepreneurship. This volume is the first effort in this research endeavor.

SLEI is a collaboration between LBAN and the Stanford Graduate School of Business that explores and expands our knowledge of the Latino entrepreneurship segment in the U.S. economy through research, knowledge dissemination, and facilitated collaboration. Since 2015, SLEI has released reports from data gathered through the annual SLEI Survey of U.S. Latino Business Owners. These national reports, designed for a wide audience of public policy makers, practitioners, media, think tanks, interest groups, and scholars, describe the current state of Latino entrepreneurship.

While the scholarship on Latino entrepreneurship is growing, SLEI has sought to accelerate and support it by providing survey data and engaging nationally prominent academics and thought leaders who study Latino entrepreneurship in one form or another. The creation of this volume came directly from the 2017 SLEI annual conference, where many participants began to leverage the data that SLEI collects to explore topics of interest and impact.

As a common theme across all chapters, the economic contributions and outcomes of Latino entrepreneurs are brought to the forefront. As Orozco notes in Chapter 13, "beyond moral or social obligations, programs are framing the support of Latino-owned entrepreneurs and firms as a national economic imperative, given their growing presence, upward trends, and significant contributions to the economy." We take on this sentiment in the naming of this book as we seek to elevate the academic scholarship and discourse in this area.

While this volume represents an important contribution to scholarship, it also constitutes a departure from basic research. Our work is important because it unifies research with education oriented to Latino entrepreneurship. We are at the nexus of theory and practice. On the education side we have the SLEI–Education Scaling program, which provides Latino entrepreneurs the concepts, enhanced business networks, and personal mentorship and a better understanding in accessing capital resources to scale their business, create jobs, and build a stronger economy. Orozco provides an overview of the education program in Chapter 13. On the research side we have the SLEI-Research program, which leverages large U.S. census data sets and collects unique national data to synthesize trends and report out the state of Latino entrepreneurship. Orozco and Perez provide an overview of the research program in Chapter 5. In intentionally creating and relating the two, we are tracking how scholarship on Latino entrepreneurs utilizes new data while improving data collection. Our work reinforces the training offered by the SLEI–Education Scaling program, establishes new research questions, and contributes to our existing thinking on ethnic entrepreneurship.

First, we represent the reciprocal influences from society and scholarship that are at the heart of the creation of both LBAN and its Stanford collaboration, SLEI. A programmatic focus on Latino entrepreneurship did not spring whole cloth from the mind of any one individual. But we acknowledge that one person, our colleague Jerry Porras, understood and recognized the pieces in the puzzle of scholars and related those to the pieces of the puzzle of educators in training nascent entrepreneurs and enabling existing entrepreneurs to grow. Porras recognized the importance of each component individually and the multiplied importance associated with bringing the two together in an organized and mutually reinforcing fashion. His efforts have produced changes through his scholarship and his students and in creating the LBAN/SLEI efforts.

Porras comprehended the importance to the United States of a robust entrepreneurial sector in the Latino community; however, he went a step further and put that vision into action. At our recent SLEI-Research conference, Porras prophesied his dream of building upon the current community of scholars and growing those with a research interest in this area fivefold over the next decade. With this goal in mind, we will move the current state of Latino entrepreneurship from the sidelines of scholarship to an important subfield within the entrepreneurship literature and discipline.

The need for action is clear. We have an urgent need, an *imperative*, for the engagement of Latinos in the economy. Labor force data indicate the important role that materials play in many sectors of the economy; however, the promise of the country for Latinos and for all of society is realized by participation across entrepreneurial activities in the name of a robust business sector. This book represents the first systematic effort to publish academic, programmatic, and policy-oriented work on the topic of Latino entrepreneurship. The chapters contained in this volume are beneficial for those interested in business, those desiring to become businesspeople, scholars who seek to work in this field, and public officials interested in better understanding the role that Latino entrepreneurship has to play in community and economic development.[1]

In this volume of Latino entrepreneurship, we take on an assets-based approach that acknowledges the historical and structural conditions that have led to the lack of intergenerational wealth among the U.S. Latino community but moves beyond that to focus on understanding the growing incidence of business creation as a course-correcting path. We explore questions that consider the economic contributions of Latinos to the U.S. economy in both rural and urban settings and within historically focused ethnic concentrations in geographic enclaves, the role of language, Latina economic mobility, and the experiences of high-growth and scaled firms,[2] among other thematic areas. We present many geographic scales, units of analysis, and research methods, including quantitative analysis, in-depth interviews, and case studies that capture a wide diversity of the Latino population. Additionally, we leverage a variety of data sources, with multiple chapters analyzing data collected from the SLEI Survey of U.S. Latino Business Owners.

In Chapter 2, "Entrepreneurs from the Beginning: Latino Business and Commerce since the Sixteenth Century," Geraldo L. Cadava provides an early historical view of Latino business and commerce, citing specific events that led to dramatic increases in the Latino population and subsequent business formation. Cadava's comprehensive overview of the history of Latino settlement and entrepreneurship in the United States provides a vital context for the rest of the chapters by highlighting the heterogeneity of the Latino population and the changing circumstances they have encountered as they try to establish their own businesses. Chapter 3, "Latino Businesses and Commerce: A Contemporary View" by Michael J. Pisani and Iliana Perez, extends the historical period of the previous chapter, providing exemplars of notable contemporary Latino business leaders. This chapter also provides a typology with which to categorize Latino-owned businesses by client base (Hispanic vs. non-Hispanic clients) and products (Hispanic vs. non-Hispanic products). Taken together, these two chapters provide the historical context for interpreting the latest data trends and case studies of Latino and Latina entrepreneurs explored in the subsequent chapters.

In Chapter 4, "The Economic Contributions of Latino Entrepreneurs," Robert W. Fairlie, Zulema Valdez, and Jody Agius Vallejo leverage data from two primary sources of nationally representative government data, the American Community Survey and the Survey of Business Owners, to provide a comprehensive analysis of the contributions of Latino business owners to the U.S. economy. The authors consider the contributions to business ownership, business income, total sales and receipts, employment, payroll, and exports. Chapter 5 by Marlene Orozco and Iliana Perez, "The State of Latino Entrepreneurship: SLEI Research and Findings," extends the discussion to include other data sets that have Latino-specific variables and entrepreneurship measures. This chapter also provides an overview of the SLEI national survey, which is utilized by nearly all of the remaining chapters. Chapters 2 through 5 serve as a collective introduction to Latino entrepreneurship, providing a sweeping overview of historical perspectives and data sources.

The chapters in Part II demonstrate that the sociohistorical conditions of a particular region matter for business formation and growth. Given the divergent economic, political, and demographic conditions across regions on the one hand and the heterogeneity of Latino communities living in those regions on the other, these perspectives situate the historical context of the previous section. In Chapter 6, "Latino Entrepreneurship in Rural America," Barbara Robles, Alfonso Morales, and Michael J. Pisani use a variety of data sources, including data from the Internal Revenue Service, the American Community Survey, SLEI, and the U.S. Department of Agriculture to determine the economic contributions of Latino farm entrepreneurs. In Chapter 7, "Shaping Success: Exploring the Evolution of Latino Businesses in Three Major U.S. Counties," Edna Ledesma and Cristina Cruz take on the three most populous Latino counties (in the Miami, Los Angeles, and Houston areas) to explore nuances in the scale of businesses and industry sectors of the different regions. Given the historical patterns of different Latino groups in these counties, Cadava's history in Chapter 2 provides the necessary contextual information with which to interpret these findings. John Sargent and Linda Matthews in Chapter 8, "Mexican American Founder Narratives at High-Growth Firms on the South Texas–Mexican Border," take a deep dive into this region by exploring high-growth firms through semistructured interviews in the deep South Texas region. The bilingual, bicultural nature of the borderlands fosters the success of these high-growth firms.

The authors in Part III investigate the social and economic factors that facilitate or impede Latino entrepreneurship. As John Sargent and Linda Matthew demonstrate in Part II, regional and larger opportunity structures intersect with business owner characteristics. Chapter 9, "Social Network Utilization among Latino-Owned Businesses," extends this approach and analyzes the role of enclaves and the social networks within to determine business outcomes. In this chapter Elsie L. Echeverri-Carroll and Marie T. Mora use the large national SLEI survey to overcome previous data limitations to explore this relationship. Pursuant to the individual as the unit of analysis, Michael J. Pisani and Joseph M. Guzman explore the relationship of immigrants and their descendants as it relates to business success in Chapter 10, "Acculturation and Latino-Owned Business Success: Patterns and Connections." Bilingualism and language use can present challenges or opportunities depending on the larger context. Chapter 11 by Alberto Dávila, Michael J. Pisani, and Gerardo Miranda, "The Business of Language: Latino Entrepreneurs, Language Use, and Firm Performance," explores these theories through analysis of the SLEI data. Part III concludes by considering the experiences of Latinas in Ruth E. Zambrana, Leticia Lara, Bea Stotzer, and Kathleen Stewart's Chapter 12, "How Can Entrepreneurship Serve as a Pathway to Reduce Income Inequality among Hispanic Women?" The supply of Latino entrepreneurs must include Latinas inclusive of the intersecting roles that structure aspirations and practices.

Part IV considers practice and policy as they relate to business programs and Latina practitioners' perspective on capital. In Chapter 13, "SLEI–Education Scaling Program: A Business Program of 'National Economic Imperative,'" Marlene Orozco explores the changing discourse of Latino entrepreneurship and the experiences of entrepreneurs who go through the SLEI-Education program through in-depth interviews. To provide next steps with possible actions and policies as a practitioner with over 25 years in senior management and investment management, Monika Mantilla brings forth the "Gacela Theory" in Chapter 14, "The G.R.E.A.T Gacela Theory: Increasing Capital and Conditions for Success for High-Potential Latino Entrepreneurs Capable of Transforming Our Economy and Our Country." In this chapter, Mantilla reviews the current state of capital access for Latino-owned businesses and the resources required to promote greater opportunity to next stage growth.

Contributions to this volume begin to reveal how public policy shapes the decision-making environment of entrepreneurship in particular industries as well as particular places. Each contributor in this volume polishes a facet of our understanding of Latino entrepreneurship. Together, we characterize and illustrate a variety of disciplinary approaches to understanding Latino entrepreneurship.

NOTES

1. This is not to deny the importance of and growth in social entrepreneurship among Latino nonprofit organizations, yet this topic is not our concern here.

2. Scaled firms are those that generate at least $1 million in annual revenue and have the potential to greatly contribute to the U.S. economy. We focus on this critically understudied segment of businesses, as previous work has commonly associated ethnic entrepreneurship to small informal and peripheral economies. The data explored in this volume show otherwise.

REFERENCES

Anderson, Benedict. 1983. *Imagined Communities: Reflections on the Origin and Spread of Nationalism.* London: Verso.

Booth, William J. 1993. *Households: On the Moral Architecture of the Economy.* Ithaca, NY: Cornell University Press.

Eisenmann, Thomas R. 2013. "Entrepreneurship: A Working Definition." *Harvard Business Review,* January 10, https://hbr.org/2013/01/what-is-entrepreneurship.

Hirschman, Albert. 1958. *The Strategy of Economic Development.* New Haven, CT: Yale University Press.

Kirzner, Israel M. 1973. *Competition and Entrepreneurship.* Chicago: University of Chicago Press.

Mora, Cristina. 2014. *Making Hispanics: How Activists, Bureaucrats and Media Constructed a New American.* Chicago: University of Chicago Press.

Morales, Alfonso. 2002. "Radio Mercado: Station Format and Alternative Models of the Audience in the U.S.-Mexico Border Region." *Journal of Borderlands Studies* 17(1):79–102.

Morales, Alfonso. 2009. "A Woman's Place Is on the Street: Purposes and Problems of Mexican American Women Entrepreneurs." Pp. 99–125 in *Wealth Creation and Business Formation among Mexican-Americans: History, Circumstances and Prospects*, edited by John S. Butler, Alfonso Morales, and David Torres. West Lafayette, IN: Purdue University Press.

Morales, Alfonso. 2012. "Understanding and Interpreting Tax Compliance Strategies among Street Vendors." Pp. 83–106 in *The Ethics of Tax Evasion: Perspectives in Theory and Practice*, edited by Robert McGee. New York: Springer.

Schumpeter, Joseph A. 1912. *The Theory of Economic Development.* Reprint, New York: Routledge, 2017.

Schumpeter, Joseph A. 1942. *Capitalism, Socialism and Democracy.* New York: Harper & Row.

Shane, Scott. 2003. *A General Theory of Entrepreneurship: The Individual-Opportunity Nexus.* Cheltenham, UK: Edward Elgar.

Valdez, Zulema, and Tanya Golash-Boza. 2017. "U.S. Racial and Ethnic Relations in the Twenty-first Century." *Ethnic and Racial Studies* 40(13):2181–209.

Williams, Colin C. 2007. "Entrepreneurs Operating in the Informal Economy: Necessity or Opportunity Driven?" *Journal of Small Business and Entrepreneurship* 20(3):309–20.

CHAPTER 2

Entrepreneurs from the Beginning: Latino Business and Commerce since the Sixteenth Century

Geraldo L. Cadava

For 500 years, from the earliest Spanish explorers to the growing league of twenty-first-century entrepreneurs, Latino business and commerce in the United States has encompassed the activities of ranchers, farmers, land colonizers, general store operators, street vendors, corporate executives, real estate developers, entertainment industry mavens, self-employed domestics, and barbers.[1] They have run businesses small and large, with zero to thousands of employees, and have served Latino and non-Latino communities all around the world. Latino businesses were at first concentrated in the southwestern portion of the United States as well as in Louisiana, Florida, and New York. By the twentieth century, however, they had spread across the United States and beyond as Latino culture, music, food, and styles became popular and widespread commodities. The Latino population in the United States increased from the late nineteenth century onward, leading to the expansion of Latino markets. Latino-owned and non-Latino businesses focused on cultivating as clients this growing group of consumers. Altogether, Latino business and commercial activities have constituted an important aspect of Latino ethnicity, politics, and community formation in the United States.

From *American Latinos and the Making of the United States: A Theme Study* (pp. 215–229). National Park System Advisory Board, for the National Park Service, U.S. Department of the Interior. Reprinted with permission.

The growth of Latino-owned enterprises and of data collected by U.S. government agencies about them has led to a wave of scholarship that has characterized Latino entrepreneurs as centrally important though under-studied members of their communities. As a country, we have focused on the heated debates over Latin American labor migration rather than the entrepreneurs who have created markets, played pivotal roles in the development of their communities, and emerged as political organizers and leaders.

Commemorating the long history of Latino business and commercial activities—through their designation as historically significant or sim-ply through greater awareness of them—poses several challenges. Such a process might entail the acknowledgment that already-recognized estab-lishments, such as the religious missions of the Spanish colonial period, had broader business and commercial significance. Alternatively, the process could involve figuring out how to locate the precise corners and parking lots where self-employed day laborers gather to find work. Even more broadly, designating such sites, since many of those who gather at them are not U.S. citizens, would require the recognition that noncitizens are capable of productive economic activity that is historically signifi-cant. Likewise, even though Latino entrepreneurship often has involved temporary activities or extremely small operations, only long-lasting and larger businesses have received recognition for their historical significance. Finally, how would one go about claiming the historical significance of businesses started by return migrants who saved money in the United States and learned successful business practices here that enabled them to engage in entrepreneurial activities in their Latin American home countries? While these issues pose certain challenges to the project of des-ignating historically significant Latino business and commercial activities, finding ways to recognize appropriately those endeavors would promote a richer understanding of the role Latinos have played in the history of American business and economics.

The establishment and growth of Latino business and commerce has mirrored the expansion of the Latino population itself. Until the late nineteenth century, the vast majority of such activities took place among Mexicans and Mexican Americans in the U.S. Southwest, the area of the United States that, until after the Mexican-American War (1848) and the Gadsden Purchase (1854), formed part of the Spanish Empire and Mexico. Other Latin American merchants conducted business during this period elsewhere in the United States in such places as Louisiana, Florida, and New York. For the most part their stay in these places was temporary, and their dealings did not contribute to the formation, settlement, or advancement of Latino communities. Rather, they were confined to trading and other mercantile activities. Then during the late nineteenth and early twentieth centuries, the immigration of Latinos to the United States and their exile from American independence movements as well as international conflicts such as the Spanish-American War and the Mexican Revolution led to the growth and diversification of Latino businesses including groceries, clothiers, and medical practices that served these new communities. By the end of World War II, Latino business and commerce had spread across the United States from Los Angeles to New York and from Chicago to Miami.

While the incorporation of Latino business and commercial activities into broader social, political, and economic patterns of the United States increased after World War II, most Latino businesses still catered primarily to Latino communities. Then from 1965 forward—after the Immigration and Nationality Act of 1965 (Hart-Celler Act), the Cuban Revolution of 1959, and violent antidemocratic repressions in Central and South American countries during the 1970s and 1980s led to the dramatic increase of U.S. Latino populations—Latino business and commerce exploded, becoming the fastest-growing sector of the U.S. small business community. Most Latino businesses still served local Latino communities, but others reached broader non-Latino communities across the United States. By the late twentieth century, thousands of businesses opened by recent Latin American immigrants joined those opened by earlier generations of Latinos in the United States, and many immigrants eventually returned to their home countries to establish their businesses there. Their activities represented the hemispheric and global reach of Latino business and commerce during the twenty-first century.

THE ECONOMIES OF NORTHERN NEW SPAIN

From its very beginning, Spanish imperial expansion in the Americas was a business venture. Spaniards mapped the land and exploited the indigenous labor that made it productive. They also extracted minerals that they sent back to the Crown, which increased their own wealth as well. From Florida to California, they established missions and ranches that became extremely profitable, as Spanish missionaries, soldiers, ordinary citizens, and indigenous peoples raised cattle and crops and then sold their meat, hides, tallow, grains, and vegetables both locally and throughout the empire. Among these men were the first Latino entrepreneurs.

Spaniards established cattle ranches as early as the sixteenth century, first near St. Augustine and Tallahassee, Florida. Tomás Menéndez Márquez owned the La Chua Ranch, which stretched thousands of square miles from the St. John's River in East Florida to the Gulf of Mexico and produced more than a third of Florida's cattle during the seventeenth century. Márquez provided hides, dried meat, and tallow to Florida's Spanish colonies as well as to Havana, demonstrating how Latino business and commercial activities reached distant markets from their earliest days. Once Márquez established his cattle business, he branched out into other commercial activities, traveling by boat to Havana and returning with goods that he traded in Florida (Bushnell 1978). Francisco Javier Sánchez became his successor, owning and operating stores, plantations, and ranches in Florida that supplied Spanish and British officials. Following paths first carved and traveled by indigenous communities, men such as Márquez and Sánchez established some of Florida's earliest commercial trading routes, trading posts, and stores, much like other Spaniards did elsewhere across the Spanish Empire's northern frontier.

If large-scale cattle ranching began in Florida, it became iconic in the Southwest. Juan de Oñate introduced cattle in New Mexico during the late sixteenth century, Captain Alonso de León and Eusebio Francisco Kino introduced cattle to Texas and Arizona during the seventeenth century, and Junipero Serra and Juan Bautista de Anza introduced cattle to California during the eighteenth century. Across the Southwest, livestock industries supplied nascent agricultural and mining operations, producing tallow for candles and hides for clothing, harnesses, and bags that carried mineral ores and water. Ranches throughout the region relied on the labor of indigenous populations, which herded cattle and sheep, slaughtered the animals, and made clothing and other goods from them. By the early nineteenth century, cattle from Spain's northern frontier were shipped to South America, leading to the rise of cattle industries there and again demonstrating early connections among distant markets. The cattle industries of northern New Spain also spawned some of the frontier's first illicit economic enterprises as cattle rustlers illegally drove cattle across imperial and national borders.

OPPORTUNITY AND CONSEQUENCE
ON MEXICAN AND U.S. FRONTIERS

Throughout the Spanish colonial period, land grants awarded by the Spanish Crown provided the grounds for business and commercial activities. After 1821, when Mexico won independence from Spain, the Mexican government continued the practice of granting lands on the country's northern frontier, particularly through the secularization of mission lands that were converted into ranchlands. From the 1820s through the 1840s, the Mexican government issued hundreds of land grants, with parcels that ranged from 4,000 to 100,000 acres each. By the time of the Mexican-American War, 800 ranchers owned more than 8 million acres of land. Some entrepreneurs divided their land for distribution among colonists and their families, who were then able to grow crops and raise animals. Other entrepreneurs developed ranches, many of which remained in operation decades after the Mexican-American War. In 1760, for example, Captain Blas María de la Garza Falcón received from the Spanish Crown a 975,000-acre land grant in Texas, which he called Rancho Real de Santa Petronila. Much of it later became the King Ranch, which at half a million acres was the largest ranch in the United States (Montejano 1987). In Arizona, Toribio Otero received a 400-acre land grant that his great-grandson, Sabino Otero, the so-called Cattle King of Tubac, expanded to include lands from Tucson to the U.S.-Mexican border city of Nogales (Sheridan 1992; Chávez-García 2004). While men received the majority of Spanish and Mexican land grants, some women became property owners as well, allowing them to achieve a measure of independence from patriarchal Mexican societies during the early nineteenth century.

The Southwest's agricultural, ranching, and mineral goods reached markets via shipping and trading networks including the 900-mile-long Santa Fe Trail and other routes connecting San Antonio with El Paso and connecting Tucson with the Mexican port town of Guaymas, Sonora. Through the mid-nineteenth century, the bulk of profits earned by Mexican-owned businesses stemmed from this trade in agricultural, ranching, and mining products. These goods were sold in small general stores, by street vendors, and by merchants who shipped them throughout the United States and Mexico. Such business ventures laid the groundwork for Latino business and commerce in later periods of American history and cemented relationships that increasingly pulled northern Mexico into the economic orb of the United States (Reséndez 2004).

During the mid-nineteenth century, the Mexican-American War and the annexation of Mexican land by the United States transformed the social, political, and economic conditions of Mexican business and commercial activities in the southwestern United States. Mexican American ranchers remained some of the wealthiest and most powerful businessmen into the 1880s, when U.S. railroad companies came to control most of their vast landholdings. Famously, California landowners, including Pio Pico and Mariano Guadalupe Vallejo, lost thousands of acres of land. In some cases, railroad, mining, ranching, and agricultural interests purchased the land, or it was claimed by squatters. In many cases, Mexican American ranchers, called Californios, offered up their land to pay legal fees incurred as part of their effort to defend their properties against encroachment. In bitterly ironic ends, the Americans facilitated the industrial growth of the U.S. Southwest with devastating consequences for Mexican Americans of all class backgrounds (Pitt 1999).

The shift from Mexican to U.S. economic and political control negatively affected many Mexican Americans living in the Southwest, but a few individuals capitalized on the new national context to develop their own business empires. Brothers Bernabé and Jesús Robles took advantage of the federal Homestead Act of 1862, which offered western land for cheap to those who would make it productive, claiming two 160-acre parcels of land that eventually became Three Points Ranch in southern Arizona. Their cattle and land made them wealthy, enabling them to purchase additional landholdings that eventually totaled 1 million acres between Florence, Arizona, and the U.S.-Mexican border, an expanse of land 134 miles long from north to south. Bernabé Robles later diversified his businesses, investing in Tucson real estate and general stores that he left to his children (Sheridan 1992).

In addition to ranches, Mexican American entrepreneurs owned wagon-based freighting businesses that moved goods across the Southwest and between the United States and Mexico. In 1856, Joaquin Quiroga established a business that hauled goods between Yuma and Tucson, Arizona, thus becoming a pioneer of the freighting industry. But by the 1870s, Tucson's Estevan Ocho (1831–1888) operated a business—Tully, Ochoa & Company—that shipped goods east as far as St. Louis, Missouri, and south as far as Guaymas, Sonora. He later opened several mercantile businesses, small mining companies, and sheep ranches that depended on his freight company to market their goods beyond Tucson. Freighting companies such as Tully, Ochoa & Company generally went out of business after the arrival of railroads, which could carry goods farther, faster, and for less money, though several other freighting businesses remained competitive by operating routes not serviced by trains.

BUSINESS AND COMMERCE IN URBANIZING LATINO COMMUNITIES AND BEYOND

While vast ranchlands and transportation industries provided the foundations of Mexican American entrepreneurship into the late nineteenth century, with their decline many Mexican Americans moved into the growing cities of the Southwest, including San Francisco, Los Angeles, Tucson, El Paso, Denver, Albuquerque, and San Antonio. White settlers arrived in these burgeoning metropolises as well and within a couple of decades played an increasingly dominant role in the social, political, and economic histories of these places. As the influence and status of Mexican Americans waned, they increasingly became seen as members of a regional working class, and the vast majority of them lived substantially segregated lives within barrios. These neighborhoods became the strongholds of Mexican American business and commerce. Tucson's Federico Ronstadt, an immigrant from Sonora, established the city's biggest carriage-building business as well as a successful hardware store. Leopoldo Carrillo, also from Tucson, became one of the city's largest real estate holders. According to the 1870 census, he was Tucson's wealthiest individual, owning almost 100 homes, ice cream parlors, and saloons and the city's first bowling alley. Because of the impressive array of his business interests, the *Tucson City Directory* simply called him a "capitalist." While Mexican entrepreneurs in these communities marketed their goods locally, they also developed commerce between the United States and Latin America. As part of his carriage business and hardware store in Tucson, for example, Ronstadt kept agents south of the border in Cananea, Nogales, Hermosillo, and Guaymas, Sonora (Sheridan 2012).

Emerging Latino communities elsewhere in the United States, especially Florida and New York, also demonstrated vibrant patterns of trade between the United States and Latin America. Cubans and Puerto Ricans first settled in Tampa and New York City as exiles from Latin America's wars for independence against Spain. They formed some of the first Caribbean Latino communities in the United States and opened a diverse array of businesses shortly after their arrival. By the late nineteenth century, Caribbean merchants had traded in U.S. ports for more than 100 years, but they did not establish communities. From the 1880s forward, though, Cuban and Puerto Rican exiles increasingly settled in southern and eastern U.S. cities.

Most famously, Cuban émigrés established cigar factories outside of Tampa. Caribbean revolutions had disrupted the business of these factories in Cuba. Furthermore, high import taxes on cigars entering the United States had curtailed their sales, a problem solved by opening cigar factories on the mainland. Vicente Martínez Ybor was the most famous proprietor of these cigar factories. Ybor and his partner Ignacio Haya created a company town—later known as Ybor City—with mutual aid societies, theaters, schools, and printing presses that grew up around the factories, which led to the rapid growth of the area as a whole (Mormino and Pozzetta 1998; Hewitt 2001).

A leader of the independence movement, the Cuban exile José Martí moved between Florida and New York during the 1880s and early 1890s and in those places became a unifying force for Caribbean Latino communities. Sotero Figueroa, a Puerto Rican exile who moved to New York City in 1889, developed a close friendship with Martí. Figueroa opened the print shop Imprenta América, from which he published several Spanish-language papers, including *El Americano* (The American) and *El Porvenir* (The Future). His press also printed Martí's paper, *Patria* (Nation). Figueroa moved to Cuba after the Spanish-American War and eventually became the director of *La Gaceta Oficial*, the newspaper of the new Cuban government. In addition to Figueroa's print shops, other Latino businesses located in New York as well, including small grocery stores, restaurants, and health centers such as the Midwife Clinic of Havana in New York City, owned and operated by the Cuban woman Gertrudis Heredia de Serra. These businesses in the urban Southwest, Florida, and New York laid the foundations of Latino business and commerce during the early twentieth century, when the U.S. Latino population increased in the aftermath of the Spanish-American War and during the Mexican Revolution.

During the late nineteenth and early twentieth centuries, wars and revolutions throughout Latin America caused Mexican, Cuban, and Puerto

Rican migrants to seek new livelihoods in the United States. Production demands in mining and agricultural industries during the World War I era held forth the promise of jobs upon arrival. Latinos settled in such cities as Los Angeles, Phoenix, Tucson, El Paso, Chicago, Detroit, Miami, and New York, generally in barrios established during the late nineteenth century.

After the Mexican Revolution, following a decade of migration and settlement, the economist Paul Taylor and the sociologists Manuel Gamio and Emory Bogardus conducted some of the first studies of Mexican communities in the United States, which offered brief references to the Mexican entrepreneurs who met the needs of their growing communities. While a few owned land and operated their own agricultural businesses, many recent Mexican immigrants joined more established community members in opening small businesses, such as bakeries, barbershops, billiards halls, and pharmacies, as well as larger ones, such as Mexican cinemas, hotels, and printing shops. Taylor concluded that despite these ventures, by the end of the 1920s Mexican business owners had not for the most part advanced economically in the United States (Taylor 1930; Gamio 1930; Valenzuela and Pinedo 2009).

The growth of Latino communities created new markets for goods, services, and information, which led many Latinos—longtime community members and immigrants alike—to open businesses in barrios that remained segregated from other areas of the city and served a primarily Latino clientele. Only a few non-Latino businesses during the early twentieth century sought Latino patronage or stocked goods that Latinos desired. Doctors in Los Angeles, for example, such as the "Doctora" Augusta Stone and Dr. Chee, the "Doctor Chino," claimed to speak Spanish and advertised their services to Mexican immigrants and Mexican Americans. Nevertheless, the segregation of Latino communities created business opportunities for aspiring Latino entrepreneurs (Sánchez 1993).

Most Latino-owned businesses were small family-owned operations that met the basic food, clothing, health, and everyday life (and death) needs of growing U.S. Latino communities. They included birthing and funeral services, tortilla factories, money transfer agencies, auto repair shops, bakeries, barbershops, and beauty salons. Demonstrating how Latino-owned businesses concentrated in barrios, the Mexican American neighborhoods of Corpus Christi, Texas, were home to stores named Loa's Shoe Shop, Juán González Funeral Home, Estrada Motor Sales, and La Farmácia Gómez, while those in Los Angeles were home to stores such as

Farmácia Hidalgo and Farmácia Ruíz. In addition, several Latinos were self-employed as lawyers, doctors, or dentists even though their numbers paled in comparison to their white counterparts. Only rarely did Latino-owned businesses operate outside of Latino ethnic enclaves or serve broader non-Latino communities. Jácome's Department Store and Federico Ronstadt's hardware and general store—both established during the late nineteenth century and located in Tucson's central business district—served a mixed clientele including Mexican Americans, Native Americans, and white settlers who moved to the city in growing numbers from the 1880s forward (Villarreal 2009; Sánchez 1993).

While most Latino businesses met basic needs, others that created cultural and leisure opportunities also increased during the early twentieth century. For example, in 1927 Rafael and Victoria Hernández, a husband and wife who immigrated to New York from Puerto Rico, opened Almacenes Hernández, which is widely regarded as the first Puerto Rican–owned record store in New York. Later during the twentieth century under new ownership the store's name changed to Casa Amadeo, and in 2001 it was listed in the National Register of Historic Places for its role in the development of New York's Latin American music scene. Musicians looking for work gathered at the store. Victor and Columbia records relied on the store owners to help them locate new talent and keep them abreast of new trends, and more generally, the store kept New York's Latino communities in tune with music from their home country. Similar stores served Latino communities elsewhere in the United States, such as the Repertorio Musical Mexicana in Los Angeles owned by Mexican immigrant Mauricio Calderón, who claimed that his store was "the only Mexican house of Mexican music for Mexicans" (Sánchez 1993).

In addition to record stores and other music industries, Latino-owned cultural and leisure enterprises including restaurants, dance halls, theaters, vaudeville houses, movie houses, bars, and cafés catered to Latino communities across the country. El Progreso Restaurant in Los Angeles enticed Mexican American customers with food prepared in a "truly Mexican style," and theaters such as Teatro Novel and Teatro Hidalgo entertained Mexican immigrants with live entertainment and films imported from Mexico. Such Latino-owned businesses often shaped the social and political relationships of their owners, who became important community leaders. For example, as the owner of Club Sofía, a popular nightclub in Corpus Christi during the 1940s, Sofía Rodríguez gained a seat on the Texas Alcohol Beverage Commission, which put her in contact with politicians who expected her to deliver Mexican American votes. Other businesses also developed political inroads among Latinos by making financial contributions to Latino civil rights and social organizations such as the Alianza Hispano Americana, founded in Tucson in 1894, and the League of United Latin American Citizens, founded in Corpus Christi in 1929 (Sánchez 1993; Villarreal 2009).

The growth of Latino businesses during the early twentieth century therefore demonstrated the role of Latinos not only as economic and cultural consumers but also as engaged social and political actors. They fought anti-Latino discrimination, debated the merits of candidates for office, and organized various community events. The immigrants among them also followed from afar the politics of their home countries, takings sides, for example, in the wars and revolutions that reshaped Latin American societies. Latinos formed several new social, political, and economic groups to engage these local and international issues, such as the Alianza Hispano Americana and the League of United Latin American Citizens and their women auxiliaries. Latino-owned businesses, especially Spanish-language newspapers and radio stations, both shaped and reflected the activities of these groups.

Print shops were some of the earliest Latino-owned businesses in the United States, dating back to the late eighteenth century, but a growing number of them were established during the early twentieth century as a result of expanded Latino communities that demanded news both from their new cities and their Latin American homelands. Several Spanish-language newspapers founded between 1910 and 1930 kept Latino communities informed, such as Ignacio Lozano's San Antonio paper *La Prensa* and his Los Angeles paper *La Opinion* and Arturo Moreno's Tucson paper, *El Tucsonense*. Lozano shipped *La Prensa* to the West and the Midwest, making it something like a national Spanish-language daily. He used the profits from his newspapers to diversify his businesses, which eventually included a publishing company, a bookstore in Los Angeles called Librería Lozano, and real estate holdings throughout the city. Moreover, printing presses such as Lozano's were precursors to Spanish-language radio and television media pioneered by such individuals as San Antonio's Raoul Cortez and Tucson's Ernesto Portillo.

EXPANDING POPULATIONS, EXPANDING MARKETS

The children of Latin American migrants who arrived between 1900 and 1930 came of age in the United States during the mid-twentieth century. New waves of migrants joined them, compelled to leave their home countries because of poor economic conditions caused by the global depression of the 1930s and also because of civil wars aggravated by U.S. military interventions. World War II was a critical turning point for U.S. Latinos and Latin American migrants alike. Latinos joined the U.S. military and returned from service, articulating new claims to citizenship and belonging bolstered by federal programs such as the G.I. Bill. These new programs enabled many of the returning servicemen to pursue higher education and move out of barrios and into areas of their cities that were more affluent. Meanwhile, Mexican and Puerto Rican migrants met U.S. labor demands as participants in guest worker programs, and other Caribbean and Central American migrants—namely Guatemalans, Cubans, and residents of the Dominican Republic—moved to the United States in increasing numbers. As during earlier periods, demographic changes within U.S. Latino communities led to new business and commercial practices.

Many Latino-owned businesses established during the late nineteenth and early twentieth centuries continued to serve Latino communities into the late twentieth century. Tampa's cigar factories operated into the 1950s; New York's Latino music and entertainment industries boomed between 1940 and 1970, eclipsing their success in earlier decades; and retail businesses such as Jácome's Department Store remained open until 1980. These businesses relied on Latino clientele who had lived in the United States for a generation or more and on trade with international markets throughout Latin America. Nevertheless, they also served new consumer markets in the United States, including recent Latin American immigrants and non-Latino consumers increasingly interested in the goods and services provided by Latino-owned businesses.

Small businesses remained the cornerstone of Latino entrepreneurial activity into the post–World War II period, and Latino consumers were still their targeted clients. During a period generally defined as an economic boom time, second- and third-generation Latinos—descendants of Latino families that had lived in the United States since the nineteenth century or the children of Latin American immigrants who had arrived during the early twentieth century—started more businesses than any previous generation of Latinos (Valenzuela and Pinedo 2009).

Entertainment industries established during the early twentieth century grew along with U.S. Latino communities. After the mass migration of Puerto Ricans to New York, the Forum Theater, which first opened its doors in 1917 to entertain Greek immigrant audiences, was renamed the Teatro Puerto Rico in 1948. Until the 1970s, the theater provided live entertainment for members of New York's Latino communities, including Puerto Rican musicians such as José Feliciano and Mexican actors such as Mario "Cantinflas" Moreno, Jorge Negrete, and Pedro Infante. New York's Palmieri family opened a corner store in the Bronx known as the Mambo Candy Shop. It became a hangout for the city's Latino musicians. Eddie and Charlie Palmieri, whose parents owned the store, themselves became famous musicians. At the same time, on the other side of the continent the Mexican American composer/musician Eduardo "Lalo" Guerrero entertained audiences in his Los Angeles nightclub, Lalo's (Singer and Martínez 2004).

Latino-owned businesses during the mid-twentieth century increasingly found markets for their goods and services beyond the Latino community because Latinos began to move out of barrios after World War II and also because of the increasing commoditization of all things Latino, especially food and music. Goya Foods, for example, began in 1936 as a small family-owned business that marketed its goods only within New York's Latino communities. Into the postwar period, non-Latino-owned chains including Safeway refused to sell Goya products. But under the leadership of Joseph A. Unanue, the U.S.-born son of Puerto Rican immigrant and company founder Prudencio Unanue, Goya Foods became the largest Latino-owned food distributor in the United States and also shipped its goods around the world, particularly to Latin America and Spain as well as other European countries. La Preferida, a Mexican-owned food company established in Chicago during the late nineteenth century, also started as a small enterprise that then expanded to market its products nationally and internationally (Valenzuela and Pinedo 2009).

New groups of Latin American migrants reinvigorated Latino business and commercial activities during the mid-twentieth century. Guatemalans fled their home country after the 1954 coup d'état that replaced the leftist leader Jacobo Árbenz Guzmán with the U.S.-backed conservative military leader Carlos Castillo Armas. Residents of the Dominican Republic fled their home country following the 1961 assassination of Rafael Trujillo, which unleashed more than a decade of social, political, and economic instability. Cubans fled their island following the Cuban Revolution through which Fidel Castro claimed power. As they settled in the United States, these new groups of Latino migrants opened businesses that served their migrant communities, including bodegas, restaurants, music clubs, and other operations.

Since the earliest years of their migration to New York, Illinois, and Florida, Cuban migrants—especially the first wave of exiles to arrive in the United States right after the Cuban Revolution, which included in general more educated and affluent exiles compared with later waves—have been regarded as a particularly entrepreneurial group of Latinos. Because Castro had limited their ability to open businesses in Cuba, many entrepreneurs were eager to flee the island. But even more than the supposed entrepreneurial orientation of early Cuban migrants, the Cold War policies of the United States aided Cubans who aspired to pursue careers in business, offering them financial aid, scholarships, and business loans. During the 1960s, Miami quickly became the hub of Cuban American business activity, especially the neighborhood that became known as Little Havana. Restaurants, clothing stores, pharmacies, fruit stands, cafés, medical centers, and service-oriented businesses such as locksmiths defined the business landscape of Miami's largest Cuban neighborhood (Valdez 2011; García 1997; Alberts 2006).

BUSINESS BOOMS AND THE GLOBALIZATION OF LATINO CULTURE

As the U.S. Latino population expanded dramatically after 1965, so did the number of Latino-owned businesses. The 1965 Immigration and Nationality Act replaced national origins quotas with a visa-granting system that extended opportunities for settlement to migrants from previously restricted countries yet continued to limit their number. Because the approximately 100,000 available visas numbered less than the millions of migrants who sought work in the United States, an increasing number of migrants, particularly from Latin America, Asia, and Africa, entered the United States without documentation from the late 1960s forward. During the 1970s and 1980s, streams of Central American refugees from civil wars in Guatemala, Nicaragua, and El Salvador also settled in the United States. Latinos from all ethnic backgrounds, especially from the 1990s onward, settled across the United States, most rapidly in the U.S. South, Northeast, and Great Plains. The overall growth of the Latino population during the late nineteenth century provided opportunities for profit both for longtime Latino business owners and new migrant entrepreneurs.

As Latino business and commercial activities increased, the U.S. government paid increasing attention to U.S. Latinos as consumers and entrepreneurs. In 1972, the U.S. government published its first "Survey of Minority-Owned Business Enterprises" and then repeated this exercise every few years, in 1982, 1987, 1992, 1997, 2002, and 2007. The 1972 survey revealed that there were about 81,000 Mexican-owned businesses in the United States. By 1987 the number of Mexican-owned businesses had jumped by almost 230 percent, to 267,000. The 1992 survey, because the 1986 Immigration Reform and Control Act had led many Latin American migrants to regularize their citizenship status, revealed another dramatic increase in Mexican business ownership: the number of Mexican-owned businesses grew by 42 percent, to 379,000. A decade later in 2002, there were more than 700,000 Mexican-owned businesses in the United States. The increase in business ownership was as dramatic among other Latino groups as it was among Mexicans. According to the U.S. Census Bureau, in 1977 there were 248,000 Latino-owned businesses, by 1987 there were 422,000, and by 1997 there were 1.2 million. By 2002 Latinos owned 1.6 million businesses, and their rate of business ownership was growing faster than the rate of ownership by any other ethnic or racial group in the United States. Acknowledging the astounding growth of Latino business and commercial activities, the U.S. Hispanic Chamber of Commerce was established in 1979 to represent the Latino business community (Valenzuela and Pinedo 2009).

The geographic distribution of Latino-owned businesses followed the residence patterns of U.S. Latino populations as a whole. Most Mexican-owned businesses were in the U.S. Southwest, though their number had grown in other areas as well such as the U.S. South, New York, and Illinois. In 1997, California and Texas alone were home to 75 percent of all Mexican-owned businesses. Meanwhile, 70 percent of Cuban-owned businesses were located in Florida; most Puerto Rican–owned businesses were in Florida, New York, and Illinois; and most businesses owned by individuals from the Dominican Republic were located in New York. After California, Texas, Florida, and New York, most other Latino-owned businesses could be found in New Jersey, Illinois, Arizona, New Mexico, Colorado, and Virginia. As Latino communities moved into suburbs, Latino-owned businesses quickly followed. For example, the Phoenix suburbs of Glendale and Mesa, which had few Latino residents in 1990, by the early twenty-first century were home to thriving butcheries, bakeries, tire shops, ice cream stores, western wear outlets, and beauty salons. Their names often invoked the Mexican states of Sinaloa, Michoacán, Chihuahua, or Sonora. The stores displayed images of Emiliano Zapata or the Virgen de Guadalupe, hung advertisements for van rides to Mexico, wired money to Latin American countries, and sold international phone cards and newspapers from Mexican border cities. As such, they helped Latino immigrants maintain connections with their home countries and served as primary points of entry into their new communities in the United States. Nevertheless, despite the suburbanization of the U.S. Latino population, most Latino businesses located in cities and five metropolitan areas alone—Los Angeles, Miami, New York City, Houston, and San Antonio—were home to more than a third of all Latino businesses in the United States (Oberle 2006).

Into the twenty-first century, the vast majority of Latino-owned businesses were still small operations that served Latino communities across the United States. Latino-owned restaurants, grocery stores, barbershops, movie houses, concert venues, publishing companies, and doctors' offices still catered to U.S. and foreign-born Latinos. Latinos also operated small businesses that served non-Latino communities, such as landscaping and housecleaning services. Latino entrepreneurs tended to be younger than non-Latino entrepreneurs. Latino-owned businesses concentrated in the retail, service, and construction sectors of the U.S. economy. Most self-employed Latinos—those who claimed to run their own business—had no paid employees and often relied on the unpaid labor of family members. Some held salaried positions but also cleaned houses, did yard work or maintenance work, or sold baked goods such as sweet bread, burritos, and tamales in their neighborhoods or at their places of employment. Sometimes Latinos borrowed money from family members, joined groups that pooled their resources, or successfully procured small business loans that enabled them to convert these side businesses into more profitable full-time occupations (Valenzuela and Pinedo 2009).

Nevertheless, despite these general trends, many differences existed among Latino business owners from different ethnic, class, and gender backgrounds. While Mexicans owned more businesses than any other

Latino group, businesses owned by Cubans were in general more profitable. Stereotypes held by Latinos and non-Latinos alike said that Cubans were the most entrepreneurially successful of all Latino groups or, conversely, that Mexicans lacked business savvy. In fact, differences resulted from the historical circumstances that would-be Mexican and Cuban entrepreneurs have encountered in the United States, namely that the anti-Castro policies of the United States have resulted in greater opportunities for Cubans. While all Latinos had difficulty securing bank loans to finance startup costs and therefore had to rely on personal savings, small loans from family members, government programs, or high-interest loans from banks that exploited ethnic communities, aspiring Latino business owners from middle-class backgrounds fared better than poor Latinos and recent immigrants. Their higher levels of education, wealthier relatives, and greater familiarity with U.S. business practices tended to give Cuban immigrants an advantage over these others.

Additionally, Latinos of particular ethnic backgrounds tended to loan money only to Latinos from similar backgrounds. When they opened their businesses, 18 percent of Latinos relied on coethnic sources of capital (i.e., Cuban, Mexican, or Nicaraguan), and only 6 percent benefited from coracial capital (i.e., Latino). Likewise, Mexicans were more likely to shop at stores owned by other Mexicans, Cubans at stores owned by Cubans, and Puerto Ricans at stores owned by Puerto Ricans. Finally, the number of Latina-owned businesses has increased faster than all other Latino-owned businesses. Nevertheless, Latina business owners have even less access to bank financing than their male counterparts, their businesses tend to be less profitable, and they concentrate disproportionately in food industries and domestic services (Li et al. 2006; Valdez 2011).

Differences among Latino entrepreneurs have resulted in highly segmented Latino business and commercial activities. In short, larger Latino-owned businesses have fared better than the small primarily sole-proprietor operations that constitute the vast majority of Latino-owned companies. Only 6.5 percent of Latino-owned businesses were large corporations, but these accounted for 40 percent of the total revenues of all Latino-owned businesses. Meanwhile, 85 percent of Latino-owned businesses were sole proprietorships, but these firms accounted for only 22 percent of total sales income.

The rise of Latino business and commerce has created opportunities for a few Latino entrepreneurs to become some of the most successful business leaders of the United States. Roberto Goizueta served as the CEO of the Coca-Cola Company for almost two decades. Arturo Moreno, owner of the Los Angeles Angels baseball team and son of the Mexican American owner of Tucson's Spanish-language newspaper *El Tucsonense*, became the first Latino to own a major U.S. sports franchise. Angel Ramos founded Telemundo, the first television station in Puerto Rico, which eventually moved to the Miami suburb of Hialeah and became the second-largest Spanish-language network in the United States.

Most Latino entrepreneurs experienced vastly different career trajectories. Surveys of Latino business owners revealed that many of them earned less than Latinos who worked in low-wage salaried positions. These business owners maintained their businesses only in order to remain autonomous from discriminatory labor markets, despite their lack of financial success. Furthermore, many Latino entrepreneurs who achieved financial success were financially successful only in relation to other Latinos, not in relation to white entrepreneurs. In general, Latino-owned businesses earned less than white-owned businesses. By the end of the twentieth century, 21 million U.S. companies generated more than $18 trillion in revenues, or almost $900,000 per company. However, 1.2 million Latino-owned businesses generated sales of $187 billion, or only $155,000 per company. Meanwhile, 40 percent of Latino-owned businesses had annual revenue of $10,000 or less. Latino-owned businesses therefore accounted for almost 6 percent of all U.S. businesses but only 1 percent of sales revenues. Moreover, comparatively few Latino entrepreneurs were included at the highest levels of corporate management. During the late 1990s, the magazine *Hispanic Business* revealed that there were only 217 executives at 118 Fortune 1,000 companies. In 2002, the number had risen to 928 executives at 162 Fortune 1,000 companies, still an extremely small number (Valdez 2011).

Despite different economic outcomes among Latino entrepreneurs and between Latino and white entrepreneurs, Texas A&M University sociologist Zulema Valdez (2011:97) has found that all Latino entrepreneurs share a "universal belief in their success." Their claims to success in some cases were linked to financial earnings but in many instances stemmed from establishing their own business, enabling them to leave behind "dirty, dangerous, or difficult" jobs or jobs where they experienced "verbal abuse, anti-immigrant sentiment, or racial or ethnic discrimination" (Valdez

2011:47–48). Others defined success in noneconomic terms, particularly women and recent immigrants who cited their mere survival, or their ability to help others.

Their universal belief in success through business ownership, despite unequal levels of economic success, highlights a central paradox in the history of Latino business and commerce and Latino history more broadly. Namely, Latino entrepreneurs, like many Latinos in general, continue to believe that progress and better lives are possible in the United States. This is why many of the immigrants among them have taken great risks to leave their home countries for the United States and continue to build lives in the United States even though they have experienced discrimination and economic inequalities here. In fact, many Latino migrants increasingly question this wisdom, saving only enough money in the United States to establish businesses in their Latin American home countries. Official recognition of Latino business and commercial activities, through their designation as historically significant, will acknowledge this paradox that has been central to not only Latino history but also U.S. history more broadly. Such recognition will acknowledge the many ways that Latinos and others have found success in the United States and also the structural inequalities that continue to prevent it from being the best country that it can be.

NOTE

1. *Note from the editors:* The establishment and growth of Latino business and commerce has mirrored the expansion of the Latino population itself. This chapter charts this growth since the sixteenth century to the nineteenth century and provides a comprehensive overview of the changing populations and conditions that inform the data presented in the subsequent chapters. For a more contemporary overview, see Chapter 3.

REFERENCES

Alberts, Heike. 2006. "Geographic Boundaries of the Cuban Enclave Economy in Miami." Pp. 35–48 in *Landscapes of the Ethnic Economy*, edited by David H. Kaplan and Wei Li. Lanham, MD: Rowman & Littlefield.

Bushnell, Amy. 1978. "The Menéndez Márquez Cattle Barony at La Chua and the Determinants of Economic Expansion in Seventeenth-Century Florida." *Florida Historical Quarterly* 56(4):411.

Chávez-García, Miroslava. 2004. *Negotiating Conquest: Gender and Power in California*. Tucson: University of Arizona Press.

Gamio, Manuel. 1930. *Mexican Immigration to the United States*. Chicago: University of Chicago Press.

García, María Cristina. 1997. *Havana USA: Cuban Exiles and Cuban Americans in South Florida, 1959–1994*. Berkeley: University of California Press.

Hewitt, Nancy A. 2001. *Southern Discomfort: Women's Activism in Tampa, Florida, 1880s–1920s*. Urbana-Champaign: University of Illinois Press.

Li, Wei, Gary Dymski, Maria W. L. Chee, Hyeon-Hyo Ahn, Carolyn Aldana, and Yu Zhou. 2006. "How Ethnic Banks Matter: Baking and Community/Economic Development in Los Angeles." Pp. 113–34 in *Landscapes of the Ethnic Economy*, edited by David H. Kaplan and Wei Li. Lanham, MD: Rowman & Littlefield.

Montejano, David. 1987. *Anglos and Mexicans in the Making of Texas, 1836–1986*. Austin: University of Texas Press.

Mormino, Gary, and Pozzetta, George. 1998. *The Immigrant World of Ybor City: Italians and Their Latin Neighbors in Tampa, 1885–1985*. Gainesville: University Press of Florida.

Oberle, Alex. 2006. "Latino Business Landscapes and the Hispanic Ethnic Economy." Pp. 149–64 in *Landscapes of the Ethnic Economy*, edited by David H. Kaplan and Wei Li. Lanham, MD: Rowman & Littlefield.

Pitt, Leonard. 1999. *Decline of the Californios: A Social History of the Spanish-Speaking Californias*. Berkeley: University of California Press.

Reséndez, Andrés. 2004. *Changing National Identities at the Frontier: Texas and New Mexico, 1800–1850*. New York: Cambridge University Press.

Sánchez, George J. 1993. *Becoming Mexican American: Ethnicity, Culture and Identity in Chicano Los Angeles, 1900–1945*. New York: Oxford University Press.

Sheridan, Thomas E. 1992. *Los Tucsonenses: The Mexican Community in Tucson, 1854–1941*. Tucson: University of Arizona Press.

Sheridan, Thomas E. 2012. *Arizona: A History*. Rev. ed. Tucson: University of Arizona Press.

Singer, Roberta L., and Elena Martínez. 2004. "A South Bronx Latin Music Tale." *Centro Journal* 16(1):193.

Taylor, Paul S. 1930. *Mexican Labor in the United States*. Berkeley: University of California Press.

Valdez, Zulema. 2011. *The New Entrepreneurs: How Race, Class, and Gender Shape American Enterprise.* Stanford, CA: Stanford University Press.

Valenzuela, M. Basilia, and Margarita Calleja Pinedo. 2009. *Empresarios migrantes mexicanos en Estados Unidos.* Jalisco: Centro Universitario de Ciencias Económico Administrativas, Universidad de Guadalajara.

Villarreal, Mary Ann. 2009. "Life on the 'Hill': Entrepreneurial Strategies in 1940s Corpus Christi." Pp. 43–60 in *An American Story: Mexican American Entrepreneurship and Wealth Creation.* West Lafayette, IN: Purdue University Press.

CHAPTER 3

Latino Businesses and Commerce: A Contemporary View

Michael J. Pisani and Iliana Perez

INTRODUCTION

With an emphasis on the postmillennial (2000 and beyond) era, this chapter updates the history and footprint of Latino businesses in the United States across recent time and space, contextualizing the recent economic contribution of Latino entrepreneurs and enterprises in the contemporary American business landscape and adding to the much longer historical overview presented by Geraldo Cadava in the previous chapter. We also introduce a novel method of classifying Latino-owned businesses (LOBs) by product and customer orientation strategy with preliminary evidence from 190 LOBs. We conclude with the historical trajectory of a single Latino-owned family business.

This chapter begins with a brief overview of four notable exemplars of contemporary Latino business leaders from three different spheres: the corporate environment, the family business, and the digital environment. The examples were chosen to highlight the increasingly visible and critical roles that Latinos play at the highest levels of corporate America, the continuing importance and legacy of Latino family businesses, and the contribution to high technology and innovation. The four are Carlos Gutierrez, former CEO of Kellogg's and U.S. commerce secretary; Antonio Rodolfo "Tony" Sanchez Jr., owner of Sanchez Oil and Gas and majority shareholder of IBC Bank; Andrea Brenholz, CEO and president of ATR International, a leader in staffing the STEM and business sectors; and Tom Chavez, serial technology entrepreneur and founder of Rapt and Krux.[1]

Carlos Gutierrez was born in Cuba in 1953, six years before the Cuban Revolution (1959) brought Fidel Castro to power. Gutierrez's father owned a pineapple plantation in Cuba that was expropriated, and the family left in 1960 for Florida. In 1975 Carlos Gutierrez began his long career with the multinational Kellogg Company (a Fortune 250 company), beginning as a sales representative and then moving into international operations with an early focus on Mexico and Latin America, leveraging his cultural capital and business acumen. By 1999 he became the CEO of the Kellogg Company (Battle Creek, Michigan), a post he held until selected by the George W. Bush administration to serve as the U.S. secretary of commerce (2005–2009). Gutierrez's post-Bush years include consulting, scholarly engagement, political involvement and media commentary, and board membership of several publicly traded companies, all on a national stage. He exemplifies the role Latinos play not only in corporate America but also in high-level government positions when Latino business leaders are tapped for their skills, experience, and knowledge.

Tony Sanchez Jr. is a descendent of the founder of Laredo, Texas; his family has remained connected to South Texas since the community's founding in 1755. Born in 1943 and educated in South Texas, Sanchez in the early 1970s expanded his father's (A. R. Sanchez) oil business, the privately held Sanchez Oil and Gas Corporation. The company made several large finds of natural gas in the South Texas region, giving rise to the company and its majority stake in the International Bank of Commerce ($12 billion in assets). Tony Sanchez's personal fortune is estimated to be more than $600 million. Ambitious beyond South Texas, Sanchez ran on the Democratic ticket unsuccessfully for Texas governor in 2002, polling 40 percent of the vote. The political defeat did not impede the family's financial success. With the next generation (A. R. Sanchez III), the family business continues with Sanchez Oil and Gas Corporation and has expanded horizontally with Sanchez Energy (begun in 2011 as a publicly traded company). Tony Sanchez's example embodies the trajectory of the Latino family business over the generations—from inheritance (from his father), business development (on his own), and handoff (to his offspring)—and the continuing legacy of family-owned businesses.

The daughter of immigrant parents from El Salvador and Poland, Andrea Brenholz is CEO and president of ATR International. Founded in 1988 by Brenholz's parents, ATR International is a leading Silicon

Valley–based firm specializing in staffing STEM and business positions. ATR International began when Brenholz's parents were tired of working for others and opened their own staffing business using the skill sets of each—engineering/IT (father) and office administration (mother). Now the fast-growing business has six offices across the United States and business alliances with partners in Canada and survived the dot.com bust by adapting and adding IT support. In 2018 Brenholz took over the family business from her parents as part of an intergenerational succession plan whereby she had been groomed for the position since her start in the business at the ground floor in marketing in 2007. Uniquely, CEO and President Andrea Brenholz represents a new face in Silicon Valley as a top female (Latina) executive and minority business leader. She is eager and well positioned to take the family-owned business to the highest levels of corporate America.[2]

From humble Hispanic origins in Albuquerque, New Mexico, Ray and Rosario Chavez sent all five of their children to Harvard University for undergraduate studies. Among them is Tom Chavez (born in 1968), who studied computer science and philosophy and then completed his doctoral degree at Stanford University in engineering-economic systems and operations research. Chavez is a serial entrepreneur, helping to create two very successful technology businesses: Rapt, a provider of yield management solutions for digital media founded in 1999, and Krux Digital, a provider of data governance (including consumer data analysis and intelligence) for websites. Rapt was sold to Microsoft in 2008,[3] where Chavez became the general manager of Microsoft's Online Publisher Business Group until he founded Krux in 2010. Krux was sold to Salesforce in 2016 for about $700 million. After Chavez's successful harvesting of these enterprises, perhaps future business ventures still lie ahead for this relatively young Latino entrepreneur. Chavez's story illustrates that all sectors of the economy, including high technology, are not only in reach of Latinos, but these emerging advanced economic sectors are also in active pursuit from talented, well-educated, and entrepreneurial-minded Latinos.

While these four examples highlight very public successes, LOBs do come in all shapes and sizes, from the informal *raspa* (shaved ice drinks) street vendor working the boulevards on a hot day to the formal business heights of information technology in Silicon Valley. Recent trends are offered in the next section.

CONTEMPORARY LOBS BY THE NUMBERS

This section provides a contemporary overview of business census data, offering a backdrop to the exploration and understanding for the context of LOBs.[4] Since 1982, the U.S. Census Bureau has reported the number of LOBs in its quinquennial Survey of Business Owners (SBO). The SBO is the most comprehensive and definitive accounting/census of businesses in the United States. The number of LOBs has increased precipitously from just under 250,000 in 1982 with sales receipts of $15 billion to over 3.3 million firms with sales receipts of $473 billion in 2012 (Figure 3.1). Of the 3,305,873 LOBs in 2012, 287,501 (8.7 percent) had paid employees; hence, most LOBs are owner-operated concerns. This percentage of LOBs with paid employees is considerably lower than the U.S. rate of 19.6 percent of all firms with paid employees. Additionally, the overall rate of growth was 46 percent for all LOBs and 26 percent for employer LOBs between 2007 and 2012; LOB growth surpassed growth of all other racial or ethnic groups (Orozco, Oyer, and Porras 2018). And in 2012, LOBs employed 2,329,553 workers and contributed $70.8 billion in payroll into the U.S. economy.

Figure 3.2 displays the average annual sales of LOBs and the percent change in LOB average annual sales over the SBO reporting periods (1982–2012). From 1982 to 1997, the average sales per LOB grow rapidly from

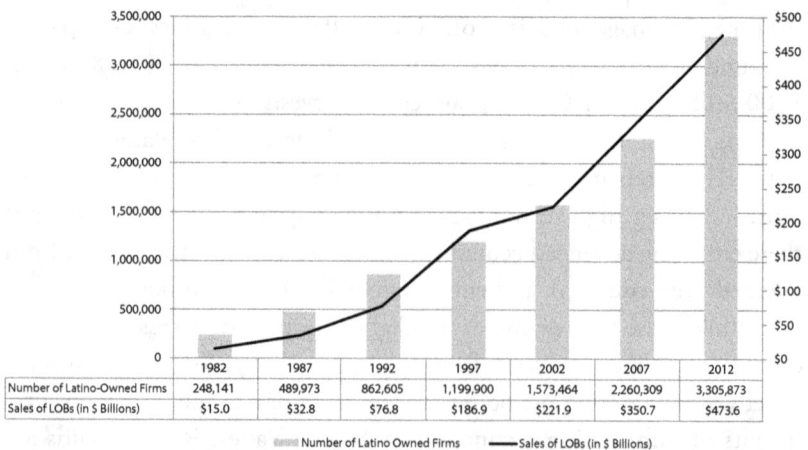

	1982	1987	1992	1997	2002	2007	2012
Number of Latino-Owned Firms	248,141	489,973	862,605	1,199,900	1,573,464	2,260,309	3,305,873
Sales of LOBs (in $ Billions)	$15.0	$32.8	$76.8	$186.9	$221.9	$350.7	$473.6

Number of Latino Owned Firms   Sales of LOBs (in $ Billions)

Figure 3.1 Total number and total sales of LOBs, 1982–2012. (Source: U.S. Census Bureau, Survey of Business Owners, various years [1982, 1987, 1992, 1997, 2002, 2007, 2012].)

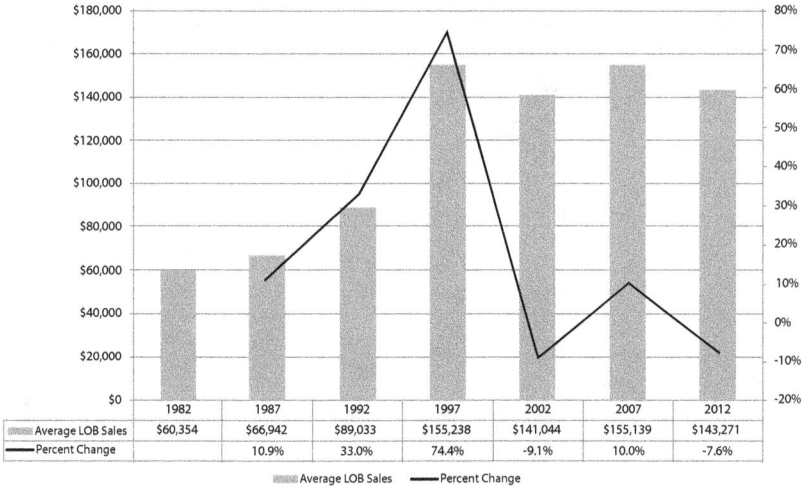

	1982	1987	1992	1997	2002	2007	2012
Average LOB Sales	$60,354	$66,942	$89,033	$155,238	$141,044	$155,139	$143,271
Percent Change		10.9%	33.0%	74.4%	-9.1%	10.0%	-7.6%

Figure 3.2 Average LOB sales and relative change, 1982–2012. (Source: U.S. Census Bureau, Survey of Business Owners, various years [1982, 1987, 1992, 1997, 2002, 2007, 2012].)

an average of $60,354 to $155,238. Thereafter, LOB average annual sales slide backwards somewhat and vacillate up and down just under its peak in 1997. The rapid pace of LOB initiation may in part explain this backwards movement and leveling off of average annual sales as new entrants begin smaller than more established firms (Dávila and Mora, 2013).

The latest 2012 SBO, the focus of this section, records 44.5 percent of LOBs as female-owned with $78.7 billion in sales (or 16.6 percent of all LOB sales). And between 2007 and 2012, the number of Latina-owned businesses expanded by 87 percent (Orozco et al. 2018). In Rhode Island, New York, and the District of Columbia, female-owned LOBs are the majority of all LOBs, 51.5 percent, 51.3 percent, and 50.3 percent, respectively. Four states comprise 71.9 percent of all LOBs and female-owned LOBs: California, Texas, Florida, and New York (Table 3.1). Five states had fewer than 1,000 LOBs in 2012: North Dakota, South Dakota, Vermont, Maine, and West Virginia. The numbers for the Dakotas is likely to change upward with the recent energy boom.

Mining the responses to the 2012 SBO provides for further observations of LOBs. Regarding educational achievement, one-third of Latino business owners are college graduates (associate degree, 5.9 percent; bachelor's degree, 15.9 percent; graduate degree, 11.7 percent). Roughly one-fifth of Latino business owners possess less than a high school education (18.9 percent) or a

TABLE 3.1 *2012 Top 10 States for All LOBs and Female-Owned LOBs*

Top 10 States	No. of All LOBs	% of Total	Top 10 States	No. of Female LOBs	% of Total
California	815,304	24.7	California	365,576	24.9
Texas	687,570	20.8	Texas	290,085	19.8
Florida	604,128	18.3	Florida	261,992	17.9
New York	266,624	8.1	New York	136,855	9.3
New Jersey	93,336	2.8	Arizona	41,725	2.8
Illinois	92,231	2.8	New Jersey	40,266	2.7
Arizona	89,383	2.7	Illinois	40,110	2.7
Georgia	56,339	1.7	Georgia	23,966	1.6
Colorado	51,141	1.5	Colorado	22,913	1.6
New Mexico	46,477	1.4	New Mexico	20,307	1.4
Top 10 Total	*2,802,533*	*84.8*	*Top 10 Total*	*1,243,795*	*84.7*

Source: 2012 Survey of Business Owners, U.S. Census.

high school education or equivalent (22.9 percent) background. The remainder have achieved vocational or trade school training (8.0 percent) or some time in college (16.6 percent). The largest age cohort for Latino business owners is the 45–54 age range (28.6 percent), followed closely by the 35–44 age group (26.8 percent). Few are younger than 25 (4.5 percent) or older than 65 (7.0 percent), with the remainder between 25 and 34 (15.9 percent) and 55 and 64 years of age (17.2 percent). Just over half (52.7 percent) of Latino business owners were born outside the United States. Most Latino business owners were able to conduct business in English (89.2 percent), and a majority could also do so in Spanish (58.2 percent).

In 2012, about half (48.5 percent) of LOBs were situated in the home and operated as home-based enterprises. This may be related to the relative youth of many LOBs, whereby one-third had been in business two years or less by 2012 and only 17.7 percent had begun operations before 2000. In regard to startup capital, more than half of LOBs (54.9 percent) began their business with less than $5,000, and fully 83.2 percent began business life with startup funds less than $25,000. More than one-quarter (28.5 percent) of Latino business owners had previously owned another enterprise, and 88.1 percent of owners founded their current business. About 4 in 10 (37.1 percent) Latino business owners spent less than 20 hours per week in their business, another 21.2 percent worked between 20 and

39 hours in their business, and the rest (41.7 percent) worked full-time or more in their business. Nearly 6 in 10 (58.3 percent) LOBs served as the owners' principal income. Not many LOBs were connected to franchise ownership (4.2 percent) or had operations outside the United States (1.7 percent). Few LOBs had a web presence (17.8 percent), and very few (5.6 percent) had e-commerce operations or sales, and of those who did engage e-commerce, only 2.0 percent did a majority of their sales online.

Only in the Miami–Fort Lauderdale–West Palm Beach metropolitan area does the share of LOBs outperform the share of the Latino population, and the greater Miami metro area contains the largest concentration of LOBs in the United States (see Table 3.2, Panel A). This result may be due in part to occupational discrimination in an ethnic enclave (Portes and Shafer 2007; see also Chapter 6 in this volume). Panel A of Table 3.2 also displays the top 10 metropolitan areas by the total number of Latinos, share of Latinos in the metro area, and the number and share of Latino enterprises. While the largest metro areas where Latinos live are as expected, LOBs generally are less represented than their aggregate numbers would suggest. This may be due in part to continuing overt financing, language, and discrimination challenges as well as problematic immigration status concerns for individuals (i.e., undocumented) and families (e.g., mixed documentation) in the absence of needed immigration reform policy that forces many Latinos into the shadows of the informal and unrecorded economy (Richardson and Pisani 2012).

South Texas encompasses the top three metro areas with the highest shares of Latinos and LOBs. Laredo, Texas, contains the highest concentration of LOBs (88.3 percent), followed by McAllen-Edinburg-Mission (86.7 percent) and Brownsville-Harlingen (78.8 percent). Still, the share of LOBs is smaller than the share of the overall Latino population, indicating that LOBs are underrepresented even in these mostly Latino communities indicative of continuing challenges as outlined above. This is also true for the top 10 most Hispanic-concentrated metro areas. The top 10 metropolitan areas with the highest concentration of Latinos and the number and share of LOBs are reported in Table 3.2, Panel B.

Recent population growth in the Southeast mostly describes the metropolitan areas with the fastest-growing Latino populations. These communities, such as Charlotte and Raleigh, North Carolina, are often described as nontraditional receiving areas or new receiving areas for Latinos. In 6 of the 10 metro areas (Charlotte, Raleigh, Atlanta, Oklahoma

TABLE 3.2 *Top 10 Metro Areas by Latino Population and LOBs*

Panel A: Top 10 Metro Areas— Largest Total Latino Population	Latino Population	Latino Share	No. of LOBs	LOB Share
Los Angeles, Long Beach, Anaheim	5,979,000	45.1	393,051	26.5
New York, Newark, Jersey City	4,780,000	23.9	339,415	15.4
Miami, Fort Lauderdale, West Palm Beach	2,554,000	43.3	423,163	47.0
Houston, The Woodlands, Sugar Land	2,335,000	36.4	164,923	27.2
Riverside, San Bernardino, Ontario	2,197,000	49.4	122,233	36.5
Chicago, Naperville, Elgin	2,070,000	21.8	89,523	9.9
Dallas, Fort Worth, Arlington	1,943,000	28.4	117,582	18.3
Phoenix, Mesa, Scottsdale	1,347,000	30.1	54,393	16.0
San Antonio, New Braunfels	1,259,000	55.7	81,126	43.3
San Diego, Carlsbad	1,084,000	33.3	62,753	21.4
Panel B: Top 10 Metro Areas— Highest Share of Latino Population	Latino Population	Latino Share	No. of LOBs	LOB Share
Laredo (Texas)	254,000	95.3	25,133	88.3
McAllen, Edinburg, Mission (Texas)	758,000	91.2	71,377	86.7
Brownsville, Harlingen (Texas)	373,000	88.7	28,839	78.8
El Centro (California)	148,000	82.3	8,029	71.7
El Paso (Texas)	676,000	81.2	52,065	77.1
Las Cruces (New Mexico)	142,000	66.8	8,429	51.7
Visalia, Porterville (California)	288,000	63.0	9,147	39.2
Yuma (Arizona)	125,000	61.6	5,136	47.4
Corpus Christi (Texas)	289,000	59.5	16,148	42.7
Salinas (California)	282,000	57.5	8,262	27.4
Panel C: Top 10 Metro Areas— Fastest-Growing Latino Population (2000–2013)	Latino Population	Latino Share	No. of LOBs	LOB Share
Charlotte, Concordia, Gastonia (North Carolina)	277,000	11.7	11,610	5.7
Raleigh (North Carolina)	132,000	10.2	5,868	5.4
Atlanta, Sandy Springs, Roswell (Georgia)	588,000	10.5	44,240	7.5

(continued)

Panel C: Top 10 Metro Areas— Fastest-Growing Latino Population (2000–2013)	Latino Population	Latino Share	No. of LOBs	LOB Share
Orlando (Florida)	645,000	28.3	61,157	26.3
Cape Coral, Fort Meyers (Florida)	133,000	19.6	12,262	18.8
Oklahoma City (Oklahoma)	167,000	36.9	7,130	5.9
Tampa (Florida)	517,000	17.7	45,490	17.5
Miami, Fort Lauderdale, West Palm Beach	2,554,000	43.3	423,163	47.0
Seattle, Tacoma, Bellevue (Washington)	355,000	9.7	11,906	4.0
Washington, DC; Arlington, Alexandria (DC, Virginia, Maryland, West Virginia)	906,000	15.3	65,997	11.6

Source: 2012 Survey of Business Owners, Pew Research Center, "Hispanic Population and Origin in Select U.S. Metropolitan Areas, 2014."

City, Seattle, and Washington, D.C.), the Latino share of businesses is significantly smaller than the Latino population share. The Latino business share is closer to the population share in three Florida communities (Fort Myers, Orlando, and Tampa). And only in the Miami, Fort Lauderdale, West Palm Beach metro area are Latino more represented as business owners than the general population, as described above. The top 10 fastest-growing metro areas are displayed in Table 3.2, Panel C.

These numbers are illustrative of the economic contributions LOBs make to the overall economy but lack contextualization. In a nutshell, LOBs are growing in importance, even more so in the present, as one of the primary engines of growth in the U.S. economy. However, LOBs are often underrepresented in their communities. If the United States is to flourish and prosper, so too must LOBs. Unleashing LOBs with concerted, supportive, and strategic public policy is paramount to unleashing the U.S. economy. To do so, the more we know and understand about LOBs, the better choices can be made to effect the best outcomes for all stakeholders.

THE LOB LANDSCAPE

The primary business association allied with Latino businesses is the U.S. Hispanic Chamber of Commerce (USHCC) and its over 200 local affiliates. While the USHCC seeks to represent all Latino businesses, the 2016 SLEI Survey of U.S. Latino Business Owners indicates that 22.8 percent of respondent Latino firms had been members of the Hispanic Chamber (either locally or nationally). Another 14.1 percent indicated that they had been a member of a Latino business-oriented nonprofit, and collectively, 36.7 percent reported belonging to a Hispanic chamber and/ or a Latino business-oriented nonprofit. The SLEI survey also notes that male LOBs join at a slightly higher rate than female LOBs. A small study of Texas-based LOBs and Hispanic Chamber membership renewal noted that female LOBs renew membership at higher rates and reported that length of time as a chamber member and business size were also determinants of membership renewal (Olivas and Frankwick 2016).

Agius Vallejo (2012:146) notes in her study of the Mexican American middle class that membership in organizations such as the Hispanic Chamber is a business "strategy to obtain more clients and increase revenues" more so than acquisition of specific skills. Beyond scaling, some small LOBs may also seek out business assistance, especially those with weaker business networks. In a 2010 survey of small businesses conducted in South Texas, 19.5 percent of LOBs had contacted the local chamber of commerce to access information about starting or running a business (Pisani et al. 2017). The connection between chamber activities and LOBs warrants further academic investigation.

Building upon and adapting the work of Curci and Mackoy (2010) and Bates and Robb (2014), LOBs can be categorized by customer- and product-based profiles. The focus is directed toward the strategic emphasis placed on the Hispanic customer and Hispanic-oriented products. This allows the construction of a two-by-two typology with four quadrants based on customers (Hispanic and non-Hispanic) and products (Hispanic and non-Hispanic). Figure 3.3 depicts the typology where four possible outcomes are observed: Hispanic customers/Hispanic products, labeled the ethnic (Hispanic) market niche; Hispanic customers/non-Hispanic products, named the ethnic (Hispanic) friendly marketplace; non-Hispanic customers/Hispanic products, labeled the ethnic (Hispanic) market "experience"; and non-Hispanic customers/non-Hispanic products, named the postethnic (Hispanic) marketplace. In marketing parlance, the quadrants can be characterized as highly segmented (quadrant 1), product integrated (quadrant 2), market integrated (quadrant 3), and highly integrated (quadrant 4). In essence, the typology reflects a continuum of LOB integration[5] (Figure 3.4).

		Primary Customer Ethnic Profile	
		Hispanic Customers	**Non-Hispanic Customers**
Primary Product Ethnic Profile	**Hispanic Product**	Ethnic (Hispanic) Market Niche *Quadrant 1:* *Highly Segmented*	Ethnic (Hispanic) Market "Experience" *Quadrant 3:* *Market Integrated*
	Non-Hispanic Product	Ethnic (Hispanic) Friendly Marketplace *Quadrant 2:* *Product Integrated*	Post-Ethnic (Hispanic) Marketplace *Quandrant 4:* *Highly Integrated*

Figure 3.3 Typology of LOBs by clientele base and product. (Adapted from Curci, Roberto and Robert Mackoy [2010], "Immigrant Business Enterprises: A Classification Framework Conceptualization and Test," *Thunderbird International Business Review*, 52[2], 107–21.)

A) The Market Integration Continuum

Ethnic Market Niche	Ethnic Friendly Marketplace	Ethnic Market Experience	Post-Ethnic Marketplace
Low	<Integration>		High

B) SLEI-Ed Participants Recorded Along the Continuum

15.8%	23.2%	5.8%	55.3%

Figure 3.4 A continuum of LOB market integration. (Source: 190 SLEI-Ed participants, 2017–2018 [cohorts 3–5].)

The typology may be operationalized to reflect businesses generally and LOBs on the ground. For example, in the highly segmented or ethnic market niche quadrant, Fiesta supermarkets (owned by Grocers Supply, a non-LOB) cater to a mostly Hispanic clientele, offering products of value to Hispanic consumers.[6] Examples of LOBs in the highly segmented space are Cidrines, a Puerto Rican-based maker of breads and pastries, and Cacique, Inc., a California-based specialty maker of Mexican cheeses, chorizos, and *cremas*; both firms target the Hispanic consumer (Figure 3.5). While Western Union (a non-LOB enterprise) has the ability to transfer money anywhere in the world, it specializes in money transfers to Mexico and Latin America, offering services in Spanish and scores of locations in Mexico and the United States. Western Union offers a non-Hispanic product—wire transfer—for an ethnic clientele engaged in sending money

		Primary Customer Ethnic Profile	
		Hispanic Customers	**Non-Hispanic Customers**
Primary Product Ethnic Profile	**Hispanic Product**	Highly Segmented: - Ethnic Media - Ethnic Foods - Ethnic Supermarkets - Ethnic Retailing - Ethnic Bakery Examples: Cidrines, Cacique, Inc.	Market Integrated: - Ethnic Restaurants - Ethnic Consulting - Ethnic Advertising Example: H Code Media
	Non-Hispanic Product	Product Integrated: - Real Estate - Medical Services - Automotive Sales & Repair - Wire Transfers Example: Ancira Enterprises	Highly Integrated: - Construction - Waste Management - Cleaning Services - Insurance - Banking, Finance - Landscaping Services Example: Nation Waste, Inc.

Figure 3.5 Typology of LOBs by clientele base and product. (Adapted from Curci, Roberto, and Robert Mackoy [2010], "Immigrant Business Enterprises: A Classification Framework Conceptualization and Test," *Thunderbird International Business Review*, 52[2], 107–21.)

and remittances from the United States to Mexico, an example of the product category. The LOB Ancira Enterprises of San Antonio is one of the largest automobile dealers in the United States, with branches in heavily Latino Laredo and Eagle Pass and majority Latino San Antonio. Because of its majority Hispanic customer base, Ancira is like Western Union and represents product integration or the ethnic friendly marketplace. Under its dealerships are vehicle makes from GM, Nissan, Ford, and Volkswagen (products that are ethnically neutral). Its founder Ernesto Ancira, who grew up in Mexico City, opened his first dealership in 1972 selling cars to the greater San Antonio population, with present annual revenues approaching $1 billion.

A market-integrated example is On the Border Mexican Grill & Cantina, a non-LOB restaurant chain that serves ethnic Mexican food and beverages targeting a primarily non-Hispanic client base, in essence re-creating the ethnic market experience. In the same category of market integrated, the LOB H Code Media specializes in creating advertising campaigns targeting Hispanic customers (its Hispanic-oriented product) for general non-Hispanic-owned businesses (its non-Hispanic business-to-business customer) in such segments as automotive, pharmaceutical, air transportation, fast food, and discount retailing segments, among others. Waste disposal is ethnically oriented by neither customer nor product class and is an example of the highly integrated or postethnic marketplace classification. Nation Waste, Inc., a LOB based in Houston with trash removal operations in Houston and Austin, is owned and operated by Maria Rios, a dynamic Latina entrepreneur originally from El Salvador.

Utilizing the nearly 200 participants in the latest three rounds of the Stanford Latino Entrepreneurship Initiative/SLEI–Education Scaling (SLEI-Ed) program from 2016–2017 (see Chapter 13), we are able to fill in a bit more of the categorical detail provided by the typology. Preselection criteria for inclusion in the SLEI-Ed program requires for-profit firms to have generated at least $1 million in revenue or have raised at least $500,000 in external funding, and preselection for nonprofit organizations requires an annual budget of at least $1 million. Additionally, SLEI-Ed participants must display a clear vision and investment in the communities they serve. Because of the SLEI-Ed training and connection to SLEI, these firms and organizations are well known to SLEI and subsequently to the authors assisting in the category placement. Although not representative of LOBs generally because they represent less than 10 percent of all LOBs by sales revenue, the SLEI-Ed participants do illustrate very high potential firms and organizations. While this may skew categorical placement, it provides a wider qualitative and first glimpse into the classification and trajectory of high-potential LOBs.

In all, the authors classified 190 SLEI-Ed firms as to the ethnic profile of the customer base (Hispanic, non-Hispanic) and the product (Hispanic and non-Hispanic). The four quadrants are represented as follows (and are embedded in Figure 3.4):

- Quadrant 1. Hispanic market niche/highly segmented (Hispanic customers/Hispanic product): 15.8 percent.
- Quadrant 2. Hispanic-friendly marketplace/product integrated (Hispanic customers/non-Hispanic product): 23.2 percent.
- Quadrant 3. Hispanic market experience/market integrated (non-Hispanic customers/Hispanic product): 5.8 percent.
- Quadrant 4. Post-Hispanic marketplace/highly integrated (non-Hispanic customers/non-Hispanic product): 55.3 percent.

As LOBs become more integrated into the economy, they tend to widen their market presence (Curci and Mackoy, 2010). This market widening includes serving a broader array of customers with a broader array of products, resulting in higher-revenue LOBs more often operating within the postethnic market space. As expected, the SLEI-Ed participants reviewed reflect a majority share in the highly integrated quadrant. Nonetheless, high-potential LOBs are found in each market segment quadrant and can be successful in fully exploiting selective market segments. However, it is illustrative that the majority of SLEI-Ed LOBs are located in quadrant 4, supporting the view of a continuum in the development and integration of LOBs into the economy (as depicted in Figure 3.4). Future research focusing on the entire scale of LOB size and scope including entrepreneur background (e.g., age, gender, nativity, education, language) will bring a fuller portrait of LOB classification; however, the high-potential LOBs represented by the SLEI-Ed participants reflect LOBs with a larger impact and footprint where the marginal effects of supportive public policy may have the largest economic returns.

These categories are not absolute but are instructive for the entire array of LOBs, and some LOBs may span more than one category if involved in multiple market segments. For example, Cantú Construction and Development Company, a major LOB builder and developer, reflects both product and high integration, as it builds homes and residential developments primarily for Latino residents in the lower Rio Grande Valley of South Texas and commercial properties in South Texas regardless of product and ethnic orientation. LOBs may find strategic success in and across the four quadrants, as the above examples reflect. The extended entrepreneurial life story of Refugio and Juanita Rochín spans much of the twentieth century and reflects businesses that spanned the highly segmented and market integrated categories within the larger backdrop of U.S. society, polity, and economy (see the box and accompanying figures).

For the Love of Family and Business: Refugio and Juanita Rochín, Hispanic Entrepreneurs in Southern California, 1929–1993

Television's Cisco Kid (Leo Carillo), Richard Nixon, California governors Goodwin Knight and Edmund "Pat" Brown, California senators Thomas Kuchel and Clair Engle, Mexican Baja California governor Braulio Maldonado, and Conrad Hilton all dined at Acapulco Gardens during its heyday (1950s–early 1960s) in Oceanside, California. Acapulco Gardens was a popular Mexican food restaurant and entertainment destination owned and run by Refugio and Juanita Rochín. The facility seated 350 patrons and hosted governors, club meetings, and even a political debate between senatorial candidates broadcast on radio. Acapulco Gardens and the Rochíns are an entrepreneurial story, a Latino story, and an American story rooted in pursuing the American dream (Figure 3.6).

Figure 3.6 Acapulco Gardens, Oceanside, California.

For Refugio, the pursuit of that dream began in 1923. At age 15 with an $8 U.S. visa, he left his hometown of San José de Gracia, Sinaloa, Mexico, for a better life in Los Angeles. One of seven children working as a pharmacy hand in Mexico, Refugio believed that greater opportunities lay ahead north of the border. He took whatever jobs he could find with his limited English-speaking ability: factory worker making tires and fertilizer, a few years spent with the railroad on a construction gang in Wyoming, farmhand, and night jobs selling cars and dry goods. In 1928 Refugio met Juanita at a social function (Alianza Hispano Americano), where he was smitten by her musical talents (e.g., piano, song) and her beauty. Juanita was born and raised in the Mexican part of town along the railroad tracks of Colton, located in San Bernardino County in southern California.

Within the year, Refugio Rochín (1908–1994) and Juanita Rodriguez (1913–1999) eloped to Mexicali, Mexico, though not without some family turmoil. Juanita's father was not happy with his daughter being "taken away" at age 15, which landed Refugio in some legal trouble and temporary incarceration (on a rape charge) when the couple returned from their vows through Calexico, California. Soon the ill feelings were mended and the charges were dropped, and Refugio and Juanita began their lives together in southern California. To make ends meet, Refugio immediately began working as a delivery boy for Juanita's uncle, who operated a grocery store and *panadería* (bakery), and within two years launched his own mom-and-pop grocery business that became the largest business of its type in Coachella and Riverside County.

Figure 3.7 Grocery store in Carlsbad, California.

Refugio and Juanita operated their first business, the grocery store in Coachella, until 1937, when they sold their Coachella store and moved to Carlsbad in search of a better climate. In Carlsbad, they capitalized on their accumulated business knowledge and bought an existing grocery store (Figure 3.7), a horizontal move.

In 1940, the Rochíns sold their grocery store in Carlsbad and purchased and operated a Mexican restaurant, El Mejicano #2, while remaining in Carlsbad. By 1942 they sold the restaurant and turned to farming pole tomatoes. Refugio did this until 1944, supplying his produce in part to Mexican braceros working in citrus and avocado fields. Because of the difficulties of farming, the Rochíns returned once again to trading in food products, opening C&R* Provisions in Oceanside, a wholesale food enterprise, followed by Rochín's Market (Figure 3.8). Next door to C&R Provisions, Acapulco Gardens was constructed in 1949 and began operations in 1950. Acapulco Gardens ran its course from 1950 to 1965.

Figure 3.8 Rochín's Market, Oceanside, California.

On the Acapulco Gardens' last day, a story ran in the local newspaper that lamented its loss:

> He [Refugio] would stand at the door, always a glad man whose face seemed to have been washed with a smile at birth. His wife [Juanita] would be at his side and they welcomed you to their home. The Acapulco Gardens stands as a vacant monument to another day. . . . It was in those days when people would wait to order his Mexican meal or a slice of his roast beef, the city's bright nightspot. Men of Oceanside and Carlsbad were honored there, politicians were introduced there, newlyweds were received there, friends were made there, athletic teams were toasted there and the good life of a good area was stimulated there. . . .

In its grand, glorious days the Acapulco Gardens belonged to everyone. No one and no city had a lock on the pleasure it dispensed. It was, its epitaph should read, a clean, good, fine place to go to eat, to drink, to feel good.

. . . "I started from scratch" he [Refugio] said, "I had no surplus cash and when business slowed down I had to refinance. So I sold the bar operation and leased it back. The rent was very high. I couldn't make ends meet." Always, from the beginning, the Acapulco Gardens had been considered a generous participant in community affairs. Its float would win parade honors, its owners would be available for work on any project and its kitchen would meet the budget of any service club. And it disturbs Rufus [Refugio] that in the end he and his restaurant were only watching and hoping rather than doing. "When things got tough, there wasn't any time to participate," he explained. "People expected us to participate. They didn't realize there was a financial problem. Now they realize it." (Grossman 1965)

The demise (bankruptcy) of Acapulco Gardens was not the end of the entrepreneurial trail for the Rochíns. They returned to Coachella and their U.S. business roots and opened and operated a mom-and-pop grocery store until retirement in 1993. Beyond entrepreneurship, *familia* (family) was also central to the Rochíns. They raised four children, three girls and one boy, in a home that valued honesty, hard work, *respeto* (respect), resourcefulness, *orgullo* (pride), humility, education, *musica* (music), and bilingualism. Family members were expected to care for each other, offer hospitality, show graciousness, look clean, and honor elders, *abuelitos/as* (grandaprents), and *primos/as* (cousins). Refugio and Juanita reminded their children that every action was a reflection on the family's reputation, honor, and status for *la familia* (the family) Rochín-Rodriguez. Refugio and Juanita Rochín would be labeled serial entrepreneurs in today's entrepreneurial ecosystem and lexicon.

All this was achieved in a social, political, and economic environment where Mexican-origin peoples in the early to mid-twentieth century sat in separate sections on buses and in theaters, had "special" (nonintegrated) swim times in community swimming pools, navigated red-lined housing and business/banking areas, held little political power or representation, and were forced to speak English in school, with punishment exercised to those who spoke Spanish in separate and unequal schools, and where *la migra* (Border Patrol) acted with impunity, rounding up Mexican-looking peoples for deportation. In this reality, utilizing an ethnic enclave to begin entrepreneurial life allowed the Rochíns to overcome the challenges of overt discrimination and eventually succeed in the mainstream business environment. This challenge, however, still remains for many Latino-owned businesses today.

The entrepreneurial and family life of Refugio and Juanita Rochín connect Latinos to the American story through serial business ownership. For a long time and through many challenges, Latinos continue to contribute to the American economy; indeed, Latino-owned businesses are at the forefront of the American business experience today.

Sources: Refugio I. Rochín, personal correspondence, October 29, 2017; Rodriguez de Rochín (1998).

*C&R stands for Castorena and Rochín. Manuel Castorena was Rochín's partner during the first year of operation.

The Rochín family story of Refugio and Juanita is a powerful one, encapsulating serial entrepreneurship within the boundary of the Latino cultural experience.[7] The Rochíns owned and operated enterprises that at one time or another occupied all four quadrants of the customer- and product-based profiles. Acapulco Gardens and El Mejicano #2 served an ethnic product to nonethnic customers (quadrant 3). The Rochíns farmed pole tomatoes for sale to Braceros; the operation provided a nonethnic product to ethnic consumers (quadrant 2). The initial foray into the grocery business in Coachella brought ethnic goods for sale for an ethnic customer base (quadrant 1), but later the grocery business moved into Riverside, supplying general products to a general population (quadrant 4). In the end, the Rochíns returned to their grocer roots in Coachella and the safety of an enclave business and community (quadrant 1). In many ways, the Rochín family businesses reflect the trajectory of LOBs presented in the chapter.

CONCLUSION

The story of Refugio and Juanita Rochín provides historical context and trajectory of Latino entrepreneurs with business operations extending nearly to the twenty-first century. This chapter brings their story further into the present through a description of contemporary Latino entrepreneurship focused on entrepreneurial profiles, statistics, and strategic business models. There is abundant room for further research on LOBs; chief among them presented in this chapter is the further development and analysis of the clientele/product typology by firm age, firm size, industry, geography, ownership gender, operational language(s), generation and immigration status, socioeconomic networks, and so on.

The importance of Latino enterprises continues to rise, and the future success of the American economy depends heavily on the success, ingenuity, and incorporation of Latino entrepreneurs. The legacies of Carlos Gutierrez, Tony Sanchez, Andrea Brenholz, Tom Chavez and scores of others past and present (as described in later chapters) may help inspire future Latinos/as to join in and succeed as entrepreneurs. The SLEI annual reports contain some of the latest data available on Latino entrepreneurship and should be consulted along with U.S. census data for the most up-to-date information concerning LOBs.

NOTES

1. The information presented on each of the three Latino business leaders comes from popular media sources.
2. The information for Andrea Brenholz was derived from a personal interview (April 2019) with the second author and from the company's public website.

3. The sales price was undisclosed; some unconfirmed estimates range upwards of $200 million.

4. The primary source of data in this section is derived from the 2012 Survey of Business Owners, U.S. Census.

5. Bates and Robb (2014) find that minority businesses that focus on a minority clientele perform worse than minority businesses that focus on a nonminority clientele, perhaps indicating a progression of market integration and performance.

6. The company information presented as exemplars of each quadrant comes from popular media sources and company websites.

7. Latino cultural experience includes migration and immigration for work, the use of social capital to move forward, life in an ethnic enclave for survival, racism and stunted opportunities, and so on.

REFERENCES

Agius Vallejo, Jody. 2012. *Barrios to Burbs: The Making of the Mexican American Middle Class*. Stanford, CA: Stanford University Press.

Bates, Timothy, and Alicia Robb. 2014. "Small-Business Viability in America's Urban Minority Communities." *Urban Studies* 51(13):2844–62.

Curci, Roberto, and Robert Mackoy. 2010. "Immigrant Business Enterprises: A Classification Framework Conceptualization and Test." *Thunderbird International Business Review* 52(2):107–21.

Dávila, Alberto, and Marie T. Mora. 2013. *Hispanic Entrepreneurs in the 2000s: An Economic Profile and Policy Implications*. Stanford, CA: Stanford University Press.

Grossman, Irv. 1965. "Closing Day." *Oceanside Blade Tribune*, June 28.

Olivas, Denisse, and Gary L. Frankwick. 2016. "Understanding Hispanic Entrepreneurial Success: An Exploratory Study." *Journal of Business Diversity* 16(1):11–22.

Orozco, Marlene, Paul Oyer, and Jerry I. Porras. 2018. "2017 State of Latino Entrepreneurship Report." Stanford Latino Entrepreneurship Initiative, Graduate School of Business, Stanford University. https://www.gsb.stanford .edu/faculty-research/publications/state-latino-entrepreneurship-2017.

Pisani, Michael J., Joseph M. Guzman, Chad Richardson, Carlos Sepulveda, and Lyonel Laulié. 2017. "Small Business Enterprises and Latino Entrepreneurship:

An Enclave or Mainstream Activity in South Texas?" *Journal of International Entrepreneurship* 15(3):295–323.

Portes, Alejandro, and Steven Shafer. 2007. "Revisiting the Enclave Hypothesis: Miami Twenty-Five Years Later." Pp. 157–90 in *The Sociology of Entrepreneurship*, edited by Martin Ruef and Michael Lounsbury. Oxford, UK: Elsevier JAI.

Richardson, Chad, and Michael J. Pisani. 2012. *The Informal and Underground Economy of the South Texas Border.* Austin: University of Texas Press.

Rodriguez de Rochín, Juanita. 1998. *Juanita: My Life with Refugio.* East Lansing: Julian Samora Research Institute, Michigan State University.

CHAPTER 4

The Economic Contributions of Latino Entrepreneurs

Robert W. Fairlie, Zulema Valdez, and Jody Agius Vallejo

INTRODUCTION

Entrepreneurial activity in the United States is generally associated with the social and economic incorporation of immigrant minorities and their descendants (Valdez 2011), facilitating their economic mobility and wealth creation (Butler and Morales 2012; Keister, Vallejo, and Borelli 2015). Entrepreneurship also fuels job creation and economic growth (Valdez 2015). An examination of Latino entrepreneurship in the United States thus contributes to our understanding of this group's economic success and contributions to the larger U.S. economy (Dávila, Mora, and Zeitlin 2014). Though many immigrant and ethnic minority groups in the United States engage in business ownership at disproportionately higher rates than non-Hispanic whites, historically Latino rates of business ownership have lagged behind all other immigrant groups. Prior research has identified several factors that contribute to low rates of business ownership among Latinos, chief among them aggregate lower levels of educational attainment and personal wealth and a lack of coethnic social capital—the information and resources found within immigrant and ethnic networks that facilitate individual or collective economic action (Guo, Chen, and Yu 2016; Fairlie and Woodruff 2010).

Recent research, however, suggests that business ownership among Latinos in the United States is undergoing a transition. Though Latinos remain underrepresented in business ownership as a share of the overall population, today Latino business ownership is growing at unprecedented rates (Dávila and Mora 2013; Dávila et al. 2014). According to the U.S. Census Bureau's Survey of Business Owners (SBO), between 2007 and 2012 Latino-owned businesses grew by 46.3 percent. Latinos now own more firms than any other ethnic minority group in the United States, and according to the 2015 "State of Latino Entrepreneurship" report, Latino-owned businesses are located across all regions of the United States, with 75 percent in majority non-Latino neighborhoods serving mostly non-Latino customers (Rivers and Porras 2015) and with a growing presence in new immigrant destinations including the rural South.

This chapter provides an overview of estimates of Latino entrepreneurship using two sources of nationally representative government data for a comprehensive picture of Latino business ownership in the United States. We provide an extensive analysis of the contributions of Latino business owners to the U.S. economy, including identifying key patterns of Latino entrepreneurship as measured by business owner income, total sales and receipts, employment, payroll, industrial clustering, and exports. As we will demonstrate, Latino-owned businesses are making significant contributions to the economy, and while disparities remain, recent numbers show rapid growth and economic progress.

METHODS AND DATA

We present estimates of Latino business ownership and contributions to the U.S. economy using data from the two primary sources of nationally representative government data providing information on business activity by race and ethnicity: the American Community Survey (ACS) and the SBO. The two data sets are considered the authoritative government sources of data on population demographics (ACS) and minority business outcomes (SBO). Combined, they provide a comprehensive picture of Latino business ownership in the United States.

The focus and coverage of the two data sets are distinctive, leading to major differences in estimates that should be briefly noted before presenting results. The ACS data focus on business ownership only when it is the main job activity of the individual, whereas the SBO data capture all business entities (based on tax records) even if they are small-scale side businesses (e.g., consulting activities or contract work) or multiple businesses owned by the same person. Hence, the ACS provides data on the number of Latinos who own businesses versus the total number of business entities that are owned by Latinos. As shown below, the total number of businesses captured in the SBO is much higher than the total number of business owners captured in the ACS. Another difference is that the ACS focuses on the income received by the business owner instead of the total sales of the business as in the SBO.

American Community Survey

The first data set that will be used is the latest five-year microdata sample of the ACS, 2011–2015. The ACS is a household survey and provides information on business ownership, income, and industries at the owner level. Individuals are included for only one year in the ACS and cannot be followed over time. The data are pooled over the five years to make the sample representative at smaller geographical levels. The ACS is one of the only nationally representative Census Bureau datasets that provides a large sample size of Latino business owners.

The ACS includes over 9 million observations for working-age adults (ages 20–64). Even after conditioning on business ownership, the sample size is very large, making it possible to explore the causes of differences in net business owner income. The ACS includes more than half a million observations for business owners and is also large enough to examine industrial concentrations.

In the ACS microdata, business ownership is measured by using the class-of-worker question that refers to the respondent's main job or business activity (i.e., activity with the most hours) at the time of the interview. Business owners are individuals who report that they are (1) "self-employed in own not incorporated business, professional practice, or farm, or (2) "self-employed in own incorporated business, professional practice, or farm." This definition includes owners of all types of businesses—incorporated, unincorporated, employer, and nonemployer firms. The samples used in this analysis include all business owners ages 20–64 (i.e., working-age adults) who work 15 or more hours per week in their businesses. To rule out very small-scale businesses, disguised unemployment, or casual sellers of goods and services, only business owners with 15 or more hours worked are included.[1] Fifteen hours per week is chosen as the cutoff because it represents a reasonable amount of work effort in the business (roughly two days per week). Note that self-employed business ownership is defined as the individual's main job activity, thus removing the potential for counting side businesses owned by wage and salary workers. Also, estimates are reported with and without the 15-hour restriction to show the robustness of disparities in business ownership rates. Finally, the self-employment information is self-reported and not based on tax or business registration filings and thus may capture a wide range of self-employment activities depending on the respondent.

Business owner income is calculated from survey questions about income sources. The main question used is "Self-employment income from own nonfarm businesses or farm businesses, including proprietorships and partnerships. Report NET income after business expenses." Most business owners report this type of income, but incorporated business owners report their earnings from the business as wage and salary earnings. For simplification and consistency in treatment, the responses to self-employment income and wage and salary earnings are combined for all business owners. The questions refer to annual income and capture the past 12 months.

Survey of Business Owners

We also use data from the 2012 SBO, which are business-level data. The SBO includes detailed information on both the business and the owner. We mainly present information about the businesses in this chapter, but detailed information in addition to race and ethnicity is available. The SBO is conducted by the U.S. Census Bureau every five years to collect statistics that describe the composition of U.S. businesses by race and ethnicity. The universe for the most recent survey is all firms operating during 2012 with receipts of $1,000 or more that filed tax forms as individual proprietorships, partnerships, employers, or any type of corporation, with the exception of a handful of industries including crop and animal production (North American Industry Classification System codes 111 and 112). The 2012 SBO also includes information on the sales, employment, payroll, and exports of the business. All estimates using the 2012 SBO are from published sources using American FactFinder.

Latino Business Ownership, Income, and Industry

American Community Survey

Estimates of the number of business owners, business ownership rates, and business owner income are first presented. All estimates are calculated from ACS (2011–2015) microdata, which as noted above is the latest available

TABLE 4.1 *Total Latino Business Ownership: American Community Survey 2011–2015*

Group	Latinos	Non-Latino Whites	Total
Population (ages 20–64)	31,247,449	121,520,318	189,464,182
Business owners	1,817,236	8,820,771	12,159,527
Percent of population	5.8%	7.3%	6.4%
Workforce (15+ hours/week worked)	21,320,868	86,387,463	130,981,496
Business owners (15+ hours)	1,692,007	8,277,854	11,388,697
Percent of workforce (15+ hours)	7.9%	9.6%	8.7%

Source: Authors calculations from American Community Survey 2011–2015 microdata.

household data from the U.S. Census Bureau on business ownership and business owner income. Table 4.1 reports estimates for Latinos, non-Latino whites, and the U.S. total. There are 12.2 million business owners in the United States. Roughly 1.8 million of these business owners are Latinos. For comparison, there are 8.8 million non-Latino white business owners in the United States.

Latinos are underrepresented in business ownership. The total Latino working-age population (defined here as ages 20–64) is 31 million. As a percentage of the population, 5.8 percent of Latinos own a business. This level of business ownership is lower than the national level at 6.4 percent and lower than the non-Latino white rate of 7.3 percent. The causes of these disparities have been studied with relatively low levels of education and wealth being identified as two of the most important factors (Lofstrom and Wang 2009; Ramirez and Hondagneu-Sotelo 2009; Fairlie and Woodruff 2010; Valdez 2011; Dávila and Mora 2013; Vallejo and Canizales 2016).

For comparison, business ownership rates are calculated for other major ethnic and racial groups (although not reported in the tables). The business ownership rate is 3.0 percent (800,000 business owners) for African Americans, 6.6 percent (800,000 business owners) for Asian Americans, and 4.8 percent for Native American/Alaskan Natives (150,000 business owners). Thus, across the five major ethnic/racial groups, Latinos represent the second-largest number of business owners but only the third-highest business ownership rate.

Additionally, we calculate business ownership rates for all Latino groups identified in the ACS. Table 4.2 reports estimates. Focusing on the

TABLE 4.2 *Business Ownership among Latino Groups: American Community Survey 2011–2015*

Group	Population (Age 20–64)	Business Owners	Business Owners/ Population
Mexican	19,414,811	1,045,540	5.4%
Puerto Rican	2,953,909	90,837	3.1%
Cuban	1,213,738	103,904	8.6%
Dominican	1,045,016	56,058	5.4%
Costa Rican	88,156	7,622	8.6%
Guatemalan	832,936	71,452	8.6%
Honduran	502,726	42,079	8.4%
Nicaraguan	262,414	21,180	8.1%
Panamanian	116,609	5,681	4.9%
Salvadoran	1,283,898	95,552	7.4%
Other Central American	27,556	1,756	6.4%
Argentinean	160,473	21,164	13.2%
Bolivian	71,007	6,089	8.6%
Chilean	92,609	8,782	9.5%
Colombian	692,695	63,977	9.2%
Ecuadorian	429,123	33,004	7.7%
Paraguayan	14,886	1,724	11.6%
Peruvian	391,308	35,063	9.0%
Uruguayan	37,840	4,970	13.1%
Venezuelan	188,661	20,210	10.7%
Other South American	19,855	1,368	6.9%
Spaniard	441,785	29,149	6.6%
All Other Span/Hisp./Lat	965,448	50,075	5.2%

Source: Authors calculations from American Community Survey 2011–2015 microdata.

largest groups, Mexican Americans have a business ownership rate that is only slightly lower than the total Latino rate. Puerto Ricans have lower rates (3.1 percent), and Cubans have higher rates (8.6 percent).

Focusing more generally on Latino business owners with a work commitment of 15 or more hours worked per week, the total number of business owners is lower but not substantially. There are 1.7 million Latino business owners after using this restriction. The total number of business owners in the United States who work 15+ hours per week is 11.4 million.

Imposing the hours worked restriction is useful for removing individuals who might be partly unemployed and just have part-time self-employment work as a method of generating some income.

Another commonly used measure of the rate of business ownership is being in the workforce. Of the total workforce that owns a business, 7.9 percent are Latino.[2] The non-Latino white rate is 9.6 percent. The similarity of these differences and the ranking across groups indicates that the relatively low rates of business ownership among Latinos are not due to higher levels of unemployment or not being in the labor force.[3]

Table 4.3 reports estimates of business owner income across groups. Latinos have substantially lower levels of business owner income than non-Latino whites. Mean business owner income is $34,500 for Latinos. This mean level of business owner income is roughly $30,000 lower than mean business owner income among non-Latino whites. The disparity in business owner income is much larger than the disparity in business ownership rates.

Low mean business owner income among Latinos is not driven by business owners working few hours. Table 4.3 also reports mean business owner income based on working 15+ hours per week. Using this restriction, mean business owner income among Latinos is $36,200. Mean business owner income among non-Latino whites is $66,600. The difference of roughly $30,000 is similar.

Examining the industry distributions of business owners provides useful information on concentrations of business owners and potentially where to target policy assistance. Table 4.4 reports industry distributions for Latino, non-Latino white, and all U.S. business owners. Latino business

TABLE 4.3 *Latino Business Owner Income: American Community Survey 2011–2015*

Group	Latinos	Non-Latino Whites	Total
Business owners	1,817,236	8,820,771	12,159,527
Mean business owner income	$34,475	$63,329	$57,357
Standard deviation	$54,115	$88,131	$83,003
Business owners (15+ hours)	1,692,007	8,277,854	11,388,697
Mean business owner income (15+ hours)	$36,246	$66,618	$60,375
Standard deviation	$55,314	$89,653	$84,575

Source: Authors calculations from American Community Survey 2011–2015 microdata.

TABLE 4.4 *Industry Distribution of Business Owners: American Community Survey 2011–2015*

Group	Latinos	Non-Latino Whites	Total
Number of business owners	1,691,501	8,273,387	11,383,483
Agriculture/extraction	1.3%	5.9%	4.6%
Construction	23.4%	17.7%	17.4%
Manufacturing	2.2%	3.9%	3.5%
Wholesale	1.9%	2.5%	2.4%
Retail	6.8%	7.7%	7.9%
Transportation	5.3%	3.5%	4.4%
Information/finance	4.9%	10.0%	8.9%
Professional services	20.8%	21.7%	21.0%
Educational services	0.8%	1.7%	1.6%
Health care and social assistance	7.8%	8.4%	8.9%
Accommodation, recreation, and entertainment	5.4%	6.2%	6.6%
Other services	19.5%	10.8%	12.9%

Source: Authors calculations from American Community Survey 2011–2015 microdata.

owners are concentrated in construction (23.4 percent) and professional services (20.8 percent). The distribution across industries is not substantially different from the distribution across industries for non-Latino whites or all U.S. business owners. Latino business owners are more concentrated in construction and other services and less concentrated in agriculture/extraction and information/finance.

These findings are important because there are advantages and disadvantages to being concentrated in a few industries. On the one hand, it is easier to create business programs that could help minority business owners because they can be targeted toward those specific industries. On the other hand, efforts could be made to create general programs that allow people of color to create and grow businesses in whatever industry makes the most sense economically. Specific initiatives, such as the Stanford Latino Entrepreneurship Initiative's Executive Program on Scaling Companies, serve as a model for such programs. Similarly, being concentrated in a few industries is advantageous if those industries grow rapidly, but not if they face economic contractions. For example, the concentration of Latino business owners in construction could create a problem if those industries experience rapid structural changes, such as the rapid impact of Uber on the taxicab industry or the massive slump in home building that occurred during the 2007–2009 recession. Creating and maintaining a business in an ethnically concentrated industry thus has its own set of unique challenges, especially in the context of structural shifts in the larger economy. Once established, Latino business owners have achieved success in growing businesses regardless of industrial concentration. Most important is that Latinos own firms in a wide range of sectors, dispelling the myth that Latino businesses are concentrated only in low-status industries.

Business owner income differs substantially across industries; however, the disparities in business owner income between Latinos and non-Latino whites are consistent for industries. Table 4.5 reports mean business owner income by industry. Latinos have lower average business owner income in every reported industry than non-Latino whites. The patterns are very consistent across all industries. This finding suggests

TABLE 4.5 *Mean Business Owner Income by Industry: American Community Survey 2011–2015*

Group	Latinos	Non-Latino Whites	Difference	Total
Number of businesses	1,691,501	8,273,387	6,581,886	11,383,483
Agriculture/extraction	$45,706	$61,696	$15,990	$60,693
Construction	$31,214	$49,805	$18,591	$45,354
Manufacturing	$46,887	$69,399	$22,512	$66,138
Wholesale	$47,481	$85,817	$38,336	$78,677
Retail	$33,659	$53,996	$20,337	$50,114
Transportation	$48,059	$61,996	$13,937	$55,050
Information/finance	$59,592	$87,173	$27,581	$82,830
Professional services	$39,000	$83,187	$44,187	$74,633
Educational services	$35,961	$40,351	$4,390	$40,547
Health care and social assistance	$51,114	$105,805	$54,691	$95,609
Accommodation, recreation, and entertainment	$38,745	$49,978	$11,233	$47,378
Other services	$21,604	$32,849	$11,245	$29,473

Source: Authors calculations from American Community Survey 2011–2015 microdata.

that the total business owner income difference between Latinos and non-Latino whites cannot be explained by differences in industry concentration alone.

As Table 4.5 shows, the top five industries with the largest mean business income gap include health care and social assistance ($54,691), professional services ($44,187), wholesale ($38,336), information/finance ($27,581) and manufacturing ($22,512). Factors that explain the gap between Latino and non-Latino business income include age of the firm, number of owners, establishment size, and differences in financing (McManus 2016).

Contributions of Latino Business Owners to the U.S. Economy: Business Ownership, Employment, and Exports

American Community Survey

What is the contribution of Latinos to the total entrepreneurial economy? One method of answering this important question is to examine the total number of business owners who are Latinos and compare that to the total number of all business owners in the United States. The Latino share of total business ownership has likely increased substantially over time, partly due to population growth (Fairlie and Robb 2008; Dávila and Mora 2013) and also because of larger structural changes in the economy and opportunity structure that have created entrepreneurial pathways for specific segments of the Latino population, such as middle-class professionals (Vallejo and Canizales 2016). We update this work by examining current contributions here.

Table 4.6 reports the share of business owners relative to the U.S. total. Latinos represent 14.9 percent of all U.S. business owners. The Latino share of total business owner income provides another measure of the contribution of Latino entrepreneurs to the economy. Similar to the estimates of the Latino contribution to total business ownership in the United States, we estimate the contribution of Latinos to total business owner income in the U.S. economy. There are 1.8 million Latino business owners (15 percent), and they have a total business owner income of $63 billion (9 percent). Table 4.6 also reports total business owner income and shares of the U.S. total for Latinos. In total, Latino business owners have nearly $63 billion in business owner income. This represents 9 percent of the total U.S. business owner income of roughly $700 billion.

TABLE 4.6 *Latino Business Ownership and Income Contributions: American Community Survey 2011–2015*

Group	Latinos		Total
Number of business owners	1,817,236	14.9%	12,159,527
Total business owner income (000s)	$62,649,379	9.0%	$697,427,911

Source: Authors calculations from American Community Survey 2011–2015 microdata.

Survey of Business Owners

Published estimates from the 2012 SBO can also be used to measure the contributions of Latino businesses to the U.S. economy.[4] As noted above, the SBO captures all business entities through tax records even if they are of small scale. The SBO also captures multiple businesses owned by the same person. Thus, the total number of businesses for Latinos and non-Latino whites are much higher than for business owners in the ACS (which focuses on main job activity).

Table 4.7 reports estimates from the SBO.[5] The number of Latino businesses in the United States is 3.3 million, which represents 12 percent of all identifiable businesses. These businesses generate a total of $473 billion in revenue (representing 4 percent of total revenue among identifiable businesses). Nevertheless, Latino firms lag behind non-Latino white firms, which represent approximately 70 percent of classifiable businesses generating almost 90 percent of total revenue. Average revenue among Latino firms is $143,271, which is substantially lower than the average revenue of $440,190 among all identifiable firms.

TABLE 4.7 *Number of Firms and Revenues among Latinos: Survey of Business Owners 2012*

Group	Latino Firms		Non-Latino White Firms		All Classifiable Firms
Number of firms	3,305,873	12.2%	18,987,918	69.9%	27,179,380
Revenue (000s)	$473,635,944	4.0%	$10,482,831,537	87.6%	$11,964,077,871
average Revenues	$143,271		$552,079		$440,190

Source: Published estimates from the Survey of Business Owners 2012. Includes all classifiable businesses by gender, race, ethnicity, and veteran status.

Clearly, Latino business owners make substantial contributions to the entrepreneurial economy in the United States. Although these are large contributions, they could be even higher as evidenced by the relatively low rates of business ownership among Latinos and low average business owner incomes among Latino business owners. If business ownership rates were increased relative to white levels or if business owner income was increased relative to white levels, the result would be a substantial increase in the total contributions made by Latino entrepreneurs to the U.S. economy.

Table 4.8 reports estimates from the SBO on the number of Latino businesses with paid employees. The majority of businesses in the United States do not hire employees; nevertheless, these businesses provide jobs for the self-employed business owner, who if not employed as a full-time wage-worker might otherwise be unemployed or underemployed. Businesses with paid employees contribute to the U.S. economy by not only providing a job for the self-employed owner but also creating additional jobs for American workers (Valdez 2015). Of the 3.3 million businesses owned by Latinos, only 7.5 percent have paid employees. In contrast, businesses owned by non-Latino whites are over twice as likely to have paid employees (19.4 percent). Although the majority of Latino and non-Latino businesses do not hire paid employees, a significant number of these businesses are creating jobs.

Table 4.9 reports estimates from the SBO on the employment size of businesses with paid employees. Although the percentage of non-Latino white businesses with paid employees is over twice that of Latino businesses, the employment size of these businesses is similar across race/ethnicity. For example, there is a difference of one percentage point or less for Latino and non-Latino white businesses that report an employment size between the middle ranges of 5 to 9 employees. A larger difference is

TABLE 4.8 *Number of Businesses with Paid Employees: Survey of Business Owners 2012*

Group	Latino Firms		Non-Latino White Firms		All Classifiable Firms
Firms with paid employees	246,773	7.5%	3,684,250	19.4%	4,539,370
Number of firms	3,305,873		18,987,918		27,179,380

Source: Published estimates from the Survey of Business Owners 2012. Includes all classifiable businesses by gender, race, ethnicity, and veteran status.

TABLE 4.9 *Employment Size of Businesses with Paid Employees: Survey of Business Owners 2012*

Group	Latino Firms		Non-Latino White Firms		All Classifiable Firms
1–4	153,637	62.3%	2,123,628	57.6%	2,643,124
5–9	46,032	18.7%	714,071	19.4%	883,891
10–19	26,384	10.7%	433,664	11.8%	529,191
20–49	14,943	6.1%	275,419	7.4%	326,596
50–99	3,719	1.5%	82,396	2.2%	94,909
100–499	1,811	.7%	48,789	1.3%	54,720
500 or more	247	.1%	6,282	.1%	6,939
Firms with paid employees	246,773		3,684,249		4,539,370

Source: Published estimates from the Survey of Business Owners 2012. Includes all classifiable businesses by gender, race, ethnicity, and veteran status.

TABLE 4.10 *Export Sales as a Percent of Total Sales: Survey of Business Owners 2012*

Group	Latino Firms		Non-Latino White Firms		All Classifiable Firms	
Businesses reporting	1,254,951	38.0%	13,381,641	70.5%	16,861,765	62.4%
None	1,115,318	88.9%	12,358,259	92.4%	15,436,879	91.5%
1–100%	33,461	2.7%	295,524	2.2%	389,090	2.3%
Don't know	106,172	8.5%	727,858	5.4%	1,035,796	6.1%

Source: Published estimates from the Survey of Business Owners 2012. Includes all classifiable businesses by gender, race, ethnicity, and veteran status.

reported for businesses with the smallest employment size (1 to 4 employees) and one of the largest employee sizes (100–499 employees). In other words, 4 percent more Latino businesses fall into this smallest employment size range than non-Latino whites (62.3 percent to 57.6 percent, respectively), whereas twice the number of non-Latino white firms fall into one of the largest employment size categories (1.3 percent compared to .7 percent).

Table 4.10 reports estimates on the percent of total sales that are exported for businesses reporting this information. Notably, a minority of Latino businesses report this information (38.0 percent). The vast majority of Latino businesses that do provide this information indicate that they do

TABLE 4.11 *Number of Businesses with $5,000 or Less or $1,000,000 or More in Sales/
Receipts: Survey of Business Owners 2012*

Group	Latino Firms		Non-Latino White Firms		All Classifiable Firms	
Firms with receipts of less than $5,000	650,017	19.7%	3,757,438	19.8%	5,442,329	20.0%
Firms with receipts of $1,000,000 +	54,867	1.7%	1,062,383	5.6%	1,262,649	4.6%
Number of firms	3,305,873		18,987,918		27,179,380	

Source: Published estimates from the Survey of Business Owners 2012. Includes all classifiable
businesses by gender, race, ethnicity, and veteran status.

not generate sales from exports (88.9 percent). Conversely, the small percentage of Latino businesses that do generate sales from exports is slightly higher than the export sales reported by non-Latino white businesses (2.7 percent to 2.2 percent, respectively).

Table 4.11 reports SBO estimates for the number of businesses reporting very low and very high sales. Latino businesses, when compared to non-Latino white businesses, are similar to each other in the percentage of businesses that report very low sales/receipts. About 20 percent of Latino and non-Latino white businesses report sales/receipts of $5,000 or less. In contrast, a markedly higher percentage of non-Latino white businesses than Latino businesses report sales at the high end. Over 1.2 million non-Latino white businesses generate sales of $1 million or more (5.6 percent). Though significantly fewer, the number of Latino businesses that report sales/receipts in excess of $1 million is not insignificant. Of the 3.3 million Latino businesses operating in the United States in 2012, fully 55,000 (1.7 percent) report sales/receipts in excess of $1 million.

CONCLUSION

Our analysis reveals that rates of Latino ownership and income are on the rise, associated with greater economic incorporation and mobility. Latino business owners are also making significant contributions to employment and exports in the United States, particularly in some economic sectors. The highlights from the analysis of ACS and SBO data are:

- There are 1.7 million Latino business owners in the United States, representing 15 percent of all business owners.
- Latinos own businesses at a rate that is roughly 20 percent lower than non-Latino whites, suggesting that contributions could be even larger.
- Latino business owners generate $62 billion in total business owner income, representing 9 percent of all business owner income in the United States.
- Latino-owned businesses generate $474 billion in total sales and revenues.
- There are 247,000 Latino firms with paid employees, representing 7.5 percent of all Latino firms.
- There are 55,000 Latino firms representing 1.7 percent of all Latino firms that generate $1 million or more in total sales/ receipts.

These findings demonstrate that Latino business owners are making significant contributions to the American economy, although some disparities remain. Several individual-level factors increase the odds of Latino business ownership, including earning a college degree and acquiring managerial (Guo, Chen, Yu 2016) or professional experience (Vallejo and Canizales 2016); access to financial capital, which may include personal savings or securing funds from friends, family, and/or banking institutions (Fairlie and Robb 2008; Fairlie and Woodruff 2010; Valdez 2011; Vallejo and Canizales 2016); and accumulating or inheriting wealth (Butler and Morales 2012; Keister, Vallejo, and Borelli 2015).

At the group-level, fostering coethnic social support and business networks for advice and mentorship (Vallejo 2009) are particularly important for immigrant and ethnic minorities. Social capital, or group-based resources and social support, provides business information and networking opportunities as well as financial aid and offers a source of coethnic labor (Valdez 2011). Successful Latino entrepreneurs also engage the business community and join organizations such as the Hispanic Chamber of Commerce. Beyond providing crucial information on funding and establishing business connections, these organizations often provide training in business and financial planning, navigating financial institutions or locating angel investors, and web development and social media tools to increase the chances of business success (Vallejo 2009; Vallejo and Canizales 2016). Recent research also demonstrates that some wealthy Latino entrepreneurs are using their wealth and social capital to create economic structures, such as Latino-owned banks, that aim to provide Latino entrepreneurs with access to capital (Vallejo 2015). Future research could more fully investigate the mechanisms—such as racial discrimination in commercial credit markets—that might hinder Latino entrepreneurship. Finally, important efforts are being made by ethnic organizations, such as the Latino Business Access Network, to create programs that aim to fill resource gaps so that Latino business owners can access social and economic capital and scale up their businesses.

ACKNOWLEDGMENTS

The authors would like to thank Arnobio Morelix, Alfonso Morales, Leticia Lara, Jerry Porras, and participants of the Stanford Latino Entrepreneurship workshop for comments and suggestions. For an earlier analysis of this chapter, see Fairlie (2018).

NOTES

1. Some unemployed individuals may report being self-employed if they sell a small quantity of goods or services while not working at their regular jobs.
2. Although not directly comparable from using slightly different definitions, Dávila and Mora (2013) find that the self-employment rate for Hispanics increased from 7.9 percent in 2000 to 9.1 percent in 2010.
3. It is not clear how informal business activity, which is shown to be relevant (e.g., see Richardson and Pisani 2012), is captured in the ACS data as self-employment, unemployment, or some other labor force activity.
4. For evidence from earlier years of the SBO, see Fairlie and Robb (2008) and Dávila and Mora (2013).
5. The SBO delineates businesses by whether they are identifiable by gender, race, ethnicity, and veteran status to rule out public corporations in which ownership status is difficult to identify.

REFERENCES

Butler, John Sibley, and Alfonso Morales, eds. 2012. *American Story: Mexican American Entrepreneurship and Wealth Creation*. West Lafayette, IN: Purdue University Press.

Dávila, Alberto, and Marie Mora. 2013. *Hispanic Entrepreneurs in the 2000s: An Economic Profile and Policy Implications*. Stanford: Stanford University Press.

Dávila, Alberto, Marie T. Mora, and Angela Marek Zeitlin. 2014. "Better Business: How Hispanic Entrepreneurs are Beating Expectations and Bolstering the U.S. Economy." Partnership for a New American Economy. http://www.newamericaneconomy.org/wp-content/uploads/2014/04/hispanic-entrepreneurs-final.pdf.

Fairlie, Rob. 2018. "Latino Business Ownership: Contributions and Barriers for U.S.-Born and Immigrant Latino Entrepreneurs." Office of Advocacy, U.S. Small Business Administration.

Fairlie, Robert, and Christopher M. Woodruff. 2010. "Mexican-American Entrepreneurship." *BE Journal of Economic Analysis & Policy* 10(1):1–44.

Fairlie, Robert W., and Alicia M. Robb. 2008. *Race and Entrepreneurial Success: Black-, Asian-, and White-Owned Businesses in the United States*. Cambridge, MA: MIT Press.

Keister, Lisa A., Jody Agius Vallejo, and E. Paige Borelli. 2015. "Mexican American Mobility: Early Life Processes and Adult Wealth Ownership." *Social Forces* 93(3):1015–46.

Lofstrom, Magnus, and Chunbei Wang. 2009. "Mexican-American Self-Employment: A Dynamic Analysis of Business Ownership." *Research in Labor Economics* 29:197–227.

McManus, Michael. 2016. "Minority Business Ownership: Data from the 2012 Survey of Business Owners." Office of Advocacy Issue Brief 12, Office of Economic Research in the Office of Advocacy, Washington, DC.

Ramirez, Hernan, and Pierrette Hondagneu-Sotelo. 2009. "Mexican Immigrant Gardeners: Entrepreneurs or Exploited Workers?" *Social Problems* 56(1):70–88.

Richardson, Chad, and Michael J. Pisani. 2012. *The Informal and Underground Economy of the South Texas Border*. Austin: University of Texas Press.

Rivers, Douglas, and Jerry Porras. 2015. "State of Latino Entrepreneurship." Stanford University. http://lban.us/wp-content/uploads/2015/11/Final-Report-.pdf.

U.S. Census Bureau. 2011–2015. *American Community Survey*. Microdata.

U.S. Census Bureau. 2012. *Survey of Business Owners and Self-Employed Persons.* American FactFinder.

Valdez, Zulema. 2011. *The New Entrepreneurs: How Race, Class and Gender Shape American Enterprise.* Palo Alto, CA: Stanford University Press.

Valdez, Zulema. 2015. *Entrepreneurs and the Search for the American Dream.* London: Routledge.

Valdez, Zulema. 2019. "The Great Recession and Precarious Wealth among Middle-Class Mexican-Origin Entrepreneurs." *Journal of Ethnic and Migration Studies.* doi: 10.1080/1369183X.2019.1592879.

Vallejo, Jody Agius. 2009. "Latina Spaces: Middle-Class Ethnic Capital and Professional Associations in the Latino Community." *City & Community* 8(2):12954.

Vallejo, Jody Agius. 2015. "Levelling the Playing Field: Patterns of Ethnic Philanthropy among Los Angeles' Middle and Upper-Class Latino Entrepreneurs." *Ethnic and Racial Studies* 38(1):125–40.

Vallejo, Jody Agius, and Stephanie Canizales. 2016. "Latino/a Professionals as Entrepreneurs: How Race, Class, and Gender Shape Entrepreneurial Incorporation." *Ethnic and Racial Studies* 39(9):1637–56.

Xuguang Guo, Wei Chen, and Andy Yu. 2016. "Is College Education Worth It? Evidence from Its Impacts on Entrepreneurship in the United States." *Journal of Small Business & Entrepreneurship* 28(1):1–26. doi: 10.1080/08276331.2015.1104452.

The State of Latino Entrepreneurship: SLEI Research and Findings

Marlene Orozco and Iliana Perez

INTRODUCTION

The growth of Latino entrepreneurship represents an important dynamic force in the American economy. Continuation and acceleration of this trend will raise living standards for Latinos (who currently have about twice the poverty rate of non-Latinos) and contribute to aggregate economic growth. Despite substantial research efforts, our understanding of Latino entrepreneurship is relatively meager. We have only a rough idea of who Latino entrepreneurs are as well as their size, how they got their start, what contributes to their success, and what policies are needed to promote further expansion. Well known surveys of business owners, such as the U.S. Census Bureau Survey of Business Owners (SBO) and the Kauffman Firm Study, occur infrequently and reach only small numbers of Latino entrepreneurs. To fill this gap, the Latino Business Action Network (LBAN), a 501(c)3 collaborated with Stanford University researchers under the umbrella of the Stanford Latino Entrepreneurship Initiative (SLEI) to create the SLEI-Research program.

Since 2015, SLEI research has conducted the nation's largest annual survey of U.S. Latino business owners. In 2017, we surveyed 5,026 Latino business owners. This annual data set provides much-needed information on the state and growth of Latino entrepreneurship, and its potential will be shown throughout this volume as researchers use this survey to explore a variety of topics. In this chapter, we highlight key distinctions among other data sets and share insights from our recent survey. We conclude with future directions of our Latino business surveys.

WHAT IS SLEI AND WHY DOES IT EXIST?

SLEI is a collaboration between the LBAN and the Stanford Graduate School of Business. SLEI (pronounced "slay") explores and expands our knowledge of the Latino entrepreneurship segment in the U.S. economy through research, knowledge dissemination, and facilitated collaboration. Since 2015, SLEI has released reports from data gathered through its annual SLEI Survey of U.S. Latino Business Owners. SLEI collects national survey data to provide researchers, policy makers, and business leaders with insights on Latino entrepreneur profiles, opportunities for growth among U.S. Latino-owned firms, and barriers that Latino entrepreneurs face in scaling up their businesses.

While the scholarship on Latino entrepreneurship is slowly growing, in the creation of this volume we sought to accelerate it by engaging nationally prominent academics and thought leaders who study Latino entrepreneurship in one form or another. We have made the SLEI data available to these researchers who have then used them, along with data independently collected, to produce the various chapters here.

On a second front, SLEI collects data from Latino business owners who go through the SLEI-Education Scaling program. This program focuses on developing the ability of Latino business owners to successfully scale their companies and serves as the basis of our ongoing longitudinal data collection efforts (more on these data and the program are presented in Chapter 13).

SOURCES OF GOVERNMENT-COLLECTED DATA

The government collects data about Latino-owned businesses using business and household surveys through the U.S. Census Bureau. The most comprehensive business survey is the SBO, which sampled about 1.75 million employer (i.e., companies with paid employees) and nonemployer businesses every five years from 1972 to 2012. The SBO includes all nonfarm businesses, with and without paid employees, filing Internal Revenue

Service tax forms as individual proprietorships, partnerships, or any type of corporation and with receipts of $1,000 or more. The data are compiled by combining data collected from businesses and business owners in the SBO with data collected from the primary economic census and administrative records. These data are then released two to three years after the year they are collected. This spacing means that we miss out on year-to-year trends, and the lag makes the data outdated. The most recent SBO was released in 2015 from data collected in 2012. The five-year schedule would indicate that the collection of new SBO data should have occurred in 2017. That did not occur. Instead, the government created the Annual Business Survey (ABS), which will be collected yearly (Department of Commerce 2017). The ABS is a consolidation of the SBO and a second survey, the Annual Survey of Entrepreneurs (ASE). The ASE focuses only on employer firms, or those with paid employees. In 2015, employer firms comprised a relatively small subset (9 percent) of the overall number of Latino businesses. Similarly, the ABS will be an annual survey that collects comprehensive data on business owner demographics and business characteristics, including financing, research, and development (Department of Commerce 2017). However, the ABS also will only consider employer firms, leaving a wide gap in knowledge on nonemployer firms, or about 9 out of every 10 Latino-owned businesses.

Other large household and individual-level data sets contain information about self-employment and business ownership. The American Community Survey (ACS) is widely used to estimate self-employment in the United States (see Chapter 4 in this volume as an example for how this data source and self-employment measure is used to estimate economic contributions of Latino business owners). The ACS produces period estimates of socioeconomic and housing characteristics based on samples of about 3.54 million addresses each year. Designed to provide estimates that describe the average characteristics of an area over a specific time period, the ACS collects survey information continuously nearly every day of the year and then aggregates the results over a specific time period—one year (populations of 65,000 or more), three years (populations of 20,000 or more), or five years (all geographic areas down to the tract and block group levels). The single-year estimates provide the most current information about areas that have changing populations, because they are based on the most current data from the previous year. The benefit of using the three-year or five-year estimates is statistical reliability, as they use larger sample sizes. The ACS identifies entrepreneurs through a survey question describing the "class of worker." The U.S. Census Bureau currently uses eight basic classifications for class of worker: private for-profit and private not-for-profit (among salaried workers), local government, state government, federal government (for government workers), self-employed not incorporated, self-employed incorporated, and unpaid family workers (for nonsalaried workers).

Another popular data set used in entrepreneurship research is the Current Population Survey (CPS). The CPS, conducted by the U.S. Census Bureau and the U.S. Bureau of Labor Statistics, is representative of the entire U.S. population and interviews about 90,000 households and 180,000 people per month. Although the CPS is typically used as a cross-sectional data set, panel data can be created by linking consecutive months or years of the survey. A unique feature of the CPS is that it follows respondents for a period of time; households from all 50 states and the District of Columbia are in the survey for four consecutive months, out for eight, and then return for another four months before leaving the sample permanently. The CPS also identifies entrepreneurs in the "class of worker" question. Class of worker indicates whether a respondent is self-employed, an employee in private industry or the public sector, in the armed forces, or works without pay in a family business or on a family farm as the primary job.

Another data set commonly used is the Survey of Income and Program Participation (SIPP), a household-based survey designed as a continuous series of national panels. Each panel includes a nationally representative sample interviewed over a multiyear period lasting about four years. The SIPP identifies entrepreneurs by asking about the type of work arrangement, whether it is work for an employer, self-employed (owns a business) work, or other. The SIPP data also contain information on the type of business the individual owns as well as business equity. Given its longitudinal nature, the SIPP has been commonly used to analyze entry and exit patterns among the self-employed (Lofstrom and Wang 2007).

The SLEI Survey of U.S. Latino Business Owners surveys more than 5,000 self-identified Latino business owners from across the country. The survey has been conducted every year since 2015 and is used as a cross-sectional data set. Respondents are asked a core set of questions, including their industry, zip code, customer base, company size, age, ownership structure, and a specialized set about company growth, including sources of capital, challenges faced, and aspirations. The majority of responses have been collected through a Qualtrics business owner panel funded by the LBAN. Other data-collection methods include convenience sampling through social media posts, outreach to business contacts derived from SLEI and LBAN newsletter readership, and an email database of over 10,000 Latino business owners.

In 2017, the SLEI Survey of U.S. Latino Business Owners was primarily administered to a proprietary business panel from Qualtrics. Of the 5,026 respondents, 97 percent of the sample comes from Qualtrics. The remainder come through convenience sampling to gather saturation at the opposite ends of business sizes: microbusinesses and scaled businesses. While the sampling procedures undertaken by Qualtrics are proprietary, our survey respondents are generally representative of Latino business owners at large in terms of industry, geography, and age of business. Although the survey slightly undersamples owners of smaller firms, we adjust for this by weighting to population targets estimated from U.S. census data (Figure 5.1). To more closely match the population of Latino-owned firms in the United States, we weight by revenues, industry, region, and number of employees (as reported in SBO 2007 and 2012). We use a statistical technique known as "raking," which uses iterative poststratification weights to match the marginal distributions of each survey sample to known population margins. We stratify based on industry, region, and firm size (in terms of both employees and revenue). We then compare the group of

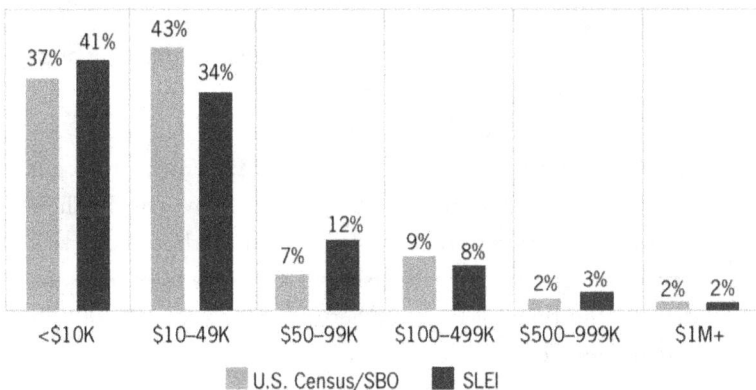

Figure 5.1 Revenue distribution for 2017 SLEI Survey of U.S. Latino Business Owners compared to 2012 U.S. Census Survey of Business Owners. (Source: SLEI Survey of U.S. Latino Business Owners 2017.)

businesses in each stratum to the comparable population of businesses in the nation. The calculations in this chapter account for firm industry and age by using fixed effects—holding industry and age constant—to ensure that differences in firm-level characteristics cannot explain other differences we observe.

Table 5.1 provides an overview of the differences among the various data sets available for use in entrepreneurship research, specifically focusing on data sets that include a Latino-specific variable. A Latino-specific variable is one in which the ethnic and/or racial background of the respondent through self-identification has been collected and is available for public use. We should note that the data sets are not always consistent in the way they define entrepreneurship. Therefore, it is extremely important that users clearly understand how entrepreneurship is defined in each particular data set, as this will impact the interpretation of the sample and the larger universe it is intended to measure. Definition must be based on the way the questions are asked in the surveys and how the data are coded. In addition, race and ethnicity are also not consistent across surveys, as is evident in Table 5.1

Estimates for the number of businesses and the self-employed vary by the type of data used and may not be comparable (see Chapter 4 in this volume for a discussion about differences between SBO and ACS figures). Table 5.2 provides a summary of the number of firms and the self-employed based on estimates from the SBO, ASE, ACS and CPS. Fairlie and Robb (2009) provide some explanations for the discrepancies between business-level and individual-level data, summarized as follows:

- Multiple businesses owned by one individual count only once in individual-level data, and businesses with multiple owners count only once in business-level data.
- Business ownership in the CPS refers to the person's main job activity. Individuals not reporting self-employment as their main job activity report self-employment in their secondary occupation. In the SBO, all businesses resulting from filing tax forms to the Internal Revenue Service with at least $1,000 in annual sales are included.
- Hours worked as a self-employed individual might exclude small-scale businesses, while the SBO data do not impose any restrictions on the size of the business other than the annual sales restriction.

TABLE 5.1 *Matrix of Entrepreneurship Datasets and Latino-Specific Variables*

Data Set	Entrepreneurship Unit of Analysis	Latino Variable	Frequency and Availability	Sample Size
Survey of Business Owners (SBO)	All firms (employer and nonemployer) and their owners. Included are all nonfarm businesses filing IRS tax forms as individual proprietorships, partnerships, or any type of corporation and with receipts of $1,000 or more.	Hispanic origin: Mexican, Mexican American, Chicano Puerto Rican Cuban Other Hispanic, Latino, or Spanish origin (fill in) Ancestry not included	Every 5 years: 1972–2012	Samples about 1.75 million employer and nonemployer businesses.
Annual Survey of Entrepreneurs (ASE)	Employer firms and their owners. Included are all nonfarm businesses filing IRS tax forms as individual proprietorships, partnerships, or any type of corporation and with receipts of $1,000 or more.	Hispanic Origin: Mexican, Mexican American, Chicano Puerto Rican Cuban Other Hispanic, Latino, or Spanish origin (fill in) Ancestry not included	Annual: 2014, 2015	Samples about 290,000 employer businesses.
American Community Survey (ACS)	Individual: Self-employed in own not incorporated business, professional practice, or farm; self-employed in own incorporated business, professional practice or farm; working without pay in family business or farm.	Hispanic Origin: Mexican, Puerto Rican, Cuban, Central or South American, or some other Hispanic origin) Ancestry: Includes 26 Hispanic categories	Every 1, 3 and 5 years. 1-year estimates available: 2010–2016; 5-year estimates available 2006–2010, 007–2011, 2008–2012, 2009–2013, 2010–2014, 2011–2015, and 2012–2016.	Samples about 3.54 million addresses each year.

(continued)

TABLE 5.1 (Continued)

Data Set	Entrepreneurship Unit of Analysis	Latino Variable	Frequency and Availability	Sample Size
Current Population Survey (CPS)	Individual: Self-employed in own not incorporated business; self-employed in own incorporated business.	Hispanic Origin: Mexican, Puerto Rican, Cuban, Dominican, Salvadorian, and other Spanish Ancestry: Includes 5 Hispanic categories	Monthly and longitudinal (4-8-4 sampling scheme is used). Summary tables available: 1940–2017. Microdata available: 1962–2017.	Interviews about 90,000 households and 180,000 people per month.
Survey of Income and Program Participation (SIPP)	Individual: Self-employed in own not incorporated business; self-employed in own incorporated business.	Hispanic Origin: Is . . . Spanish, Hispanic, or Latino? Ancestry not included.	The duration of each panel ranges from 2½ years to 4 years. Ongoing since 1983. Current operation is the 2014 panel.	Sample size ranges from about 14,000 to 52,000 interviewed households per panel.
SLEI Survey of U.S. Latino Business Owners	Latino business owners.	Hispanic Origin: Mexican, Mexican American, Chicano/a, Puerto Rican, Cuban, Central American (fill in), South American (fill in), and Other (fill in).	Annual: 2015–2017.	Samples about 5,000 Latino-owned businesses.

TABLE 5.2 *Estimates of the Number of Business and Self-Employed in the United States*

Survey	Type of Business	2012	2014	2015	2016	2017
SBO	Nonemployer firms	All: 22,201,902 Latino: 3,018,372	N/A	N/A	N/A	N/A
	Employer firms	All: 5,424,458 Latino: 287,501	N/A	N/A	N/A	N/A
	All firms	All: 27,626,360 Latino: 3,305,873	N/A	N/A	N/A	N/A
ASE	Employer firms	N/A	All: 5,437,782 Latino: 298,563	All: 5,531,169 Latino: 312,738	N/A	N/A
ACS (1-year estimates)	Total self-employed (incorporated and unincorporated)	All: 17,437,492 Latino: 2,307,823	All: 17,688,178 Latino: 2,594,769	All: 17,897,803 Latino: 2,475,084	All: 18,250,542 Latino: 2,594,769	N/A
CPS	Total self-employed (incorporated and unincorporated)	All: 15,093,736 Latino: 1,671,063	All: 15,011,891 Latino: 1,783,015	All: 15,542,615 Latino: 2,000,236	All: 16,050,258 Latino: 2,118,703	All: 15,702,247 Latino: 2,149,231

- SBO/SMOBE data refer to businesses that existed at any point in the calendar year. The CPS instead refers to self-employed business ownership at the time of the survey. Thus, the CPS is likely to capture fewer business owners because there is a considerable amount of volatility in business ownership.
- The CPS and the SBO/SMOBE may also differ in how likely they are to capture some occupations, such as sales and real estate agents. These individuals may report working for an employer instead of self-employment on the CPS questionnaire even when they file as sole proprietors.

To summarize, the SBO was the most comprehensive survey of business owners, given that it captured all business activity over $1,000 regardless of business size or whether or not it was a person's main job activity. The other data sets (ACS, CPS, SIPP) are not focused on businesses characteristics but instead focus on individual characteristics; as a result, they likely underestimate business activity and fail to include important business variables. Given the recent replacement of the SBO with the ASE, researchers interested in entrepreneurship will have no choice but to resort to using other data sets to consider both employer and nonemployer business activity.

Finally, there are other data sets that are regional in nature or are limited by small sample sizes of Latino-owned businesses. As noted earlier, SLEI's most recent surveys have more than 5,000 self-identified Latino business owners across the United States. This allows us to disaggregate various segments within the larger group (i.e., intragroup comparisons), including firm size, geography, gender, age, and immigrant status of entrepreneurs. As an example, in the 2017 report we were able to create a DACA-comparable group by considering immigrant millennials who came to the United States as children. If we only use governmental or existing data, we are limited to questions that were asked rather than having the flexibility to spotlight thematic survey questions.

In 2015, a group of faculty researchers across the country who study Latino entrepreneurship in various forms came together for the first SLEI research convening. It was in this meeting that researchers provided feedback on question content to be asked at a six-month follow-up survey to respondents of the 2016 Survey of U.S. Latino Business Owners. These themes focused on company growth, capital acquisition, capital use, language use, and business responses to the 2016 presidential election.

SLEI DATA: SOME KEY FINDINGS

Table 5.3 summarizes the key findings from the SLEI Survey of U.S. Latino Business Owners, 2015–2017. These surveys provide comprehensive insights into an increasingly important and growing segment of businesses in the United States. Our latest projection estimates that there were roughly 5 million Latino-owned businesses in 2016. This projection used data from the 2007 and 2012 SBO and the 2007, 2012, and 2016 ACS one-year sample surveys. Changes in population and the number of self-employed individuals and businesses between 2007 and 2012 were used to predict the number of Latino businesses in 2016 (the latest year of data available in the ACS) so long as the patterns persist in a five-year period.

To obtain forecasts of the number of Latino-owned firms in the United States, we estimated a two-stage model. First, the total number of firms in the United States among all owners, regardless of ethnicity, was modeled as a function of population growth and the proportion of self-employed individuals, controlling for industry and geography. Second, the proportion of all Latino-owned firms was modeled as a function of the Latino population as a proportion of the total population and proportion of self-employed individuals, again controlling for industry and geography. The forecast number of all business for 2016 was estimated to be 34.4 million, and the forecast number of Latino businesses was estimated to be 6.6 million. We knew that our 2012 total business projection was inflated by 13 percent and that the Latino business projection was inflated by 24 percent (based on 2012 SBO numbers). Therefore, we adjusted the 2016 projection accordingly and ultimately estimated that there were about 5 million Latino businesses (both employer and nonemployer) in 2016.

Furthermore, SLEI surveys explore the profile of the Latino entrepreneur and examine the opportunities and barriers in funding that Latino business owners face as they launch and grow their enterprises. Before launching our own data collection to supplement existing data, we

TABLE 5.3 *Key Findings from the SLEI Survey of U.S. Latino Business Owners*

2015 SLEI Survey	
Key Findings	Statistics
A multitrillion-dollar opportunity gap	In 2012 alone, if all LOBs averaged the same yearly sales per firm as all NLOBs, $1.38 trillion would have been added to the economy.
Diverse customers and industries	There are no discernable differences in the industries of LOBs and NLBOs. Eighty percent of Latino firms sell to a mixture of both Latino and non-Latino customers.
An entrepreneurial mind-set	Growth mentality is present, but 54% of surveyed LOBs have businesses that are either growing slowly or not growing at all, revealing a disconnect between goals and reality.
Internal motivations affect ownership and capital	While half of those surveyed believe they could grow faster if they had additional capital, 67% are concerned about losing control of their business.
Capital awareness and engagement	LOBs are likely to use conventional institutional capital sources, and many are unaware of government funds and programs, having never heard of the following: 22%, SBA; 51%, SBIC; 5%, SBIR.
2016 SLEI Survey	
Key Findings	Statistics
Located everywhere	Latino firms are located all over the United States, with 75% in majority non-Latino neighborhoods serving mostly non-Latino customers.
Immigrant success	Immigrants own 29% of Latino firms, with 40–50% being businesses with more than $1 million in revenue
Organizational membership	Scaled firms are more integrated into the ecosystem, as shown by their numerous formal business memberships.
Reliance on internal funding	Fifty percent of Latinos at both startup and growth stages solely utilize internal funding sources, regardless of size.
Banks leveraged at growth stage	Of the firms that received external funding, one-third mostly use regional bank and business loans at early state, while two-thirds mostly use regional bank and business loans at growth stage.

(continued)

2017 SLEI Survey	
Key Findings	Statistics
National banks provide minimal bank loans	National banks provide less loan funding to Latino-owned businesses, relative to other external funding sources and other demographic groups.
Latinas are leading the way	Latina-owned companies are increasing in number, having growth 86% between 2007 and 20012. However, Latina entrepreneurs face a funding ceiling, as many feel they are not qualified for funding.
Immigrant millennial success	Successful Latino immigrant entrepreneurs are more likely to be millennials who came as children to the United States, representing 86% of scaled firms.
International in reach	Latino-owned businesses are international in reach. Among Latino firms surveyed, 9% have international clients. This is more than any other demographic group.

recognized some big-picture trends about Latino-owned businesses. First, from the SBO trends and census population data, we know that the rate at which new Latino firms are being created is outpacing Latino population growth. From those same data sources, we also know that Latinos are starting businesses at a higher rate relative to all other demographic groups. Still, scaling remains a challenge, as our most recent survey data reveal that about 3 percent of Latino-owned businesses are generating at least $1 million or more in annual revenue per year. We define this group as scaled firms, which serves as one benchmark for measuring the success of businesses in our survey. By comparison, there are 6 percent scaled firms in the nonminority population in the United States.

In 2015, we reported on the immense opportunity gap of $1.38 trillion left on the table if only Latino-owned businesses were as large as their counterparts (Rivers et al. 2015). In today's dollars that is about $1.47 trillion that could be added to the U.S economy. One pathway forward is to acknowledge the processual nature of growth and its concomitant moments of choice and need for resources. Thus, the SLEI-Research program explores the opportunities and challenges facing the Latino segment of the business population by exploring experiences with capital and other resources such as organizational participation.

SLEI SURVEY OF U.S. LATINO BUSINESS OWNERS 2017

The 2017 SLEI Survey of U.S. Latino Business Owners considers only entrepreneurs of Latino origin. As such, we leverage other data sources, namely the SBO and the ASE, a collaboration of the Kauffman Foundation and the U.S. Census Bureau, which provide a comparative lens among other demographic groups when possible. The latter data source focuses only on employer firms, or those that have paid employees, which makes up 9 percent of the Latino business ecosystem. Still, employer firms can serve as yet another measure of success. Employer firms are more likely to be scaled firms, but not all employer firms are scaled firms.

The first key finding considers the role of national banks. Among employer firms, only 12 percent of Latino businesses access national bank loans, compared to 18.4 percent for white-owned, 15.3 percent for Asian-owned, and 14.2 percent for black-owned firms. The SLEI survey asks about several types of external funding sources, including institutional sources of funding such as banks at both the national and local levels, allowing for comparisons across funding types and different Latino profiles. Figure 5.2 shows the external funding types used across Latino profile groups by age, gender, nativity, and revenue. We find that bank loans are accessed at very low rates to grow Latino businesses, although we see greater use of local bank loans relative to the national bank loans (see

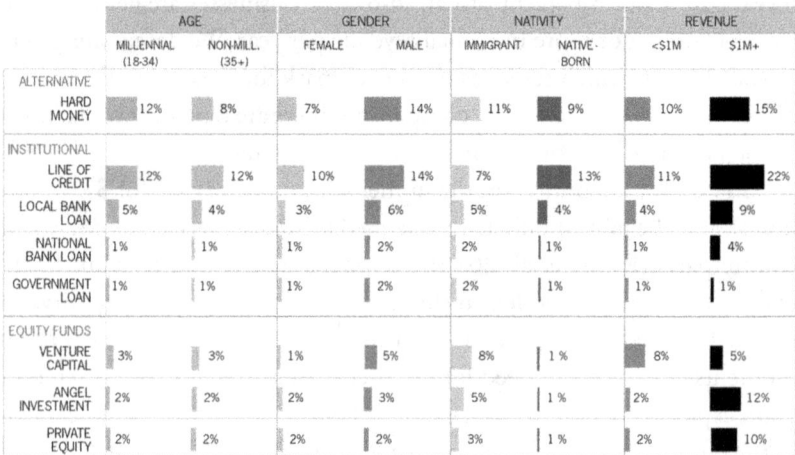

	AGE		GENDER		NATIVITY		REVENUE	
	MILLENNIAL (18-34)	NON-MILL. (35+)	FEMALE	MALE	IMMIGRANT	NATIVE-BORN	<$1M	$1M+
ALTERNATIVE								
HARD MONEY	12%	8%	7%	14%	11%	9%	10%	15%
INSTITUTIONAL								
LINE OF CREDIT	12%	12%	10%	14%	7%	13%	11%	22%
LOCAL BANK LOAN	5%	4%	3%	6%	5%	4%	4%	9%
NATIONAL BANK LOAN	1%	1%	1%	2%	2%	1%	1%	4%
GOVERNMENT LOAN	1%	1%	1%	2%	2%	1%	1%	1%
EQUITY FUNDS								
VENTURE CAPITAL	3%	3%	1%	5%	8%	1%	8%	5%
ANGEL INVESTMENT	2%	2%	2%	3%	5%	1%	2%	12%
PRIVATE EQUITY	2%	2%	2%	2%	3%	1%	2%	10%

Figure 5.2 External funding used by all Latino firms to grow their business. (Source: SLEI Survey of U.S. Latino Business Owners 2017.)

Chapter 13 in this volume for an extended discussion on banks and the desire of Latino entrepreneurs to have banking relationships). We also see higher use of lines of credit including personal and business lines, which can come from banks.

Among all external funding sources, government funding has the lowest rate of use among Latino-owned businesses. The low use rates of banks and government funding indicate that Latino-owned firms are not being funded through traditional financial institutions. There are many possible reasons for this (see Chapter 11 in this volume for findings related to language and access to financial capital, and see also Chapter 14, which represents a Latina's experience in investment management). Banks may be unwilling to take the risk on smaller firms, as we see slightly higher use among scaled firms. On the other hand, this may also have to do with how prepared Latino business owners are in accessing external funds. In the SLEI survey, we asked about the materials that Latino entrepreneurs had on hand for their businesses. On average, about one out of every three Latino firms reported having the necessary materials. For example, 36 percent of scaled firms have a business plan available, whereas only 20 percent of nonscaled firms have this funding material available. Still, these are low rates for all Latino firms, which may be why we see workshops tailored to these business outputs.

In addition to the outcome measure of business success through scaled and unscaled revenue categories, we construct additional measure of success through profit growth. Among Latino firms surveyed, 62 percent reported increased profits in the last 12 months. Firms that experienced profit growth were more likely to have secured a national bank loan. As such, there is an evident link between acquiring institutional funding and experiencing profit growth. Instead, we see other funding types, such as hard money, filling in the gaps. Hard money is secured from private sources and is less regulated than more formal business loans, and interest can range from 12 to 18 percent. In contrast, interest rates for the average bank loan range from 4 to 13 percent. Because hard money funding sources are typically easier to access, they may be more attractive for the business owner despite higher interest rates.

In a second key finding, we highlight the rapid growth in number of Latina-owned firms (see Chapter 12 in this volume for more about Latina entrepreneurship). Latinas play an important role in creating new businesses, representing nearly half of the growth of all U.S. Latino-owned firms. Between 2007 and 2012, the number of Latina-owned firms grew 87 percent. Between 2007 and 2015, Latina-employer firms grew in number by 44 percent. While the growth rate in the number of Latina-owned firms remains healthy, they tend to be smaller than male-owned firms. Among the 3 percent of scaled firms, 30 percent are owned by women. Latinas are less represented in the construction industry, which makes up 4 in 10 of the scaled firms and are more frequently found in the "other services" industry classification as compared to male-owned firms.

We hypothesize a few reasons why we have seen a surge in Latina entrepreneurship. First, Latinas are achieving higher education at a greater proportion compared to their male counterparts. There is also a growing wage gap among Latinas. The average woman working full-time earns 80 cents on the dollar paid to men. Latinas earn 53 cents on the dollar (UnidoUS and National Partnership for Women and Families 2018). In interviews with SLEI-Ed Latinas, some of them recount stories of working hard, generating lots of money for someone else, and not getting promoted. There is also the dynamic of changing gender role expectations, such as the Mexican-American women street vendors in Chicago who negotiated home and workplace gendered expectations and transformed both institutional values and their lives (Morales 2009). Taken together, these experiences and changing expectations may be compelling Latinas to start their own businesses. Certainly, we must contend with instances in which ethnic entrepreneurs are pushed into entrepreneurship rather than pulled, as these opportunistic stories would have us believe. Still, the higher rates of educational attainment among Latina entrepreneurs relative to the general Latino population debunks sole accounts of Latinas being pushed into entrepreneurship because a limited skill set precludes them from competing in the primary labor market.

Our survey findings further show that despite their high levels of business creation, Latinas feel that they are not qualified to access funding from financial institutions at higher percentages when compared to men. When considering only those entrepreneurs who would like national bank loans, we reveal some barriers to accessing this type of funding for both Latinas and Latinos, including not knowing how to get it, not having a relationship or contact, and not feeling qualified. Figure 5.3 depicts these barriers. The largest gap is found among small firms compared to scaled firms, where 60 percent of unscaled firms feel they are not qualified. There is another gap among men and women whereby 40 percent of women

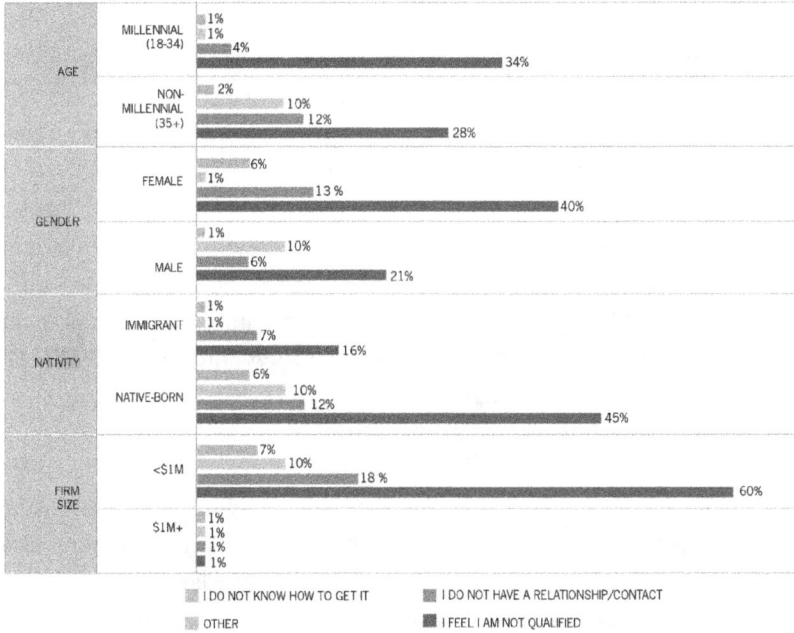

AGE

MILLENNIAL (18-34)
- 1%
- 1%
- 4%
- 34%

NON-MILLENNIAL (35+)
- 2%
- 10%
- 12%
- 28%

GENDER

FEMALE
- 6%
- 1%
- 13%
- 40%

MALE
- 1%
- 10%
- 6%
- 21%

NATIVITY

IMMIGRANT
- 1%
- 1%
- 7%
- 16%

NATIVE-BORN
- 6%
- 10%
- 12%
- 45%

FIRM SIZE

<$1M
- 7%
- 10%
- 18%
- 60%

$1M+
- 1%
- 1%
- 1%
- 1%

I DO NOT KNOW HOW TO GET IT   I DO NOT HAVE A RELATIONSHIP/CONTACT

OTHER   I FEEL I AM NOT QUALIFIED

Figure 5.3 Barriers to national bank loans across Latino groups. (Source: SLEI Survey of U.S. Latino Business Owners 2017.)

feel they are not qualified compared to 21 percent of men. This gap holds among women even when compared to men with similarly sized firms, so it is not just because Latina firms are smaller that they feel less qualified. Other research has shown a similar self-doubt about qualifications among women who think they are not qualified to run for political office even when having the same educational, occupational, and professional success compared to men (Lawless 2015). Among Latina entrepreneurs, gendered perceptions of qualifications may result in a funding ceiling both external and self-imposed, preventing more Latinas from reaching their full business potential.

As the next key finding, we consider the profile of immigrants compared to native-born Latinos. In the 2017 survey, we consider millennial immigrants who came to the United States before their 16th birthday to parallel a DACA-comparable group. Given the timely topic of DACA in the news, we considered it important to investigate this group in our data set. Surprisingly, we found that for Latino entrepreneurs, a DACA-comparable group is overrepresented among owners of immigrant businesses earning

$1 million or more annually. That is, this group is likely to have scaled firms. More specifically, we find that 86 percent of immigrant scaled firms are owned by millennials who immigrated before age 16 and that 29 percent of all scaled firms are owned by immigrant millennials who arrived before age 16. We hypothesize a few reasons why this might be.

First, research has found that immigrants arrive with a sense of "immigrant optimism" that propels earlier generations to perform well in school and have high ambitions (Escobar 2006). Second, we may also be seeing processes of psychological acculturation whereby immigrants develop an emotional attachment to their host culture (Singh and DeNoble 2004). Finally, because these immigrants arrived as children, they developed during their formative years in the American school system, learning English, and many are also taking advantage of expanded opportunities of higher education. Taken together, these are likely to play a role in the success of young immigrant entrepreneurs. As a final structural note as to what may facilitate entrepreneurship, federal and state laws do not require proof of immigration status for an individual to start a business.

In the 2015 survey, we found that Latino businesses were well integrated into the mainstream economy; they are located all over the United States, with more than three-quarters in non-Latino neighborhoods serving mostly non-Latino customers. In the 2017 analysis of the SLEI Survey of U.S. Latino Business Owners, we found that Latino entrepreneurs have the highest rate of business clients and customers outside the United States. Among all Latino firms (from the SBO), 9 percent have international clients, and 28 percent have clients throughout the United States. This also holds true among employer firms (from the ASE), where 4.5 percent of Latino firms have clients outside the United States compared to 4 percent for Asian-owned, 2 percent for white-owned, and 1.9 percent for black-owned firms.

LOCATIONS OF LATINO-OWNED BUSINESSES

Figure 5.4 shows the 2017 survey sample of over 5,000 Latino businesses plotted on a U.S. map. While merely a subset of Latino businesses, this figure shows us that they are located in new entrepreneurial gateways across the country not commonly associated with entrepreneurship. While Latino firms of all sizes definitely cluster in Latino-dense states such as California,

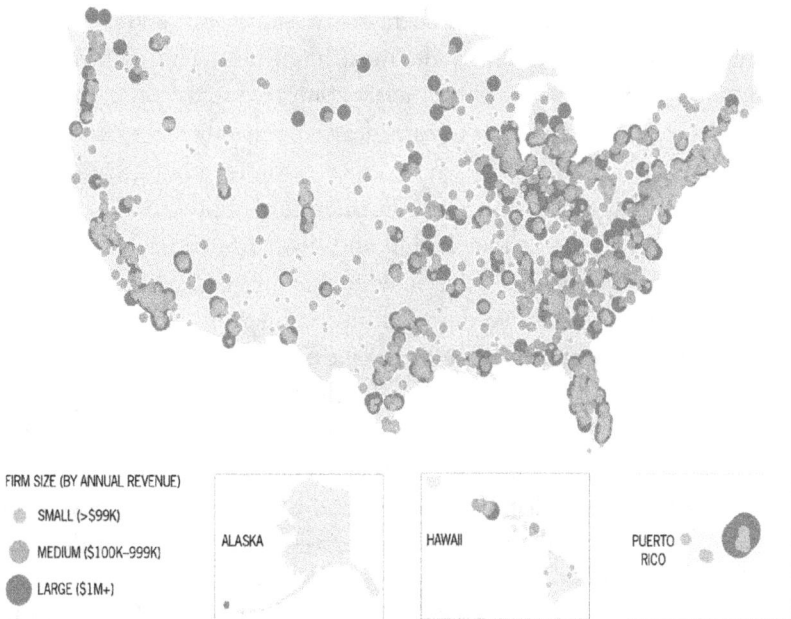

FIRM SIZE (BY ANNUAL REVENUE)

- SMALL (>$99K)
- MEDIUM ($100K-999K)
- LARGE ($1M+)

ALASKA

HAWAII

PUERTO RICO

Figure 5.4 Location and sizes of Latino firms in the U.S., 2017. (Source: SLEI Survey of U.S. Latino Business Owners 2017.)

Texas, Florida and New York, Latino firms—and large ones too—are increasingly being established in the South and the Midwest. For a detailed breakdown on these and other SLEI survey findings, refer to the *State of Latino Entrepreneurship* reports for 2015, 2016, and 2017.

CONCLUSION

It is important to note the larger context in which the SLEI findings are situated. Latino entrepreneurship is growing while catching up to other demographic groups. Latino-owned firms make up 12 percent of all U.S. firms, but Latinos represent 17.6 percent of the total U.S. population. An important factor in this catch-up game is the relatively lower level of wealth in the Latino community and the funding barriers facing Latino entrepreneurs (Butler, Morales, and Torres 2009). In contrast, the Asian community has higher levels of wealth and is seeing greater success in entrepreneurial outcomes. In a study on U.S. black-, Asian-, and white-owned businesses, minority entrepreneurship researchers Fairlie and Robb (2008) find that a high level of startup capital is the most important factor contributing to the success of Asian-owned businesses compared to the other groups.

Another important factor to consider is that nearly half of U.S.-born Latinos are younger than 18. We find great promise among Latino millennials in scaling their businesses. Furthermore, a poll from Harvard's Institute of Politics finds that Latino and black millennials show twice as much interest as white millennials in starting their own businesses (Lesonsky 2015). As the younger Latino population comes of age, we may see this segment of the population take on entrepreneurial dynamism that has been on a slow decline overall in the United States.

The continued work of SLEI is of great importance, as policy recommendations on minority entrepreneurship often call for the collection of data to inform knowledge about trends and disparities in business ownership. Collecting data is a very costly venture, especially when the goal is to make the sample nationally representative of the projected universe. Researchers have heavily relied on the SBO as a census of businesses in the United States. With its replacement focusing only on employer firms, researchers and others interested in business data will need to look to the other data sets described in this chapter, heeding the discrepancies in business-level and individual-level data.

Furthermore, it has been noted that a "lack of sufficient and frequent data on the characteristics and status of business ownership has hampered the identification of trends that could inform solutions aimed at reducing the nation's overall decline in entrepreneurship, as well as strengthen entrepreneurship among people of color" (Klein 2017:23). The consolidated efforts at the federal government to collect small business data at the employer firm level and the dissolution of the SBO make it all the more imperative that SLEI continue to gather annual research on Latino entrepreneurs at all firm size levels to better understand persistent challenges and growth opportunities.

REFERENCES

Butler, John S., Alfonso Morales, and David Torres. 2009. *An American Story: Mexican American Entrepreneurship and Wealth Creation.* West Lafayette, IN: Purdue University Press.

Department of Commerce, U.S. Census Bureau. 2017. "Submission for OMB Review: Comment Request; Annual Business Survey." *Federal Register* 84(28). https://www.govinfo.gov/content/pkg/FR-2019-02-11/pdf/2019 -01717.pdf.

Escobar, Gabriel. 2006. "The Optimistic Immigrant: Among Latinos, the Recently Arrived Have the Most Hope for the Future." Pew Research Center, May 30. https://www.pewresearch.org/2006/05/30/the-optimistic -immigrant/.

Fairlie, Robert W., and Alicia M. Robb. 2008. *Race and Entrepreneurial Success: Black-, Asian-, and White-Owned Businesses in the United States*. Cambridge, MA: MIT Press.

Fairlie, Robert W., and Alicia M. Robb. 2009. "Entrepreneurship, Self-Employment and Business Data: An Introduction to Several Large, Nationally-Representative Datasets." IZA Discussion Paper No. 4052.

Klein, Joyce A. 2017. *Bridging the Divide: How Business Ownership Can Help Close the Racial Wealth Gap*. FIELD at the Aspen Institute. https://www .aspeninstitute.org/publications/bridging-divide-business-ownership-can -help-close-racial-wealth-gap/.

Lawless, Jennifer L. 2015. "Female Candidates and Legislators." *Annual Reviews Political Science* 18:349–66.

Lesonsky, Rieva. 2015. "Fewer Millennials Want to Start a Business." Small Biz Daily, December 8. https://www.smallbizdaily.com/fewer-millennials-want -start-business/.

Lofstrom, Magnus, and Chunbei Wang. 2007. "Mexican-Hispanic Self-Employment Entry: The Role of Business Start-Up Constraints." *Annals of the American Academy of Political and Social Science* 612(2):32–46.

Morales, Alfonso. 2009. "A Woman's Place Is on the Street: Purposes and Problems of Mexican American Women Entrepreneurs." Pp. 99–126 in *An American Story: Mexican American Entrepreneurship & Wealth Creation*, edited by J. S. Butler, A. Morales, and David L. Torres. West Lafayette, IN: Purdue University Press.

Rivers, Douglas, Remy Arteaga, Tiq Chapa, and Jessica Salinas. 2015. *State of Latino Entrepreneurship: Research Report 2015*. Stanford Latino Entrepreneurship Initiative. http://lban.us/wp-content/uploads/2015/11/Final -Report-.pdf.

Singh, Gangaram, and Alex DeNoble. 2004. "Psychological Acculturation of Ethnic Minorities and Entrepreneurship." Pp. 279–89 in *Ethnic Entrepreneurship: Structure and Process*, Vol. 4, *International Research in the Business Disciplines*.

Emerald Group Publishing Limited. https://doi.org/10.1016/S1074-7877 (03)04013-3.

UnidosUS and National Partnership for Women and Families. 2018. "Beyond Wages: Effects of the Latina Wage Gap: Fact Sheet." National Partnership for Women & Families. http://www.nationalpartnership.org/our-work/resources /economic-justice/fair-pay/latinas-wage-gap.pdf.

PART II

MACRO PERSPECTIVES: A REGIONAL APPROACH

CHAPTER 6

Latino Farm Entrepreneurship in Rural America

Barbara Robles, Alfonso Morales, and Michael J. Pisani

INTRODUCTION

Most of the landscape of the United States is rural, which sustains a vibrant agricultural industry in small localities, across the nation, and around the world. However, as farmers and ranchers are aging, succession planning is a topic of importance across the country, and the concern is with who will become the farmers and ranchers of the future. Only recently have those farming careers become desirable again as local and regional food systems have increased in importance and especially in visibility. Many of these farms, especially in border states such as California, New Mexico, and Texas, employ tens of thousands of the Latino community, but those farms and associated agricultural enterprises are often owned by these Latinos as well (the second author's family has farmed and ranched in West Texas since 1867). The U.S. Department of Agriculture (USDA) recognizes the increasing importance of Latino-owned farms (USDA 2014), but a firmer understanding of the factors associated with such ownership and especially more research on agriculture-related business are needed.

Important research on Latino farm labor continues to grow and diversify (Morales 2009a, 2009b; Richardson and Pisani 2017:chap. 1), but there has not been a parallel increase in data or reporting on the business or the employer side of agriculture (Minkoff-Zern 2016; Zarrugh 2007) or with respect to Latino farmer participation in USDA grants or technical assistance programs. When investigating the Latino entrepreneurial sector, particularly in regard to agricultural business, a majority of the research produced has been on self-employment or business ownership in larger cities, with little or no work describing business ownership in rural areas or smaller cities proximate to most agricultural enterprises. Furthermore, the research to date has been limited mostly to case studies scattered rather randomly across the country, some largely excluding the border states that have the majority of Latino farms. Finally, there are incomplete measures of Latino farm ownership.

Our work provides a useful corrective to this situation—albeit only a first step in the right direction. In short, this chapter provides a method for estimating Latino farm income by combining data from the Internal Revenue Service (IRS) Schedule F, with Hispanic population density from the American Community Survey (ACS). We examine the share of Schedule F (farm entrepreneurs) filers in both urban and rural places with relatively large Latino populations and from these data relate farm income to a variety of independent variables, such as household structure and education. First, we will turn to a brief review of Latino participation in the agricultural economy of the United States (Chapter 4 in this volume specifies general economic contributions).

The majority of people who work on and run Latino farms in the United States are either first-generation Mexican immigrants or have at least one parent or grandparent who emigrated from Mexico (Lewis, Martinez, and Coronado 2017; Minkoff-Zern 2016; Pisani et al. 2017). However, as we will infer, this does not mean all are in new or relatively new enterprises. Still, while the term "migrant workers" in the United States is used to primarily represent different farmworkers traveling across the country in various seasons, it has now become synonymous with Latino workers migrating from Mexico, California, or South Texas (Lewis et al. 2017; Richardson and Pisani 2017). Over 6,500 H-2A workers, nearly all from Mexico, have been authorized for Michigan—up from just 442 just one decade ago—and now Mexican immigrants comprise 60 percent of the farmworker population in the state (Lewis et al. 2017). Most workers in Michigan and other states across the country do not immigrate to the United States by themselves. Often, this migration is network driven by friends or family already living in the destination state (Zarrugh 2007). These previous connections or accumulated social capital help these people begin their own businesses, since before they venture into self-employment they often shadow someone in their community or work in their prospective trade (Zarrugh 2007). This is one reason why self-employed Latino workers are often older and married and speak better English compared to the rest of their community. Across the United States, nearly 90 percent of all Hispanic-owned businesses are own-account ventures, meaning that the owner is the only paid employee. Additionally, Mexican immigrants who live in border states are 1.9 times more likely to be self-employed than people who settle in northern states (Dávila, Mora, and Hales 2009). These Latino workers have similar cultural ties and histories, many of which drive these individuals to self-employment.

Communication and language barriers are frequently cited problems in accessing resources associated with business formation, yet a common language can help generate the relationships producing businesses that serve coethnics. Language plays two roles in accessing services. First, seekers of services develop an understanding and practice of business or farming concepts such as regulations, techniques, expectations for accounting practices, and so on. Swisher et al. (2007) show how communication plagues laborers, contractors, and extension professionals alike in their relationships with each other. Research shows that 90 percent of Latino farmworkers prefer to learn in Spanish (Gonzales and Jeanetta 2013); while not business owners, a similar desire is likely. In this regard, we know that along with documentation, speaking English is highly related to making a Latino entrepreneurial business more economically successful (Pisani et al. 2017; see also Chapter 11, this volume). This language barrier can impede business formation across the gradient of the formation process in terms of accessing supportive relationships, comprehending the variety of practices required, and accessing grants and loans, and thus transforming aspiration to practice becomes more viable with new relationships and subsequent knowledge of practices and resources (Minkoff-Zern 2016; Swisher 2017). Making this information available in native languages (such as Spanish) is the first step to a more equitable agricultural system.

As indicated in Chapter 13 of this volume, Latino entrepreneurs tend to have higher levels of education and socioeconomic status relative to the general Latino population. Nonetheless, Latino people in the United States, especially those who have immigrated in recent generations, tend to have far lower education levels and socioeconomic status than their white American-citizen counterparts. This relationship continues to be more stratified, as data from rural California shows that when more Latino people move into a community and non-Latino white people move out, the median education level and income decrease. Poorer areas also tend to have lower-performing schools that do not effectively help or properly prepare students for higher education or career opportunities.

In the 1970s and 1980s the USDA advanced programs for the conversion of Mexican farmworkers into owner-operators of cooperative farms. Many participants were defined as farmers, but the programs did not always produce entrepreneurship, instead occasionally producing sharecropping arrangements, which triggered new law enforcement efforts (Rochín 1986). Pisani et al.'s (2017) work in South Texas explores this sector of Latino business as needs-driven and found that many of these people began their business with less than $1,000 in startup funds. This ability to start a business with little income is appealing to many people. Many nascent entrepreneurs reduce labor expenses of hiring by employing family members (DePhelps et al. 2005; Pisani et al. 2017; Zarrugh 2007). In the Alvarez Farms case, the help of 11 members of his family grew a 20-acre farm to over 120 acres over the course of 25 years, becoming one of the largest direct-to-market farms[1] in the state of Washington (DePhelps et al. 2005). However successful these necessity-driven businesses become, they do not always prove profitable, and the absence of human capital resources and social relationships impedes increased opportunities available with respect to credit, grants, and technical assistance. Nonetheless, as in the Alvarez case and in data analyzed below, we know that some Latino farm enterprises have survived founding processes that defeat small business generally to find some measure of success and opportunity.

It remains the case that business formation frequently follows from the important idea of *confianza* (trust) often found among Latinos (Zarrugh 2007), yet such familiarity can also inhibit growth and experimentation with new practices. Food and agricultural businesses are often highly regulated by local, state, and federal government agencies, and Latino owners may take a substantial amount of time and experience in substituting interpersonal trust for knowledge and subsequent trust in agencies and regulatory bodies (Morales 2012). Research now a decade old indicates that Latino business owners are more likely to use cash due to their distrust in banks (Morales 2012). More recent research indicates that Latinos have little trust in the USDA, a USDA that boasts about grants for non-white farmers. Yet only 14.4 percent of Latino USDA grants have been awarded as of July 2015, with most applicants told that their applications contained insufficient information (Minkoff-Zern 2016). Thus, it is no wonder that Pisani et al. (2017) find that self-employed Latinos are likely to trust their friends and families in making most business decisions. And this makes sense. These coethnics are the same people who brought them to the United States, gave them a path of a business to follow, and worked for them at their business. Coethnics are a principle source of knowledge and resources in the absence of successful experience and examples in government organizations.

These communication lines need to be opened and trust needs to commence being built in order to start to build the capacity of the agricultural/food-based Latino business community in the United States. This line of communication and means of assistance will not be useful until people in the Latino agricultural community can begin to trust these larger entities, and this takes time—so much so that research has not been able to identify where to start (Gonzalez and Jeanetta 2013). The Small Farms Program at Washington State University has begun to explore routes that will help build trust and create access (Ostrom, Cha, and Flores 2010). Some of its most important findings indicate the processual nature of correcting these problems. The interactions between problems must be addressed; cross-sectional/informational approaches are insufficient. It is simply not enough to translate pamphlets and presentations for potential farmers into Spanish; instead, a steady investment in process is required, recognizing no firm intervals in such processes and instead recognizing sensitivity to context and interest. Instead of dense power points with difficult vocabulary, workers, specifically in the Latino community, responded much better to hands-on face-to-face learning in their first language.

Latino farmers also need more than general overviews, so the Small Farms Program split workers into groups and brought in bilingual professionals to discuss topics such as finances and other important aspects to running a business. They paired farming couples individually with bilingual business students who helped them create a business plan. Ostrom et al. (2010) found that most beneficial were program elements that conveyed support professionals to farmers and taught them on their actual land. Programs such as these take substantial time and resources, but once in place participants will follow the experience of previous generations of white farmers who conveyed lessons to each other and learned from extension services and other professionals more swiftly. Once trust is built frequently and systematically between nascent Latino agricultural/food businesses, then the learning curve will steepen as it has toward creating an equitable agricultural system in the United States.

Clearly, the literature on farm enterprises is thin and lacking, especially with respect to our understanding of Latino farm entrepreneurs, where they are found, and what outcomes they may be enjoying. It is to this question that we direct our attention. So, we turn now to our research methods and subsequent data analyses to describe the correlates of farm entrepreneurship, in keeping with our effort to describe such as well as proscribe ideas to enhance the prospects for Latino farm enterprises.

METHODS: SCHEDULE F EMPIRICAL RESULTS FOR LATINO-ORIENTED ZIP CODES

In the absence of direct measurement, qualitative or quantitative, we have elected to deploy data from multiple sources directed to the most fine-grained scale that we could determine could still provide reliable estimates. Thus, we selected zip code–level data from the ACS five-year estimates (Census Bureau) and IRS statistics of income individual tax data. This relatively uncommon strategy draws from the 43,000 zip codes in the United States. Among these, over 60 percent report some farm income as identified by Schedule F filings. The latest agricultural survey[2] (2012) does not permit public use of farm income microdata by ethnicity. Using Hispanic population density from the ACS data as a proxy for Latino population density and the Schedule F farm income declaration for income tax filers for the 2013 tax year, we estimate a logistic regression to determine the likelihood of select independent variables in association with declared farm income.

As we are the first investigators to explore the connection between Schedule F filers and Latinos, this analysis is exploratory. The dependent variable is the Schedule F filer available through public-use data from the IRS. We operationalized the Schedule F filer as the share of Schedule Fs filed vis-à-vis all filers by zip code; all zip codes in our analysis contain some share of Schedule F filers. As logistic regression requires a dichotomous dependent variable, we coded all shares of Schedule F tax filers at the level of .01 (or 1.0 percent) or higher as equal to 1, otherwise 0.[3]

We selected a priori the following set of independent variables obtained from the IRS (tax year 2013) and the ACS (2011–2015) by zip code level. While these variables were selected a priori, they were selected in part from the literature (Pisani and Guzman 2016; Thompson 2011) and in part from each author's direct experience in Hispanic agriculture.

The selected variables include, by zip code, the share of (a) married couples, (b) females, (c) populations over age 65, (d) populations with a high school education or higher, (e) unpaid family workers, (f) families with children, (g) populations speaking Spanish, (h) foreign-born populations, (i) populations identified as poor, (j) populations engaged in agriculture, and (k) populations located in rural areas.[4] Additionally, adjusted gross income, average household size (by number of persons), median age, and the number of form 1099 Misc. filers by zip code are included. These variables were included based on the authors' collective experiences in rural America, experience with research on Latino issues, and availability of data via the IRS and the ACS.

As we are interested in locations with Hispanic populations, we selected zip codes populated with Latinos comprising 20 percent or more of the population. We selected zip codes excluding Puerto Rico, which presents unusual definitional and service concerns. We feel that this is justified given the exploratory nature of this research. We also avoided the definitional question of who counts as a Latino farmer.[5] Instead, we infer participation by examining the density of the Latino population at various levels: 20 percent and higher (n=3,500 zip codes), 30 percent and higher (n=2,229 zip codes), 40 percent and higher (n=1,517 zip codes), and 50 percent and higher (n=1,053 zip codes). The higher the density level, the more likely the Latino influence. The descriptive statistics for farm income by Hispanic density zip code is provided in Table 6.1.

Descriptive Statistics

Texas and California comprise the bulk of the zip codes with more heavily concentrated Latino populations.[6] This population concentration ranges from 49.5 percent for zip codes at the 20 percent level of Hispanic resident to 63.1 percent at the 50 percent level of Hispanic residents. Just under half of the zip code residents are married couples or women. Residents over 65 years of age are 11–13 percent of the population; this percentage increases as the density of Latinos decreases, reflecting the relative youth of the Latino population (Patten 2016). This relative youth is also reflected by the median age of higher-density Latino zip codes as well as the number of children and number of persons in the household. Educational attainment reflects the challenges of Hispanics to close the education gap, though those with a high school education represent two-thirds to more than three-quarters of residents in the studied zip codes, with the increase

TABLE 6.1 *Descriptive Statistics by Zip Codes with Farm Income for TY2013 by Hispanic Population Density for IRS Data Merged with ACS and SLEI 2015 Survey*

Name of Variables—Mean (Std. Dev.) *	Percentage of Hispanics in Zip Code							
	50%+	SLEI 50%+	40%+	SLEI 40%+	30%+	SLEI 30%+	20%+	SLEI 20%+
% Married couples	46.6 (12.2)	47.75 (9.08)	46.9 (12.4)	49.03 (10.17)	47.41 (12.5)	49.51 (9.62)	48.0 (12.8)	48.94 (8.73)
% Female	49.5 (4.1)	50.02 (2.82)	49.6 (4.0)	49.78 (2.69)	49.7 (4.1)	49.32 (3.17)	49.8 (4.3)	48.94 (3.59)
% Over 65	11.4 (6.1)	13.95 (3.9)	11.8 (6.0)	14.56 (4.98)	12.2 (5.9)	14.41 (4.69)	12.9 (6.0)	14.41 (4.54)
% HS ed+	67.7 (12.5)	73.64 (10.98)	70.6 (12.2)	74.89 (9.92)	73.9 (11.9)	75.37 (9.46)	77.8 (11.7)	76.51 (8.97)
% Unpaid family workers	0.2 (0.5)	0.16 (0.31)	0.2 (0.5)	0.17 (0.3)	0.2 (0.5)	0.19 (0.28)	0.2 (0.6)	0.18 (0.27)
% Families w/kids	35.9 (10.3)	31.13 (9.06)	34.9 (9.9)	29.83 (9.16)	33.6 (9.6)	30.1 (8.54)	32.1 (9.8)	29.54 (7.77)
% Spanish speaking	56.6 (16.7)	55.27 (19.56)	49.6 (17.9)	48.65 (20.47)	42.0 (18.8)	43.25 (21.2)	33.2 (19.2)	36.88 (21.41)
% Foreign born	27.5 (14.9)	12.97 (12.9)	25.7 (14.2)	12.28 (11.67)	23.7 (13.7)	12.08 (10.77)	20.9 (13.1)	11.76 (9.58)

% Poor	25.3 (10.4)	24.46 (6.48)	23.6 (10.4)	23.31 (6.68)	21.8 (10.4)	22.22 (6.69)	19.9 (10.3)	21.6 (6.5)
% Agriculture	8.7 (13.8)	11.6 (9.96)	8.1 (12.9)	11.01 (8.99)	7.4 (11.9)	10.84 (8.68)	6.5 (10.9)	9.42 (8.23)
Adjusted Gross Income ($)								
$1–$24,999	5952.2 (533.02)	3559.23 (2735.72)	5627.7 (5176.0)	3167.14 (2514.36)	5191.2 (4833.0)	3107.27 (2374.02)	4678.0 (4411.4)	3276.95 (2233.06)
$25,000–$49,999	3202.3 (2809.2)	1805.77 (1342.13)	3106.0 (2765.5)	1646.29 (1228.13)	2954.7 (2443.3)	1681.36 (1168.71)	2747.2 (2466.7)	1854.92 (1219.97)
$50,000–$74,999	1242.9 (1153.5)	821.54 (633.33)	1284.6 (1210.6)	748 (569.55)	1302.2 (1211.1)	779.09 (543.63)	1303.7 (1197.1)	861.86 (573.16)
$75,000–$99,999	595.1 (611.8)	470.77 (379.63)	647.4 (666.8)	428 (337.75)	692.1 (698.0)	440.45 (320.85)	734.8 (729.7)	493.9 (341.78)
$100,000–$199,999	563.3 (694.4)	476.15 (392.86)	656.0 (793.0)	438.57 (344.04)	760.3 (910.0)	443.86 (322.44)	874.1 (1051.3)	500.34 (353.89)
$200,000+	118.2 (248.2)	97.69 (93.01)	141.7 (269.5)	93.43 (84.95)	178.7 (328.6)	98.86 (77.32)	226.0 (409.1)	122.37 (118.06)
Household size	3.2 (0.6)	2.96 (0.35)	3.2 (0.5)	2.89 (0.37)	3.1 (0.5)	2.86 (0.36)	2.9 (0.5)	2.82 (0.33)
Median age	33.4 (6.1)	33.86 (4.7)	34.0 (6.0)	35.24 (6.78)	34.8 (5.9)	35.36 (6.19)	36.0 (6.3)	36.14 (5.81)
Number of 1099 Misc. filed	5574.8 (5137.8)	4117.08 (3463.69)	5626.2 (5159.1)	3915.09 (3108)	5645.2 (5257.7)	4300.39 (2934.44)	5701.9 (5526.4)	4604.61 (3011.89)

(continued)

TABLE 6.1 *(Continued)*

Name of Variables—Mean (Std. Dev.) *	Percentage of Hispanics in Zip Code							
	50%+	SLEI 50%+	40%+	SLEI 40%+	30%+	SLEI 30%+	20%+	SLEI 20%+
Location: Rural	18.0 (0.4)	100.0	18.0 (38.8)	100.0	20.0 (0.4)	100.0	21.0 (0.4)	100.0
N = (number of obs)	1,053	26	1,517	35	2,229	44	3,500	59
Top 4 States Share								
California	30.5	0	29.6	0	27.2	0	23.9	0
Florida	6.6	0	7.1	0	7.4	0	7.5	1.7
New Mexico	9.0	30.8	7.8	34.3	6.2	29.5	4.6	22.0
Texas	32.6	42.3	30.2	42.9	28.0	50.0	25.9	47.5
Total 4 State Share	78.7	73.1	74.7	77.1	68.8	79.5	61.9	71.2

* Variable mean and standard deviation are in parentheses.

associated with a decrease in Latino population density (Krogstad 2016a; Lopez 2009). As education is highly correlated with earnings, fewer high school or higher-educated residents in zip codes with denser Latino populations are in poverty (Lopez, Morin, and Krogstad 2016). Unpaid family workers remain essentially unchanged over the Latino density groups. The reporting of miscellaneous income appears similar across Latino density zip codes, increasing somewhat as density declines. This may be the result of more off-the-books transactions in Latino populations (Richardson and Pisani 2012).

The presence of Spanish-speaking residents is much larger for zip codes with higher-density Hispanic populations, as expected (Krogstad, Stepler, and Lopez 2015). Also expected is the larger share of foreign-born residents in higher-density Latino zip codes, because many Latinos are relatively recent arrivals in the United States (Flores 2017). Noting Latinos' contribution to agriculture, the more densely populated a zip code by Latino residents, the higher the incidence of agricultural activity (Passel and Cohn 2016; Pisani and Guzman 2016). Yet rising shares of adjusted gross income are reflected in less densely populated Latino zip codes, perhaps illustrating the inequality between workers and owners in this sector. Finally, there is an inverse relationship between Latino population density and rural location, signifying that Latino residents within zip codes with Schedule F filers reside in more urban environments (Krogstad 2016b).

Focusing on the SLEI data reported in Table 6.1, we explore the difference between varying densities of Hispanic population and their corresponding sociodemographic characteristics by zip codes. We use ACS ZCAT data for the socioeconomic demographic variables merged with zip codes for reported farm income (Schedule F) on tax returns (see Figure 6.1). We then merge this data with zip codes in the rural Latino-owned business (LOB) SLEI data. The major differences between the tax return (IRS) data and the SLEI survey data appear in the adjusted gross income categories, where the smaller sample size decreases the number of tax filers by income category. In addition, Texas and New Mexico remain represented in the SLEI data in comparable percentages to the farm income tax data. The SLEI data for California and Florida appear to have higher urban representation of LOBs. The SLEI data provides a higher representation of the Hispanic demographic with more than a high school education compared to the farm income tax data, which disappears as Hispanic density in zip codes (20 percent plus). The percent of foreign-born demographic

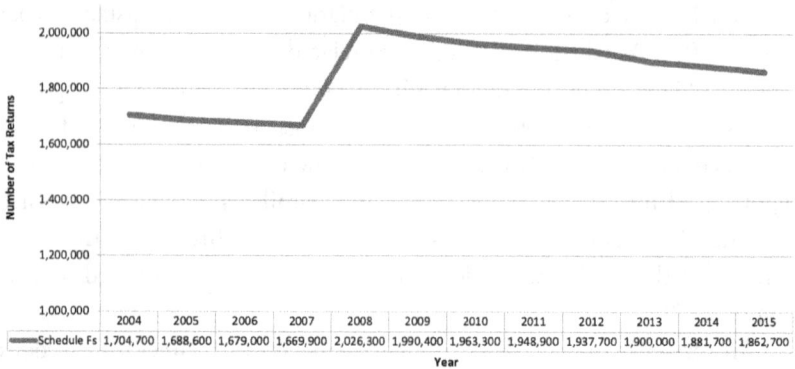

Figure 6.1 Schedule F: US Farm Income Tax Returns by Tax Year. (Source: Internal Revenue Service [IRS].)

is higher for each of the Hispanic density zip codes for the farm income tax data compared to SLEI data.

Logistic Regression Results

For the most part, eight of the independent variables are significant throughout the various levels of Latino population density (Table 6.2).[7] The positive and significant coefficients across the levels of Latino density are percent of married couples, percent of agricultural activities, and agricultural income between $75,000 and $99,999. This suggests that the likelihood in the increased share (≥.01) of Schedule F filers at the zip code level is significantly associated with greater numbers of married couples, higher levels of agricultural activities, and middling adjusted gross incomes ($75,000–$99,999). These data reveal the absence of research on middle-scale farm operators, an absence noted elsewhere in this volume. This indicates that as Hispanic population densities increase from 20 percent to 50 percent, the explanatory variables predicting increases in Schedule F filers display robust significance with minimal variation.

Significantly reducing the odds of the share of Schedule F filers (.01<) at the zip code level includes percent of high school or higher-educated residents, percent of foreign-born filers, adjusted gross income between $50,000 and $74,000, median age of residents, and an urban location. The results suggest that as education rates rise for the high school educated and beyond, the odds of Schedule F filers declines. An increase in the percentage of foreign-born residents reduces the

TABLE 6.2 Logistic Regression Results for Schedule F Share Filing (1 = .01 or above) by Zip Codes with Farm Income and Hispanic Population Density

	Percentage of Hispanics in Zip Code							
	50%+		40%+		30%+		20%+	
Variables	Coeff.	Exp(β)	Coeff.	Exp(β)	Coeff.	Exp(β)	Coeff.	Exp(β)
Constant	5.363	39.325‡	1.856	1.279	6.184	102.474†	9.951	4517.871†
% Married couples	.086	1.089†	.075	1.078†	.089	1.094†	.097	1.102†
% Female	.013	1.013	.021	1.021	.006	1.006	.005	1.005
% Over 65	.060	1.062*	.021	1.021	.004	1.004	.021	1.021
% HS ed+	−.043	.958†	−.041	.959†	−.061	.940†	−.094	.910†
% Unpaid family workers	−.108	.898	−.073	.930	−.027	.973	−.037	.964
% Families with children	−.020	.980	.010	1.010	−.004	.996	−.040	.960†
% Spanish speaking	−.013	.988	−.011	.989	−.006	.994	−.006	.994
% Foreign born	−.079	.924†	−.085	.919†	−.102	.903†	−.121	.886†
% Poor	−.008	.992	−.002	.998	−.013	.987	−.025	.976†
% Agriculture	.021	1.022*	.031	1.032†	.028	1.029†	.033	1.034†
Adjusted Gross Income ($)								
$25,000–49,999	.000	1.000	.000	1.000	.000	1.000	.000	1.000
$50,000–74,999	−.004	.996†	−.003	.997*	−.003	.997†	−.003	.997†
$75,000–99,999	.005	1.005‡	.004	1.004‡	.004	1.004†	.004	1.004†
$100,000–199,999	.000	1.000	−.001	.999	−.001	.999‡	−.001	.999†
$200,000+	−.001	.999	.000	1.000	.000	1.000	.001	1.001*

(continued)

TABLE 6.2 (Continued)

	Percentage of Hispanics in Zip Code							
	50%+		40%+		30%+		20%+	
Variables	Coeff.	Exp(β)	Coeff.	Exp(β)	Coeff.	Exp(β)	Coeff.	Exp(β)
Avg. household size	-.184	.832	-.213	.808	-.551	.576‡	-.283	.753
Median age	-.095	.909†	-.016	.984	-.039	.962*	-.069	.933†
Number of 1099 Misc. filed	.000	1.000	.000	1.000‡	.000	1.000†	.000	1.000†
Location (rural = 1)	-1.696	5.453†	-1.610	5.004†	-1.555	4.734†	-1.535	4.642†
Model Statistics								
-2LL	659.719†		971.231†		1396.640†		2166.564†	
Cox & Snell R²	.420		.428		.450		.464	
Nagelkerke R²	.609		.613		.637		.652	
N	1,053		1,517		2,229		3,500	

Reference categories: Adjusted gross income = $1–24,999, location = rural.

†, ‡, * denote statistical significance at the .01, .05, and .10 levels, respectively.

likelihood of filing a Schedule F tax form. Adjusted gross income in the range of $50,000 to $75,000 decreases the odds of filing a Schedule F tax form, as does an increase in median age of residents. Finally, residents in urban-based zip codes are less likely to file a return indicating farm income (i.e., Schedule F). The logistic regression model parameters and statistics are robust.

In order to ascertain the robustness of the logistic model results, we ran four separate zip code samples conditional on Hispanic population presence. The largest zip code sample, with the number of observations at 3,500, was zip codes where the Hispanic population totaled 20 percent or more. Each subsequent subsample contained tighter thresholds for the Hispanic population residing in the following population-dense zip codes: 30 percent or more, 40 percent or more, and 50 percent or more. None of the estimated coefficients changed signs with statistical significance. However, the 50 percent or more sample generated less statistical significance in tax filers with 1099 Misc. income (contract/independent filers), while the age variable for the population over 65 becomes significant at the 10 percent level. In addition, the model goodness-of-fit statistics did not substantially change over the various subsamples.

THE RURAL LANDSCAPE OF LATINO-OWNED BUSINESS FROM SLEI 2016 SURVEY

Because of the small sample size of rural LOBs in the SLEI data set, this section offers some preliminary, descriptive, and selective insights into the rural character of Hispanic enterprises. Utilizing SLEI data collected in the fall of 2016, we explore the nature of LOBs in rural areas as identified by rural zip codes from the IRS. The nationally representative survey was conducted in two rounds, the first in the fall of 2016 and the second in the spring of 2017 (described elsewhere in this volume). To correct unevenness in survey collection, associated weights were calculated and included in the data set. In all, 4,787 were surveyed in the fall with an additional follow-up survey of 616 chosen from the original respondents to explore most focused issues.

Rural LOBs comprised 5.5 percent (weighted n=247) of the fall 2016 SLEI respondents. Three-quarters of these respondents were from four states: California (19.4 percent), Florida (9.7 percent), New York

(8.5 percent), and Texas (37.7 percent). Additionally, more than two out of three rural Latino business operators are of Mexican origin (70.4 percent). Furthermore, rural LOBs are majority male-owned (66.2 percent male, 33.8 percent female) and averaged 42.5 years of age. These industry segments in which these rural LOBs operate are professional business services (32.8 percent), construction (19.4 percent), manufacturing (12.6 percent), leisure and hospitality (11.5 percent), and trade, transportation, and utilities (8.5 percent). Over 75 percent of operators of rural LOBs are involved in business (e.g., Hispanic Chamber of Commerce, general chambers of commerce, trade associations) and civic (e.g., local boards) organizations.

Business initiation came mostly from the owner/operator (68.0 percent) and somewhat in association with others (20.6 percent), and 59.2 percent of business revenues for rural LOBs surpass $1 million annually. The remainder possess revenues in the following ranges: $500,000 to $1 million, 11.4 percent; $100,000 to $500,000, 12.3 percent; and less than $50,000, 17.1 percent,. Beyond revenues, 78.8 percent of rural LOBs reported profits for the previous year, 4.2 percent reported losses, and 16.9 percent reported breaking even. Rural LOBs by number of employees are as follows: no employees, 27.9 percent; 1 to 9 employees, 36.3 percent; 10 to 49 employees, 15.8 percent; 50 to 99 employees, 11.5 percent; and 100 to 499 employees, 8.5 percent. Finally, the customer base of rural LOBs is mixed, with the following breakdown: all Latino, 7.7 percent; over half Latino, 20.9 percent; about half Latino/non-Latino, 25.2 percent; less than 50 percent Latino, 38.8 percent; and no Latinos, 7.5 percent.

The more focused SLEI follow-up survey respondents from the spring of 2017 record 8.4 percent (weighted n=51) of the resurveyed businesses as being located in rural areas. As discussed more fully in Chapter 10 in this volume, rural LOBs have a slightly lower rate of generational connection to the United States than their urban LOB counterparts.[8] Rural operators of LOBs are English dominant as reported in their language use with employees and customers: 48.9 percent of LOBs report speaking just English to employees, 32.0 percent report speaking mostly English and some Spanish, 32.3 percent report speaking just English to customers, and 48.7 percent report speaking mostly English and some Spanish to customers. This is in part a reflection of language competency, whereas rural Latino business owners report a 95.0 percent rate of fluency in English and a 59.7 percent rate of fluency in Spanish. Additional observations concerning language usage are informative; see Chapter 11 in this volume for further analyses on this topic.

Latino Farmers

The number of Latino farmers is on the rise. The quinquennial agricultural census notes impressive increases in the number of Hispanic principal farm operators, averaging 32.2 percent per census from 1987 through 2012 (Figure 6.2).[9] Latino farmers farmed 21 million acres and sold nearly $9 billion in agricultural goods in 2012 (Figure 6.3). The production of beef cattle occupied 36 percent of Latino farmers, the largest farm commodity by output. This growth is in contrast to the general decline in the number of farmers in the United States; from 2007 to 2012, the overall number of farmers dropped by 4 percent.[10] Compared to all farmers in the latest agricultural census, Latino farmers were similar as to average age (57.1 years), gender (88 percent male), and farming as the primary occupation (47 percent). Differences exist as far as rate of farmers who worked at least one day off the farm (Latinos have higher rates of off-farm work, 68 percent vs. 61 percent), and Latino farmers have significantly less tenure on their present farm than U.S. farmers (Latino farmers with 10 years or more on their present farm in 2012 was 62 percent and for all other farmers was 78 percent). Additionally, Hispanic farms tend to be smaller (58 percent had farms smaller than 50 acres) and bring fewer agricultural goods to market (68 percent had annual agricultural sales under $10,000) than U.S. farmers as a whole.[11]

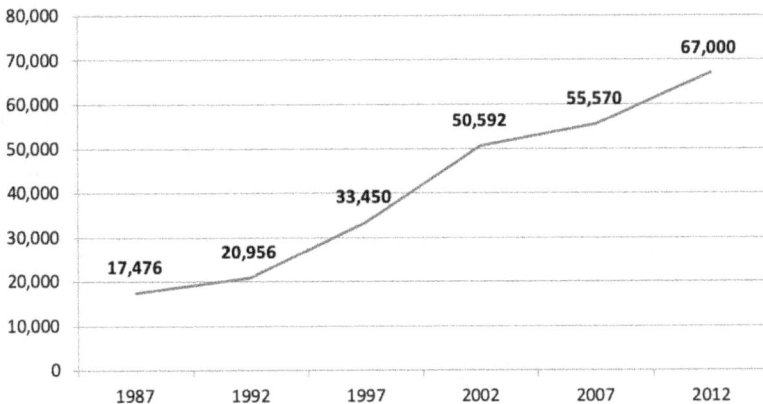

Figure 6.2 Number of Latino principal farm operators. (Source: 1987, 1992, 1997, 2002, 2007, 2012 Agricultural Census, USDA.)

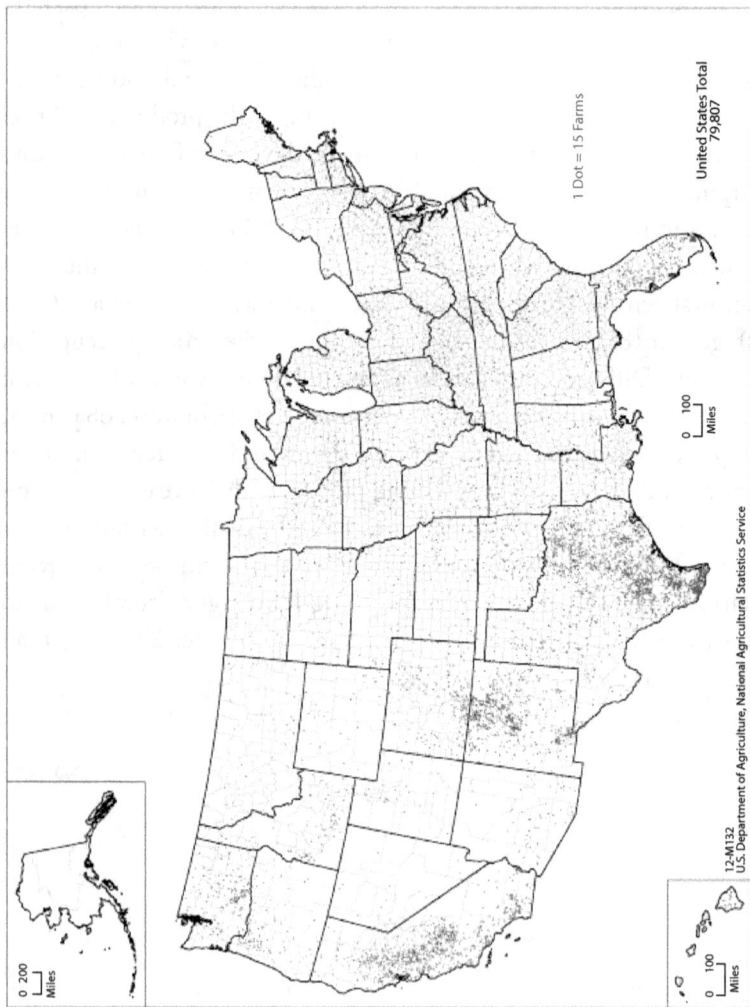

Figure 6.3 Number of farms with Spanish, Hispanic, or Latino origin operators, 2012. (Source: USDA, Agricultural Census 2012.)

1 Dot = 15 Farms

United States Total
79,807

0   100
Miles

12-M132
U.S. Department of Agriculture, National Agricultural Statistics Service

0   200
Miles

0   100
Miles

Six states represent areas with the greatest share of Latino farmers selected through our study of Schedule F filers at or above the 1 percent level in zip codes with at least 50 percent Hispanic population. The states and the number of counties included by the zip codes are California, 14 counties; Colorado, 5 counties; Florida, 4 counties; New Mexico, 21 counties; Texas, 72 counties; and Washington, 7 counties. For these states, we report Latino farm and operator characteristics as recorded in the 2012 agricultural census. Texas has the largest number of Latino farm operators, totaling 34,264 (or 51.1 percent of all Latino farm operators), and New Mexico has the largest share of Latino farmers within a state at 35.5 percent of all New Mexican farmers (Table 6.3, Panel A). Because more than one operator may operate a farm, there are fewer farms than operators. In each of the six states, the share of Latino farms is greater than the number of operators, indicating fewer Latino farm operators vis-à-vis farms in general. Average farm size is larger for Latino farms in more pastoral environments (e.g., Colorado, New Mexico, and Texas) and smaller in more crop/tree-intensive areas (e.g., California, Florida, and Washington). Finally, average annual market value for agricultural goods of Latino farmers is highest in California and is above the state market value average in Colorado, Florida, and Washington. Latino farmers in New Mexico have the lowest average market sales compared to New Mexico state farmers at just 48.6 percent of sales.[12]

Occupationally, Latino farmers in California have the highest rate of full-time farm work (58.4 percent), but a substantial majority of Latino farmers earn income with off-farm work in each of the six states (Table 6.4). A majority of Latino farmers have been on their present farms for more than a decade, with the greatest tenure noted in New Mexico and Colorado. While the average age of Latino farmers is slightly below the national average, principal Latino farmers are much older relatively than Latinos in general. Latino farmers in Washington state have the youngest age profile. Finally, more than a third of farm sales fall below $1,000 in Colorado, New Mexico, and Texas, indicating farms that may be experiencing a combination of crop, animal, and/or land valuation or rental price volatility combined with local economic stagnation (Burns et al., 2018). Most farms have annual sales less than $100,000, and only in California and Washington do 10 percent of Latino farms generate $500,000 or more in annual sales.

Five other states have zip codes with Schedule F filers above 1 percent and Hispanic densities above 50 percent. When aggregating by county as

TABLE 6.3 *2012 Latino Farm Characteristics of States with Schedule F Filers above 1% and At Least One County with a Hispanic Population of 50% or More*

Panel A

Farm Characteristic

States	Number of Farm Operators		Number of Farms		Ave. Size of Farm (acres)		Ave. Market Value	
	Latinos	Latinos as a % of Total	Latinos	Latinos as a % of Total	Latinos	Latinos as a % of Total	Latinos	Latinos as a % of Total
California	15,123	12.4	12,030	15.5	202	61.6	$546,617	99.8
Colorado	3,255	5.6	2,733	7.6	500	56.8	$247,486	115.1
Florida	6,668	9.1	5,100	10.7	130	65.0	$242,477	150.3
New Mexico	13,195	35.5	9,962	40.3	731	41.8	$50,111	48.6
Texas	34,264	9.2	26,465	10.6	347	66.3	$61,262	60.1
Washington	2,981	5.0	2,381	6.4	193	48.7	$426,202	174.1

Panel B

Farm Characteristic

	Number of Farm Operators		Number of Farms		Ave. Size of Farm (acres)		Ave. Market Value	
	Latinos	Latinos as a % of Total	Latinos	Latinos as a % of Total	Latinos	Latinos as a % of Total	Latinos	Latinos as a % of Total
Iowa	584	0.5	499	0.6	275	79.7	$272,855	78.5
Kansas	990	1.1	862	1.4	533	71.4	$542,055	181.4
Nebraska	494	0.7	414	0.8	670	73.9	$250,072	54.2
Oklahoma	1,749	1.5	1,508	1.9	255	59.6	$43,961	49.5
Oregon	1,489	2.6	1,267	3.6	165	35.9	$301,237	218.6

Source: 2012 Agricultural Census, USDA.

TABLE 6.4 *2012 Latino Farm Operator Characteristics of Eight States with Schedule F Filers above 1% and At Least One County with a Hispanic Population of 50% or More*

Operator Characteristics	California	Colorado	Florida	New Mexico	Texas	Washington
Primary Occupation (%)						
Farming	58.4	46.3	50.0	42.4	38.9	52.5
Other	41.6	53.7	50.0	57.6	61.1	47.5
Days worked off farm (%)						
None	35.8	30.9	30.7	33.6	27.3	33.7
1 or more	64.2	69.1	69.3	66.4	72.7	66.3
Years on Present Farm (%)						
2 years <	6.0	4.1	6.6	4.4	5.8	8.7
3–4 years	8.5	6.7	10.2	5.8	8.4	12.0
5–9 years	24.3	18.9	25.6	14.4	23.3	25.1
10+ years	61.2	70.3	57.6	75.4	62.6	54.3
Age Group (%)						
35 <	8.5	6.5	9.1	6.0	8.0	10.9
35–44	15.5	10.4	15.0	9.1	14.1	21.2
45–64	54.9	55.8	50.5	49.6	52.6	50.9
65+	21.1	27.3	25.4	35.2	25.3	17.0
Ave. age years	60.1	56.7	54.3	58.8	54.8	51.4
Farm Sales in Dollars (%)						
1,000 <	16.7	37.9	27.9	43.1	39.6	28.9
1,000–2,499	4.9	10.9	10.3	14.7	15.8	11.1
2,500–4,999	7.0	10.2	10.2	11.7	12.8	9.7
5,000–9,999	9.2	10.3	11.5	11.5	11.7	8.4
10,000–49,999	23.8	17.7	22.1	12.2	13.8	15.3
50,000–99,999	10.3	5.4	5.6	2.5	2.0	4.1
100,000–249,000	10.0	3.6	4.8	2.3	1.9	8.2
250,000–499,999	5.5	1.8	2.8	1.1	1.0	4.3
500,000+	12.6	2.2	4.7	0.9	1.4	10.0
N	15,123	3,255	6,668	13,195	34,264	2,981

Source: 2012 Agricultural Census, USDA.

above, these states and numbers of counties are Iowa, one county; Kansas, three counties; Nebraska, two counties; Oklahoma, one county; and Oregon, two counties. In these states, Latino farmers comprise between 0.5 and 2.6 percent of all farmers and between 0.6 and 3.6 percent of all farms (see Table 6.3, Panel B). Farm size is greater in the midwestern plains and smallest in Oregon but comparatively smaller than non-Hispanic farms. Relative to non-Hispanic farms, the average market value of Latino farms is robust in Kansas and Oregon and much weaker in Iowa, Nebraska, and Oklahoma.

Only in Oregon are more than half of Latino farmers engaged in full-time farming; the majority of Latino farmers in Iowa, Kansas, Nebraska, and Oklahoma farm as a secondary occupation (see Table 6.5). Given the secondary nature of many Latino farmers in these five states, about two-thirds are employed off the farm. A clear majority of Hispanic farmers in these five states have worked their farms for 10 years or more; though relative to large Latino farming states and non-Hispanic farmers, Latino farmers in these five states are relatively younger, with ages averaging mostly in the low 50s. Finally, farm sales below $1,000 ranged from 23.2 percent of Latino farms in Nebraska to 37.9 percent of farms in Iowa. Indeed, over 90 percent of Latino farms in Oklahoma had sales less than $50,000, with Nebraska having the lowest rate of Hispanic farmers, with sales below $50,000 at 63.7 percent. Most farms are small-scale concerns, as relatively few farms have sales above $500,000.

Farm sales and income volatility are related to several factors. The most dominant among these factors are crop versus animal production and large- versus small-scale farming. Input price volatility, crop production dependencies on weather and irrigation access and market force, and animal susceptibility to infectious diseases cause farm sales and income to vary depending on the locale and the size of the farm. In addition, Key, Prager, and Burns (2017) report that the educational attainment level of the principal farm operator is negatively correlated with total income volatility. Disadvantaged and nascent farmers will be pooling their farm income with off-farm income as they increase their farm-operating knowledge and skill set as a means of mitigating farm operation market cycles and local economic conditions. Access to farm subsidy programs and technical assistance in farm lending opportunities also contribute to smoothing farm income.

TABLE 6.5 *2012 Latino Farm Operator Characteristics of Other States with Schedule F Filers above 1% and At Least One County with a Hispanic Population of 50% or More*

Operator Characteristics	Iowa	Kansas	Nebraska	Oklahoma	Oregon
Primary Occupation (%)					
Farming	40.6	43.9	42.5	35.8	57.8
Other	59.4	56.1	57.5	64.2	52.2
Days Worked Off Farm (%)					
None	37.2	34.4	34.8	27.4	33.4
1 or more	62.8	65.6	65.2	72.6	66.6
Years on Present Farm (%)					
2 years <	6.0	4.0	8.5	5.4	7.4
3–4 years	11.5	6.1	4.5	11.3	8.7
5–9 years	13.3	20.0	23.7	25.0	25.5
10+ years	69.2	69.9	63.3	58.3	58.4
Age Group (%)					
35 <	11.1	9.0	16.4	12.3	9.3
35–44	20.9	16.5	16.4	19.7	19.3
45–64	43.5	47.7	44.9	48.7	54.8
65+	24.5	26.8	22.3	19.3	16.6
Ave. age years	53.5	55.2	52.9	51.3	51.5
Farm Sales in Dollars (%)					
1,000 <	37.9	27.1	23.2	31.5	26.8
1,000–2,499	6.0	7.4	4.3	10.5	11.7
2,500–4,999	5.4	9.0	6.5	12.0	10.8
5,000–9,999	10.6	9.3	12.3	11.8	10.4
10,000–49,999	12.4	24.4	17.4	24.6	20.0
50,000–99,999	4.8	5.7	7.2	4.8	6.1
100,000–249,000	7.2	7.9	11.1	1.4	6.5
250,000–499,999	7.0	3.2	6.8	0.7	2.4
500,000+	8.6	5.9	11.1	2.7	5.4
N	584	990	494	1,749	1,489

Source: 2012 Agricultural Census, USDA.

In summary, we have deployed a novel combination of data and methods that have produced a number of suggestive findings. However, we wish to focus here on the inverse relationship we have found between Latino-dense areas, which have a higher incidence of agricultural activity, and income, typically higher in the Schedule F data associated with less Latino-dense areas. This finding opens the door for further research on a number of questions to which we now turn.

NEW RESEARCH OPPORTUNITIES

We identify here four opportunities for new research. Clearly research is needed on Latino farmers, yet it is also clear that Latino *farming* should be as important to study, as we need an understanding of how Latinos constitute businesses, producing, marketing, and expanding farm enterprises, in order to begin to disaggregate components of our empirical findings.

First, we have contextual questions. As more nascent and younger farm operators enter into the agriculture sector, the need for further research on those agricultural subsectors with the highest growth potential and the most significant technological changes is apparent. The current farm-to-table movement indicates that more organic farming will be demanded as well as more all-season crop harvesting. Indoor farms or covered farming, which can increase urban farming movements, along with aqua-culture farming and other new organic farming methods will continue to increase (Greene et al. 2017; Agrilyst 2018). Currently, short supply lines are on the rise, as are new technologies to reduce costs of irrigation and harvest cycles. Drone technology is increasingly used in farm crop production (Mazur 2016). How Latino farmers are participating in various methods and using various technologies or marketing opportunities is unclear—and this is a topic of substantial importance not just to employment and income but also to the cost, quality, and availability of food as well as to the ecological sustainability of farm practices.

How does demand for agricultural products vary by density of Latino participation? One demand-side question is in the composition of supply chain partners (including cross-border supply chains from Mexico). The farmers' profit or loss may be associated with the composition demand-side businesses (restaurant/retail/food processors and the like). Regional economic analyses and programming can help Latino farmers access markets and relationships that improve profits. Another demand-side question has a very different unit of analysis; instead of organizations, it is individuals. Food accessibility and problems accessing healthy food is an important demand-side problem (i.e., food deserts; Roubal and Morales 2016). Such problems often plague those of low to moderate incomes and minority-dense communities. Access problems can be reconfigured as opportunities that drive new ways of farming and subsequent creation of value-added activities and products. As more direct-to-consumer sales (farmer's markets, roadside stands, and food trucks/mobile kiosks) occur, the opportunities to provide more technical assistance and create collaborative public-private relations are emerging. The farm-to-table movement creates a unique opening to connect with Latino farm operators in multiple venues. The rural areas adjacent to urban areas and those rural areas serving micropolitan cities and towns are underresearched in terms of understanding the dynamics of farm-to-market/farm-to-table supply chains for small farm operators (Pressman, Oberholtzer, and Dimitri 2013; Hendrickson and Porth 2012). In this regard as Key (2016) reports,

> Consumers have more opportunities to purchase food directly from producers, with 8,268 farmers' markets operating in 2014, up 180 percent since 2006. DTC [direct-to-consumer] marketing—where producers engage with consumers face-to-face at roadside stands, farmers' markets, pick-your-own farms, onfarm stores, and community-supported agricultural arrangements (CSAs)—is a substantially different business model from traditional marketing and is one that could help some farmers survive and prosper in a risky and competitive business environment.

One example of the data collection, reporting, and relationship building is in the Metrics + Indicators for Impact (MIFI) program (mifimarkets .org) sponsored by the University of Wisconsin–Madison. Based on decades of scholarship on marketplaces (Morales, Balkin, and Persky 1995; Morales 2009a, 2009b, 2011; Suerth and Morales 2018), MIFI shows the utility of self-consciously creating purpose-based multidisciplinary teams to work with local farmers markets in identifying goals, advancing practices of data collection and evaluation, and revising or developing strategies to achieve those goals. Moreover, such knowledge and practice benefit participants broadly, not just Latinos. Still, much more interdisciplinary research that brings to bear different expertise is required to better grasp Latino participation, or lack thereof, in financing, capital access, and government-sponsored programs as well as local initiatives that often fly below the radar.

However important such programs, given the research gap on Latino farmers at the national level (Swisher et al. 2007), one research approach would be to create a research team composed of university scholars, extension professionals, representatives of 4-H and Future Farmers of America state and/or national organizations (and the students from those organizations at the local level), along with trade associations that sponsor, for instance, farmers markets in various locales. Such a team of researchers would provide (or assist in) data collection and also identify potential networks and emerging farm-to-table/farm-to-market innovations.

As we consider what our research revealed, we can identify another important thread of new research needed on how Latinos access USDA grants and technical assistance programs. One working hypothesis is associated with program design and implementation and assumes that unintended barriers to USDA support are created by insufficiently considered programs and impeded further by uneven abilities of Latinos to interact with and navigate existing programs and personnel. Demand-side problems may be due to language, education level, socioeconomic status, and previous cultural experiences. Many of these barriers might be attributed to insufficient attention to how Latino farmers practice business and interact with existing programs. However, this assumption requires research of its own, and the existing capacity of rural development research is stretched thin. Furthermore, USDA programs are frequently understaffed and insufficiently funded and thus are diminished in their ability to follow up inquiries and increase trust between the Latino agricultural community and the U.S. government, and surely other factors contribute. In order to build the capacity of this increasingly important sector of the American population and business, steps have to be taken to identify and understand Latino farmers and capacitate academic and government actors for the interactive processes they must engage to work with Latinos.

Finally, we have left open important definitional questions. New research must also work at identifying Latino farmers. As indicated elsewhere in Chapter 5 of this volume, Latino entrepreneurs tend to have higher levels of education and socioeconomic status relative to the general Latino population. While we can only speculate, it may be that some new

Latino farmers are finding opportunities to engage in agricultural entre-preneurship in the context of an aging farm owner population. We surely need more work on this question, as it may mean different approaches to government technical assistance and grant programs. Furthermore, we have very little hard data on the number of farmworkers who transition to farm operators/owners and little to none on the Latino path to farm operator (Rochin 1986; Rochin 2013). Some ethnographies exist but are rare (see Chapter 2 in this volume). This gap in our research should be closed in order to have a better understanding of the role that farm labor plays in the eventual farm ownership dynamic. In addition, we have no data on Latino farm wealth where states play a significant role in mining and resource extraction rights for farm/ranch owners.

Such research opens the doors to understanding interactions between farming and associated communities—rural or urban. A variety of nonfarm-related activities can become problems for farm operations. Take, for instance, the recent increase in fracking. We have no data-oriented information on how this has impacted Latino farmers. However, we do know that fracking has changed the landscape of rural America. A *Los Angeles Times* article in 2014 reported that the former small town of Carrizo Springs, Texas, with a population of 5,700 boomed to over 40,000 with the advent of fracking in the Eagle Ford Shale formation. "The region is set to reap more than $90 billion in the next decade" (Hennessy-Fiske 2014). Since 2014 the world market for oil has been through boom-bust cycles, with implications for fracking growth and sustainability. We have little information on how this has impacted the Latino small towns and farm/ranch operators in the Eagle Ford Shale area.

Ultimately, farm and ranch operators in rural America and those operators turning to alternative farming and ranching systems (aqua-ponics, urban farming, free-range animal production, etc.) indicate that the agricultural sector is changing. We know that food access and short supply chains are part of national security concerns. As more weather-related disasters occur and as more food safety issues arise from imports, local place-based growers and ranch operators become more essential to the well-being of urban populations. Combine these economic landscape transformations with a changing demographic profile of the United States, and the economic opportunities and sustainability of the agricultural sector are potentially high-growth spaces for the Latino farm and ranch operators. We look forward to being among the investigators of these questions.

ACKNOWLEDGMENTS

The authors would like to thank Daniel Besinaiz for his assistance with the bibliography and Chloe Green for her work on the literature review. Arnobio Morelix, Marlene Orozco, and Refugio Rochin all provided careful reading and helpful comments.

NOTES

1. Direct market refers to farmers who sell product at farmers markets, roadside stands, and the like.
2. The USDA deploys an agricultural census every five years. The latest census was conducted in 2017–2018.
3. The cut-off point for the .01 share of Schedule F filers includes 49.3 percent of zip codes below .01 and 50.7 percent of zip codes .01 share or more.
4. Rurality varies widely. California does not have a rural area, as defined by the U.S. Census Bureau, the USDA, and the Office of Management and Budget. By the current definition, rural areas comprise open country and settlements with fewer than 2,500 residents; areas designated as rural can have population densities as high as 999 per square mile or as low as 1 person per square mile.
5. The U.S. Economic Development Agency approach is that a business qualifies as Hispanic-owned if 51 percent or more owned or assets are controlled by a self-identified Hispanic.
6. In aggregating the zip codes by 50 percent Latino population and Schedule F filers above the 1 percent threshold by county, the following number of counties by state are: California, 14; Colorado 5; Florida, 4; Iowa, 1; Kansas, 3; Nebraska, 2; New Mexico, 21; Oklahoma, 1; Oregon, 2; Texas, 72; and Washington, 7.
7. A fractional logistic regression was also estimated utilizing the same set of independent variables and the share value of the dependent variable (Schedule F filers). The fractional logistic regression results are similar to the logistic regression results reported in this section, as most readers are familiar with this statistical tool. The fractional logistic result reinforces the use of the .01 share as the cutoff value for the dichotomous dependent variable (Schedule F) in the logistic regression as appropriate.
8. The generation score for each group is 7.7 for rural LOBs and 8.0 for urban LOBs. The difference is not statistically significant.

9. The first data from the 2017–2018 agricultural census was released in April 2019. In this census, there was a change in reporting from principal operator to principal producer for Hispanic farms. Not all data has been released from this survey as this chapter goes to press.

10. The bulk of the data for this paragraph is derived from *Hispanic Farmers* (USDA 2014).

11. We highlight the April 2019 release of the 2017–2018 agricultural census numbers for Hispanic principal producers in this note. In 2017, there were 90,344 Hispanic principal producers, 71.0 percent male on average 5.4 years old, farming 77,416 farms on 26 million acres of land. The average farm size was 336.4 acres producing $186,936 in farm sales or $14.5 billion in farm sales in 2017. Beef cattle continued to be the number one agricultural activity of Hispanic farmers (USDA 2019). This shows a marked increase in the number of Hispanic principal farmers.

12. Hispanic principal producers (90,344) number over 1,000 in 11 states in the 2017–2018 agricultural census. These are Arizona (1,153), California (11,192), Colorado (3,192), Florida (5,805), Idaho (1,002), Kansas (1,016), New Mexico (10,220), Oklahoma (2,160), Oregon (1,612), Texas (33,508), and Washington (2,268).

REFERENCES

Agrilyst. 2018. "The State of Indoor Farming—2018." https://www.agrilyst.com /stateofindoorfarming2017/#cta.

Burns, Christopher, Nigel Key, Sarah Tulman, Allison Borchers, and Jeremy Weber. 2018. "Farmland Values, Land Ownership, and Returns to Farmland, 2000–2016." ERR-245. U.S. Department of Agriculture, Economic Research Service. https://www.ers.usda.gov/webdocs/publications/87524/err -245.pdf?v=43153.

Dávila, Alberto, Marie T. Mora, and A. D. Hales. 2009. "Earned Income along the U.S.-Mexico Border." Pp. 107–20 in *Labor Market Issues along the U.S.-Mexico Border*, edited by M. T. Mora and A. Dávila. Tucson: University of Arizona Press.

DePhelps, Colette, Cinda Williams, John Foltz, John Potter, Cynthia Selde, and Karen Faunce. 2005. "Sowing the Seeds for a Better Future: Alvarez Farms." Northwest Direct Farmer Case Study No. 12. Rural Roots Inc., Moscow, ID.

Flores, Antonio. 2017. "Facts on U.S. Latinos, 2015." Pew Research Center Hispanic Trends, September 18. http://www.pewhispanic.org/2017/09/18/facts-on-u-s-latinos/.

Gonzalez, Eleazar U., and Stephen C. Jeanetta. 2013. "Latino Farmers and USDA Agents Talk about Challenges to Access and Use of USDA Programs." Cambio de Colores—Proceedings of the 11th Annual Conference Latinos in the Heartland: At the Crossroads: ¿Incorporation or Marginalization? https://mospace.umsystem.edu/xmlui/bitstream/handle/10355/48941/2013-GonzalezJeanetta.pdf?sequence=1&isAllowed=y.

Greene, Catherine, Gustavo Ferreira, Andrea Carlson, Bryce Cooke, and Claudia Hitaj. 2017. "Growing Organic Demand Provides High-Value Opportunities for Many Types of Producers." *Amber Waves* (January–February). https://www.ers.usda.gov/amber-waves/2017/januaryfebruary/growing-organic-demand-provides-high-value-opportunities-for-many-types-of-producers/.

Hendrickson, Mary, and Mark Porth. 2012. "Urban Agriculture—Best Practices and Possibilities." Division of Applied Social Sciences, University of Missouri–Extension. http://extension.missouri.edu/foodsystems/documents/urbanagreport_072012.pdf.

Hennessey-Fiske, Molly. 2014. "Fracking Brings Oil Boom to South Texas Town, for a Price." *Los Angeles Times*, February 15. http://www.latimes.com/natioin/la-na-texas-oil-boom-20140216-story.html.

Internal Revenue Service. 2013. "Individual Income Tax Data." https://www.irs.gov/statistics/soi-tax-stats-individual-income-tax-statistics-2013-zip-code-data-soi.

Key, Nigel. 2016. "Local Foods and Farm Business Survival and Growth." *Amber Waves* (March). https://www.ers.usda.gov/amber-waves/2016/march/local-foods-and-farm-business-survival-and-growth/.

Key, Nigel, Daniel Prager, and Christopher Burns. 2017. "Farm Household Income Volatility:

An Analysis Using Panel Data from a National Survey." ERR-226. U.S. Department of Agriculture, Economic Research Service. https://www.ers.usda.gov/webdocs/publications/82564/err-226.pdf?v=42787.

Krogstad, Jens Manuel. 2016a. "5 Facts about Latinos and Education." Pew Research Center. http://www.pewresearch.org/fact-tank/2016/07/28/5-facts-about-latinos-and-education/.

Krogstad, Jens Manuel. 2016b. "Key Facts about How the U.S. Hispanic Population is Changing." Pew Research Center. http://www.pewresearch.org

/fact-tank/2016/09/08/key-facts-about-how-the-u-s-hispanic-population-is -changing/.

Krogstad, Jens Manuel., Renee Stepler, and Mark Hugo Lopez. 2015. "English Proficiency on the Rise among Latinos; U.S. Born Driving Language Changes." Pew Research Center. http://assets.pewresearch.org/wp-content /uploads/sites/7/2015/05/2015-05-12_hispanics-english-proficiency _FINAL.pdf.

Lewis, Barry, Rubén Martinez, and Juan David Coronado. 2017. "Farmworkers in Michigan." Julian Samora Research Institute Research Report No. 59. Michigan State University. https://jsri.msu.edu/upload/publications/research -reports/RR59%20final.pdf.

Lopez, Mark Hugo. 2009. "Latinos and Education: Explaining the Attainment Gap." *Pew Hispanic Center.* http://assets.pewresearch.org/wp-content/uploads /sites/7/reports/115.pdf.

Lopez, Mark Hugo, Rich Morin, and Jens Manuel Krogstad. 2016. "Latinos Increasingly Confident in Personal Finances, See Better Economic Times Ahead." Pew Research Center, June 8. http://assets.pewresearch.org/wp -content/uploads/sites/7/2016/06/PH_2016.06.08_Economy-Final.pdf.

Mazur, Michal. 2016. "Six Ways Drones Are Revolutionizing Agriculture." *MIT Technology Review*, July 20. https://www.technologyreview.com/s/601935 /six-ways-drones-are-revolutionizing-agriculture/.

Minkoff-Zern, Laura-Anne, and Sea Sloat. 2017. "A New Era of Civil Rights? Latino Immigrant Farmers and Exclusion at the United States Department of Agriculture." *Agriculture and Human Values* 34: 631–43.

Morales, Alfonso. 2009a. "A Social Currency Approach to Improving the Health Related Quality of Life for Migrant Workers." *Journal of Southern Rural Sociology* 24(1):92–112.

Morales, Alfonso. 2009b. "A Woman's Place Is on the Street: Purposes and Problems of Mexican American Women Entrepreneurs." Pp. 99–125 in *Wealth Creation and Business Formation among Mexican-Americans: History, Circumstances and Prospects*, edited by John S. Butler, Alfonso Morales, and David Torres. West Lafayette, IN: Purdue University Press.

Morales, Alfonso. 2011. "Public Markets: Prospects for Social, Economic, and Political Development." *Journal of Planning Literature* 26(3):3–17.

Morales, Alfonso. 2012. "Understanding and Interpreting Tax Compliance Strategies among Street Vendors." Pp. 83–106 in *The Ethics of Tax Evasion: Perspectives in Theory and Practice*, edited by Robert McGee. New York: Springer.

Morales, Alfonso, Steven Balkin, and Joe Persky. 1995. "The Value of Benefits of a Public Street Market: The Case of Maxwell Street." *Economic Development Quarterly* 9(4):304–20.

Ostrom, Marcia, Bee Cha, and Malaquías Flores. 2010. "Creating Access to Land Grant Resources for Multicultural and Disadvantaged Farmers." *Journal of Agriculture, Food Systems, and Community Development* 1(1):89–106.

Passel, Jeffrey S., and D'Vera Cohn. 2016. "Size of U.S. Unauthorized Immigrant Workforce Stable after Great Recession." *Pew Research Center Hispanic Trends*, November 3. http://assets.pewresearch.org/wp-content/uploads/sites/7/2016/11/02160338/LaborForce2016_FINAL_11.2.16-1.pdf.

Patten, Eileen. 2016. "The Nation's Latino Population Is Defined by Its Youth." *Pew Research Center Hispanic Trends*. http://assets.pewresearch.org/wp-content/uploads/sites/7/2016/04/PH_2016-04-20_LatinoYouth-Final.pdf.

Pisani, Michael J., and Joseph M. Guzman. 2016. "The Exceptional One Percent: US Farmworker and Business Owner." *Journal of Agriculture, Food Systems, and Community Development* 6(2):225–42.

Pisani, Michael J., Joseph M. Guzman, Chad Richardson, Carlos Sepulveda, and Lyonel Laulié. 2017. "Small Business Enterprises and Latino Entrepreneurship: An Enclave or Mainstream Activity in South Texas?" *Journal of International Entrepreneurship* 15(3):295–323.

Pressman, Andy, Lydia Oberholtzer, and Carolyn Dimitri. 2013. "Urban Agriculture in the United States: Baseline Findings of a Nationwide Survey." USDA Alternative Farming Systems Information Center. https://attra.ncat.org/attra-pub/summaries/summary.php?pub=558.

Richardson, Chad, and Michael J. Pisani. 2012. *The Informal and Underground Economy of the South Texas Border.* Austin: University of Texas Press.

Richardson, Chad, and Michael J. Pisani. 2017. *Batos, Bolillos, Pochos, and Pelados: Class and Culture on the South Texas Border.* Rev. ed. Austin: University of Texas Press.

Rochín, Refugio I. 1986. "The Conversion of Chicano Farmworkers into Owner-Operators of Cooperative Farms, 1970–85." *Rural Sociology* 51(1):97–115.

Roubal, Anne, and Alfonso Morales. 2016. "Chicago Marketplaces: Advancing Access to Healthy Food." Pp. 191–212 in *Cities of Farmers: Problems, Possibilities and Processes of Producing Food in Cities,* edited by Julie Dawson and Alfonso Morales. Athens, University of Iowa Press.

Suerth, L., and Alfonso Morales. 2018. "What Are the Broader Societal Benefits of Community Food Systems Development?" *Journal of Community Development* 48 TBD.

Swisher, M. E., Mark Brennan, Mital Shah, and Joysee Rodriguez. 2007. "Hispanic-Latino Farmers and Ranchers Project." CREES Report. U.S. Department of Agriculture, https://nifa.usda.gov/sites/default/files/asset/document/hispanic _full_report.pdf.

Thompson, Diego. 2011. "'Somos del Campo': Latino and Latina Gardeners and Farmers in Two Rural Communities of Iowa—A Community Capitals Framework Approach." *Journal of Agriculture, Food Systems, and Community Development* 1(3):3–18.

U.S. Census Bureau. *American Community Survey, 2011–2015, 5 Year Estimates.* https://www2.census.gov/programs-surveys/acs/summary_file/2015/data/5 _year_entire_sf/.

United States Department of Agriculture. 2014. *Hispanic Farmers.* ACH 12-11. https://www.agcensus.usda.gov/Publications/2012/Online_Resources /Highlights/Hispanic_Farmers/Highlights_Hispanic_Farmers.pdf.

United States Department of Agriculture. 2019. *2017 Census of Agriculture.* https://www.nass.usda.gov/Publications/AgCensus/2017/Full_Report /Volume_1,_Chapter_1_US/usv1.pdf.

Zarrugh, Laura H. 2007. "From Workers to Owners: Latino Entrepreneurs in Harrisburg, Virginia." *Human Organization* 66(3):240–48.

CHAPTER 7

Shaping Success: Exploring the Evolution of Latino Businesses in Three Major U.S. Counties

Edna Ledesma and Cristina Cruz

INTRODUCTION

Latinos[1] are changing the demographic distribution of the United States. There are about 56 million Latinos in the United States, accounting for 17 percent of the total U.S. population (Flores 2017; Lopez 2014). Of these 56 million, about 37 million are U.S. born, and 19 million are foreign born (Flores 2017). After increasing for four decades, from 1960 to 2000, the share of foreign-born Latinos in the United States began decreasing at the turn of the twenty-first century (Flores 2017). Nevertheless, in the same time frame the U.S. Latino population has increased ninefold and is projected to increase to 119 million, 29 percent of the total population, by 2060 (Flores 2017; Lopez 2014; Rios, Vazquez, and Miranda 2012).

The Latino population is concentrated in the southern United States (Figure 7.1). According to the U.S. Census Bureau, in 2010 the top three counties with the highest number of Latinos were Los Angeles County, California (48 percent Latino); Harris County, Texas (42 percent Latino); and Miami–Dade County, Florida (65 percent Latino) (U.S. Census Bureau 2010) (Table 7.1).[2] Using the 2016 Stanford Latino Entrepreneurship Initiative (SLEI) Survey of U.S. Latino Business Owners, the study focuses on these top three counties to explore the profiles of Latino owned businesses.

California and Texas each hold a minority-majority population (Lopez 2014). In 2014, Latinos surpassed whites as the largest racial and ethnic group in California (Lopez 2014), and it is estimated that based on current

135

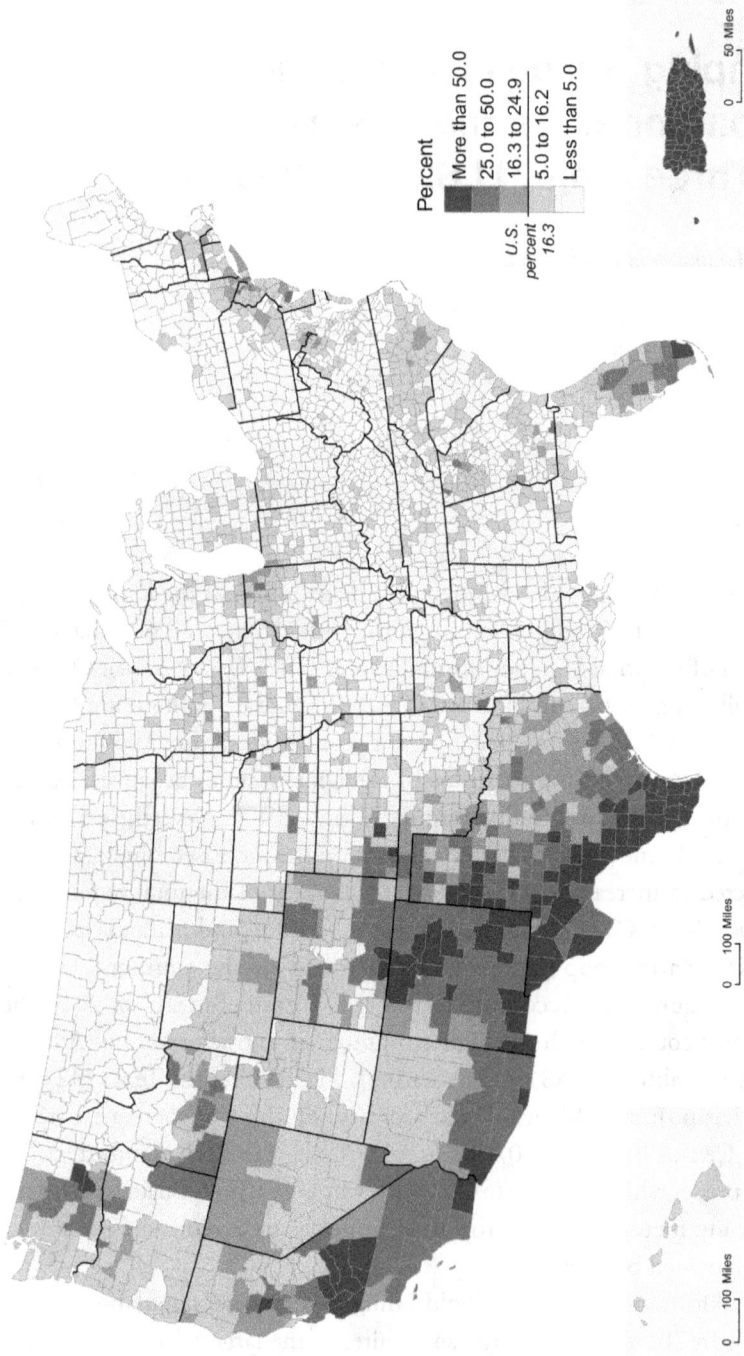

Figure 7.1 Latino population as a percent of total population by county: 2010. (Reprinted from Ennis, Ríos-Vargas, and Albert [2011].)

Percent

More than 50.0
25.0 to 50.0
16.3 to 24.9
5.0 to 16.2
Less than 5.0

U.S. percent 16.3

0   50 Miles

0   100 Miles

0   100 Miles

TABLE 7.1 *Top 10 Counties of Total Latino Population*

1	Los Angeles County, CA	4,760,974
2	Harris County, TX	1,731,046
3	Miami–Dade County, FL	1,648,630
4	Cook County, IL	1,273,631
5	Maricopa County, AZ	1,162,596
6	Orange County, CA	1,042,752
7	Bexar County, TX	1,033,722
8	Riverside County, CA	1,031,958
9	San Bernardino County, CA	1,030,532
10	San Diego County, CA	1,021,896

Source: Lopez 2014; U.S. Census Bureau 2010.

population growth rates, Texas will follow (Lopez 2014). Although at the state level Latinos account for 22 percent of the population in Florida, the minority population is about 48 percent, indicating that Florida is following a similar demographic shift as the other two states (U.S. Census Bureau 2010).

Latinos of Mexican origin are the largest Latin American group in the United States (Flores 2017), accounting for nearly two-thirds of the U.S. Latino population (López 2015). Since 1980, the Mexican-origin population has nearly quadrupled (López 2015). Today, unlike other migrants, Mexicans are dispersed in all 50 of the U.S. states (Rosenblum et al. 2012). Of all Mexicans in the United States, 33 percent are foreign born, and 42 percent have been in the United States for over 20 years (López 2015). Nevertheless, nuances within the Latin American origin profile of the Latino population in the United States could present lessons on the variations of entrepreneurialism and business profile among this population.

Latino demographic trends are significant in reinforcing how the Latino presence in the United States will continue to impact the shape, character, and form of cities (Rios et al. 2012). The national profile for Latinos, however, is changing in regions beyond the border, particularly in the Midwest and the Southeast (U.S. Census Bureau 2010). This change will be defined by the younger generations, since today nearly 6 out of 10 Latinos are millennials or belong to younger generations, in comparison to 4 out of 10 whites (Flores 2017). Given these changes, this study aims to provide insights on how Latino businesses are currently operating in counties with a large number of Latinos. Lessons on their operation and sector distribution might shed light for policy makers as Latinos expand into other regions of the country.

This chapter aims to contribute to a particular gap in the literature that explores the evolution of Latino-owned businesses in areas with high concentrations of Latinos. Portes' research showed that ethnic enclaves in Miami provide immigrants with a path for upward mobility (Wilson and Portes 1980). Yet as discussed by Orozco in Chapter 13, little research has been done on Latino businesses in other areas of large Latino concentrations such as Los Angeles and Houston. In Chapter 9, Echeverri-Carroll and Mora used the 2016 SLEI data and found that nationwide, Latinos represented the majority of customers for nearly one-third (31.4 percent) of Latino business owners operating in enclaves and only one-fifth (20.8 percent) of those outside of enclaves, showing that the relationship between location in a Latino enclave and the likelihood of having Latinos as the majority of customers is positive and statistically significant. Nevertheless, the 2016 SLEI data shows that 75 percent of Latino firms are in majority non-Latino neighborhoods, outside Latino enclaves. This chapter therefore aims to explore the nuances in the geospatial distribution of the businesses relative to Latino enclaves in three selected counties.

POLITICAL AND ECONOMIC CONTEXT

Political and economic contexts are important for understanding a more comprehensive profile of Latino businesses within the three geographic focuses of this study. A state-level profile[3] is important, as policies at this level play a critical role in defining the economic climate of counties. The following overview of the uniqueness or similarities across these three different states explains particular nuances in the study findings of the industry sectors and business growth within the three county study areas.

California

California, a progressive state, is considered to be high cost for doing business. Unlike Texas and Florida, California has a state income tax. Nevertheless, this high cost is offset by the state's economic strength. California's economy is performing well due to consistent job growth and a long-term low unemployment rate, and construction and major service industries, at both the high- and less-skilled levels, are projected to continue to drive growth over the next decade (Public Policy Institute of California 2018). California is also a high-benefit state: workers on average earn 11 percent more than the national average, but the output per worker for the state is 14 percent above the national average (Public Policy Institute of California 2018).

Between 2011 and 2016, California enacted over 50 policy measures to address a variety of progressive agendas such as taxations, workers' rights, safety net programs, infrastructure and housing, and environmental issues (Perry 2017). Supporters argued that these policy changes would raise wages for low-wage workers, increase access to health insurance, lower wage inequality, and reduce carbon emissions, while critics predicted that these policies would slow down economic growth and reduce employment (Perry 2017).

A study by the University of California–Berkeley found that employment and gross domestic product growth were not negatively affected by the policies, and wage inequality declined modestly (Perry 2017). Between 2011 and 2016, California's gross domestic product grew by 17.2 percent (Perry 2017). Yet, a number of challenges remain, with 10 percent of workers being unemployed, underemployed, or discouraged,[4] a number that remains above pre–Great Recession levels (Public Policy Institute of California 2018).

Texas

Texas, a conservative state, is frequently promoted as a business-friendly state with strong job creation (Jillson 2014). Texas labor laws create a favorable business climate with less red tape, in addition to having no state income tax and lower housing costs than California, making it an attractive place to live and do business (Rechtin 2014). Texas's economic growth has occurred parallel to the state's population growth. Between 1980 and 2011, Texas's population grew by 79 percent (11 million people), more than double the rate of growth of the nation as a whole (McNichol and Johnson 2012). Even during the Great Recession, Texas outperformed California and Florida in job growth (Jillson 2014).

In 2003 Texas passed one of the most prominent economic development initiatives to emerge from the political process in recent years, the Texas Enterprise Fund, which appropriated $295 million in funds to be used primarily for "deal-closing" incentives, what critics sometimes refer to as "corporate welfare" ("Texas Politics—Political Economy" 2018). What was particularly controversial about the bill was that it took money from the emergency Economic Stabilization Fund (also known as the Rainy Day Fund), to fund economic growth through grants and subsidies to attract new businesses ("Texas Politics—Political Economy" 2018).

The Texas model, however, is not a helpful model for economic growth for the rest of the country (McNichol and Johnson 2012). Although Texas workers are more productive than other workers in the United States, they receive less pay for their labor and face thinner social safety nets when they stumble (Jillson 2014). About 1 out of every 10 hourly wage jobs in Texas pays at or below the minimum wage, more than in any other state (McNichol and Johnson 2012). The Texas model is therefore a low-wage economy with greater income inequality than the average for the nation (Jillson 2014).

Florida

Florida, a conservative state, does not have a state income tax but does have a corporate income tax. Although on the surface this tax policy profile might depict Florida as a more middle-of-the-road model when compared to California and Texas, its economic profile paints a different picture. In 2015, the Institute of Taxation and Economic Policy[5] ranked Florida as having the second most unfair, or "regressive," tax system in the nation, second only to Washington, D.C. (Keystone Research Center 2018). Furthermore, Florida has significant income disparities between the rich and the poor (Keystone Research Center 2018).

Florida's economy has recovered from the Great Recession; however, the levels of economic security have not improved (Bustamante 2017). With few good jobs, the Florida economy is promoting low-wage and low-quality jobs at the expense of workers' economic security, disproportionately impacting women and people of color (Bustamante 2017). In 2016, one in five Florida workers was paid at or below $10 an hour, the highest share of low-wage workers in the past 11 years (Bustamante 2017).

DATA: LATINO DIVERSITY, SECTORS, AND BUSINESS SCALE

The 2016 SLEI survey collected data from about 4,800 Latino business owners. According to the survey, the top three states with largest number of Latino businesses were California (24 percent), Texas (15 percent), and Florida (15 percent). Using the 2016 SLEI data set, this study zooms into the top three counties with total Latino population, all located within these three states, to explore the profile of Latino-owned business in a smaller geographic context. After narrowing down the SLEI data set, the sample size for this study was reduced to 726 survey respondents: 333 in Los Angeles County, 67 in Harris County, and 326 in Miami–Dade County.[6]

According to the 2016 SLEI report, 75 percent of Latino firms are in majority non-Latino neighborhoods, outside Latino enclaves. We were particularly interested in exploring this finding geospatially by mapping the distribution of the survey respondents within the three-county study sample. The 2016 SLEI survey collected geographic data regarding business locations at the zip code level. Using the 2016 American Community Survey data, the study compared the demographic profile of each county, looking specifically at the percentage of Latinos in the total population, and the concentration of the 2016 SLEI survey respondents at the zip code level.

The geographic classifications and the declared Latin American origin, or Latino type, were the independent variables in the analysis. Using descriptive statistics, the study explores the relationship of these two variables to the total number of employees over a five-year period and the company industry classification.

GEOGRAPHIC FOCUS

Los Angeles County

Los Angeles County, California, has a total population of about 10 million people (U.S. Census Bureau 2016b) and contains the city of Los Angeles, the second most populous city in the United States (U.S. Census Bureau 2010) with about 3.8 million people (U.S. Census Bureau 2016b). In Los Angeles County, 48 percent of the population is Latino (U.S. Census Bureau 2016b) (Table 7.2). Per capita income for Los Angeles County ($29,301) is just short of the U.S. average ($29,829) (U.S. Census Bureau 2016b). The per capita income of Latinos in Los Angeles County is $16,749, while non-Hispanic whites alone make $34,982, almost twice the Latino per capita average (U.S. Census Bureau 2016b) (Table 7.3).

TABLE 7.2 Population by Race

Los Angeles County

	Los Angeles County		California		United States	
	Count	Percentage	Count	Percentage	Count	Percentage
Total population	10,057,155		38,654,206		313,55,162	
Non-Hispanic	5,195,507	52%	23,750,224	64%	260,909,226	83%
Non-Hispanic white	2,687,787	27%	14,837,242	38%	197,362,672	62%
Non-Hispanic black	801,182	8%	2,724,286	7%	44,088,615	14%
Non-Hispanic Asian	1,413,105	14%	6,122,435	16%	19,663,833	6%
Latino	4,861,648	48%	14,903,982	39%	52,199,107	17%

Harris County

	Harris County		Texas		United States	
	Count	Percentage	Count	Percentage	Count	Percentage
Total Population	4,434,257		26,956,435		313,55,162	
Non-Hispanic	2,578,653	58%	16,543,285	61%	260,909,226	83%
Non-Hispanic white	1,382,851	31%	11,705,684	43%	197,362,672	62%
Non-Hispanic black	821,066	19%	3,134,962	12%	44,088,615	14%
Non-Hispanic Asian	293,797	7%	1,161,742	4%	19,663,833	6%
Latino	1,855,604	42%	10,413,150	39%	52,199,107	17%

Miami–Dade County

	Miami–Dade County		Florida		United States	
	Count	Percentage	Count	Percentage	Count	Percentage
Total Population	2,496,435		19,934,451		313,55,162	
Non-Hispanic	872,576	35%	15,127,597	76%	260,909,226	83%
Non-Hispanic white	383,551	15%	11,080,426	56%	197,362,672	62%
Non-Hispanic black	425,650	17%	3,078,918	15%	44,088,615	14%
Non-Hispanic Asian	35,841	1%	511,264	3%	19,663,833	6%
Latino	1,623,859	65%	4,806,854	24%	52,199,107	17%

Source: U.S. Census Bureau 2016a.

TABLE 7.3 *Income Indicators (in 2016 Inflation-Adjusted Dollars)*

Los Angeles County

	Los Angeles County	California	United States
Median family income	$64,824	$72,952	$67,871
Per capita income	$29,301	$31,458	$29,829
Per capita income for Latino	$16,749	$17,013	$17,323
Per capita income for white alone	$34,982	$35,519	$32,770

Harris County

	Harris County	Texas	United States
Median family income	$63,720	$64,585	$67,871
Per capita income	$29,301	$27,828	$29,829
Per capita income for Latino	$16,749	$16,640	$17,323
Per capita income for white alone	$34,982	$29,749	$32,770

Miami–Dade County

	Miami–Dade County	Florida	United States
Median family income	$50,373	$59,139	$67,871
Per capita income	$24,515	$27,598	$29,829
Per capita income for Latino	$21,890	$19,727	$17,323
Per capita income for white alone	$26,609	$30,505	$32,770

Source: U.S. Census Bureau 2016a.

Looking at the spatial distribution of Latinos within Los Angeles County, the areas with the highest concentration of Latinos are in the southeast and northwest regions (Figure 7.2). The sample distribution of the 2016 SLEI survey respondent depicts a similar concentration of Latino-owned businesses across the county with a southeastern concentration (Figure 7.3).

Harris County

Harris County, Texas, has a population of about 4.4 million (U.S. Census Bureau 2016a) and is home to the city of Houston, the fourth most populous city in the United States with a population of about 2.2 million (U.S. Census Bureau 2016a). At the county level, Latinos account for 42 percent of the total population (U.S. Census Bureau 2016a) (see Table 7.2). The per capita income at the county level ($29,301) is slightly lower than the national average ($29,829) (U.S. Census Bureau 2016a). Looking

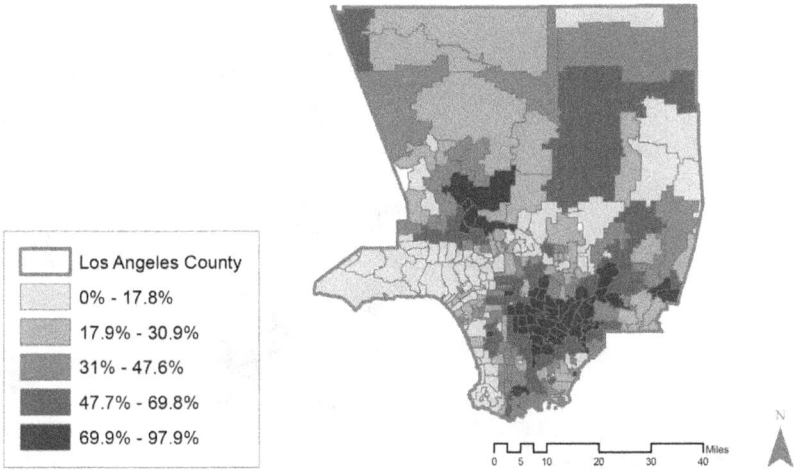

Figure 7.2 Latino population in Los Angeles County by zip code. (Source: U.S. Census Bureau 2010.)

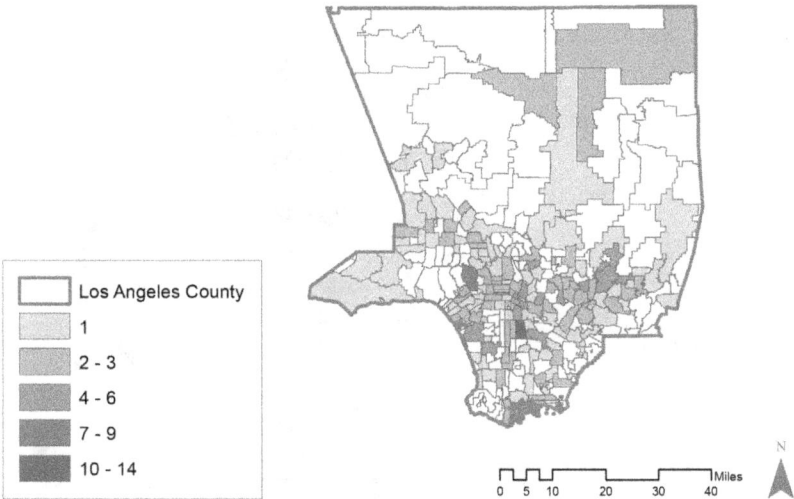

Figure 7.3 Total sample size by zip code. (Source: SLEI Survey of U.S. Latino Business Owners 2016.)

at income indicators by race, the per capita income of Latinos for Harris County is an estimated $16,749, while non-Hispanic whites only average $34,982 (U.S. Census Bureau 2016a) (see Table 7.3).

Looking at the percentage of Latino population by zip code, we find that higher concentrations reside on the east side of Harris County

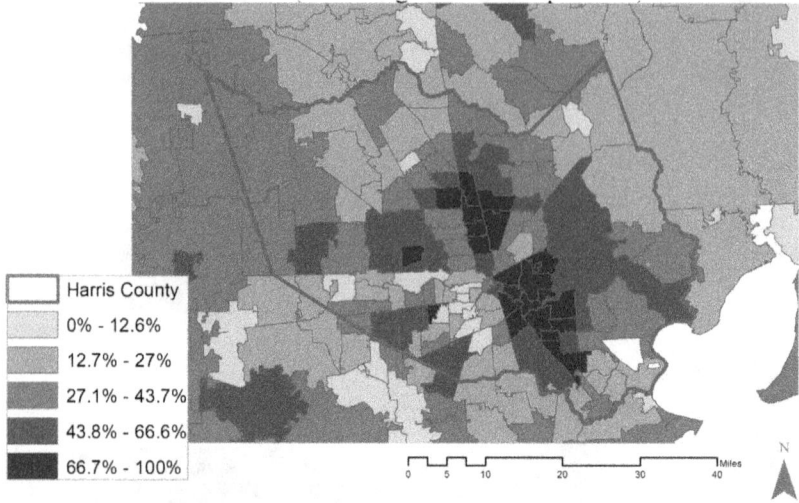

Figure 7.4 Latino population in Harris County by zip code. (Source: U.S. Census Bureau 2010.)

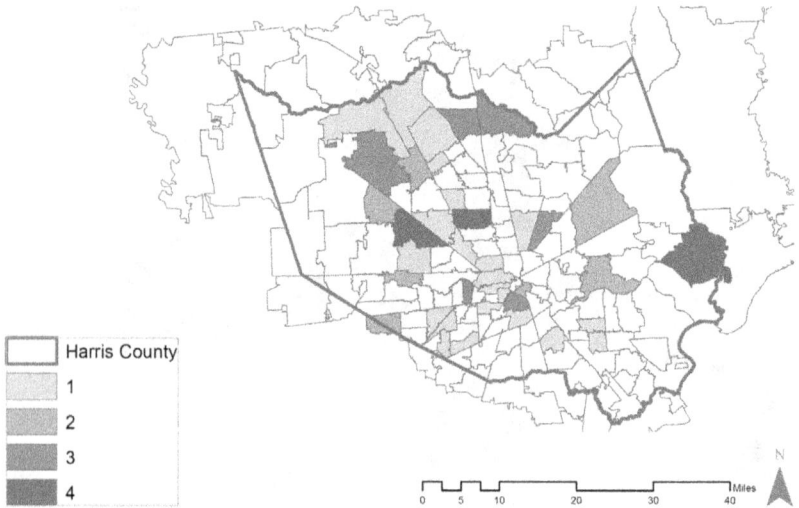

Figure 7.5 Total sample size by zip code. (Source: SLEI Survey of U.S. Latino Business Owners 2016.)

(Figure 7.4). A mapping of the 67 survey respondents shows the sample ringing areas of high percentages of Latinos, supporting the theory that Latino-owned businesses are located outside Latino enclaves. For Harris County, we find more Latino businesses located on the periphery of the county boundary (Figure 7.5).

Miami–Dade County

Miami–Dade County has a total population of about 2.5 million people (U.S. Census Bureau 2016a) and contains the city of Miami, which has a total population of about 400,000 people (U.S. Census Bureau 2016a). In Miami–Dade County, 65 percent of the population is Latino (U.S. Census Bureau 2016a) (see Table 7.2). Per capita income in Miami–Dade County ($24,515) is also slightly lower than the U.S. average ($29,829) (U.S. Census Bureau 2016a). The per capita income of Latinos in Miami–Dade County ($21,890) is higher than both the state ($19,727) and national ($17,323) averages (U.S. Census Bureau 2016a) (see Table 7.3).

The Latino profile by zip code across Miami–Dade County shows a western concentration (Figure 7.6). Unlike Los Angeles County and Harris County, Miami–Dade County had the widest Latino business sampling across most of the county zip codes. Furthermore, the largest concentration of the survey respondents was seen predominately in the central region of the county (Figure 7.7).

Within the Latino population in Miami–Dade County the largest group is Cubans, who account for more than half (53 percent) of the Latino population, or 34 percent of the total population ("Hispanics by Country of Origin in Miami–Dade" 2011). Yet within the SLEI data, Cubans represent 17 percent of the Latino business owners in Miami–Dade County. Mexican-origin Latinos account for approximately 2 percent

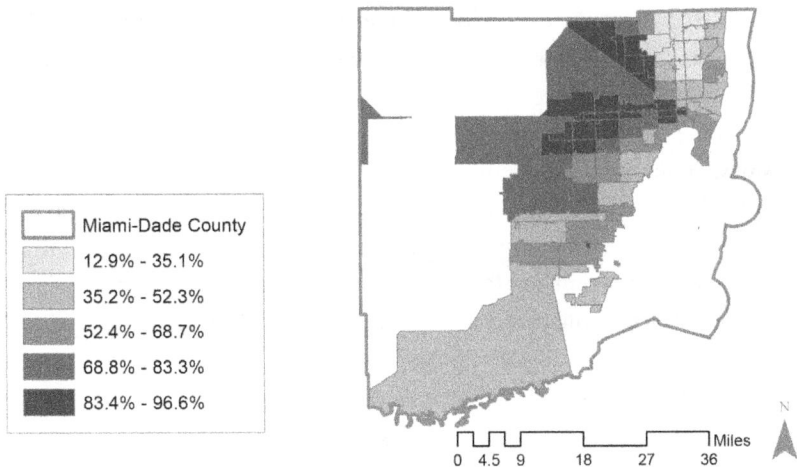

Figure 7.6 Latino population in Miami–Dade County by zip code. (Source: U.S. Census Bureau 2010.)

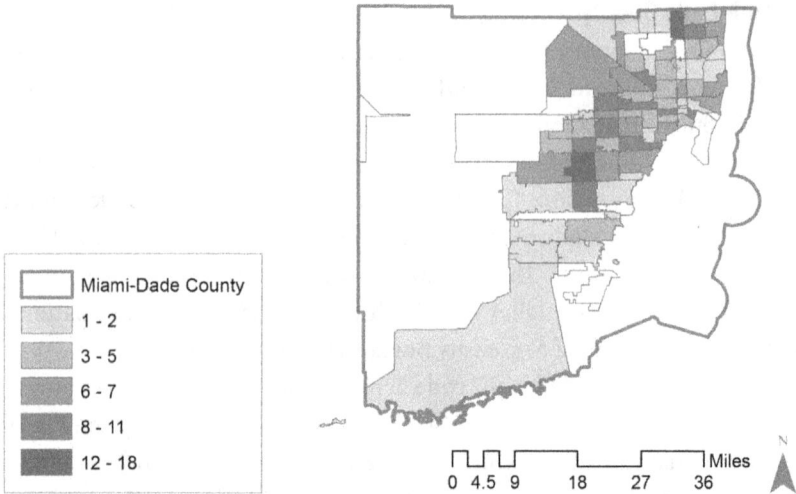

Figure 7.7 Total sample size by zip code. (Source: SLEI Survey of U.S. Latino Business Owners 2016.)

of the total population in Miami–Dade County, but they account for more than half (54 percent) of the SLEI respondents for that county.

INDUSTRY SECTORS BY COUNTY

The 2016 SLEI survey classified business industries into 10 categories that parallel the North American Industry Classification System, the standard classification system used by the U.S. government to register businesses for the purpose of collecting, analyzing, and publishing data related to the U.S. business economy (U.S. Census Bureau 2017). All 10 industries classified in the 2016 SLEI survey were found within the Harris, Los Angeles, and Miami–Dade County sample. Within the aggregate three-county sample, the largest (29 percent) sector among Latino businesses was professional business services, construction was the second (16 percent), and trade, transportation, and utilities ranked third (12 percent).

Looking only at Harris County, the county with the smaller sample size, the top three sectors present a slightly different profile from the aggregate average. Professional business services also account for the largest sample (28 percent), other services trail second (15 percent), and manufacturing is the third-largest industry sample (11 percent) (Table 7.4).

TABLE 7.4 *Industry Sectors*

Industry Sectors by County

Industry	Harris County		Los Angeles County		Miami–Dade County		Three-County Sample	
	Count	Percentage	Count	Percentage	Count	Percentage	Total	Percentage
Construction	5	7%	40	12%	71	22%	116	16%
Education and health services	3	4%	25	8%	9	3%	37	5%
Financial activities	5	7%	24	7%	15	5%	44	6%
Information	3	4%	25	8%	19	6%	47	6%
Leisure and hospitality	5	7%	13	4%	12	4%	30	4%
Manufacturing	7	10%	40	12%	22	7%	69	9%
Natural resources and mining	6	9%	2	1%	2	1%	10	1%
Other services (except public administration)	10	15%	45	14%	21	6%	76	10%
Professional business services	19	28%	98	29%	95	29%	212	29%
Trade, transportation, and utilities	4	6%	21	6%	60	18%	85	12%
	67	100%	333	100%	326	100%	728	100%

(continued)

TABLE 7.4 (Continued)

Industry Sectors by Latin Origin

Industry	Mexican		Cuban		Puerto Rican				Other	
	Count	Percentage	Count	Percentage	Count	Percentage	Total		Count	Percentage
Construction	101	21%	6	8%	4	12%	5		5	4%
Education and health services	23	5%	5	6%	1	3%	5		5	4%
Financial activities	28	6%	7	9%	3	9%	6		6	4%
Information	31	6%	3	4%	0	0%	13		13	9%
Leisure and hospitality	14	3%	5	6%	3	9%	7		7	5%
Manufacturing	46	9%	12	16%	4	12%	9		9	6%
Natural resources and mining	6	1%	1	1%	0	0%	4		4	3%
Other services (except public administration)	44	9%	6	8%	6	18%	24		24	17%
Professional business services	139	29%	20	26%	9	26%	48		48	35%
Trade, transportation, and utilities	53	11%	12	16%	4	12%	18		18	13%
	485	100%	77	100%	34	100%	139		139	100%

Source: SLEI Survey of U.S. Latino Business Owners 2016.

The top three sectors for Los Angeles County were professional business services (29 percent), with other services second at 14 percent, and construction and manufacturing both tied as the third-largest sectors, each capturing 12 percent of the sample (see Table 7.4).

Like the other two counties, professional business services also accounted for the largest sample size (29 percent) in Miami–Dade County. Construction accounts for a large portion of the industry (22 percent), ranking second in the county sample; the trade, transportation, and utilities industry follows third (18 percent) (see Table 7.4).

Although all three counties had professional business services as their largest business industry classification, nuances among the sample present parallels the aforementioned spatial distribution of businesses across the counties. For instance, the location of businesses in the urban periphery in Harris County might be linked to the prevalence in manufacturing. The prevalence of trade, transportation, utilities, and construction industries is an indicator of Latino entrepreneurialism with the development field in Miami–Dade County that is not seen across the other two counties sampled.

INDUSTRY SECTORS BY LATINO- OR HISPANIC-ORIGIN TYPE

Looking at the three-county agglomerate, we were interested in profiling the business industry sector distribution by Latino origin classifications. The SLEI survey classified Latino owners under four categories: Mexican, Mexican American, Chicano/a; Puerto Rican; Cuban; and other.[7] It is important to note that the sample universe for the three counties increased by 13 respondents, as these respondents identified with more than one Latin origin.

Consistent with the national demographic profile of Latinos, business owners of Mexican origin account for the largest respondent group (66 percent) within Harris, Los Angeles, and Miami–Dade Counties. Looking at the predominate business industries within this Latino classification, the study found that professional business services was the largest sample (29 percent) among Mexicans; the construction industry was second (21 percent), and trade, transportation, and utilities was third (11 percent) (see Table 7.4).

The Latin American origin classification of "other" Latino types was the second-largest response (19 percent). Within this group, the top three business industry sectors were professional business services (35 percent), other services (17 percent), and trade, transportation, and utilities (13 percent). It is interesting to note that among this Latin American–type group, construction (4 percent) ranked second to last (see Table 7.4).

Business owners of Cuban origin (10 percent) ranked third. Like in the other Latin American sample types, professional business services (26 percent) ranked first; trade, transportation, and utilities and manufacturing industries tied for second, each representing 16 percent of the sample (see Table 7.4).

Looking specifically at the industry classification by Latin origin, the highest-ranking industry, professional business services, did not differ from the three-county aggregate in each county. Where we find nuances in the distribution is with the construction industry, which ranked second among Latinos of Mexican origin and those classified as "other" but was not a top-ranking industry among Cubans.

Although the study sample depicts a heterogeneous Latino business owner population, the predominately Mexican-origin sample in all three counties might provide insight regarding the entrepreneurialism of this particular subset of Latin origin population. For instance, as discussed earlier, although Cubans account for the majority of the Latino population in Miami–Dade County, this group did not account for the majority of the Latino business owners in the sample. Furthermore, businesses operated by predominately Mexican origin owners might affect the consumer base for the various industry concentrations.

BUSINESS GROWTH BY COUNTY

Success rate of new businesses in the United States vary by scale, yet nevertheless, the rate of success for new businesses decreases over time. In the United States, it is estimated that 69 percent of new businesses will survive at least two years; however, almost half of all new businesses have a chance of failing within the first five years of operation (Adams 2011). This five-year threshold is therefore a critical time to monitor the scale and operation of businesses.

Looking at the evolution of a business over time, a potential proxy to explore success is business growth through increase in the number of employees. The 2016 SLEI survey provides insights into business growth over a five-year period (2011 and 2016). In 2011, the percentage of Latino-owned businesses with zero employees in Harris County was 15 percent, a percentage that doubled in 2016. Looking at the next business size classification, this study found that 36 percent of Latino business owners in Harris County employed one to nine people in 2011. In 2016, this percent increased to 48 percent of the sample (Table 7.5).

The change in employee numbers with the Los Angeles County sample has a similar profile as Harris County. In 2011, Latino businesses with zero employees accounted for 8 percent of the sample; this number increased nearly threefold (21 percent) in 2016. The percentage of businesses with one to nine employees increased minimally by 3 percent between 2011 and 2016 (see Table 7.5).

For businesses with zero employees in Miami–Dade County, the percentage increased from 5 percent to 12 percent between 2011 and 2016. Like the other two counties, the number of businesses with 1 to 9 employees increased in the five-year sample period. The scaling down of Latino-owned businesses in Miami–Dade County is evident in the decrease of businesses with 1,000 or more employees. According to the survey, in 2011, 24 percent of businesses operated at this scale; however, in 2016 the number decreased to zero (see Table 7.5).

Overall, all three counties saw a rise in owner-operated businesses with zero employees over the five-year study period. Businesses with 1 to 10 employees also saw a rise, while those with 500 or more employees saw a decline in number of employees over time. The prevalence and rise of small businesses in these three counties might be an indicator of the entrepreneurialism of Latino business owners, but at the same time the decline of larger businesses should be addressed by providing support mechanisms for small business owners such as small business loans.

BUSINESS GROWTH BY LATINO TYPE

We also looked at the number of employees over time by Latino type to explore potential indicators of business success among different Latinos. Within the three-county sample, Latinos of Mexican origin are the largest group. According to the survey, 33 percent of these business owners employed 1 to 9 others in 2016; this figure rose slightly from 30 percent in 2011. Within the five-year period, the study also found that

TABLE 7.5 *Number of Employees in 2016, 2015, and 2011 by County*

Harris County

Number of Employees	2016		2015		2011	
	Count	Percentage	Count	Percentage	Count	Percentage
Zero	20	30%	10	15%	10	15%
1 to 9	32	48%	29	43%	24	36%
10 to 49	8	12%	19	28%	24	36%
50 to 99	4	6%	1	1%	3	4%
100 to 499	3	4%	5	7%	2	3%
500 to 999	0	0%	2	3%	2	3%
1000+	0	0%	1	1%	2	3%
	67	100%	67	100%	67	100%

Los Angeles County

Number of Employees	2016		2015		2011	
	Count	Percentage	Count	Percentage	Count	Percentage
Zero	71	21%	32	10%	25	8%
1 to 9	132	40%	127	38%	123	37%
10 to 49	47	14%	73	22%	64	19%
50 to 99	52	16%	44	13%	50	15%
100 to 499	26	8%	39	12%	34	10%
500 to 999	2	1%	11	3%	27	8%
1000+	3	1%	7	2%	10	3%
	333	100%	333	100%	333	100%

Miami–Dade County

Number of Employees	2016		2015		2011	
	Count	Percentage	Count	Percentage	Count	Percentage
Zero	38	12%	18	6%	15	5%
1 to 9	97	30%	79	24%	78	24%
10 to 49	59	18%	62	19%	46	14%
50 to 99	42	13%	26	8%	40	12%
100 to 499	87	27%	57	17%	22	7%
500 to 999	3	1%	70	21%	48	15%
1000+	0	0%	14	4%	77	24%
	326	100%	326	100%	326	100%

Source: SLEI Survey of U.S. Latino Business Owners 2016.

owner-operated businesses with zero employees doubled. There was also a significant drop in the number of businesses with 1,000 employees; in 2011 these accounted for 13 percent of the sample, while in 2016 the number dropped to less than 1 percent (Table 7.6).

The business profile among Latinos of Cuban origin depicts a scaling down of businesses over the past five years. Starting with businesses with no employees, the number grew from 5 percent to 21 percent between 2011 and 2016. Furthermore, while in 2011 businesses with 500 or more employees accounted for nearly 20 percent of the sample, businesses of this scale were no longer present in 2016. The sample distribution showed absorption of these larger businesses across the categories of 1 to 9 and 10 to 49 employees (see Table 7.6).

Latinos classified as "other," the second-largest sample within the three-county study, also depict a decrease in scale of businesses. Within the five-year period, businesses with zero employees grew from 8 percent to 22 percent of the sample; this business scale absorbed the majority of the change within the sample. Larger businesses with 500 to 999 employees and those with 1,000 or more employees dropped from accounting for a combined 18 percent of the sample in 2011 to less than 2 percent in 2016 (see Table 7.6).

Much like in the analysis of business growth across the three counties, the profile reflected a similar trend when exploring this variable relative to the various classifications of Latin American origin. The decline in number of larger businesses over the five-year period is an indicator of the higher risks that Latino business face in reaching longevity and growth through their employee size. Businesses with over 1,000 employees were scarce among Mexicans and were not present in the 2016 sample.

DISCUSSION AND PUBLIC POLICY CONSIDERATIONS

During and after the Great Recession between 2007 and 2017, the growth rate of Latino businesses in the United States outpaced that of non-Latino groups (Orozco, Oyer, and Porras 2017). Although they are growing at a faster pace, growth is particularly challenged by a number of factors such as the current opportunity gap[8] between Latino-owned and other businesses and low access to financial institution–based loans (Orozco et al. 2017).

TABLE 7.6. *Number of Employees in 2016, 2015, and 2011 by Latin Origin*

Mexican, Mexican American, Chicano/a

	2016		2015		2011	
Number of Employees	Count	Percentage	Count	Percentage	Count	Percentage
Zero	79	16%	38	8%	33	7%
1 to 9	161	33%	152	31%	144	30%
10 to 49	72	15%	99	20%	89	18%
50 to 99	76	16%	46	9%	59	12%
100 to 499	91	19%	74	15%	36	7%
500 to 999	4	1%	62	13%	62	13%
1000+	2	0%	14	3%	62	13%
	485	100%	485	100%	485	100%

Cuban

	2016		2015		2011	
Number of Employees	Count	Percentage	Count	Percentage	Count	Percentage
Zero	16	21%	5	6%	4	5%
1 to 9	31	40%	24	31%	22	29%
10 to 49	16	21%	18	23%	11	14%
50 to 99	5	6%	10	13%	16	21%
100 to 499	9	12%	9	12%	9	12%
500 to 999	0	0%	6	8%	3	4%
1000+	0	0%	5	6%	12	16%
	77	100%	77	100%	77	100%

Puerto Rican

	2016		2015		2011	
Number of Employees	Count	Percentage	Count	Percentage	Count	Percentage
Zero	5	15%	3	9%	2	6%
1 to 9	19	56%	16	47%	13	38%
10 to 49	3	9%	5	15%	8	24%
50 to 99	5	15%	4	12%	4	12%
100 to 499	2	6%	6	18%	4	12%
500 to 999	0	0%	0	0%	3	9%
1000+	0	0%	0	0%	0	0%
	34	100%	34	100%	34	100%

(continued)

Other

	2016		2015		2011	
Number of Employees	Count	Percentage	Count	Percentage	Count	Percentage
Zero	31	22%	15	10%	12	8%
1 to 9	57	40%	51	36%	54	38%
10 to 49	26	18%	34	24%	27	19%
50 to 99	12	8%	11	8%	15	10%
100 to 499	15	10%	13	9%	9	6%
500 to 999	1	1%	16	11%	11	8%
1000+	1	1%	3	2%	15	10%
	143	100%	143	100%	143	100%

Source: SLEI Survey of U.S. Latino Business Owners 2016.

National banks provide less loan funding for Latino businesses relative to other external funding sources and other demographic groups, and the Small Business Administration is the lowest funding source for Latino businesses (Orozco et al. 2017). Latino business owners rely heavily on hard money, therefore bearing more personal financial risk in starting a business (Orozco et al. 2017).

The 2016 SLEI survey showed that although California, Texas, and Florida were the top three states with the largest number of Latino businesses at California (24 percent), Texas (15 percent), and Florida (15 percent), these states do not necessarily correlate with the states that provide the most external funding[9] sources for Latino businesses (Orozco et al. 2017). Although the study found that Latino businesses have the lowest number of business loans, nine times the number of Latino businesses that currently have government-backed loans would want to have them (Orozco et al. 2017).

Based on the 2016 SLEI survey, Latino businesses in Florida appeared to be the best funded, as the state ranked in the top five for all seven categories of external funding. Latino businesses in Texas had a high rate of funding in all external funding categories except venture capital. In contrast, Latino businesses in California appeared to be underrepresented in several categories of external funding sources such as private equity, venture capital, government funding, and local banks (Orozco et al. 2017).

This study found that Los Angeles County, Harris County, and Miami–Dade County all saw a rise in Latino businesses with zero employees between 2011 and 2016, meaning that within the sample group, more businesses had zero employees in 2016 than they did in 2011. Additionally, businesses with 500 or more employees declined in number over the five-year period. States and local municipalities could support Latino businesses by providing access to government-backed loans to decrease the high-risk financial burden of these business owners. Furthermore, providing communities and small business owners with financial literacy education could also help address the opportunity gap for Latino business owners in these regions.

Although the post–Great Recession economies of California, Texas, and Florida have all recovered, their growth projection by industry sectors differ. Recent employment growth in California has been led by construction, accommodation and food services, health care, and other services, and these industries are likely to continue to grow (Public Policy Institute of California 2018). In Florida, employment growth in the fastest-growing regions has been largely driven by low-wage jobs (Bustamante 2017). Both Texas and California are projected to be driven by high-skilled knowledge and innovation-based economies (Jillson 2014; Public Policy Institute of California 2018).

According to the 2016 SLEI Survey, Latino businesses in the United States span a variety of industries and are mostly concentrated in those with the highest-projected growth rates: construction, other services (except public), and professional/business services (Orozco et al. 2017). This study found that professional business services was their largest business industry classification for Latino businesses in Los Angeles County, Harris County, and Miami–Dade County, a key sector with projected growth nationwide. The prevalence of trade, transportation, and utilities and construction industries in Miami–Dade County support the national projection growth of low-wage jobs in Florida.

As the economy continues to demand a more high-skilled workforce, education will play a crucial role in helping these three counties remain economically competitive. Furthermore, promoting education is a key strategy for addressing inequality and ensuring economic opportunity for a wide range of people (Public Policy Institute of California 2018).

CONCLUSION: PLANNING FOR LATINO ECONOMIC DEVELOPMENT

In summary, the mapping of the county sample showed different spatial distributions relative to where Latinos reside. In the case of Los Angeles County, the location of Latino businesses appeared to be concentrated in or near areas of high concentration of Latinos; in Harris County, we find more businesses located on the periphery of the county boundary outside of Latino enclaves; and relative to the other two counties, Miami–Dade County showed Latino businesses distributed over a wider range of zip codes across the county, with a concentration of Latino businesses outside Latino enclaves. Mapping the spatial distribution might help address location opportunity gaps for Latino businesses. Although the 2016 survey showed that across the United States Latino businesses tend to locate in non-Latino enclaves (Orozco et al. 2017), the contrast in distribution between Miami–Dade County and the other two counties depicts it as a region with easier entry into the business market.

Two key findings were extracted from profiling industry sectors. First, the study found that all three counties had professional business services as their largest business industry classification, supporting the findings of the 2016 SLEI survey profile of Latino businesses across the United States. This study found that professional business services were also the largest industry when we looked at the industry classification by Latin origin. Nuances emerged within the Latin-origin classification when looking at the second-largest industry sample. For instance, although the construction industry ranked second among Latinos of Mexican origin and those classified as "other," it was not a top-ranking industry among Cubans. The most predominant industries for Cubans, after professional business services, were trade, transportation, and utilities and manufacturing. Cubans therefore appear to be able to enter larger industries, making them a key Latin-origin group to further profile to better understand entry into these markets. Furthermore, with Cubans typically concentrated in the Florida region, this finding reinforces the recommendation to explore Miami–Dade County due to its wider spatial distribution of Latino business locations.

Second, the analysis of business growth between 2011 and 2016 found that the number of businesses with zero employees grew across all three counties and among all of the Latin-origin groups. Given that more

Latino-owned businesses had zero employees in 2016 than in 2011, the study finds that Latino businesses in these regions are not able to easily scale up. Furthermore, the evolution of businesses with over 1,000 employees was particularly telling. Businesses owned by Latinos of Mexican origin went from 13 percent of all Mexican-owned businesses to less than 1 percent between 2011 and 2016 (see Table 7.6). At the county level, Miami–Dade County saw the most extreme evolution in the downscaling of these businesses; within the same five-year time frame, the total of businesses with over 1,000 employees went from 77 (24 percent) to zero. Local and county municipalities could address this decline in business scale by providing support mechanisms such as government-backed small business loans and financial literacy support.

Ultimately, diverse representation of industry sectors and business growth were found across the study regions of Los Angeles County, Harris County, and Miami–Dade County. However, a key limitation to this study is that it is not necessarily the case that Latino-dense counties are ideal types for understanding successful operation of Latino entrepreneurship. Nevertheless, focus on these areas was important for capturing a wider profile sample. Through the nuances between the counties and Latin origin of the business owners, we begin to better understand potential vulnerabilities and strengths of Latino businesses in counties with the largest number of Latinos and shed light on these issues to address their needs, social and institutional, to help them facilitate sustainable operation over time. Furthermore, this study limited its analysis to the top three counties with the largest number of Latinos in the United States; future research could focus on those counties with over 1 million Latinos to capture a wider context in profiling industry and growth for Latino businesses (see Table 7.1).

Latinos compose the largest and fastest-growing ethnic minority in the United States (Rios et al. 2012). Yet the literature has given little attention to their contributions in the growth of urban areas—both cities and counties—and, more specifically, to Latino issues of "the right to the city" (Brenner 2000; Douglass and Friedmann 1998; Friedmann 2002; Holston 1999; McCann 2002; Mitchell 2003; Purcell 2003, 2008; Rios 2013; Rios et al. 2012). Latino communities need to be up front and engaged in the discussion of economic development, urban and regional planning, and related fields. One pervasive barrier to the inclusion of this demographic in planning practice is the lack of understanding in the ways that these communities construct spaces (Rios et al. 2012). As economic drivers, cities have the potential to support economic and social diversity through local policy. In addressing local economic development, in particular that of minority owned businesses, cities should be aware of the unique nuances that support or hinder their success.

> Among Cubans in South Florida, Central Americans in Houston, Puerto Ricans in New York, and Mexicans . . . *everywhere*, history has conspired to create an endlessly fascinating set of relationships between people and place, the present and the past, and the dueling hopes and fears for the future. The future prosperity of this country relies on the education and hard work of the coming Latino plurality. The future happiness of those millions will depend in large part on whether the communities that become their homes are coherent, operational, humane, and a real way, *theirs*. (Suarez 2012:xviii)

NOTES

1. The term "Latinos" refers to a pan-ethic group that generally identifies with Latin American countries (Rios et al. 2012). In addition to "Latino," other common terms such as "Hispanic" and "Chicano" are used in some cases to refer to more regional specific distinctions (U.S Census Bureau 2012). For the purpose of consistency, this chapter uses the term "Latino" as the common designation.

2. While these counties have the highest number of Latinos by count, they are not the largest by proportion. Nevertheless, these counties are important because of their sheer count of Latinos more so than their percent Latino.

3. According to the 2010 U.S. census, California and Texas are the states with the largest population; California has 37.3 million people, and Texas has 25.3 million. Florida has 18.8 million people, making it the state with the fourth-largest population (Grieco et al., 2012). Latinos compose 37.6 percent of the total population in both California and Texas and 23 percent in Florida (U.S. Census Bureau 2010). Economic data reveals similar patterns: California has 2.8 million businesses, the highest number of businesses in any state; Florida is second, with 2.4 million; and Texas is third, with 2.0 million (U.S Census Bureau 2012).

4. "Discouraged" refers to those who would like to work but have dropped out of the labor force.

5. The Institute of Taxation and Economic Policy developed the Tax Inequality Index to measure the effects of each state's tax system on income inequality. The index aimed to answer the following question: Are incomes more or less equal after state taxes than before taxes? For each state, the index compares incomes by income group before and after state and local taxes (counting the tax savings from deducting state and local taxes on federal tax returns). The index for each state equals one minus the average of the following ratios: (1) the after-tax income of the richest 1 percent as a share of pretax income over the after-tax income of the poorest 20 percent as a share of pretax income, (2) the after-tax income of the richest 1 percent as a share of pretax income over the after-tax income of the middle 60 percent as a share of pretax income, and (3) the after-tax income of the best-off 20 percent as a share of pretax income over the after-tax income of the poorest 40 percent as a share of pretax income, half-weighted. States with regressive tax structures have negative tax inequality indexes, meaning that incomes are less equal in those states after state and local taxes than before. States with progressive tax structures have positive tax inequality indexes; incomes are more equal after state and local taxes than before (The Institute on Taxation and Economic Policy 2015).

6. The total number of cases selected for this study within each of the three counties relative to the total number of respondents for each of the states in the sample universe of the 2016 SLEI survey is 36 percent from California in Los Angeles County, 14 percent from Texas in Harris County, and 48 percent from Florida in Miami–Dade County.

7. Latin-origin classification as "other" includes people of Latin origin who are not Mexican, Cuban, or Puerto Rican.

8. Opportunity gap is defined by the difference between the average annual revenues of Latino versus non-Latino owned firms (Orozco et al. 2017).

9. External funding categories in the SLEI 2016 survey include lines of credit, local/national banks, government loans, venture capital, angel investment, private equity, and hard money.

REFERENCES

Adams., Diana. 2011. "Global Entrepreneurial Costs & Success Rates." http://www
.bitrebels.com/lifestyle/global-entrepreneurial-costs-success-rates-infographic/.

Brenner, Neil. 2000. "The Urban Question as a Scale Question: Reflections on Henri Lefebvre, Urban Theory and the Politics of Scale." *International Journal of Urban and Regional Research* 24(2):361–78.

Bustamante, Alí. 2017. "State of Working Florida 2017." Center for Labor and Research Studies. https://risep.fiu.edu/state-of-working-florida/state-or-working-florida-2017.pdf.

Douglass, Mike, and John Friedmann, eds. 1998. *Cities for Citizens: Planning and the Rise of Civil Society in a Global Age.* Chichester, NY: Wiley.

Ennis, Sharon, Merarys Ríos-Vargas, and Nora Albert. 2011. "The Hispanic Population: 2010." U.S. Census Bureau. https://www.census.gov/prod/cen2010/briefs/c2010br-04.pdf.

Flores, Antonio. 2017. "Facts on U.S. Latinos, 2015." Pew Research Center's Hispanic Trends Project, September 18. http://www.pewhispanic.org/2017/09/18/facts-on-u-s-latinos/.

Friedmann, John. 2002. *The Prospect of Cities.* Minneapolis: University of Minnesota Press.

Grieco, Elizabeth, Yesenia D. Acosta, G. Patricia de la Cruz, Christine Gambino, Thomas Gryn, Luke J. Larsen, Edward N. Trevelyan, and Nathan P. Walters. 2012. "The Foreign-Born Population in the United States: 2010." U.S. Census Bureau. https://www2.census.gov/library/publications/2012/acs/acs-19.pdf.

"Hispanics by Country of Origin in Miami–Dade." n.d. Miami-Dade County, https://www.miamidade.gov/planning/library/reports/data-flash/2011-hispanics-by-origin.pdf.

Holston, James, ed. 1999. *Cities and Citizenship.* Durham, NC: Duke University Press.

The Institute on Taxation and Economic Policy. 2015. "Who Pays? A Distributional Analysis of the Tax System in All 50 States." https://itep.org/wp-content/uploads/whopaysreport.pdf.

Jillson, Cal. 2014. *Lone Star Tarnished.* New York: Taylor and Francis.

Keystone Research Center. 2018. "Tax Fairness: An Answer to Florida's Budget Problems." http://keystoneresearch.org/sites/default/files/FL_TaxFairness_0.pdf.

López, Gustavo. 2015. "Hispanics of Mexican Origin in the United States, 2013." Pew Research Center's Hispanic Trends Project, September 15. http://www.pewhispanic.org/2015/09/15/hispanics-of-mexican-origin-in-the-united-states-2013/.

Lopez, Mark Hugo 2014. "In 2014, Latinos Will Surpass Whites as Largest Racial/Ethnic Group in California." Pew Research Center, January 24. http://www

.pewresearch.org/fact-tank/2014/01/24/in-2014-latinos-will-surpass-whites-as-largest-racialethnic-group-in-california/.

McCann, Eugene J. 2002. "Space, Citizenship, and the Right to the City: A Brief Overview." *GeoJournal* 58(2–3):77–79. https://doi.org/10.1023/B:GEJO.0000010826.75561.c0.

McNichol, Elizabeth, and Nicholas Johnson. 2012. "The Texas Economic Model: Hard for Other States to Follow and Not All It Seems." Center on Budget and Policy Priorities, April 4. https://www.cbpp.org/research/the-texas-economic-model-hard-for-other-states-to-follow-and-not-all-it-seems.

Mitchell, Don. 2003. *The Right to the City: Social Justice and the Fight for Public Space*. New York: Guilford.

Orozco, Marlene, Paul Oyer, and Jerry Porras. 2017. P. 28 in *State of Latino Entrepreneurship 2017*. Research report. Stanford Latino Entrepreneurship Initiative.

Perry, Ian. 2017. "California Is Working: The Effects of California's Public Policy on Jobs and the Economy since 2011." Center for Labor Research and Education. http://laborcenter.berkeley.edu/california-is-working/.

Public Policy Institute of California. 2018. " Economy: California's Future." http://www.ppic.org/wp-content/uploads/r-118sbr.pdf.

Purcell, Mark. 2003. "Citizenship and the Right to the Global City: Reimagining the Capitalist World Order." *International Journal of Urban and Regional Research* 27(3):564–90. https://doi.org/10.1111/1468-2427.00467.

Purcell, Mark. 2008. *Recapturing Democracy: Neoliberalization and the Struggle for Alternative Urban Futures*. New York: Routledge.

Rechtin, M. 2014. "What's So Tempting about Texas to Toyota?" *Automotive News*, May 5. http://www.autonews.com/article/20140505/retail01/140509934/whats-so-tempting-about-texas-to-toyota%3f.

Rios, Michael. 2013. "From a Neighborhood of Strangers to a Community of Fate." Pp. 164–76 in *Transcultural Cities Border Crossing and Placemaking*, edited by J. Hou. New York: Routledge.

Rios, Michael, Leonardo Vazquez, and Lucrezia Miranda. 2012. *Diálogos: Placemaking in Latino Communities*. Milton Park, Abingdon, UK: Routledge.

Rosenblum, Marc, William Kandel, Clare Seelke, and Ruth Wasem. 2012. "Mexican Migration to the United States: Policy and Trends." Congressional Research Services. https://fas.org/sgp/crs/row/R42560.pdf.

Suarez, R. 2012. "Forward: A People, of People, Makes Its Place." Pp. xv–xviii in *Diálogos: Placemaking in Latino Communities*, edited by Michael Rios, Leonardo Vazquez, and Lucrezia Miranda. New York: Routledge.

"Texas Politics—Political Economy." 2018. Liberal Arts Instructional Technology Services. https://www.laits.utexas.edu/txp_media/html/pec/print_pec.html.

U.S. Census Bureau. 2010. https://www.census.gov/2010census/.

U.S. Census Bureau. 2012. American Community Survey. https://www.census.gov/programs-surveys/acs.

U.S. Census Bureau. 2016a. American Community Survey. https://www.census.gov/acs/www/data/data-tables-and-tools/data-profiles/2016/.

U.S. Census Bureau. 2016b. American FactFinder. https://factfinder.census.gov/faces/nav/jsf/pages/index.xhtml.

U.S. Census Bureau. 2017. "North American Industry Classification System." https://www.census.gov/eos/www/naics/.

Wilson, Kenneth L., and Alejandro Portes. 1980. "Immigrant Enclaves: An Analysis of the Labor Market Experiences of Cubans in Miami." *American Journal of Sociology* 86(3):295.

CHAPTER 8

Mexican American Founder Narratives at High-Growth Firms on the South Texas–Mexican Border

John Sargent and Linda Matthews

INTRODUCTION

Research on Latino-owned businesses (LOBs) in the United States consistently identifies two major trends. First, the number of LOBs is rapidly increasing. The Stanford Latino Entrepreneurship Initiative (SLEI) 2015 research report found that the number of LOBs increased from 1.2 million in 1997 to 3.3 million in 2012. Second, the same report found that LOBs are much smaller than firms owned by non-Latino whites. Only 1.9 percent of LOBs but 4.9 percent of non-LOBs (NLOBs) exceed 1 million in annual revenue. In 2012 the average LOB generated $155,806 in sales versus $573,806 for NLOBs. From 1997 to 2012 LOB sales per firm increased by $564 versus $146,727 for NLOBs. A major focus of the SLEI 2015 and 2016 reports as well as much of the research in the field of minority entrepreneurship explores the dynamics limiting the growth of firms owned by Latino, African American, and other minority entrepreneurs (Butler, Morales, and Torres 2009; Dávila and Mora 2013; Fairlie and Robb 2008; Valdez 2011).

In this study we address the challenges of LOBs and growth. We believe that our contribution falls into three main areas. First, we conducted semistructured interviews with 14 Latino entrepreneurs leading companies that are currently experiencing rapid growth and/or have experienced rapid growth in the past (we use the terms "Latino" and "Hispanic" interchangeably throughout this chapter). We believe that the systematic exploration of how these entrepreneurs have been able to create rapidly growing companies provides important insight for scholars, practitioners, and public policy makers interested in closing the performance gap. Second, we incorporate research from the management and economics literature on high-growth firms (HGFs) as the theoretical framework for this study. We believe that this lens provides value in that it facilitates comparisons between LOBs and the mainstream literature. Finally, this study is set in a unique region of the United States. Located in deep South Texas on the U.S.-Mexican border, the McAllen-Edinburg-Mission (MEM) metropolitan statistical area (MSA) has a number of distinguishing characteristics (Richardson and Pisani 2017). A key finding from our study is that many of our sample entrepreneurs are successful due to their ability to combine "generic" entrepreneurial skills with their in-depth knowledge of the bilingual, bicultural nature of the borderlands.

This chapter continues as follows. In the second section we provide a brief review of the HGF and Latino entrepreneurship literature. In the third section we provide a description of the history and demographics of the MEM MSA. In the fourth section we describe our research methodology and in the fifth section our results. The concluding section provides a discussion of our findings, theoretical implications, and suggestions for further research.

HIGH-GROWTH FIRMS, LOCATION, AND LATINO ENTREPRENEURS

The systematic study of small and midsize HGFs began in 1979 with the publication of *The Job Generation Process* by David Birch. This study utilized a national database to track the birth, growth, contraction, and death of U.S. companies. Birch (1979) concluded that firms with fewer than 100 employees were responsible for 82 percent of all net new jobs created in the United States from 1969 to 1976. The small firm job creation hypothesis was controversial, and a number of authors challenged Birch's methodology and findings (Kirchhoff and Phillips 1998; Brown, Hamilton, and Medoff 1990; Davis, Haltiwanger, and Schuh 1996). In 1994 Birch joined with one of his main critics to address a subset of these controversies. Birch and Medoff (1994) found that firms starting with at least $100,000 in sales that experienced average yearly sales growth of at least 20 percent over a four-year period were responsible for 70 percent of all job creation over the 1988–1992 period. Only 4 percent of firms in their data set fit this high-growth "gazelle" category. The finding that a limited number of small, medium, and large HGFs rather than simply small firms were responsible for a large percentage of job creation has been largely supported by subsequent research. Acs and Tracy (2008) found that HGFs with fewer than 20 employees represented 93.8 percent of all HGFs and accounted for 33.5 percent of all HGF job creation, HGFs with 20 to 499 employees represented 5.9 percent of firms and 24.1 percent of HGF job growth, and HGFs with 500 or more employees represented only .3 percent of HGFs but 42.4 percent of net new HGF job creation.

The last three-plus decades of research has resulted in a generally accepted set of stylized facts that are often used to describe the HGF phenomena (Coad et al. 2014). First, firm growth rates tend to resemble a tent-shaped Laplace distribution. In other words, the majority of firms are not growing at all, but a small percentage are growing rapidly, and at the other end of the distribution, a small number are rapidly contracting. Second, the use of different indicators such as sales or employment growth results in a far from identical set of firms qualifying as HGFs. Third, HGFs tend to be younger than the average firm in each major size category. Fourth, HGFs are broadly distributed across the economy and are not overly represented in technology-intensive industries. Last but not least, HGFs tend to grow in short bursts; HGFs in one period often do not qualify as HGFs before or after their high-growth period.

Much of the research that has provided the empirical foundation for these stylized facts comes from the economics discipline. Researchers in the field of strategic management have produced their own set of largely complementary findings. As summarized by Demir, Wennberg, and McKelvie (2017), the following factors appear to serve as strategic drivers of HGF growth:

1. *Human capital of the founder.* Studies have found a positive relationship between the education level, managerial experience, and domain expertise of the founding entrepreneur and high growth. Domain expertise includes both industry and entrepreneurial experience.
2. *Strategy.* In general, research indicates a positive relationship between formal strategic planning, the pursuit of a differentiation strategy, and HGF status.

3. *Human resource management.* Demir et al. (2017) identified 11 studies that focus on the relationship between human resource management practices and high-growth. In broad terms, these studies find that effective employee selection practices, investing in employee training, and well-designed managerial and employee incentive systems are positively related to high growth.

4. *Innovation.* There does not appear to be a straightforward relationship between innovation and growth. Some studies have shown a positive relationship between innovation indicators such as R&D spending, patents, and rapid growth (especially with manufacturing firms). However, Hölzl (2009) found a positive relationship between investments in innovation and high growth only in firms located in countries close to the technological frontier. Demir et al. (2017:447) conclude that the links between product and process innovation and high growth are "poorly studied" in the HGF literature.

5. *Capabilities.* Demir et al. (2017:447) refer to capabilities as denoting "an ability to purposefully enact resources, practices, and processes as well as to change, modify, and replace these in order to achieve certain goals or ends beneficial to the firm." These authors found a handful of studies showing a positive relationship between capabilities (managerial, financial, and innovation) and HGF status.

There has been surprisingly little attention paid in either the economics or strategic management literature to contextual factors, such as the location of HGFs. One notable exception is the Acs et al. (2008) study. These authors utilize two large data sets to create perhaps the most comprehensive database of HGFs in the United States used in academic research to date. They found relatively little variation in the ratio of HGFs to total firms across census regions, states, MSAs, and counties. However, the range of variation tended to be greater in midsize and smaller MSAs and counties. In the smallest counties, the ratio of the number of HGFs to the total number of firms ranged from .99 percent to 3.33 percent. In another study of HGF location, Motoyama and Danley (2012) examined firms included on the Inc. 500 list. They found that the highest concentration of HGFs in a large MSA was in Washington, D.C., followed by Salt Lake City, Austin, San

Francisco, and Boston. The authors did not find a uniform trend of increasing concentration of HGFs over time or strong correlations between Inc. 500 firm density and venture capital investment, academic R&D funding, federal R&D funding, or patents per capita. They found a positive relationship between Inc. 500 firm density and the ratio of high-tech to total employment as well as the number of science and engineering graduates in the area. In another study of Inc. 500 firms, Li et al. (2016) found a higher concentration of HGFs in counties with larger average establishment size, higher educational attainment, and more natural amenities. A lower concentration of HGFs was found in counties with higher income growth, higher-paying industries, and more banks per capita.

In addition to understanding the influence of contextual factors on HGFs, another underexplored topic within the HGF literature is the ethnicity/race of the founding entrepreneur. A search of Google Scholar and Business Source Premier using such keywords as "high-growth firm," "Hispanic," and "Latino" did not find a single study published in a peer-reviewed journal on Latino HGFs. As previously mentioned, one of the primary themes in the limited research on Latino entrepreneurs is the difficulties these individuals face in growing new ventures. For example, Dávila, Mora, and Zeitlan (2014) found that the increase in the number of Hispanic entrepreneurs occurred at the same time the monetary rewards for pursuing entrepreneurship for Hispanics decreased when measured relative to non-Hispanic whites. In 1990, self-employed Hispanics earned 25 percent less than non-Hispanic entrepreneurs. By 2012 this gap increased to 43.1 percent.

Lofstrom and Wang (2006, 2007) address additional challenges facing Hispanic entrepreneurs. They found stark differences in the educational achievement, total annual earnings, and household wealth of Hispanic Mexicans and non-Hispanic whites. Only 9 percent of self-employed Mexican Hispanics had earned a college degree versus 38 percent of self-employed non-Hispanic whites. The median household wealth stood at $36,537 for the Mexican Hispanic self-employed sample versus $135,036 for the self-employed non-Hispanic white sample. The authors argue that these factors shape the type of industries the two groups choose to enter and sort industries into low, medium, or high barrier to entry categories utilizing measures of financial capital requirements and educational attainment measures. They found over a four-year period that Mexican Hispanics were more likely to enter low-barrier-to-entry industries versus non-Hispanic whites (4.4 versus 2.9 percent). In contrast, the entry rate for Mexican Hispanics in medium-barrier (1.8 percent) and high-barrier industries (.2 percent) is significantly lower than the entry rate for non-Hispanic whites (3.4 percent and 1.9 percent, respectively). Perhaps due to the intense competition characteristic of low-barrier-to-entry industries, Lofstrom and Wang (2006) report that yearly exit rates for Mexican Hispanics was 20.5 percent versus 11 percent for non-Hispanic whites.

The 2015 and 2016 SLEI reports provide additional data and insight regarding the growth challenges faced by Latino entrepreneurs. As mentioned, LOBs are considerably smaller than NLOBs. The report discounts two explanations for these size differences. First, there are not large differences in the average size of firms in industries that LOBs are most likely to enter as compared to those with a higher ratio of NLOBs. Second, only 20 percent of LOBs state that they have a "mostly Latino" customer base and are not limited by the size of the local ethnic marketplace. The authors preferred explanation for the small size of LOBs is the preference of Latin entrepreneurs to start businesses for internal reasons as compared to the pursuit of market opportunities, limited initial financial resources, difficulties in accessing external financing, a preference to not accept outside capital, and a lack of awareness of government programs that provide grants for small businesses. The 2016 SLEI report compared scaled and nonscaled Latino-owned firms. Scaled firms were defined as those that met one or more of the following criteria: at least $1 million in annual revenue, employs 50 or more people, or has grown substantially over the last five years. Scaled firms were more likely to have immigrant and highly educated owners, tap into more sources of capital, make greater use of external capital, and have larger networks. They also found that "Latino owners of all firms, regardless of scale, report similar reasonings to become entrepreneurs and similarly high expectations for their firm's growth" (SLEI 2016:17).

In this section we briefly reviewed the HGF and Latino entrepreneurship literature. HGF studies tend to focus on the contribution of these firms to employment and revenue creation as well as their primary characteristics and growth strategies. There have been very few HGF studies with a focus on minority entrepreneurs. The influence of the local context on the founding and growth of HGFs is another underexplored topic in the literature. Finally, research on Latino entrepreneurs tends to emphasize the rapid increase in the number of LOBs (often in low-barrier-to-entry industries) and the profound differences in the performance of LOBs and NLOBs.

THE RESEARCH CONTEXT: THE SOUTH TEXAS BORDERLANDS

The MEM MSA represents a somewhat unique location in which to examine the influence of the local context on the emergence and development of HGFs. The MEM MSA has the lowest per capita personal income of any MSA in the United States, and 33.5 percent of residents live below the poverty line (U.S. Census 2017). Hispanics/Latinos account for 91.3 percent of the local population, and an estimated 82.3 percent of residents speak Spanish at home (U.S. Census 2017). Educational attainment is low, with 62.1 percent of the population ages 25 or older with at least a high school diploma and 16.7 percent with at least a bachelor's degree (vs. national averages of 88.4 percent and 32.5 percent, respectively) (U.S. Census 2017). Mean hourly wages are 30 percent lower than the national average (Bureau of Labor Statistics 2017), and a significantly lower percentage of individuals are employed in high-paying occupational groups such as management, business and finance operations, computer and mathematical, architecture and engineering, and legal when compared to national averages. A significantly higher percentage are employed in low-paying occupational groups such as education and training, health care support, and personal care and service. There are no publicly listed companies headquartered in the MEM MSA.

The region is a major center for trade between the United States and Mexico. In 2017 the Hidalgo port of entry was the highest-volume entry point for fruit and vegetable imports from Mexico to the United States (USA Trade Online 2018). In addition, as of December 2017, 116,980 individuals were employed in *maquiladoras* directly across the border in Reynosa (a city of roughly 1 million people) (INEGI 2018). Not only do goods and services cross the border in large volumes, but so do illegal drugs and people without legal permission to enter the United States (smuggling has been a major regional industry since at least the 1840s; see Díaz 2015). With over 3,000 employees, U.S. Customs and Border Protection is one of the largest employers in the region. For the fiscal year ending in September 2017, the U.S. Border Patrol reported that the Rio Grande Valley sector experienced the highest number of overall apprehensions (other than Mexican apprehensions) and nonresident alien deaths compared to any other sector on the U.S.-Mexican border (U.S. Border Patrol 2017). The sector is also the primary entry point into the United States for families and unaccompanied minors fleeing gang violence in Central America. While these statistics give the impression of a general state of lawlessness, crime statistics show that the MEM MSA has a lower rate of violent crime per 100,000 population (287) than several other large MSAs in Texas such as Houston (559), San Antonio (460), and Dallas (318) (Solomon 2015).

Several of the characteristics of the MEM MSA are related to the HGF research findings given in the section above titled "High-Growth Firms, Location, and Latino Entrepreneurs." For example, Demir et al. (2017) found a positive relationship between the human capital of the founder (including formal education) and high growth. Motoyama and Danley (2012) found a positive relationship between Inc. 500 firm density and the ratio of high-tech to total employment and the number of science and engineering graduates in an area. Given the low per capital incomes, low levels of educational attainment, and the above average percentage of people working in low-paying occupational groups, research would suggest that HGF firm density will be low in the MEM MSA. While we do not test HGF firm density directly, our study provides considerable insight into the characteristics of HGFs that have emerged in a Latino-dominated economically and educationally challenged region on the U.S.-Mexican border.

RESEARCH METHODS

For purposes of this study we define HGFs as firms with at least $100,000 in initial sales that then experienced an average annual increase in the number of employees and/or sales of at least 20 percent over a three-year period. In our sample we include firms that experienced rapid growth in the most recent three-year period as well as in more distant periods. One of the main challenges facing researchers studying low-frequency phenomena such as small and midsize HGFs is to identify a valid sample. We adopted a number of strategies to locate locally owned Latino HGFs. First, the authors have been faculty members at the public university in the MEM MSA since 1997. The first author has taught entrepreneurship classes since 2005, and a standard requirement for students is to interview an entrepreneur and write up a case study of that person's experience. We identified entrepreneurs from the case write-ups who qualified as HGFs given our definition. Second, when we interviewed entrepreneurs from the initial list, we asked if they would recommend other business owners they knew who were leading HGFs. Third, we interviewed the presidents of the McAllen,

Mission, and Edinburg economic development corporations as well as the presidents of the McAllen and Mission chambers of commerce and asked for their help to identify HGF founders. Finally, we reviewed the business section of the local paper as well as specialized business publications with the goal of identifying additional HGF entrepreneurs.

We developed a semistructured interview questionnaire based on common themes identified in the mainstream HGF literature (see Appendix 8.1). Topics include company history, the founder's background, the founder's preference for growth and if this preference had changed over time, measures of sales and employment growth, whether the company had experienced consistent or erratic growth, growth goals in the next five years, significant growth barriers, strategies to overcome barriers, whether the entrepreneur had received support from government agencies such as the local Small Business Development Center during startup, why they chose to locate their business in the MEM MSA, similarities and differences in creating an HGF locally compared to larger cities such as San Antonio and Austin, and who they rely on for business advice. Follow-up questions were used to explore these and other topics. Interviews were conducted primarily by the lead author and took place during the summers of 2016 and 2017 at the entrepreneurs' places of business. The interviews typically lasted from 45 to 75 minutes. Detailed notes were taken during and immediately after the interviews.

FOUNDER BACKGROUND, GROWTH BARRIERS, AND CREATING A LATINO HGF IN THE MEM MSA

Table 8.1 provides information on the founder (gender, age at the time of the interview, education, and birthplace), and his/her company (industry, startup year, and number of employees at the time of the interview). There are 13 males and 1 female in our sample. Nine of the 14 had earned a college degree, often from the local public university in disciplines such as finance and marketing. Only 1 individual, a Monterrey native who attended Monterrey Tec, earned a degree from a private institution. Only 2 individuals had earned graduate degrees. One of these interviewees was a second-generation member of a family-run firm. He worked full-time at the family's restaurants and completed his MBA over a six-year period, taking one class at a time. The other individual dropped out as a college

TABLE 8.1 *Sample Profile*

Gender, Age, Education	Birthplace	Industry	Startup Year	Employees
Male, 47, UTPA,[1] marketing	Reynosa	insurance agency	2001	38
Male, 29, attended UTPA	Guadalajara	auto care	2012	12
Male, 48, UTPA finance	Mercedes,[3] Texas	banking, auto care, agriculture, real estate	1920	57
Male, 52, UTPA finance	Weslaco,[3] Texas	low cost housing, fast food, construction, insurance, etc.	1976	92
Male, 45, UTPA economics	Reynosa	warehousing, freight forwarding, trucking	1997	100
Male, 45, Monterrey Tec,[2] business administration	Monterrey	restaurants	1997	300
Male, 43, UTPA MBA	Sinaloa[4]	restaurants	1987	1,400
Male, 25, UTPA graphic design	Roma,[3] Texas	web design and development	2014	10
Male, 56, attended UTPA	McAllen	freight brokerage, trucking	1993	100
Male, 48, UTPA marketing/economics	Cuba	electronics retailer	1992	88
Female, mid-40s, did not complete university degree at UTSA	McAllen, raised in Reynosa	food producer	2012	5
Male, 44, high school graduate	Edinburg	sporting goods accessories	2011	31

	Beeville,[5] Texas	fast-food franchisee	1987	600
Male, 54, Texas State graduate, computer information systems				
Male, 50, UTPA dropout, returned 20 years later to obtain BA/MBA	Rio Bravo,[6] Mexico	service provider for developmentally disabled	2004	360

1. UTPA stands for the University of Texas Pan American. This university merged with the University of Texas at Brownsville in 2015 to form the University of Texas Rio Grande Valley.

2. Monterrey Tec, officially known as the Instituto Tecnológico de Estudios Superiores de Monterrey, is a large internationally recognized private university located in the state of Nuevo Leon roughly 150 miles from the MEDM MSA.

3. Mercedes, Weslaco, and Roma are all small cities located on or close to the U.S.-Mexican border close to the MEM MSA.

4. Sinaloa is a state located on Mexico's west coast.

5. Beeville is a small town located about 180 miles north of the MEM MSA.

6. Rio Bravo is a border city located about 15 miles east of Reynosa.

freshman to take a full-time job. After 20+ years working and growing his startup to 140+ employees, he returned to the local public university and completed his undergraduate degree in management, followed by an MBA from the same institution. In the spring of 2017 he completed his first semester of a weekend/online doctoral program in leadership. One of his primary motivations for returning to school is to be a better example for his children. Four individuals in our sample had not completed a college degree, including 1 who ended his formal education immediately after high school.

Seven of the 14 founders are immigrants, including 1 from Cuba. The ages these individuals moved to the United States varied from 5 to the late 20s. The one female in our sample was born in McAllen but raised in Reynosa. As a child she spent the great majority of her time in Reynosa and only moved to the Texas side of the border when her parents insisted that she attend high school in McAllen and improve her English.

Consistent with the literature, sample HGFs compete in a wide range of industries. Only one is in a technology intensive industry (web design and digital marketing). There are several serial entrepreneurs in our sample. One individual currently serves as the CEO and major stockholder of a growing bank while maintaining at least three side businesses. Another individual serves as the CEO of a nonprofit. He and his team have set up several for-profit enterprises in industries such as fast food, insurance, back office services, and construction. The profits from these enterprises help finance the activities of the nonprofit. Another individual started a freight brokerage firm in the 1990s. This company recently merged with a similar firm in the Pacific Northwest with the goal of the combined company going public. The founder has maintained his ownership position in the larger company but stepped down from an operational role. In 2015 he started a rapidly growing trucking company serving the international trade community. There are also two second-generation entrepreneurs operating as part of family firms. In one company, the father is a very successful Mexican customs broker in Reynosa serving the maquiladora industry. The son set up U.S.-based warehousing and trucking companies that complement the father's Reynosa operation. The second family company competes in the restaurant industry. The father established the first restaurant in Sinaloa in the 1970s and, after expanding in Mexico, set up U.S. operations in the early 1980s in Los Angeles. The U.S. operation was sold to a large franchisor, after which the family established a new restaurant concept. This business has expanded to include three separate but related restaurant chains. The son currently serves as CEO and has led the expansion of the company in the MEM MSA and adjacent regions.

In the rest of this section we focus on our interviewees' responses in three areas: founder background and startup details, major growth barriers, and founder views of the similarities and differences in creating an HGF in the MEM MSA as compared to locations in central Texas such as San Antonio and Austin. Exhibit One contains short summaries of the background and startup details of seven of our sample Latino HGFs. The entrepreneurs not included in Exhibit One also have notable startup experiences. The founder of the auto care business grew up in Guadalajara, where his father required him and his brother to work on the family car to earn their allowance. During this time, the founder "had a passion for creating money" and sold candy at school to his classmates as well as miniature cars at the local flea market. In the United States his first job was at Burger King (he left due to a dispute with the manager), followed by a position with a produce broker. After a particularly frustrating day he came home and told his wife he was done with produce. His wife told him he loved cars and should open a car care business. The female entrepreneur in our sample grew up in an upper-class family in Reynosa. After graduating from high school, she attended a university in San Antonio. She fell in love, got married, had children, did not complete her degree, ended up divorced, and moved back to the MEM MSA. An aunt of hers had produced a specialized food product for more than 30 years in Mexico. While in San Antonio the female entrepreneur made this product at her home and gave or sold it to friends. Back in the MEM MSA she started and ran a restaurant for two years. After she sold the restaurant, the new owner came to her and said that the customers continued to ask for the product. Encouraged, a friend and fellow entrepreneur convinced her to participate in a *Shark Tank*–like competition run by one of the local economic development corporations. She won the competition and obtained significant seed capital. The funds were used to set up a production facility, and she initially sold her product to a number of small local companies. She then competed in a new product contest sponsored by a large regional grocer. She placed second at the event and soon thereafter obtained a contract to sell her product at 50+ stores.

Exhibit One: *Selected Founder Background, Startup Details*

Male, dropped out of college, freight brokerage, founded in 1993. The founder attended the local university for a year and a half before dropping out. He worked at a truck stop and eventually obtained a managerial position. The truck stop rented out offices to a number of businesses, including small brokerage firms. He became friends with one of the brokers and became interested in the industry because his friend was always on the phone talking to business people from around the country. The founder left his position at the truck stop and obtained a position as a broker, and over the next several years he worked for three brokerage companies. With the third company his brother-in-law kept telling him he was making a lot of money for his boss and should ask for a raise. He did, and the request was turned down. As a result, he and his brother-in-law decided to open their own brokerage company. His father-in-law (a successful insurance agent) lent them $500,000 to get started. The company grew very quickly and at one time was the largest Hispanic-owned brokerage firm in Texas.

Male, high school graduate, sports accessories, founded in 2011. The founder was a full-time postal service employee. He had a personal need for a product as part of an activity he pursued during his spare time. The wait time to obtain the item online was from 10 to 20 weeks, and the price was high. As a result, the founder decided to see if he could make the product at home. He obtained the required materials and produced the first prototype using the oven in his kitchen to complete the molding process (his spouse was not pleased). In 2011 they moved to a larger home, and production began in their two-car garage. Initial sales were primarily through eBay. By 2013 they had outgrown the garage and moved to a larger shop. In 2013 the founder retired from the postal service and dedicated himself full-time to the business. By 2015 they had outgrown the shop and moved into a larger facility. By 2017 they were again planning to move to a larger facility.

Male, college graduate, insurance, founded in 2001. The founder was born in Reynosa but immigrated to McAllen when he was five. After graduating from the local university, he quickly became one of the top salespeople for a national industrial products distributor. His immediate boss stated that he was going to be promoted to run the company's Mexican operation. His boss was fired before the offer was formalized. After unsuccessfully interviewing for the Mexican position with his new boss, on the flight home from San Antonio the founder sat next to a distant relative who was coming to the valley to identify a franchisee for a well-known insurance company. By the end of the flight he was offered the position. He was not particularly excited about the possibility. He discussed this at dinner with his mother and brother. While he was talking, his brother wrote a check for $20,000 for the franchise fee and startup costs and handed it to him (his brother was employed by a large multinational in an engineering position; he later joined his brother as co-owner). The first year was very difficult; his wife told him he was a *pendejo* (a stupid person) and that he should have opened a Subway. By the late 1990s the agency was among the top 10 producers in the country. The founder set up his own agency selling policies from multiple companies in 2001.

Male, college graduate, electronics, founded in 1992. The founder immigrated from Cuba when he was 11. The family intended to settle in Miami but came to McAllen on what was supposed to be a two-week trip so his mother could see her sisters for the first time in 20 years. They ended up staying. Middle class in Cuba, the family struggled financially. For several years father and son sold electronics at one of the local flea markets to make extra money. The founder attended the local university on a full athletic scholarship while continuing to sell at the flea market. His parents had saved $17,000 to be used for his college education, not anticipating that he would have a scholarship. After graduation he used these funds as well as merchandise from the flea market to open his first electronics store in McAllen.

Married couple, college graduates, fast-food franchisee, founded in 1987. The founding couple met in high school in a small town 70 miles north of the MEM MSA. Both came from families of modest means and worked at the local fast-food franchise. The franchise owner was a major influence on the couple and helped convince the founder to attend college (he was the first in his family to obtain a college degree). On a business trip to McAllen, the founder stopped by the local restaurant of the same national chain (a run-down location and one of the lowest-performing restaurants in the franchise system). The couple ended up buying the store with $18,000 they had saved in a tennis can and a loan cosigned by their former employer.

Male, college dropout when company was founded, service provider for individuals with developmental disabilities, founded in 2004. The founder immigrated from Mexico when he was 10 with his mother and siblings. Family income was significantly below the poverty line for the next several years. After high school the founder enrolled at the local public university. He needed a job, so he went to the university's placement office and soon thereafter obtained a part-time position as a driver at a company for the developmentally disabled. His intention was to drive in the morning, attend class, and then drive in the evenings. He was offered a full-time position soon thereafter and dropped out of school. After two decades of working in the industry the founder became CEO of a large organization in the same industry. He attended a session about how to get an operating license. The owner found out and immediately fired him and two colleagues. Unable to obtain a loan, they self-financed the launch of their business.

Male, college graduate, banking, founded in 1920. The bank existed for 80 years, with one branch serving a rural community northeast of the MEM MSA. The entrepreneur remembers accompanying his father (a farmer) to the bank as a child and being very impressed. He earned a finance degree at the local university and was hired as a credit analyst at a large locally owned bank. After six years he joined a national firm as a financial adviser. After six years there he was hired by a different national financial firm and joined its investment group. He eventually became the manager for the entire South Texas region. In 2000 he joined another financial firm and eventually managed a portfolio that approached $1 billion. The great majority of these funds came from Mexican companies and investors in Monterrey. In 2007 he left this opportunity and dedicated himself full-time to the ventures he and his brother had started (at one time his brother was chairman and CEO of a large locally owned bank). Given that the brothers were generating excess cash throughout their careers, in 1991 they purchased a car wash. Over the next 15 years they acquired 32 additional locations. In addition, they purchased 3,000 acres of farmland that they actively manage. The brothers also purchased a number of commercial properties that they renovated and leased out. They purchased shares in the bank in 2001. Serving on the board of directors, the founder helped design and implement a growth strategy. The brothers bought additional shares in 2007, and the founder took over as CEO in 2014.

Exhibit Two contains short profiles of the types of growth barriers encoun-tered by our Latino HGF founders. The first example provides an especially intriguing lens into the dynamics faced by many companies competing in the MEM MSA. This includes the challenges of competing with rivals that employ undocumented individuals and operate on a cash basis. Another interesting example of the nature of the MEM MSA market was provided by the founder of the insurance company. He stated that competition from national companies was intense in traditional areas such as home and car insurance. To compete, they like to "swim against the current" and focus on nontraditional areas such as insurance for mobile homes. While these homes may only be worth $20,000 to $30,000, if owners want to obtain a home improvement loan they often cannot because the property is not insured. The company had recently established a call center, and one of the goals was to use bilingual local employees to sell insurance to Spanish-speaking customers in the Texas panhandle. The founder of the company serving the developmentally disabled also viewed the company's ability to interact with Spanish-speaking consumers in central Texas as one of its primary competitive advantages in those markets.

Exhibit Two: *Major Growth Barriers*

Auto care, 12 employees, founded in 2012. The founder stated that the biggest barrier to business in the area was the nature of the local market. McAllen is not a Mexican city, but it is also not an American city. "To figure out what the consumer wants in the area businesswise is very difficult. . . . "You can't have a product just for the Mexican consumer or just for locals." Another barrier is that "businesses in the area give away their services." The founder stated that he doesn't understand how many of the company's competitors make money. He believed that many of these companies hire undocumented individuals, pay them less than the minimum wage (often under the table), and even then often go out of business in short order. Due to this type of competition, when formal companies try to charge what their services are worth, customers say prices are too high. He stated that his company's prices are the highest in the area but are still 40 percent lower than in locations such as San Antonio and Austin. One of the company's goals is to treat a customer with a Nissan Sentra and a customer with much more expensive car the same. He stated that many individuals in the MEM MSA come from lower-class backgrounds. When they are able to buy their own car, they are very proud; it's a sign that they have made it. He stated that this type of customers responds to great customer service.

Warehousing, trucking, founded in 1997. The founder indicated that market conditions, finding capable employees, and government were all major factors slowing growth. The company was strongly impacted by what the U.S. and Mexican governments were doing on the international bridge. Accessing financing was not a growth barrier. He stated that there had been multiple times when he requested a loan and the banks would say yes, but then the paperwork would require a second lean in order to get 100 percent financing. He didn't like this and instead would put in his own money to cover 20 percent of the loan. Finding capable management was also not a major growth barrier. Many of his supervisors and managers had been with him for more than 10 years.

Restaurants, 300 employees, founded in 1997. The founder stated that major growth barriers included their inexperience, lack of knowledge, and shallow networks. When asked if access to finance was a barrier, he stated no. He and his partners paid cash to get the first restaurant started. After that, "Once the bankers saw the numbers the loans kept coming." A significant number of their customers are from Mexico. The peso devaluation, the security situation, and Donald Trump and his anti-Mexican talk had contributed to a major drop in demand. Middle- and upper-class Mexicans who might have vacationed on South Padre Island are now going to Cancun. Also, if Mexican nationals have a bad experience with U.S. Customs at the international bridge, that will have a strong impact on whether or not they come back. At times "the Border Patrol is not nice. . . . In the end it affects everything. . . . Everybody should be worried about this."

Electronics, 88 employees, founded in 1992. In addition to U.S. sales, the company acts as a distributor for Mexico and other Latin American countries. To support this operation, the founder maintained an account at the Reynosa branch of a large multinational bank. In 2008 the branch manager was threatened and provided details on his largest customers to the Zeta drug cartel. From that point on the founder believed that he was and continues to be a kidnapping target. At that time he began receiving threats from individuals calling his business. He began communicating on a regular basis with local law enforcement (the police department staked out his house during one period), hired a federal agent who provided protection services when off duty, and attended a "two-week survival training" where he learned tactics such as how to dress casually, regularly change his day-to-day routine, and reduce/eliminate his presence on the web. He limits his travel in Mexico and continues to view as risky what most people believe are relatively safe cities such as Monterrey. Changes to the banking laws that made it difficult for Mexican nationals to maintain bank accounts in U.S. border cities and the negative perception of the Trump administration with this same group represent additional growth barriers. The founder stated that a significant number of Mexicans living in the area were self-deporting.

Restaurants, 600 employees, founded in 1987. When asked about major growth barriers, the founder stated, "We limit ourselves." The company was transitioning from a mom-and-pop operation to a professionally run firm. The founder did not view obtaining new financing as a major growth barrier. The regulatory environment was a concern with changes such as the Affordable Care Act and new food labeling regulations. These were not major issues but needed to be addressed. The founder stated that there was a positive business climate in Texas, and with the changes shaping the Rio Grande Valley there was room for those who wanted to be a part of it.

Services for the developmentally disabled, 360 employees, founded in 2004. The most significant growth barrier was the lack of Medicaid funding. Individuals who fit the Medicaid criteria may have to wait up to 10 years before they actually receive services due to insufficient funding.

We found three other themes that emerged from our questions in regard to growth barriers as being particularly noteworthy. The first is that many of our Latino HGF founders did not view access to finance as an issue. One interviewee stated that "once the bankers saw the numbers the loans kept coming." The second was the dependence of the MEM MSA economy on the Mexican economy and the quality of U.S.-Mexico relations. A number of our interviewees stated that the election of the Trump administration had resulted in fewer Mexican nationals purchasing their goods and services. One stated that the change of U.S. president had contributed to their worst quarterly performance ever. Another mentioned that he was aware of a number of Mexican nationals who were "self-deporting" due to the perception of increased anti-Mexican sentiment emanating from the U.S. government. The security situation in Mexico also represented a growth barrier for a number of our sample LHBOs. Our bank CEO mentioned that one reason he had left his position working with large Mexican firms and wealthy Mexican nationals in 2007 was due to his perception of deteriorating market conditions in Mexico resulting from the violence associated with the drug trade. Another of our interviewees dramatically cut back on business travel south of the border after receiving kidnapping threats and experiencing the trauma caused by the kidnapping of a close friend's relative. One of the trucking firms in our sample is authorized to transport goods in the Mexican interior. However, the firm is not willing to put its vehicles at risk and instead focuses on the drayage business (i.e., moving goods across the international bridges).

Exhibit Three contains a number of excerpts from our interviewees regarding the advantages and disadvantage of building an HGF in the MEM MSA as compared to large cities in central Texas. Surprisingly, there was little mention of the lack of wealth in the local community as a major factor limiting growth. One dynamic that was mentioned by a number of our interviewees with businesses that served local consumers is that competition is less intense in the MEM MSA as compared to larger cities. This was viewed as a major benefit, especially during the startup and early growth phases.

Exhibit Three: *Challenges of Creating an HGF in the MEM MSA Compared to Cities in Central Texas*

Insurance, 38 employees, founded in 2001. The founder stated, "The Valley is the last frontier." The cost of living is low, the cost of labor is low, and housing is available for a reasonable price. He stated that if you include everybody within 250 miles from McAllen, there are 25 million people. "The Valley is a great place for us [i.e., Hispanics]. We have access to two countries, and Mexican nationals are very fond of the Valley. . . . The culture will take you in."

Social enterprise with multiple for-profit affiliated companies, 92 employees, founded in 1976. The CEO stated that it is easier in the area. There is a younger pool of talent, and it is an easier environment to work in because it is a smaller community.

Banking, founded in 1920. Our interviewee stated that there were differences; for too long the contribution made by the region to growth in Texas was ignored. The founder stated that with developments such as Space X (the company is building a launch facility in the area), the medical school (established at the public university in the region in 2016), and the new Texas A&M campus (scheduled to open in 2018), the area was positioned for rapid growth over the next 10–20 years. Other businesses associated with traditional industries such as farming and serving the Winter Texan community will also do well. He stated that the area is a great place to be for those looking for opportunity and to raise a family.

Warehousing, trucking, founded in 1997. The founder stated that the nature of his business requires it to be on the border. When he got married the first question from his wife was whether they could move to San Antonio. He said no; the next question was whether they could live on South Padre Island. He said that his would require him to commute all the time. He left it with his wife that "We'll play it by ear" (they have been married for 10 years and continue to live in the MEM MSA).

Restaurants, 600 employees, founded in 1987. The founder stated that "I believe here in the area there is more opportunity. I believe there are fewer people competing in the market; to put it bluntly, you have the opportunity to be a bigger part of something in this type of community. Here they are looking for people that want to be involved." They had "glanced" at other areas such as the Dallas–Fort Worth metroplex, but "there is the opportunity to be part of something good here if you are doing things for the right reasons. . . . There is a great deal of need and opportunity."

Services for the developmentally disabled, 360 employees, founded in 2004. The founder stated that the valley is very different. Everybody in central Texas thinks that the valley is in Mexico. However, he has found communication and cooperation to be better in the area as compared to other locations in the state. Individuals at one of his competitors in the area had been very helpful, and they continue to cooperate when doing so helps patients. In contrast, they had tried to set up group homes in Central Texas. The neighbors complained about having people with disabilities in the community. They received eviction notices and eventually shut down three group homes.

TOWARD A BETTER UNDERSTANDING OF LATINO HGFS AND THE BORDERLANDS

The goal of this study has been to increase our collective understanding of HGFs in general and Latino HGFs operating along the U.S.-Mexican border in particular. Rather than develop and test formal hypotheses, we utilized an inductive methodology to gain a detailed understanding of our sample entrepreneurs and their experiences in creating a rapidly growing firm. One of the standard recommendations for researchers utilizing qualitative methodologies is to continue to collect data until common themes emerge and little additional information is gained from more interviews or additional time in the field. We have not reached that point with our exploration of Latino HGFs in the borderlands. Our interviewees each have a unique story to tell regarding the start and growth of their companies. We found little consistency in major growth barriers encountered, views toward the advantages and disadvantages of the MEM MSA as a location for HGFs, and other areas covered in our interviews. The lack of common themes and the significant variation across our sample is in and of itself a valuable finding. Further study is clearly needed before we can arrive at well-supported conclusions that could be used for robust theory development or public policy recommendations.

We do believe that it is useful, even with the limitations discussed in the prior paragraph, to evaluate information gleamed from our interviewees and compare those insights to the list of HGF stylized facts discussed by Coad et al. (2014), the drivers of HGF growth summarized in Demir et al. (2017), and research on Latino entrepreneurs. Mainstream research suggests that HGFs are broadly distributed across the economy and are not overall concentrated in technology-intensive industries. In our study we found only one firm, a web design and development company, that qualifies as a technology-intensive HGF. This company grew rapidly in its first three years, but whether it continues to grow remains an open question. Sample firms compete in a diverse set of industries, with bias toward those involved in one form or another with international trade and Mexico.

Another stylized fact presented by Coad et al. (2014) is that HGF growth is often erratic. The methodologies used to support this conclusion often do not allow researchers to explore the reasons for this volatility. Our results do not fully support the erratic growth hypothesis. Some firms clearly experienced steady growth over long periods. For those experiencing erratic growth, the reasons for the volatility appear to be highly idio-syncratic. The growth (or lack thereof) of the company serving the needs of the developmentally disabled was dependent on the amount of federal funding administered by the State of Texas. The brokerage company in our sample was strongly impacted by the drop in demand resulting from the Great Recession starting in 2007. In contrast, the banker/real estate developer in our sample was able to buy commercial real estate at attractive prices and carve out a compelling comparative advantage for the bank he leads during the same recession.

In their review article Demir et al. (2017) argues that the human capital of the founder serves as a driver of firm growth. This includes the founder's education level, managerial experience, and domain expertise. An interesting finding from our study is the relatively low level of formal education within our sample as well as the nature of that education. As mentioned, only 9 of the 14 interviewees had earned a college degree, and only 1 graduated from a private institution. We would attribute this level of formal education to the backgrounds of the founders; the majority of our interviewees came from lower-class or lower middle-class backgrounds where it was rare for the parents to have a college degree. Shaped by their environment, formal education at elite higher educational institutions at either the undergraduate or graduate level is not part of the educational background of our sample entrepreneurs. However, the narratives suggest that the entrepreneurs each developed deep domain expertise and manage-rial experience early in their careers. The founder of the company serving the needs of the developmentally disabled as well as our serial entrepreneur turned bank CEO were promoted to top managerial positions in large companies in their respective industries. The founder of the insurance company in our sample took his franchise operation from founding to one of the top-performing locations in the country before starting his own insurance agency.

A widely recognized characteristic of Mexican and Mexican American culture is the importance of family. One of the dynamics that emerges from our sample is the importance not only of the human capital of the founder but also the complementary skill sets and capital provided by family members. The Latino HGF fast-food franchise was founded and led by a husband/wife team. The banker in our sample and his brother both pursued successful careers in large institutions while coinvesting in and managing car washes, farm operations, and a real estate company.

The largest restaurant chain is a classic Mexican/Mexican American family business operated by multiple generations where family and business dynamics continuously intermingle. The freight brokerage was started due to a brother-in-law pushing the founder to ask for a raise and then to do something about it when his boss said no. Startup funds were provided by the father-in-law, and the entrepreneur and his brother-in-law served as co-CEOs for many years.

Another factor that we believe is a major strength for the entrepreneurs is their knowledge of border culture, the idiosyncrasies of Hispanic consumers in the area, and their bilingual abilities. The founder of the Latino HGF serving the needs of the developmentally disabled has expanded to central Texas through forming relationships with Hispanic consumers in those locations. The banker and his brother have a long track record of providing financial services to Mexican consumers (many of whom purchase second homes and invest in businesses in the MEM MSA) as well as other border residents. The company with the greatest number of employees in our sample specializes in providing authentic Mexican food to largely Mexican and Mexican American Spanish-speaking consumers. Our interview at the freight brokerage was interrupted a number of times by urgent telephone calls during which our interviewee would respond in Spanish. It is difficult to imagine these entrepreneurs being as successful as they are without an in-depth knowledge of border culture, the proclivities of consumers in the borderlands, and Spanish-language fluency.

The SLEI 2015 report found that only 20 percent of Hispanic-owned businesses served a "mostly Latino" consumer base. In contrast, our Latino HGF entrepreneurs serving the local consumer market targeted Mexican American and Mexican consumers. While the location of this study is somewhat unique, Hispanics are currently the largest minority group in the United States, and their numbers are rapidly increasing. In the Hispanic-dominated minority-majority communities common in states such as Texas, California, and Florida, the assumption that specializing in serving the needs of ethnic consumers places on upper limit on growth may be outdated. We believe this is an important question for future research.

One of the areas of inquiry in this study was to better understand the challenges of creating and managing Latino HGFs in an economically disadvantaged MSA as compared to larger cities with well-developed entrepreneurial ecosystems such as Austin and Dallas. We received a wide range of responses from our interviewees in regard to this line of questioning. The

Latino HGF serving the developmentally disabled assisted Hispanic clients in larger cities but stated that the business climate was better along the border. The company's growth was primary coming from the border rather than central Texas. The fast-food franchisee believed that there were unmet needs in the community and a relatively low level of competition and that community leaders were proactively looking for capable businesspeople to champion. During our interview the entrepreneur leading the largest employer in our sample stated when the company opens new restaurants in the MEM MSA and surrounding areas, they are immediately profitable due to the strong brand recognition with local consumers and visitors from Mexico. This was not the case with San Antonio locations, where it took much longer to build a loyal consumer base. We believe that much more research using a variety of methodologies needs to be done to better understand how local environments shape the frequency of occurrence and characteristics of HGFs.

To conclude, in this study we utilized an inductive, qualitative methodology to explore the dynamics of Latino HGFs operating in the MEM MSA. Inductive methodologies are particularly valuable for identifying relationships between variables that can feed into deductive, quantitative studies. Our research has identified a number of factors that we believe merit further exploration, such as rethinking the relationship between measures of human capital and its relationship to firm growth and the creation of Latino HGF competitive advantage through a focused strategy of serving the wants and needs of the rapidly growing Latino community. We hope this study serves to spark additional study of high-growth LOBs, especially those operating in minority-majority communities. While our sample size is small and our conclusions are tentative, we are encouraged by the frequency with which individuals from lower-class and lower middle-class families have been able to create HGFs and in the process generate considerable wealth for themselves and their communities. As mentioned by our interviewees, people in other parts of the country may "think that deep South Texas is part of Mexico," and even some local residents consider the area "the last frontier." At the same time, our data suggest that the MEM MSA has more than its fair share of bright, ambitious individuals who move from lower to middle class and above in a relatively short period of time through their entrepreneurial activities. As shown by other recent research (Chetty et al. 2017), our study finds that the American Dream is alive and well in South Texas.

REFERENCES

Acs, Zoltan, William Parsons, and Spencer Tracy Jr. 2008. *High Impact Firms: Gazelles Revisited.* Study prepared for the U.S. Small Business Administration, Office of Advocacy, Washington, DC. http://www.sba.gov/advo/research /rs328toto.pdf.

Birch, David. 1979. *The Job Generation Process.* Report prepared for the U.S. Department of Commerce, Economic Development Administration, Washington, DC.

Birch, David, and James Medoff. 1994. "Gazelles." Pp. 159–67 in *Labor Markets, Employment Policy and Job Creation,* edited by L. C. Solmon and A. R. Levenson. Boulder, CO: Westview.

Brown, Charles, James Hamilton, and James Medoff. 1990. *Employers Large and Small.* Cambridge, MA: Harvard University Press.

Bureau of Labor Statistics. 2017. "Occupational Employment and Wages in McAllen-Edinburg-Mission." gttps://www.bls.gov/regions/southwest /newsrelease/occupationalemploymentandwages_mcallen.htm.

Butler, John, Alfonso Morales, and David Torres. 2009. *An American Story: Mexican-American Entrepreneurship and Wealth Creation.* West Lafayette, IN: Purdue University Press.

Chetty, Raj, John Friedman, Emmanuel Saez, Nicholas Turner, and Danny Yagan. 2017. "Mobility Report Cards: The Role of Colleges in Intergenerational Mobility." http://www.equality-of-opportunity.org/papers/coll_mrc_paper .pdf.

Coad, Alex, Sven-Olov Daunfeldt, Werner Hölzl, Dan Johansson, and Paul Nightingale. 2014. "High-Growth Firms: Introduction to the Special Section." *Industrial and Corporate Change* 23(1):91–112.

Dávila, Alberto, and Marie Mora. 2013. *Hispanic Entrepreneurs in the 2000s: An Economic Profile and Policy Implications.* Stanford, CA: Stanford University Press.

Dávila, Alberto, Marie Mora, and Angela Zeitlin. 2014. *How Hispanic Entrepreneurs Are Beating Expectations and Bolstering the U.S. Economy.* New York: Partnership for a New American Economy.

Davis, Steven, John Haltiwanger, and Scott Schuh. 1996. "Small Business and Job Creation: Dissecting the Myth and Reassessing the Facts." *Small Business Economics* 8(4):297–315.

Demir, Robert, Karl Wennberg, and Alexander McKelvie. 2017. "The Strategic Management of High-Growth Firms: A Review and Theoretical Conceptualization." *Long Range Planning* 50:431–56.

Díaz, George. 2015. *Border Contraband: A History of Smuggling across the Rio Grande.* Austin: University of Texas Press.

Fairlie, Robert, and Alicia Robb. 2008. *Race and Entrepreneurial Success: Black-, Asian- and White-Owned Businesses in the United States.* Cambridge, MA: MIT Press.

Hölzl, Werner. 2009. "Is the R&D Behavior of Fast-Growing SMEs Different? Evidence from CIS III Data for 16 Countries." *Small Business Economics* 33:59–75.

INEGI (Instituto Nacional de Estadística y Geografía). 2018. "Indicadores de establecimentos con programa IMMEX. Cifras durante diciembre, 2017." www.inegi.org.mx/sistemas/bie.

Kirchhoff, Bruce, and Patricia Green. 1998. "Understanding the Theoretical and Empirical Content of Critiques of U.S. Job Creation Research." *Small Business Economics* 10(2):153–69.

Li, Minghao, Stephan Goetz, Mark Partridge, and David Fleming. 2016. "Location Determinants of High-Growth Firms." *Entrepreneurship and Regional Development* 28(1–2):97–125.

Lofstrom, Magnus, and Chunbei Wang. 2006. *Hispanic Self-Employment: A Dynamic Analysis of Business Ownership.* Discussion Paper No. 2101. The Institute for the Study of Labor, Bonn, Germany.

Lofstrom, Magnus, and Chunbei Wang. 2007. "Mexican-Hispanic Self-Employment Entry: The Role of Business Start-Up Constraints." *Annals of the American Academy of Political and Social Science* 613:32–46.

Motoyama, Yasuyuki, and Brian Danley. 2012. *The Ascent of America's High-Growth Companies: An Analysis of the Geography of Entrepreneurship.* Kansas City, MO: Kauffman Foundation.

Richardson, Chad, and Michael Pisani. 2017. *Batos, Bolillos, Pochos, and Pelados: Class and Culture on the South Texas Border.* Rev. ed. Austin: University of Texas Press.

SLEI (Stanford Latino Entrepreneurship Initiative). 2015. *State of Latino Entrepreneurship.* http://lban.us/wp-content/uploads/2015/11/Final-Report-.pdf.

SLEI (Stanford Latino Entrepreneurship Initiative). 2016. *State of Latino Entrepreneurship.* https://www.gsb.stanford.edu/faculty-research/publications/state-latino-entrepreneurship-2016

Solomon, Dan. 2015. "The FBI's List of the Most Dangerous Cities in Texas." *Texas Monthly,* January 22. http://www.texasmonthly.com/the-daily-post/the-fbis-list-of-the-most-dangerous-cities-in-texas/.

USA Trade Online. 2018. United States Census Bureau. https://usatrade.census.gov.

U.S. Border Patrol. 2017. "Sector Profile—Fiscal Year 2017 (Oct. 1st through Sept. 30th)." https://www.cbp.gov/sites/default/files/assets/documents/2017 -Dec/USBP%20Stats%20FY2017%20sector%20profile.pdf.

U.S. Census. 2017. "American Community Survey Data on Educational Attainment." https://www.census.gov/hhes/socdemo/education/data/acs/

Valdez, Zulema. 2011. *The New Entrepreneurs: How Race, Class, and Gender Shape American Enterprise*. Stanford, CA: Stanford University Press.

APPENDIX 8.1
Semistructured Interview Questions

Date: _____

Start Time: _____

Interviewee: _____

Position: _____

Company: _____

Date company founded: _____

Company history/highlights: _____

Founder Background

Age: _____

Hometown: _____

Education: _____

Prior employment: _____

How/why did you select this industry/business? _____

Do you have an ownership interest in other businesses? _____

If so, please describe the ventures. _____

With this company, was growth always a goal? Why? _____

Has the goal of growing the company changed over time? If so, how
 and why? _____

Growth Measures

	2014	At time of interview
*Employees**		
*Sales Growth^*		

If the firm develops the way you would like it to, how many employees
 and what would be the level of sales five years from now? _____

Employees: _____

Sales: _____

How would you characterize the consistency of growth at this company
 since the start of 2013? Consistent, steady growth or dramatic swings
 up and down? _____

If there have been varying growth rates, what have been the reasons for the
 slowdown and/or decline in growth? _____

How did you and the company respond? _____

Growth Barriers

On a scale of one to five with one not at all and five a very significant factor, how would you rate the following factors as significant growth barriers?

Market conditions _____

Finding capable employees _____

Government _____

Access to finance _____

Capable management _____

Which one of these factors (or others) represents the most significant growth barrier for this company? _____

What are you doing to address this growth barrier? _____

Did this company receive support from local, state, or federal government entities during the startup and/or early growth stages? If so, what form did this assistance take? _____

Why did you choose to locate your business in the area? _____

What is similar or different about creating a high-growth company in the area as compared to cities such as San Antonio, Houston, Austin, Dallas, etc. _____

Who do you go to for advice about how to grow your business and/or help solve crucial challenges? _____

Could you suggest other entrepreneurs leading high-growth business in the McAllen-Edinburg-Mission area who might be willing to talk to us for our study? _____

End Time: _____

PART III

MICRO PERSPECTIVES: INDIVIDUAL AND GROUP-LEVEL ANALYSIS

CHAPTER 9

Social Network Utilization among Latino-Owned Businesses

Elsie L. Echeverri-Carroll and Marie T. Mora

INTRODUCTION

As one of the country's fastest-growing racial/ethnic minority groups, the Pew Research Center reports that Latinos accounted for more than half (54 percent) of the U.S. population growth between 2000 and 2014 (Krogstad 2017). Preliminary data from Pew further shows that Latinos continued to account for more than half (51 percent) of the U.S. population growth between 2016 and 2017 (Krogstad 2017). With the growing presence of Latinos, it is not surprising that Latino business owners (LBOs) represent one of the fastest-growing segments of the business economy. To illustrate, Tareque et al. (2016) estimate that between 1996 and 2015, the share of LBOs more than doubled, from 5.6 percent to 14.0 percent, while the share of non-Latino white business owners decreased from 86.0 percent to 72.0 percent (Tareque et al. 2016; see also McManus 2016). Still, as discussed by Dávila and Mora (2013), Latino population growth alone does not fully explain the growing numbers of LBOs; business ownership tendencies have intensified within the Latino population as well.

A host of literature further argues that business opportunities increase for Latinos located in areas with a large coethnic population, presumably related to their competitive advantage in understanding the preferences, culture, and language of consumers and employees. For example, Dávila and Mora (2013) find that each percentage point increase in the share of Latinos in a metropolitan area enhanced the chances of self-employment for Latino immigrants by 0.1 percentage point in 2007 (although this effect weakened to 0.03 percentage points in 2010). At the same time, little consensus exists in the literature that LBOs have more successful business outcomes in geographic areas with a large presence of Latinos than those in other areas.

The widely used ethnic enclave hypothesis maintains that business success depends on the social resources available from coethnic support networks (for a classic study, see Wilson and Portes 1980). However, a relative dearth in the literature exists with respect to understanding the extent of coethnic networks and their impact on the performance of minority-owned firms, generally due to data limitations. Indeed, one of the key limitations of testing the ethnic enclave hypothesis is that nationally representative large-scale databases appropriate for proving this hypothesis remain rare (e.g., Bates 2011). It is not surprising, then, as noted by Dávila and Mora (2013), that existing literature both supports and questions the view that business opportunities improve for minorities in areas with a large coethnic presence. In his literature review, Bates (2011:177) concludes that "empirical applications of these theories [the immigrant and minority entrepreneurship sociological literature] to specific business situations has been complex and typically messy." Moreover, Dávila and Mora (2013) point out that most nationally representative large-scale data sets, such as the American Community Survey, exclude important measures of business outcomes for entrepreneurs, such as profits. When included, nonresponse rates tend to be high due to the common aversion of small-business owners to reporting such outcomes in questionnaire forms (e.g., Bates 1994; Bates and Robb 2008).

In this chapter, we fill this research void by analyzing restricted-use data from a new initiative—the 2016 Stanford Latino Entrepreneurship Initiative (SLEI)—which as discussed in Chapter 5 contains detailed information on Latino-owned businesses operating in 2016, including their utilization of seven types of social networks (e.g., belonging to organizations such as the Hispanic Chambers of Commerce). The data set also has a 100 percent response rate to the question "In the past 12 months, did this business have profits, have losses, or break even?" Moreover, the SLEI data identify the zip codes where the businesses operated, allowing us to examine how enclaves relate to profit outcomes when controlling for characteristics of the owners and firms.

Three questions drive our empirical analyses: (1) Do LBOs located in areas with a large presence of Latinos have a higher probability of business success (measured in terms of having positive profits and paid employees) than those located in areas with a relatively few Latinos? (2) Does the use of social networks affect business outcomes, and if so do these business outcomes differ between immigrants and natives? (3) Does location in a coethnic enclave enhance networking usage among LBOs?

LITERATURE REVIEW: TESTING THE ETHNIC ENCLAVE HYPOTHESIS

For over four decades, one of the most predominant views in the field of minority entrepreneurship has been the ethnic enclave hypothesis, which maintains that ethnic business owners have competitive advantages when operating in areas with large concentrations of coethnic populations (e.g., Light 1972; Wilson and Portes 1980; Aldritch et al. 1985). Bates (2011:177) describes this work in the following way: "Broadly influential sociological studies portrayed successful ethnic entrepreneurs as members of supportive co-ethnic networks providing captive customers, loyal employees, financing to their business ventures, and various other perks; these valuable resources derived, in varying degrees, from explicit social resources embedded in these networks."

At the same time, other scholars note that enclaves can dampen the success of some ethnic business owners (e.g., Aguilera 2009; Aldrich and Waldinger 1990 ; Razin and Langlois 1996; Portes and Landolt 1996; Portes 1998; Geertz 1963; Sanders and Nee 1987; Bates 1994; Yuengert 1995; Flota and Mora 2001; Mora and Dávila 2005; Dávila and Mora 2013). Portes and Landolt (1996) and Portes (1998) point out that relying on ethnic networks can be costly to business owners, as community obligations may result in counterproductive decisions for the success of their business. In this regard, Geertz (1963) explains that successful entrepreneurs in coethnic spaces may be approached by individuals in the community looking for favors such as loans, employment, and other resources that may not be beneficial to the firm.

Sanders and Nee (1987) highlight that if ethnic enclaves become overcrowded, firms can benefit from relocating to other areas with less competition. Operating in regions with intense competition with a less affluent customer base can also create difficult environments in which to grow successful firms (Aguilera 2009; Waldinger and Aldrich 2006). Moreover, some authors associate the likelihood of overly competitive markets for small firms with high business failure rates and low returns for owners of the surviving businesses (Waldinger and Aldrich 2006; Bates 1997).

Bates (2011), for example, believes that the high density and strong ties of small-world networks create both positive and negative consequences for entrepreneurs. Since dense networks tend toward conformity, they promote familiar routines in a context of homogeneous relationships, often constraining business owners' autonomy, creativity, and innovation (Gargiulo and Benassi 2000). Finally, other scholars, including Yuengert (1995), Flota and Mora (2001), and Mora and Dávila (2005), note that some ethnic entrepreneurs might be reluctant to leave the "safety net" of the enclave, such that their limited geographic mobility dampens their potential business outcomes.

Fluency in a country's majority language also plays a role. For example, using the Public Use Microdata Areas (PUMAs) in the 1980 U.S. decennial census, Torres (1988) discusses how proficiency in English strongly relates to higher income among self-employed workers in the United States, possibly reflecting the positive consequences of being oriented toward markets beyond those serving their coethnics. In his view, extending one's social ties beyond the enclave provides more diverse information and access to new ideas and opportunities as well as mainstream resources. Mora and Dávila (2005) further discuss how English-fluent ethnic entrepreneurs in the United States have an advantage in enclaves over their counterparts with limited English proficiency because they can communicate with their coethnics as well as with the general population.

Other authors study the concept of ethnic enclaves not in terms of whether they directly enhance or hinder business opportunities and outcomes for minority entrepreneurs but rather in terms of factors that pull or push them to coethnic enclaves. For instance, minority entrepreneurs might perceive an economic advantage in tapping into ethnic resources (e.g., capital access through networks), understanding the culture and language of customers and employees, and serving coethnic markets. In this case, pull factors move minorities into business ownership in coethnic enclaves. The counterfactual argument is that ethnic business owners (especially immigrants) choose to serve and locate in coethnic enclaves because they encounter disadvantages in the broader labor market stemming from perceived lower levels of human capital, particularly among those with limited majority-language fluency; that is, traditionally disadvantaged minorities may turn to business ownership as a survival strategy due to push factors.

Discrimination can also play a role in the location decisions of ethnic entrepreneurs. Following a Becker-type model in which discrimination increases with the visibility of minorities, Dávila and Mora (2013) note that the push factors would likely be stronger in enclaves than outside. Similarly, Borjas and Bronars (1989) find that minority entrepreneurs often self-select into minority-market segments because consumer discrimination limits their range of business ventures that non-Hispanic whites tend to patronize. In such cases, as noted by Fairlie and Lofstrom (2013:26), "higher rates of business ownership are not so much the result of signs of success but represent a reflection of blocked opportunities in wage/salary employment."

Given the mixed evidence on how enclaves relate to the success of minority-owned businesses, in an upcoming section of this chapter we empirically analyze two measures of business success among Latinos: the likelihood of having positive profits and the likelihood of being an employer firm. Because the literature identifies issues of particular relevance to immigrants (such as the role of limited English fluency), part of this analysis considers differences in business outcomes between foreign-born and U.S.-born LBOs. We also examine the role of enclaves in the usage of social networks by LBOs.

We focus on employer firms as one measure of business success in light of their impact on creating employment opportunities beyond those created for the business owner. The literature reports that nonemployers (which account for more than 80 percent of businesses in the United States) tend to have weaker performance measures, including being less likely to generate positive profits, use financing, and report higher revenues (e.g., Rosoff and Terry 2015; Dávila and Mora 2013; Davis et al. 2009). Moreover, only about 3 percent of nonemployer firms migrate to employer firm status (Davis et al. 2009).

DATA AND METHODOLOGY

SLEI Data and Measuring Ethnic Enclaves

To test whether LBOs located in coethnic enclaves have higher probabilities of earning positive profits, having paid employees, and utilizing social and business networks than those located in areas with relatively few Latinos when controlling for other owner- and firm-level characteristics, we employ the 2016 restricted-use SLEI data set. Chapter 5 of this volume contains more information on the SLEI methodology and sample characteristics.

As a proxy for ethnic enclaves, we estimate the proportion of Latinos among the population in the county in which the LBOs operate. To identify these counties, we use a crosswalk produced by the U.S. Department of Housing and Urban Development (2017), which maps zip codes to counties. While over half (55.1 percent) of the zip codes in this Department of Housing and Urban Development crosswalk correspond to a single county, the remaining zip codes correspond to multiple counties, ranging between 2 and 10 counties. In our sample of LBOs, the vast majority (83.6 percent) have zip codes corresponding to a single county; the remaining cover between 2 and 6 counties. In such cases, following Wilson and Din's (2018) methodology, we use the county with the largest share of the zip code's population in our analysis. For example, one of the LBOs in our SLEI sample had a zip code covering three counties, one of which has two-thirds of the zip code's population (66.6 percent), while the other two counties each contain a small share of the population (13.2 percent and 20.2 percent). Thus, we assign the LBOs located in that particular zip code to the county with two-thirds of the population. In the end, we assign the 2,569 zip codes where the 4,322 LBOs in our sample operate to 724 counties.

Models Estimated and Variables of Interest

Beyond business outcomes, we test whether LBOs operating in Latino enclaves tend to utilize social and business networks more than their counterparts in other areas. We consider seven network variables: four involve business-organization memberships (for Latino business organizations, government organizations, other business organizations, or any business organization), and three pertain to the networks through which LBOs secure funding to grow their businesses (family/friends, banks/financial institutions, and venture capitalists/angel investors).

The empirical models for the likelihood of earning positive profits, being an employer firm, and using social networks control for standard human capital and demographic characteristics of the LBOs, including age, gender, education (namely whether the owner had a four-year college degree or higher prior to owning the business), and immigrant status. Moreover, as noted earlier, one important variable usually missing in nationally representative studies is the extent of business owners' networks. The SLEI data allow us to measure the impact of several network indicators, including membership in various business and government organizations (discussed in more detail below) and using networks of friends and family, banks, venture capital firms, or angel investors to fund business growth. Note that the use of these networks is not mutually exclusive; some LBOs belong to multiple business organizations and secure funding from multiple sources.

In addition, the models include firm-level characteristics, namely the firm's age, size (proxied by categories of the amount of revenue in the past 12 months), and industry using a set of 10 binary variables (construction; education and health services; financial activities; information; leisure and hospitality; manufacturing; natural resources and mining; professional business services; trade, transportation, and utilities; and other services except public administration). The importance of controlling for industry has been discussed elsewhere; for example, Dávila and Mora (2013) caution that ethnic enclave benefits may vary according to the industry sector in which the business operates (e.g., owners of Mexican restaurants in predominantly non-Latino white areas versus self-employed Mexican plumbers).[1] We also control for the unemployment rate in the county as a proxy for local labor market conditions, a conventional proxy in the literature.

In our empirical analyses, we employ logistic regression to estimate the models, clustering the robust standard errors by county to address the clustered nature of certain variables. For example, intraclass correlation occurs because some LBOs operate in the same county, meaning they have identical values for the enclave and unemployment measures. Because these correlations might result in inaccurate estimates of the statistical significance of coefficients, we account for clustering inherent in the data.

SAMPLE CHARACTERISTICS AND EMPIRICAL RESULTS

Table 9.1 provides selected descriptive statistics of the LBOs in our SLEI sample (column 1) as well as for U.S. natives and immigrants (columns 2 and 3). On average, in 2016 LBOs operated in counties where nearly 4 out of 10 (38.8 percent) residents were Latino. This proportion was statistically indistinguishable between native and immigrant LBOs and

TABLE 9.1 *Summary Statistics for Latino Business Owner and Firm Characteristics by Owner's Nativity*

	All LBOs	Natives	Immigrants
A. Outcome Variable			
(%) Positive profits in last 12 months	72.49	70.48	76.37*
(%) Employer in 2016	12.25	11.98	12.78
B. Owner Characteristics			
1. *Demographics*			
(mean) Age	40.43	40.61	40.08
(%) Female owner	49.98	50.33	49.29
(%) Immigrant owner	34.11		
2. *Human Capital*			
(%) Education: At least a 4-year degree	50.90	49.21	54.16
3. *Networks*			
(%) Membership in:			
Latino business organizations	30.52	28.72	34.01
Government business organizations	11.90	12.23	11.27
Other business organizations	33.35	34.82	30.49
(%) Sources of funding for growth:			
Family, friends, or personal savings	54.44	55.98	51.47
Local, regional, or commercial bank loans	25.30	23.44	28.90*
Venture capital or angel investors	11.45	9.51	15.19**
C. Firm Characteristics			
(mean) Firm age	10.57	10.63	10.45
(%) Revenues in last 12 months			
Low (< $10,000)	22.23	23.08	20.58
Medium ($10,000 to $99,999)	58.16	57.01	60.38
High (≥ $100,000)	19.61	19.90	19.04
(%) Majority Latino customers	26.31	24.96	28.90
(mean) Hispanic proportion of county population	0.388	0.397	0.370
n	4,322	2,705	1,617

Source: 2016 SLEI survey and U.S. Census Bureau's American Community Survey 2013-2017 Five-Year Demographic Profile Tables DP03 and DP05.

Notes: *, **, *** indicate significant difference of means at the 0.1, 0.05, and 0.01 levels, respectively. Latino business organizations include Latino chambers of commerce and Latino business-oriented nonprofits. Government business organizations include economic development organizations and local government boards. Other business organizations include general chambers of commerce, trade associations, and local nonprofits. Majority-Latino customers indicates that more than 50% of customers or clients were Latino. Population includes noninstitutionalized civilians ages 16 to 64, inclusive.

considerably higher than the roughly 18 percent representation of Latinos among the U.S. population. On the surface, the relatively high share of Latinos for LBOs fits with the literature that ethnic enclaves tend to host higher shares of ethnic entrepreneurs. Later in this section, we test whether Latino enclaves relate to the success of LBOs, other things being the same.

Speaking of business outcomes, Table 9.1 indicates that nearly three-quarters (72.5 percent) of all LBOs in our sample earned positive profits in the past 12 months, an outcome that varied slightly between native and immigrant LBOs (70.5 percent vs. 76.4 percent, respectively). Moreover, about one of eight (12.3 percent) of the LBOs in our sample had paid employees in 2016, with little difference between native and immigrants LBOs (12.0 percent and 12.8 percent, respectively). In fact, with few exceptions, Table 9.1 shows that most of the characteristics do not significantly differ between U.S.-born LBOs (who represented two-thirds, or 65.9 percent, of our sample) and foreign-born LBOs (who represented one-third, or 34.1 percent).[2]

As noted earlier, an advantage with the SLEI data set is the inclusion of network variables for growth-funding sources and business-organization memberships. Table 9.1 shows that the majority of LBOs (54.4 percent) tend to tap into informal networks (i.e., families, friends, and their own personal savings) to secure funding for growth, compared to a minority who secure funding from formal networks (25.3 percent from banks/financial institutions and 11.5 percent from venture capital/angel investors). Moreover, while a minority of LBOs belong to any formal business organization, those who do tend to be members of Latino or other non-government organizations compared to government organizations; LBO membership in these three organization types were 30.5 percent, 33.4 percent, and 11.9 percent, respectively.

Table 9.1 further shows that on average, native and immigrant LBOs in the SLEI data were about 40 years old, and their firms were around 12 years old. Women (as well as college graduates) represented about half of the LBOs. In terms of revenue, slightly over one-fifth (22.2 percent) of the LBOs had revenues below $10,000 in the last 12 months, and about one-fifth (19.6 percent) had revenues over $100,000.

The industry mix variables indicate that over half of the LBOs were in three sectors: professional business services (23.8 percent), other services except public administration (18.5 percent), and construction (15.3 percent). Four industry groups (education and health services, leisure and hospitality, manufacturing, and trade, transportation, and utilities) each represented between 7 percent and 10 percent of the LBOs, while three sectors (information, financial activity, and natural resources and mining) each accounted for less than 5 percent.

Latino Customers and Latino Enclaves

As seen in Table 9.1, Latinos represent the majority of customers for just over one-fourth (26.3 percent) of LBOs in our sample. While conventional wisdom holds that Latino-owned companies in Latino enclaves serve more Latino clients than those in other areas by virtue of location, until the SLEI data it was difficult to empirically demonstrate this relationship. For insight, we estimate a logistic regression with the dependent variable equal to one for LBOs with Latinos representing the majority of their customers; it equals zero otherwise. The regressors include our enclave measure (i.e., the Latino proportion of the county's population), owner- and firm-level characteristics, and the county unemployment rate.[3] (To conserve space, the results are not shown but can be obtained from the authors.)

This exercise indicates that LBOs in Latino enclaves have a positive and statistically significant likelihood of serving a Latino majority of their clientele, other things being the same. This finding is important and contributes to the literature because it empirically demonstrates that LBOs operating in ethnic enclaves tend to cater to Latino customers more frequently than otherwise similar firms outside of enclaves. Because a logical extension is whether ethnic enclaves relate to the success of LBOs, we now turn to such an analysis while accounting for other owner- and firm-level characteristics that affect business outcomes.

More Detailed Analyses of Business Outcomes

Table 9.2 presents the logistic regression results for our two business outcomes of interest: the probability of generating positive profits (columns 1 and 2) and the probability of having paid employees (columns 3 and 4). We first regress these two outcomes of interest on the ethnic enclave variable along with other standard characteristics of the owners (e.g., education, age, gender, and birthplace) and firms (age, revenues, Latino customer base, and industry) as well as the county unemployment rate to capture local labor market conditions (Model A). We then add the variables for the use of networks regarding business organization memberships and sources of funding for growth (Model B, the full model). The rationale for estimating two models is to consider whether the inclusion of networking variables affects the estimated relationship between enclaves and business outcomes, as enclaves themselves presumably affect networking opportunities.

As seen in Table 9.2, we do not find evidence that Latino enclaves (proxied by the proportion of Latinos among the county population) significantly relates to the likelihood of earning positive profits (columns 1 and 2) or being an employer firm (columns 3 and 4 of Table 9.2) among LBOs in the SLEI data set, controlling for other observable characteristics. At the same time, despite being statistically insignificant at conventional levels, all of the enclave coefficients are positive, inconclusively suggesting potential benefits of ethnic enclaves on business outcomes. It follows that our results do not provide significant support for the ethnic enclave hypothesis with respect to these two business success measures, in line with other studies using large databases (e.g., Bates 1994; Aguilera 2009).

Other interesting findings in Table 9.2 pertain to the networking variables in Model B (columns 2 and 4), information that was not possible to explore using large data sets until now. Admittedly, as with the enclave results, we cannot test for causality versus correlation. Still, these results indicate that being part of a Latino business organization relates to a greater likelihood of having positive business outcomes among LBOs in terms of earning positive profits and having paid employees. Moreover, the probability of LBOs generating positive profits is positively associated with formal networks through commercial banks/financial institutions used to fund company growth and is negatively associated with informal networks (i.e., relying on family, friends, or personal funds). These findings align with previous studies showing that greater capitalization characterizes the small firms most likely to operate profitably (e.g., Fairlie and Robb 2008; Bates and Robb 2014). Of course, we realize that the direction of causation is a potential issue here, as the most successful firms are likely those positioned to secure funding through formal networks as opposed to informal networks for additional growth.

With respect to the LBO characteristics, other things being the same, Table 9.2 shows that younger LBOs tend to have better business outcomes than their older counterparts, as do men versus women with respect to earning positive profits (the latter being a standard finding in the literature). The coefficients on education, immigrant status, having a majority Latino customer base, and the local unemployment rate are not statistically significant at conventional levels when controlling for other characteristics.

TABLE 9.2 *Logistic Regression Analysis of Restricted (A) and Full (B) Models for the Likelihood of Having Positive Profits in the Last 12 Months and Being an Employer in 2016*

	Regression Coefficients			
	Positive Profits		Employer in 2016	
Independent Variables	A	B	A	B
Proportion of Latino population in the county	0.195	0.180	0.096	0.099
Membership in business organizations				
Latino business organizations		0.444**		0.251*
Government business organizations		−0.110		−0.206
Other business organizations		0.189		0.246
Age	−0.019***	−0.017**	−0.014**	−0.014***
Female owner	−0.539***	−0.484***	−0.157	−0.160
Education: At least a 4-year degree	0.179	0.096	0.118	0.094
Immigrant owner	0.236	0.210	0.053	0.068
Sources of funding for growth				
Family, friends, or personal savings		−0.386**		−0.012
Local, regional, or commercial bank loans		0.391*		0.028
Venture capital or angel investors		−0.100		−0.302**
Firm age	−0.004	−0.010	0.017***	0.014***

Revenues in last 12 months				
$10,000 to $49,999	0.533***	0.522***	1.213***	1.225***
$50,000 to $99,999	0.997***	0.930***	1.269***	1.259***
≥ $100,000	0.602***	0.592***	2.299***	2.315***
Majority Latino customers	−0.036	−0.066	0.020	0.011
Unemployment rate by county	0.193	−0.160	−0.069	0.116
Constant	1.141**	1.245**	−2.907***	−2.937***
Adjusted Wald test for industry controls (df=9)	12.31	7.42	11.00	11.33
Pseudo R^2	0.054	0.072	0.082	0.086
X^2(df)***	69.49(20)	88.67(26)	287.23(20)	305.90(26)
−Log pseudolikelihood	2,405.30	2,360.28	1,480.33	1,473.31
n	4,293	4,293	4,293	4,293

Source: 2016 SLEI survey and U.S. Census Bureau's American Community Survey 2013–2017 Five-Year Demographic Profile Tables DP03 and DP05.

Notes: *, **, *** indicate significance at the 0.1, 0.05, and 0.01 levels, respectively. Latino business organizations include Latino chambers of commerce and Latino business-oriented nonprofits. Hispanic proportion of the population is measured at the county level. Government business organizations include economic development organizations and local government boards. Other business organizations include general chambers of commerce, trade associations, and local nonprofits. Majority Latino customers indicate that more than 50% of customers or clients were Latino. Robust standard errors are clustered by county. Revenues in the last 12 months less than $10,000 are omitted from the category for the revenue variables. Ten industry sectors are included as controls, with "other services (except public administration)" as the omitted category, and are not presented to conserve space.

Consistent with the literature, firm size as measured by revenues was significantly associated with the likelihood of business success among LBOs for both outcomes. More established enterprises (measured by the firm's age) also enhanced the odds of being an employer firm.

While not shown to conserve space, none of the industry variables individually or as a group are statistically significant except for the financial industry in the case of being an employer firm. (The details are available from the authors.) Therefore, it appears that the effects of industry on business success for the LBOs in the SLEI sample may work through other observable characteristics in Table 9.2 (such as the owner and firm age).

Robustness of Our Enclave Findings

To test whether the lack of conventional statistical significance for our enclave variable (measured at the county level) on the two LBO business success measures is robust with respect to other measures of ethnic enclaves, we estimate the business outcome models using two different spatial units for the enclaves: PUMAs and commuting zones. We also use the location quotient, which provides a concentration measure of the Latino population in a given area by comparing that area's Latino population proportion to the national average.[4] Information on these additional measures, the methodology used to incorporate them into the research design, and the results from these analyses can be found in Appendix 9.1. In all, these results show that the lack of support for the ethnic enclave hypothesis we report in Table 9.2 is robust to different ethnic enclave specifications.

Empirical Results for Latino Immigrants versus Natives

We next explore whether the findings for LBO business outcomes differ between businesses owned by Latino immigrants versus natives by estimating Model B separately for these two groups; the logistic regression results from this exercise are reported in Table 9.3. This exercise indicates that combining the two groups masks the role of ethnic enclaves and certain networks on the likelihood of immigrant LBOs' success. The positive, significant coefficient (1.908, $p \leq 0.001$) on the enclave measure suggests that among immigrant LBOs, those in counties with high shares of Latinos have a greater likelihood of generating positive profits than those in other areas. Note, however, that the significant relationship between Latino enclaves and the odds of having positive profits holds only for foreign-born LBOs; it does not hold for U.S. natives. It also does not hold with respect to the likelihood of having paid employees. In all, these results do not provide broad support for the ethnic enclave hypothesis for LBOs in general, but they provide evidence that operating in ethnic enclaves may yield additional benefits for immigrant entrepreneurs compared to their native counterparts. Future research should continue to investigate such differences.

Table 9.3 further suggests that the relationship between certain social networks and business outcomes differs between native and immigrant LBOs in the SLEI data set. Belonging to Latino business organizations relates to a greater likelihood of success in terms of earning positive profits and being an employer among immigrant LBOs, but this was not the case among natives. The issue of why foreign-born Latino entrepreneurs belonging to Latino business organizations appear to have an advantage over their U.S.-born counterparts is a topic worthy of future exploration. One possible explanation is self-selection into such organizations; Echeverri-Carroll and Kellison (2012) have reported on the low participation of LBOs in Hispanic chambers of commerce. Moreover, Table 9.3 indicates that among native LBOs, membership in a government business organization relates to lower odds of being an employer firm, again perhaps due to selection into such organizations. This was not the case for immigrants or for the likelihood of having paid employees, indicating the complexity of social networks in the success of Latino entrepreneurs.

Other networking variables indicate that as with LBOs in general, having strong relationships with commercial banks relates to a heightened likelihood of having positive profits for native LBOs, and relying on family, friends, or personal funds to grow the business relates to a lower likelihood. Again, we realize that the issue regarding the unclear direction of causation is present here. Still, the odds of having paid employees seems to be unrelated to networks utilized to fund growth for both immigrants and natives, with the exception of the utilization of venture capital or angel investors by native Latinos, which had a negative relationship.

Younger native LBOs have a greater likelihood of earning positive profits and having paid employees than their older counterparts, as was the case for younger immigrant LBOs in terms of having paid employees, where other things held constant. Moreover, similar to results reported in other studies, among natives-owned firms in the SLEI data set, those owned by Latinas were less successful with respect to both business outcomes, which was not the case among immigrants in this sample. The lack of a significant

TABLE 9.3 Logistic Regression Analysis of Full Model for the Likelihood of Having Positive Profits in the Last 12 Months and Being an Employer in 2016 by Owner's Nativity

| | Regression Coefficients | | | |
| | Positive Profits | | Employer in 2016 | |
Independent Variables	Natives	Immigrants	Natives	Immigrants
Proportion of Latino population in the county	−0.299	1.908***	0.279	−0.295
Membership in business organizations				
Latino business organizations	0.329	0.817**	0.203	0.480**
Government business organizations	−0.151	0.056	−0.479**	0.224
Other business organizations	0.248	0.155	0.250	0.385
Age	−0.023***	−0.001	−0.013*	−0.023**
Female owner	−0.683***	−0.298	−0.357**	0.196
Education: At least a 4-year degree	−0.010	0.258	0.139	−0.063
Sources of funding for growth				
Family, friends, or personal savings	−0.535**	0.120	0.036	−0.102
Local, regional, or commercial bank loans	0.680***	0.093	−0.105	0.303
Venture capital or angel investors	−0.151	−0.284	−0.495**	−0.299
Firm age	−0.017	0.011	0.008	0.038***

Revenues in last 12 months				
$10,000 to $49,999	0.530**	0.573*	1.325***	1.275***
$50,000 to $99,999	0.796**	1.554***	1.416***	1.163***
≥ $100,000	0.843***	0.036	2.304***	2.547***
Majority Latino customers	-0.114	0.313	-0.106	0.219
Unemployment rate by county	2.937	-12.495	-7.345	17.197*
Constant	1.855***	-0.079	-2.431***	-4.120***
Adjusted Wald test for industry controls (df=9)	22.20***	15.47	17.27**	4.75
Pseudo R^2	0.112	0.108	0.089	0.135
X^2(df)***	99.13(25)	87.55(25)	205.34(25)	182.21(25)
–Log pseudolikelihood	1,530.66	721.39	951.69	490.51
n	2,680	1,613	2,680	1,613

Source: 2016 SLEI survey and U.S. Census Bureau's American Community Survey 2013–2017 Five-Year Demographic Profile Tables DP03 and DP05.

Notes: *, **, *** indicate significance at the 0.1, 0.05, and 0.01 levels, respectively. Latino business organizations include Latino chambers of commerce and Latino business-oriented nonprofits. The Hispanic proportion of the population is measured at the county level. Government business organizations include economic development organizations and local government boards. Other business organizations include general chambers of commerce, trade associations, and local non-profits. Majority Latino customers indicates that more than 50% of customers or clients were Latino. Robust standard errors are clustered by county. Revenue in the last 12 months less than $10,000 is the omitted category for the revenue variables. Ten industry sectors are included as controls, with "other services (except public administration)" as the omitted category, and are not presented to conserve space.

effect for gender among foreign-born Latinos raises some questions about the SLEI sample, as Dávila and Mora (2013) found that both U.S.-born and foreign-born Latinas were more likely to be microentrepreneurs than their male counterparts.

Other factors predicting positive profits tend to follow the same patterns as observed in Table 9.2 for LBOs overall for both Latino immigrants and natives, with the exception of the age of firms. This variable does not significantly relate to business outcomes except for the likelihood that Latino immigrant–owned enterprises had paid employees, ceteris paribus. In contrast, we find that native LBOs experience jointly significant industry effects on both measures for business success. Future research should investigate why the longevity of LBOs might play a different role in the success of firms owned by Latino immigrants than those owned by their U.S.-born counterparts. It might be that the correlation between firm age and the time immigrants have spent in the United States plays a role. Individual industry variables also have statistically insignificant effects on LBO outcomes, although as a block of variables industry has a jointly nonsignificant effect on the likelihood of business outcomes (at least for these two measures) among immigrant LBOs.

Extension: Determinants of Social Network Utilization

The previous sections of this chapter assessed whether ethnic enclaves (as measured by the proportion of Latinos among the county population) significantly relate to business outcomes for LBOs in the SLEI data set; our empirical analysis did not provide broad empirical evidence to support this relationship. At the same time, as noted earlier in this chapter, many studies have found that ethnic enclaves relate to a greater incidence of business ownership among racial ethnic minorities and immigrants—a relationship often assumed to be driven by social networks. An unanswered question is whether operating in ethnic enclaves strengthens the likelihood of networking among LBOs. The SLEI data allow us to provide empirical insight into this question at the national level as opposed to individual case studies on specific cities or regions within the United States.

Therefore, we next test the relative importance of enclaves for the likelihood that LBOs use social networks by treating the seven aforementioned networking variables as dependent variables in logistic regression models, with the regressors being the same ones we used in our analyses of business outcomes (namely, our enclave measure plus the characteristics of the business owners and firms, including industry, and the county unemployment rate). Table 9.4 displays the results.

As shown in the first row of Table 9.4, as with the other business outcomes for LBOs discussed earlier, operating in ethnic enclaves is not significantly related to social network utilization, controlling for other owner- and firm-level characteristics of LBOs (although the coefficients are positive for five of the seven networking variables). Instead, LBOs' networking activities significantly relate to other individual and firm variables rather than enclaves per se. For example, younger LBOs tend to network more with respect to five of the seven network measures than their older counterparts, which could explain why this group of LBOs tends to be more successful in terms of its business outcomes, as observed in our analysis earlier in this chapter.

The coefficient for women is negative for six of the seven networking variables (the exception being for informal networking, that is, family, friends, and personal savings to fund growth), suggesting that Latina entrepreneurs may be at a disadvantage relative to LBO men in terms of accessing formal networks to enhance their business success. More educated LBOs also have a greater likelihood of tapping into formal networks, as do Latino owners of older firms, compared to otherwise similar firms. Table 9.4 further indicates that having a majority of customers of Latino descent relates to the probability of belonging to Latino business organizations and using personal networks for funding for growth. Industry is jointly significant only for the likelihood of belonging to Latino business organizations and for using bank loans to fund business growth. The latter finding makes sense, as financial institutions often consider industry when assessing credit risk. Finally, small firms owned by Latinos (those with annual revenues below $50,000) and large firms (those with annual revenues of $100,000 or more) tend to rely less on networks than do midsize firms (those with annual revenues between $50,000 and $99,999).

In all, these results suggest that ethnic enclaves do not directly relate in a statistically significant manner to business outcomes or network utilization among LBOs in the SLEI data set, accounting for other observable owner- and firm-level characteristics. These results align with previous studies finding little support for the ethnic enclave hypothesis. As such, despite the well-documented incidence of ethnic entrepreneurship in

TABLE 9.4 *Logistic Regression Analysis of Restricted Model for the Likelihood of Networking with Seven Networking Measures*

	Regression Coefficients						
Independent Variables	Hispanic Business Org.	Government Business Org.	Other Business Org.	Any Business Org.	Personal Network Funding	Bank Loan Network Funding	VC or Angel Network Funding
% Latino population in the county	0.372	0.571	0.379	-0.129	-0.032	0.013	0.462
Age	-0.045***	0.010	0.027***	-0.016**	-0.011	-0.029***	-0.060***
Female owner	-0.136	-0.148	-0.122	-0.278*	0.258**	-0.400**	-0.380
Immigrant owner	0.263*	-0.114	-0.237	0.113	-0.212*	0.205	0.485**
Education: At least a 4-year degree	0.309**	0.552**	1.002***	0.844***	-0.098	0.567***	0.837***
Firm age	0.036***	0.009	0.025***	0.039***	-0.011	0.025***	0.018*
Revenues in last 12 months							
$10,000 to $49,999	0.040	0.354	-0.097	0.032	-0.236	0.198	0.063
$50,000 to $99,999	0.661***	0.898***	0.378	0.690***	-0.108	0.679**	0.764**
≥ $100,000	0.240	0.628**	-0.149	0.075	0.041	0.233	0.201
Majority Latino customers	0.568***	-0.037	-0.302*	0.276*	0.436***	0.249	-0.096
Unemployment rate by PUMA	-7.006	-18.814	-7.122	-5.876	-8.257	-0.718	8.723
Constant	-0.532	-3.340***	-2.387***	-0.138	1.384***	-1.531***	-1.566***

Adjusted Wald test for industry controls (df=9)	26.23***	9.81	3.95	13.81	13.56	31.40***	16.81*
Pseudo R^2	0.107	0.055	0.102	0.094	0.035	0.088	0.111
X^2(df)***	139.83(20)	39.07(20)	125.00(20)	127.75(20)	52.72(20)	101.75(20)	129.88(20)
–Log pseudolikelihood	2,372.19	1,478.76	2,469.12	2,699.11	2,870.02	2,227.48	1,373.17
n	4,293	4,293	4,293	4,293	4,293	4,293	4,293

Source: 2016 SLEI survey and U.S. Census Bureau's American Community Survey 2013–2017 Five-Year Demographic Profile Tables DP03 and DP05.

Notes: *, **, *** indicate significance at the 0.1, 0.05, and 0.01 levels, respectively. The Hispanic proportion of the population is measured at the county level. Latino business organizations include Latino chambers of commerce and Latino business-oriented nonprofits. Government business organizations include economic development organizations and local government boards. Other business organizations include general chambers of commerce, trade associations, and local nonprofits. Majority Latino customers indicates that more than 50% of customers or clients were Latino. Robust standard errors are clustered by county. Revenue in the last 12 months less than $10,000 is the omitted category for the revenue variables. Ten industry sectors are included as controls, with "other services (except public administration)" as the omitted category, and are not presented to conserve space.

enclaves, our findings based on SLEI data do not uncover additional benefits for Latino-owned firms with respect to networking and enhanced business outcomes

That said, we recommend that future research continue to analyze the relationship between network usage and ethnic enclaves while further considering other socioeconomic and demographic dimensions. For example, while we use gender as one of our control variables, it remains of interest whether the absence of the enclave effect on network usage holds for both men and women. Moreover, additional analyses focusing on the age of the owners and firms are warranted beyond being included as control variables, particularly as age presumably plays a role in the types of networks that LBOs access when seeking funding for growth.

CONCLUSION

Although their population growth has slightly tapered off, Latinos continue to account for more of the nation's overall population growth than any other racial/ethnic group, according to the Pew Research Center (Krogstad 2017). The rapid growth of the Latino population as well as an intensification of business ownership activities among Latinos have been cited as main factors in explaining the growth of LBOs over the past few decades (e.g., Dávila and Mora 2013; Tareque et al. 2016).

The ethnic enclave literature argues that LBOs' competitive advantages emerge from their geographic proximity to coethnic customers and potential networking relationships. In this view, business creation and success relate not only to human and financial capital but also to the relative abundance of social capital available to minority entrepreneurs in ethnic enclaves. However, probing the relationship between business success and coethnic location via networks has been difficult due to the lack of data capable of measuring the extent of business networks. Moreover, most of the studies that use large representative databases define ethnic enclaves as broad geographical areas, such as at the state level. The restricted-use SLEI database allows us to overcome these constraints, because beyond being a national database, it includes several measures of networks and the zip codes of the firms' locations. Moreover, it has a 100 percent response rate regarding whether firms have positive, negative, or zero profits, information usually missing in large databases or plagued with low response rates.

In this chapter, using logistic regression analysis of the likelihood of having positive business outcomes among LBOs in the SLEI data set, overall we do not find that ethnic enclaves (defined as the Latino proportion of a county's population) relate to the likelihood of generating positive profits or being an employer firm (the exception being the case of Latino immigrants, who have greater odds of having positive profits when located in enclaves). We also find that the odds of using social networks does not depend on the exposure to Latino enclaves per se and instead appears to hinge on other observable characteristics of the owners (such as age and gender) and businesses (such as the age of the firms).

This chapter contributes to the ethnic enclave literature in several ways. One way is empirically demonstrating that businesses serving mainly Latino customers tend to be located in areas with a relatively high proportion of Hispanics. This relationship has been assumed in the literature but not directly tested using large data sets until now. However, our results find little broad support for other benefits of operating in ethnic enclaves (except for immigrants).

Depending on data availability (perhaps through future SLEI surveys), future studies should investigate how the utilization of networks by ethnic business owners relates to their longevity and other long-term measures of success. Understanding the economic prospects associated with various LBO location choices can shed light on whether public policies that expand entrepreneurial opportunities for this group would facilitate their economic mobility and incorporation into communities with different demographic compositions.

Moreover, our analysis provides important policy considerations related to a variety of issues surrounding potential training programs. For example, we find that younger LBOs tend to network more than older ones. It may be that younger LBOs rely more on social media to network than do older LBOs; entrepreneurial training programs should take the owner's age into consideration in terms of the needs of small businesses. We also find that Latina entrepreneurs tend to network less than their male counterparts. Thus, entrepreneurial training programs, especially those designed for women-owned businesses, should consider helping business owners to expand their entrepreneurial networks. In all, entrepreneurial training programs designed to increase business networks should consider both the characteristics of the entrepreneurs and theirs firms to expand networking rather than offering a "one size fits all" framework.

ACKNOWLEDGMENTS

Evan Johnston and Erica Mirabitur, the research associates who worked on preparing and presenting the complex data for analysis, deserve special recognition. Both displayed great intelligence in analyzing, organizing, and interpreting the detailed data. We also acknowledge this volume's editors and Susan Pozo for their helpful comments as well as those of the participants at the 2017 and 2018 SLEI Faculty Convening workshops and the American Society of Hispanic Economists' session at the 2018 Western Economic Association International annual meetings.

NOTES

1. Similarly, Aldrich and Waldinger (1990) and others show that small minority-owned businesses differ from other businesses in their distribution across industries, since they are greatly overrepresented in the retail and service sectors, as opportunities arise in these industries because minority population growth provides the consumer base to which ethnic business owners sell. Differences in distribution across industry sectors may also reflect the level of barrier to entry (Lofstrom and Bates 2007; Lofstrom and Wang 2009). However, with our data we cannot test for the effect of low- versus high-barrier sectors, because the SLEI survey aggregates industry categories in such a way that key low- and high-barrier sectors cannot be accurately identified.

2. The relatively low share of immigrant-owned businesses raises some concerns about the nationally representative nature of the SLEI sample, as most studies on LBOs identify that immigrants comprise a disproportionate share (e.g., Dávila and Mora 2013). At the same time, the SLEI data set represents the only large data set that includes key variables of interest, such as the array of social and business networks. Future research should attempt to identify the sources of discrepancy and whether they impact the empirical results.

3. Specifically, the regressors include whether the owner had a college education as well as age, gender, immigrant status, and firm age; four levels of revenues (less than $10,000 [base], $10,000–$49,000, $50,000–$99,000, and more than $100,000), the unemployment rate in the PUMA; and a set of binary variables indicating 10 industry sectors.

4. Commuting zones delineate space based on commuting patterns of the area, and they do not rely on arbitrary boundaries imposed by city or county borders. The U.S. Census Bureau creates and uses PUMAs—containing 100,000+ people—to disseminate estimates for the American Community Survey. The location quotient equals the proportion of Latinos among the spatial unit's population divided by the proportion of Latinos among the U.S. population. The denominator is 0.176043, which comes from the U.S. Census Bureau, American Community Survey 2013–2017 Five-Year Demographic Profile, Table DP05.

5. The 1999 data are used because the Census Bureau no longer produces these files. These data are archived here at http://web.archive.org/web /20120914150518/http://www.census.gov/geo/www/tiger/zip1999.ht.ml. These data are made available by the Equality of Opportunity Project, http:// www.equality-of-opportunity.org/data/.

REFERENCES

Aguilera, Michael. B. 2009. "Ethnic Enclaves and the Earnings of Self-Employed Latinos." *Small Business Economics* 33(4):413–25.

Aldrich, Howard, John Cater, Trevor Jones, David McEvoy, and Paul Velleman. 1985. "Ethnic Residential Concentration and the Protected Market Hypothesis." *Social Forces* 63(4):996–1009.

Aldrich, Howard E., and Roger Waldinger. 1990. "Ethnicity and Entrepreneurship." *Annual Review of Sociology* 16:111–35.

Bates, Timothy. 1994. "Social Resources by Group Support Networks May Not Be Beneficial to Asian Immigrant-Owned Small Businesses." *Social Forces* 72(3):671–89.

Bates, Timothy. 1997. *Race, Self-Employment and Upward Mobility*. Baltimore: Johns Hopkins University Press.

Bates, Timothy. 2011. "Minority Entrepreneurship." *Foundations and Trends in Entrepreneurship* 7(3–4):151–311.

Bates, Timothy, and Alicia Robb. 2008. "Analysis of Young Neighborhood Firms Serving Urban Minority Clients." *Journal of Economics & Business* 60(1):139–48.

Bates, Timothy, and Alicia Robb. 2014. "Small-Business Viability in America's Urban Minority Communities." *Urban Studies* 51(13):2844–62.

Borjas, George J., and Stephen G. Bronars. 1989. "Consumer Discrimination and Self-Employment." *Journal of Political Economy* 97(3):581–605.

Chetty, Raj, and Nathaniel Hendren. 2018. "The Impacts of Neighborhoods on Intergenerational Mobility II: County-Level Estimates." *Quarterly Journal of Economics* 133(3): 1163–228.

Dávila, Alberto, and Marie T. Mora. 2013. *Hispanic Entrepreneurs in the 2000s: An Economic Profile and Policy Implications.* Stanford, CA: Stanford University Press.

Davis, Steven J., John Haltiwanger, Ron S. Jarmin, C. J. Krizan, Javier Miranda, Alfred Nucci, and Kristin Sandusky. 2009. "Measuring the Dynamics of Young and Small Businesses: Integrating the Employer and Nonemployer Universes." Pp. 329–66 in *Producer Dynamics: New Evidence from Micro Data,* edited by Timothy Dunne, J. Bradford Jensen, and Mark J. Roberts. Chicago: University of Chicago Press.

Dorn, David. 2019. "1990 Counties to 1990 Commuting Zones [Data file]." https://www.ddorn.net/data.htm.

Echeverri-Carroll, Elsie L., and J. Bruce Kellison. 2012. *Survey of Texas Hispanic-Owned Businesses with Paid Employees.* Technical Report, Bureau of Business Research and IC² Institute.

Fairlie, Robert W., and Alicia Robb. 2008. *Race and Entrepreneurial Success: Black-, Asian-, and White-Owned Businesses in the United States.* Cambridge, MA: MIT Press.

Fairlie, Robert W., and Magnus Lofstrom. 2013. "Immigration and Entrepreneurship." IZA Discussion Paper No. 7669.

Flota, Chrystell, and Marie T. Mora. 2001. "The Earnings of Self-Employed Mexican Americans along the U.S.-Mexico Border." *Annals of Regional Science* 35(3):483–99.

Gargiulo, Martin, and Mario Benassi. 2000. "Trapped in Your Network? Network Cohesion, Structural Holes, and the Adaptation of Social Capital." *Organization Science* 11(2):183–96.

Geertz, Clifford. 1963. *Peddlers and Princes.* Chicago: University of Chicago Press.

Krogstad, Jens Manuel. 2017. "U.S. Hispanic Population Growth Has Leveled off." Pew Research Center, August 3. http://www.pewresearch.org/fact-tank/2017/08/03/u-s-hispanic-population-growth-has-leveled-off/.

Light, Ivan. 1972. *Ethnic Enterprise in America.* Berkeley: University of California Press.

Lofstrom, Magnus, and Chunbei Wang. 2009. "Mexican-American Self-Employment: A Dynamic Analysis of Business Ownership." Pp. 197–227 in *Ethnicity and Labor Market Outcomes: Research in Labor Economics* 29, edited by Amelie F. Constant, Konstantinos Tatsiramos, and Klaus F. Zimmermann. Bingley, UK: Emerald Group Publishing.

Lofstrom, Magnus, and Timothy Bates. 2007. "African Americans' Pursuit of Self-Employment." IZA Discussion Paper No. 3156.

McManus, Michael. 2016. *Minority Business Ownership: Data from the 2012 Survey of Business Owners Issue Brief.* Washington, DC: U.S. Small Business Administration Office of Advocacy.

Mora, Marie T., and Alberto Dávila. 2005. "Ethnic Group Size, Linguistic Isolation, and Immigrant Entrepreneurship in the U.S." *Entrepreneurship & Regional Development* 17:389–404.

Portes, Alejandro. 1998. "Social Capital: Its Origins and Applications in Modern Sociology." *Annual Review of Sociology* 24(1):1–24.

Portes, Alejandro, and Patricia Landolt. 1996. "The Downside of Social Capital." *American Prospect* 94(26):18–21.

Razin, Eran, and André Langlois. 1996. "Metropolitan Characteristics and Entrepreneurship among Immigrants and Ethnic Groups in Canada." *International Migration Review* 30:703–27.

Rosoff, Stephanie, and Ellie Terry. 2015. "The Financial Experiences of Nonemployer Firms: Evidence from the 2014 Joint Small Business Credit Survey." Community and Economic Development Discussion Paper No. 03-15, Community and Economic Development Department, Federal Reserve Bank of Atlanta.

Sanders, Jimy M., and Victor Nee. 1987. "Limits of Ethnic Solidarity in the Enclave Economy." *American Sociological Review* 52:745–73.

Tareque, Inara, Arnobio Morelix, Robert W. Fairlie, Joshua Russell-Fritch, and E. J. Reedy. 2016. "The Kauffman Index 2016: Main Street Entrepreneurship." Kaufman Foundation. https://papers.ssrn.com/sol3/Papers.cfm?abstract_id=2872901.

Tolbert, Charles M., and Molly Sizer. 1996. "U.S. Commuting Zones and Labor Market Areas: A 1990 Update." Report No. AGES-9614. Washington, DC: U.S. Department of Agriculture

Torres, David L. 1988. "Success and the Mexican American Businessperson." In *Research in the Sociology of Organizations*, Vol. 6, edited by Samuel B. Bacharach. Greenwich, CT: JAI.

U.S. Census Bureau. *American Community Survey 2013–2017: Five-Year Demographic Profile Tables DP03 and DP05.* http://factfinder.census.gov.

U.S. Department of Housing and Urban Development. 2017. *HUD USPS Zip Code Crosswalk Files.* ZIP-COUNTY Crosswalk Type, 1st Quarter 2017. https://www.huduser.gov/portal/ datasets/ usps_crosswalk.html.

Waldinger, Robert and Howard Aldrich. 2006. "Trends in Ethnic Businesses in the United States." Pp. 59–78 in *Ethnic Entrepreneurs: Immigrant Business in Industrial Societies,* edited by Roger Waldinger, Howard Aldrich, and Robin Ward. Newbury Park, CA: Sage.

Wilson, Kenneth L., and Alejandro Portes. 1980. "Immigrant Enclaves: An Analysis of the Labor Market Experience of Cubans in Miami." *American Journal of Sociology* 86(2):295–319.

Wilson, Ron, and Alexander Din. 2018. "Understanding and Enhancing the U.S. Department of Housing and Urban Development's ZIP Code Crosswalk Files." *Cityscape: A Journal of Policy Development and Research* 20(2):277–94.

Yuengert, Andrew M. 1995. "Testing Hypotheses of Immigrant Self-Employment." *Journal of Human Resources* 30(1):194–204.

APPENDIX 9.1

For robustness checks regarding our proxy for Latino enclaves (the proportion of Latinos among a geographic area's population), we estimate models for business success using different geographical areas, including counties, PUMAs, and commuting zones. We also use the location quotient, which compares the proportion of the population that is Latino to the national average in a geographical area. This appendix describes how we assigned each LBO zip code to PUMAs and to commuting zones.

From Zip Codes to PUMAs

The U.S. Census Bureau uses PUMAs for the American Community Survey. These geographies contain 100,000+ people. We use a crosswalk from the Missouri Census Data Center to match the SLEI data LBO zip codes to PUMAs. For zip codes that do not correspond to a single PUMA, we use the crosswalk's allocation factor, which indicates the proportion of the zip code's population within each PUMA. More specifically, we designate the PUMA that contains the largest proportion of the zip code's population as the LBO's PUMA.

From Zip Codes to Commuting Zones

The commuting zone delineates space based on commuting patterns of the area, not relying on arbitrary boundaries imposed by city or county borders. This concept, developed by Tolbert and Sizer (1996), is more organic in the sense that demarcations come from human activity (i.e., natural movement of residents). Following Chetty and Hendren (2018),[5] we link the zip codes of SLEI data LBOs to corresponding counties using their 1999 crosswalk. We then use Dorn's crosswalk to link counties to corresponding commuting zones (Dorn 2019). The Latino population data come from the U.S. Census Bureau American Community Survey 2013–2017 five-year estimates.

Results

TABLE 9.A.1 *Results with Latino Population Proportion in PUMA*

Coefficients on the Latino-enclave measure for the dependent variable of positive profits.

	MODEL			
Measure of Enclave for PUMA	A	B	B: Natives	B: Immigrants
Latino proportion of population	−0.002	−0.002	−0.006	0.010
Location quotient	−0.028	−0.032	−0.114	0.170

Notes: *, **, *** indicate significant difference of means at the 0.1, 0.05, and 0.01 levels, respectively. These models control for owner- and firm-level characteristics. Standard errors are clustered at the PUMA level.

Coefficients on the Latino-enclave measure for the dependent variable of employer status.

	MODEL			
Measure of Enclave for PUMA	A	B	B: Natives	B: Immigrants
Latino proportion of population	−0.000	−0.000	0.001	−0.003
Location quotient	−0.001	−0.002	0.019	−0.045

Notes: *, **, *** indicate significant difference of means at the 0.1, 0.05, and 0.01 levels, respectively. These models control for owner- and firm-level characteristics. Standard errors are clustered at the PUMA level.

Coefficients on the Latino-enclave measure for the seven networking measures.

	Network Type						
	Business Organization				Network Funding		
Measure of Enclave for PUMA	Latino	Gov	Other	Any	Personal	Bank	VC/ Angel
Latino proportion of population	0.002	0.006	0.004	−0.004	0.000	−0.001	0.001
Location quotient	0.033	0.107	0.062	−0.063	0.006	−0.022	0.020

Notes: *, **, *** indicate significant difference of means at the 0.1, 0.05, and 0.01 levels, respectively. These models control for owner- and firm-level characteristics. Standard errors are clustered at the PUMA level.

TABLE 9.A.2 *Results with Commuting Zones (CZ)*

Coefficients on the Latino-enclave measure for the dependent variable of positive profits.

| | MODEL | | | |
Measure of Enclave for CZ	A	B	B: Natives	B: Immigrants
Latino proportion of population	−0.117	−0.159	−0.608	1.610*
Location quotient	−0.021	−0.028	−0.107	0.283*

Notes: *, **, *** indicate significant difference of means at the 0.1, 0.05, and 0.01 levels, respectively. These models control for owner- and firm-level characteristics. Standard errors are clustered at the commuting-zone level.

Coefficients on the Latino-enclave measure for the dependent variable of employer status.

| | MODEL | | | |
Measure of Enclave for CZ	A	B	B: Natives	B: Immigrants
Latino proportion of population	−0.210	−0.214	−0.008	−0.506
Location quotient	−0.037	−0.038	−0.001	−0.089

Notes: *, **, *** indicate significant difference of means at the 0.1, 0.05, and 0.01 levels, respectively. These models control for owner- and firm-level characteristics. Standard errors are clustered at the commuting-zone level.

Coefficients on the Latino-enclave measure for the seven networking measures.

| | Network Type | | | | | | |
| | Business Organization | | | | Network Funding | | |
Measure of Enclave for CZ	Latino	Gov	Other	Any	Personal	Bank	VC/ Angel
Latino proportion of population	0.587	0.891	0.526	0.108	−0.321	−0.616*	0.456
Location quotient	0.103	0.157	0.093	0.003	−0.056	−0.108*	0.080

Notes: *, **, *** indicate significant difference of means at the 0.1, 0.05, and 0.01 levels, respectively. These models control for owner- and firm-level characteristics. Standard errors are clustered at the commuting-zone level.

CHAPTER 10

Acculturation and Latino-Owned Business Success: Patterns and Connections

Michael J. Pisani and Joseph M. Guzman

INTRODUCTION

The patterns and connections between acculturation and success in Latino-owned businesses (LOBs) is the focus of this chapter. The growth of the number of Latinos and LOBs in the United States has increased markedly over the past 40 years. Continued growth perhaps approaches 5 million LOBs today,[1] far outpacing relative business growth elsewhere more generally. This growth in population and LOBs is in concert with the movement of Hispanic people as immigrants into the United States as well as expanding native Hispanic families over many generations. Foreign-born Latinos were 35 percent of the U.S. Latino population in 2013; however, the share of foreign-born Latinos is in relative decline, indicating that the peak of Hispanic immigration has passed and that endogenous growth of Latinos will become more important over time as to the ultimate size and shape of the Latino population (López and Patten 2015). Nonetheless, the mix of Latino immigrants and Latino natives abound, providing a natural experiment of the impact of acculturation on one segment of Latinos: business owners.

In this chapter we seek to explore the relationship between acculturation[2] and LOB success. We suggest that acculturation refers to how immigrants and their descendants change with each generation in regard to the structure of the host society (Portes and Rumbaut 2014; Richardson and Pisani 2017). In the present case, does generational affinity to the United States create space for enhanced LOB success, or does it detract from LOB success? In essence, our research question posits this question: *What role, if any, does acculturation play in LOB success?* The remainder of this chapter is organized as follows. Section 2 reviews the pertinent literature for measuring acculturation over generations and presents a discussion of LOB business and associated success. Next, we detail the data used in this chapter followed by calculated patterns and connections of acculturation and LOB success. The last section concludes the chapter with a focus on policy considerations.

LITERATURE REVIEW

In this chapter there are two pertinent areas of literature we pull from: acculturation and Latino entrepreneurship. These are explored below.

Acculturation

There is considerable scholarly and public interest on the topic of immigrant acculturation and integration in receiving nations. Portes and Rumbaut (2014:71) suggest that acculturation "occurs by the diffusion of [societal] values and norms," and by "osmosis, as it were, these new cultural forms are gradually absorbed by immigrants, bringing them closer to the majority." Bean, Brow, and Bachmeier (2015:17) build upon this definition, arguing that it is a "process by which the characteristics of members of immigrant groups and the members of a given receiving society come to resemble one another." Portes and Rumbaut (2014:71) further suggest that the acculturation process "may be seen as irreversible though it may take different lengths of time for different groups."

As assimilation or acculturation occurs over time (and geographical space), the process is characteristically understood within the framework of family generations. While the concept of generation is relatively simple, the operationalization of generation is not. That is, the measure of generation has been muddied by competing definitions including half-generation counts. Even a standard definition of when the first generation begins—with the immigrant or immigrant children—may be confusing. In its simplest terms, the first generation is thought to include the immigrants themselves, the second consists of their U.S.-born children, and the third consists of native-born children of native-born parents. One does not have to consider very many cases, however, before realizing that there is a great deal of complexity in measuring generational status. For example, one's father may have been born in the United States, but his or her mother may have been born abroad. Similarly, any of the four grandparents could have been born in the receiving or sending country. Out of such situations arise some very complex issues describing an individual's generational status.

Richardson and colleagues (Richardson and Pisani 2017; Richardson and Resendiz 2006) use the generation score (GS) based on the birth location of three generations as a proxy for determining acculturation in Hispanic populations. In doing so, they were able to study acculturation among Hispanics in South Texas along several cultural markers—lifestyle in Mexico vis-à-vis the United States, communication rates with family in Mexico, friendship patterns (Anglos and Latinos), language usage (Spanish, English), traditional health and celebration practices (e.g., use of *manzanilla* tea, singing "*las mañanitas*" at birthdays)—as well as political, economic, and crime-related dimensions.

For example, lower GSs were significantly associated with greater use of Spanish, more frequent communication with family abroad, and higher levels of in-group (Latino) friendships, illustrating lower rates of acculturation for language, family connections, and friendships and vice versa, where higher GSs were associated with greater use of English, less communication with family abroad, and more out-group friendships. Whereas GSs were not significantly associated with eating tamales or using piñatas for celebrating birthdays, indicating that these cultural artifacts survive the acculturation process. Use of the GS as a proxy for acculturation proved robust in South Texas in the most Hispanic of Hispanic regions in the United States; hence, we argue that this measure, explained in more detail below, is an appropriate tool in the study of Latino acculturation more broadly.

Latino Entrepreneurship

Much of the Latino entrepreneurship literature is represented by many of the authors of this volume. As such, we provide only a brief overview of the literature here. While the literature on Latino entrepreneurship[3] is in its infancy, there are a handful of studies that help shape the current state of knowledge. Because of the ongoing flow of immigration from Mexico and other sending countries, enclave or immigrant community entrepreneurship has been a sustained focus of study. Essentially, an ethnic market enclave reflects coethnic immigrant, coethnic-origin enterprises (from employees through the supply chain) serving coethnic customers (immigrants or coethnic origin) in a coethnic neighborhood or region.

Portes and Haller (2005), Light (2005), Malkin (2004), and Striffler (2007) examined different immigrant groups in the United States and found that successful immigrant communities offer newly arrived coethnics help in securing informal sources of credit, insurance, child support, English-language training, job referrals, job placement, support networks, and employment assistance (including self-employment assistance). There are many variations of an ethnic enclave; for example, there may be variations in ownership structure, staffing patterns, and ethnic origins. There is much discussion of the economic returns to entrepreneurs in ethnic enclaves and whether the market protection offered by coethnics generates better returns than outside the ethnic enclave (Zhou and Logan 1989). Aguilera (2009) argues that ethnic self-employment in enclaves may reduce potential earnings or be benign, depending on the business location and origin of the immigrant entrepreneur. Regardless, ethnic enclaves exist and persist throughout the U.S. economy (Pisani et al. 2017).

More generally, Calo (1995) uncovered direct relationships between Latino self-employment and greater educational attainment, higher English proficiency, additional work experience, and Latino population enclaves. The use of social networks for ethnic entrepreneurs is a common recurring finding in other national contexts.[4] Rochín et al. (1998) have examined rural Latino[5] self-employment in California. Rochín (2013:89) notes that structural conditions (e.g., high unemployment, limited educational attainment, and high concentration of agricultural workers) heavily influence self-employment outcomes, resulting in Latinos being "self-employed as part of their own means for survival." In her study of middle-class Mexicans in the Los Angeles area, Vallejo (2012:54) notes that a "significant majority of the second generation who grew up middle class have parents who built successful small businesses after they migrated to the United States, oftentimes servicing the ethnic community." Vallejo (2012:57) further suggests that "business ownership is a strategy to circumvent disadvantages in the labor market that emerge from not having gone to college."

Recent research has also confirmed the importance of foreign-language acquisition for the creation of immigrant enterprises. In her qualitative study of Polish immigrant entrepreneurs in the United Kingdom, Knight (2015) uncovered the importance of English-language facility as an important factor in business startup, and without such English-language skills many Polish

immigrants were reconciled to work in Polish enterprises. Coethnic employment and customer patterns are also a common refrain in the literature
(Ilhan-Nas, Sahin, and Cilingir 2011). Shinnar, Aguilera, and Lyons (2011),
Yang et al. (2011), and Curci and Mackoy (2010) suggest that financial
performance may improve when ethnic entrepreneurs widen their customer
base beyond coethnics, particularly in diverse demographic environments.
Conversely, these authors argue that to operate exclusively within the ethnic
population zone, ethnic entrepreneurs may forgo business opportunities.
Yet, ethnic familiarity may have a strong hold on many ethnic entrepreneurs
as a business safe haven because of immigration status, language facility, kinship ties, and accumulated social capital, which may weaken (or even deter)
the incentive for financial gain outside the ethnic community.

Verdaguer (2009) focuses on Salvadoran and Peruvian Latino entrepreneurs in the metropolitan Washington, D.C., area. Noting different
trajectories and resource bases of Salvadorans and Peruvians, Verdaguer
(2009) finds heterogeneity in entrepreneurship endeavors and outcomes
and cautions against sweeping pan-ethnic descriptions. In her study of
Harrisonburg, Virginia, Zarrugh (2007) uncovered enclave Latino self-
employment as a response to blocked employment paths, partially a result
of racism. This result is supported by Dávila and Mora (2013), who also
note that this is especially true for Hispanic immigrant entrepreneurs.
Wang and Li (2007) argue that English-language ability is a determinant
of self-employment for Latinos, and Borjas and Katz (2007) suggest that
Latinos over time make steady economic progress. Fairlie and Miranda
(2017) find that growth-oriented Hispanic-owned business startups are
more likely to hire employees at a faster rate than Anglo startups, perhaps
suggesting that there may by some connection between opportunity-driven
Latino enterprises and the presence of paid workers.

In this chapter, we are able to explore competing perspectives of assimilation as either a straight-line event or some variant of immigrant selection
regarding LOB success.

DATA SOURCES AND DESCRIPTIVE STATISTICS FOR GENERATION SCORE

The primary data source utilized in this chapter is derived from the nationally
representative Stanford Latino Entrepreneurship Initiative (SLEI) surveys of

2016 and 2017 (as described in Chapter 5). In all. 4,787 individuals were surveyed in the fall, with an additional follow-up survey of 616 chosen from the original respondents. The follow-up spotlight survey allowed for additional questions including those surrounding the birth location of three generations (respondent, parents, and grandparents). With this additional information, the GS (a proxy for acculturation) was calculated.[6]

The GS was created to allow for greater simplicity. For example, Bean et al. (2015) use the following generation measures: 1.0 for a person who immigrated to the United States, 1.5 for a person who immigrated to the United States before age 14, 2.0 for a person born in the United States with at least one foreign-born parent, and 3.0 for a person born in the United States with at least two foreign-born grandparents. Telles and Ortiz (2008:73) operationalize generation as 1.0 for a foreign born person, 1.5 if the foreign born person immigrated at an early age, U.S.-born children of two immigrant parents as generation 2.0; those with one immigrant parent and a U.S.-born parent of any generation as 2.5; anyone with one second-generation parent and one who was second generation or more is codified as generation 3.0; and generation 4.0 designates anyone with at least three of four grandparents born in the United States. Other authors have similarly confusing measures that parse generation by quarter points and extend to a generation 5.0 (i.e., ancestors).

This mix of native and foreign heritage has resulted in multiple definitions of generations, which make comparison across studies challenging. With such methodological confusion, we have offered and established in the literature the parsimonious measure of generation that we label GS (see Pisani 2012, 2013, 2014; Pisani and Richardson 2012; Pisani and Sepulveda 2012; Richardson and Pisani 2012, 2017; Richardson and Resendiz 2006). The use of the GS does away with the need to name each generation and the confusion of generational mixing. The generational status of any two individuals can now be compared directly by looking at the values of their GS. Most importantly, use of the GS provides a greater degree of variation in generational status compared to extant approaches; as such, data are not lost with the GS compared to other approaches with more limited and/or differently definitional generational-status categories. Additionally, the computed GS may be used for more robust empirical analyses than less precise or inconsistent categorical variables.

This GS is calculated by allotting a total of four points to each generation born in the United States, from respondent to grandparent. If a respondent is born in the United States, for example, he/she is assigned four points (zero if born outside the United States). Two points are allocated for each parent born in the United States (zero otherwise), and one point is allocated for each grandparent born in the United States (zero otherwise). This produces a GS range of 0 (all foreign-born) to 12 (all U.S.-born).[7] Tabulation of the GS is displayed in Table 10.1. Knowledge of the birth origins of the respondent, respondent's parents, and respondent's grandparents in Hispanic populations has not been problematic in previous research (Richardson and Pisani 2017).

We complement the SLEI sample with the 2006 Latino National Survey (LNS). The LNS is a national representative sample of 8,634 adult Latinos randomly selected from the universe of 11 million Hispanic households in the United States collected via a computer-assisted telephone interview. The 2006 LNS provides a baseline comparison of the general Latino population to that of LOBs and has been adroitly employed by many researchers (see Gershon and Pantoja 2014; Fraga et al. 2012). Importantly, the 2006 LNS also allows for the construction of the GS.

Together, we report the GS of the SLEI data (unweighted and weighted) and the 2006 LNS data for select demographic variables (Table 10.2). In each instance (i.e., gender, education, and English- and Spanish-language ability), respondent SLEI Latino business owners report significantly higher GSs than LNS respondents. This indicates that a much higher level of acculturation is present for Latino business

TABLE 10.1 *Tabulation of the Generation Score*

	Birthplace		
	Outside U.S.	U.S.	Possible Scores
Respondent	0	4	0 or 4
Respondent's parents			
Mother	0	2	0 or 2
Father	0	2	0 or 2
Respondent's grandparents			
Maternal grandmother	0	1	0 or 1
Maternal grandfather	0	1	0 or 1
Paternal grandmother	0	1	0 or 1
Paternal grandfather	0	1	0 or 1
Total Generation Score	*0*	*12*	*0 to 12*

TABLE 10.2 *Descriptive Statistics: Generation Score (GS) by Data Source*

SLEI Variable	GS SLEI Unweighted	GS SLEI Weighted	GS LNS	LNS Variable
Gender				
Male	8.1	7.9	3.0	Male
Female	8.4	8.2	3.4	Female
Education (Prior to Owning Business)			Education	
Less than high school	8.0	5.6	2.0	None
High school	8.1	8.6	1.9	8th grade ≤
Trade, technical, or vocational school	7.9	6.9	2.6	Some high school
Some college	8.3	9.3	3.1	GED
AA/AS	8.1	7.7	3.2	High school grad
BA/BS	8.3	8.5	4.3	Some college
MA/MS+	8.2	7.0	4.1	BA/BS
			4.0	Graduate or professional degree
English-Language Ability			Speak English	
Fluent	8.4	8.2	3.3	Very well
Advanced	7.4	6.8	2.3	Pretty well
Conversational	6.1	5.5	1.7	Just a little
Basic	8.0	7.4	1.4	Not at all
Know a few words, at most	7.0	7.0	—	—

Spanish-Language Ability		
Fluent	7.8	7.8
Advanced	8.3	7.8
Conversational	8.7	8.7
Basic	9.1	8.4
Know a few words, at most	8.8	8.0
Mean GS	8.23 (2.41)	8.00 (2.45)
N	616	8,634

Speak Spanish	
Very well	3.9
Pretty well	6.0
Just a little	8.0
Not at all	8.7
—	—
Mean GS	3.22 (3.44)
N	N

Note: *Italics* denotes significant differences within the selected respondent group at $P \leq .10$.

owners than the general Latino population. Some other trends for both data sets are also present. A higher level of educational attainment generally follows those with higher GSs. English-language ability generally increases with GS—a positive relationship. And Spanish-language ability generally increases with a decrease in GS—an inverse relationship. Hence, for language, more acculturated Latinos have more developed English-language ability, and those respondents with closer natal ties to their Latin American home or ancestral country possess greater Spanish-language ability. Finally, the average GS is reported at the bottom of the table for both samples.[8]

Beyond the descriptive statistics, the SLEI data allows a fuller look into LOB patterns and connections as reflected by firm size and ownership, financing, language utilization, business challenges, desirability of business ownership, and the inauguration of Donald Trump as U.S. president. These patterns and connections with regard to acculturation are developed in the next section using the 2016–2017 SLEI data.

PATTERNS AND CONNECTIONS

In this section, we report on patterns and connections between several categories of LOB operations and GS utilizing weighed data. These include ownership, firm size and location, sources of business loan information, business investment solicitation, frequency of contact with capital providers, language use and ability, business challenges, self-employment alternatives, and the potential impact of the 2016 presidential election.

Ownership, Firm Size, and Location

While nearly 90 percent of LOBs in the sample are owned by a single owner, co-owned firms (7.17) possess a significantly lower GS score than single-owned LOBs (8.08).[9] There are no statistically significant differences among LOBs by Latin American origin or heritage.[10] A majority of LOBs in the sample (63.0 percent, N = 604) had fewer than 10 employees, with own account businesses (i.e., no employees) recording the highest GS (8.77). Enterprises with 50 or more employees, 100 or more employees, 500 or more employees, and 1,000 or more employees are progressively owned by entrepreneurs with lower GSs. Hence, larger enterprises are significantly more likely to be owned by entrepreneurs with a lower GS.[11]

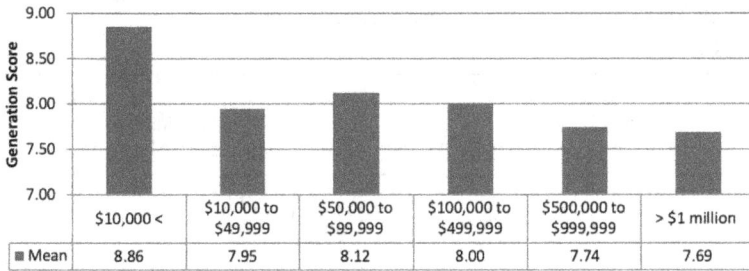

Figure 10.1 Mean generation score and LOB revenue. *Note:* Comparison of means ANOVA, $F = 2.394$, $p = .020$, $n = 604$. (Source: SLEI Survey of U.S. Latino Business Owners 2017.)

Figure 10.1 displays the GS by annual LOB revenue. Of significant note, the largest revenue LOBs are those with the lowest mean GS, and this pattern holds for all revenue categories except the $50,000–$99,999 revenue business. The State of Latino Entrepreneurship reports (Rivers et al., 2016; Orozco, Oyer, and Porras 2018) indicate a strong association with immigrant ownership and scaled LOBs. Specifically, about half of LOBs with $1 million or more in revenue are immigrant owned, which would help explain the lower GS at the highest revenue category, a pattern reflected in Figure 10.1. This result may in part be based on the model of immigrant optimism (Fernández-Reino 2016), where immigrants are positively selected into the immigration process and as such possess a higher abundance of skills that can be transferred more easily into entrepreneurial ventures. In support of this view, Dávila and Mora (2013) argue that self-employed immigrant Latinos are positively selected in times of U.S. macroeconomic growth, and Escobar (2006) notes that the most recently arrived Latino immigrants are the most optimistic.

Sources of Business Loan Information

Three sources of information on business loans were significantly different along the GS measure, though these findings are tempered by a low response rate (which occurred for this chapter section only). These sources of information are gleaned from business mentors, the Internet, and online courses/workshops (Table 10.3). For these three significant instances, a higher mean GS score was associated with their use. Access to business mentorship may be associated with a longer U.S. connection and social network established over time. Use of the Internet and online courses may be the result of Internet access, which disproportionately and negatively

TABLE 10.3 *Sources of Information for Business Loan Information and Mean Generation Score*

	Chamber of Commerce	Trade Association	Tandas	Family & Friends	Business Mentor	Internet Search	Online Course/ Workshops
Yes	7.40	7.61	5.00	8.12	9.45	8.73	10.16
No	8.15	8.12	8.08	8.05	7.85	7.65	7.84
F	—	—	—	—	15.592	13.724	25.491
P	n/s	n/s	n/s	n/s	.000	.000	.000
Yes %	9.3	8.3	0.0	44.6	14.7	39.9	10.4
N	278	278	278	278	278	278	278

Source: SLEI Survey of U.S. Latino Business Owners 2016–2017.

Note: n/s = not significant; analysis, comparison of means, ANOVA.

impacts foreign-born Latinos as compared to native-born Latinos (Lopez, Gonzalez-Barrera, and Patton 2013). Interestingly, there were no meaningful differences for accessing business loan information from chambers of commerce, trade associations, *tandas* (self-help rotating saving and loan groups), and family and friends. Of all the sources of information accessed, the most common were the use of family and friends (44.6 percent) and an Internet search (39.9 percent), both readily accessible sources of information. Certainly, more investigation into these findings will shed a more definitive answer (see also Chapter 9 in this volume).

Solicited Investments in Growing the Business

Family and friends comprised the most common group (52.3 percent) in which LOBs sought investment in growing their businesses (Table 10.4). About one-fifth of respondent LOBs indicated that they had solicited funds from a local bank or credit union, a commercial bank, or venture capitalists, and fewer still had solicited funds from microlenders and angel investors. Across the spectrum of investment solicitation, there were no significant differences with GS. This may in part be a response to the fundamental difficulties associated with financing LOBs (Dávila and Mora 2013; see also Chapter 13 in this volume) and may be a function of average resource similarities for the majority of LOBs.

More research in this area is needed to better understand the financing needs of LOBs holistically and across generations and with immigrants. Additional insights may be provided through bifurcated class structures,

TABLE 10.4 *Solicited Investments in Growing the Business and Mean Generation Score*

	Family & Friends	Local Bank/ Credit Union	Commercial Bank	Microlenders	Venture Capitalists	Angel Investors
Yes	8.04	8.16	7.83	8.02	8.28	8.06
No	7.96	7.96	8.05	8.00	7.93	7.99
F	—	—	—	—	—	—
P	n/s	n/s	n/s	n/s	n/s	n/s
Yes %	52.3	19.9	22.0	16.6	20.9	14.4
N	604	604	604	604	604	604

Source: SLEI Survey of U.S. Latino Business Owners, 2016–2017.

Notes: n/s = not significant; analysis, comparison of means, ANOVA.

where Vallejo (2012) suggests that middle-class Latinos may have stronger ties and networks to poorer Latinos rather than higher-resourced Latinos. Also, the concept and practice of microlenders is much more common in immigrant source countries, so microlenders may be a more familiar pathway for immigrant entrepreneurs. And those LOBs that are able to solicit funds from commercial banks, venture capitalists, and angel investors may possess a differentiated network, as immigrants are more heavily represented in scaled LOBs.

Contact with Capital Providers

For a majority of LOBs, only two categories of capital providers were contacted at least annually; these were commercial and local banks and credit unions (Table 10.5). More than half of Latino business owners have never met with an angel investor or a microlender, and half have never met with a venture capitalist. Hence, commercial banks and local banks and credit unions are at the forefront of contact with LOBs. There are significant differences in mean GS for each category. Generally, those business owners who meet monthly or weekly with capital providers tend to have a lower GS. Latino business owners who meet weekly with their capital providers possess the lowest GSs. Importantly, this result may be in line with the many immigrant Latino business owners who also operate scaled firms or firms with the potential for scaling. More research and study are needed in this area to better understand LOB contact with capital providers, especially those providers with little present contact with LOBs.

TABLE 10.5 *Frequency of Contact with Capital Providers and Mean Generation Score*

	Venture Capitalists	Angel Investors	Microlenders	Commercial Banks	Local Banks/ Credit Unions	Debt Capital
Never	7.87	8.07	8.08	8.51	8.25	8.18
Annually	9.08	8.60	8.06	8.44	8.58	8.67
Quarterly	8.61	8.07	8.42	7.60	7.73	7.43
Monthly	7.67	7.38	7.57	7.76	7.98	8.02
Weekly	6.78	7.09	7.49	7.33	7.51	7.00
F	11.822	4.171	1.965	5.209	3.663	4.746
P	.000	.002	.098	.000	.006	.001
Never %	46.7	56.8	54.5	26.3	27.5	59.1
N	604	604	604	604	604	604

Source: SLEI Survey of U.S. Latino Business Owners 2016–2017.

Note: Analysis, comparison of means, ANOVA.

Spanish- and English-Language Use and Ability

Language use with employees and clients is the focus of this section. Those LOBs with owners who are fluent in English report never using Spanish exclusively with either workers or clients. Fluent English Latino business owners report using just English or mostly English for the majority of conversations with employees (65.4 percent) and with clients (61.9 percent). A combination of English and Spanish is used with employees about one-quarter of the time and with clients about one-fifth of the time. The use of mostly Spanish is used sparingly, 7.4 percent of the time with employees and 12.3 percent of the time with clients.[12]

Similar to English-fluent LOBs, Latino business owners who are fluent in Spanish report never using Spanish exclusively with either workers or clients. For those LOB owners fluent in Spanish, a little over half conduct business with their employees in mostly Spanish or a balance of Spanish and English, with nearly the remainder conducted in English or mostly English.[13] Even if the Latino business owner is fluent in Spanish, about half (45.9 percent) of all business with customers is conducted in English or mostly English. Nevertheless, for fluent Spanish-speaking Latino business owners, Spanish is still widely used with business clients.[14]

TABLE 10.6 *Languages Used to Conduct Business with Employees and Clients by Mean Generation Score*

	Employees		Clients	
	GS	% Response	GS	% Response
Just English	8.13	31.6	8.57	33.9
Mostly English, some Spanish	8.04	28.1	7.61	29.7
Half English, half Spanish	7.41	27.5	7.75	22.8
Mostly Spanish, some English	8.87	8.5	7.75	12.9
Just Spanish	—	—	—	—
I don't have employees (clients)	8.84	4.3	9.48	0.7
F	4.025		4.014	
P	.001		.001	
N	604		604	

Source: SLEI Survey of U.S. Latino Business Owners 2016–2017.

Note: Analysis, comparison of means, ANOVA.

Generally, the pattern of English use and fluency and higher mean GS holds and vice versa for Spanish use and fluency and lower mean GS (Table 10.6). Overall, 45.4 percent of respondents indicated that they were fluent in both Spanish and English. In terms of business revenue, bilinguals represented 47.0 percent of LOBs with revenues greater than $100,000, and bilinguals were the majority (51.0 percent) of high-revenue LOBs, those firms with $1million or more in sales.[15]

These findings in this chapter on language and acculturation complement the product-customer dichotomy offered in Chapter 3 and Chapter 11 focused on bilingualism. As the typology offered in Chapter 3 used exploratory SLEI education data, further research may explore the connection between language use and product deployment to determine how languages may facilitate or obstruct access to the noncoethnic marketplace. This may also be the case for bilingualism, as the next chapter analyzes whether dual-language acquisition hinders or aids access to the marketplace through market institutions.

Business Challenges

Form a small challenge to a large challenge, more than half of LOBs were concerned with factors that posed challenges to business operations in nine areas: finances, marketing, growth in customers, growth in the number of employees, the general economy, competition, technology, the political climate, and accounting systems (Table 10.7). There was a significant difference in GS for five business challenges that pose a challenge for business growth. These are challenges associated with finances, the general economy, technology, the political climate, and accounting systems. It is difficult to discern a pattern across the significant challenges, though it appears some large challenges exist more so for lower GS Latino business owners with regard to the political climate and accounting systems. This may be due to the timing of the survey and the election and inauguration of President Donald Trump and accounting systems keeping pace with business scaling, both impacting immigrant business owners. In further regard to accounting, perhaps less assimilated LOBs are a bit more challenged with institutional accounting and bookkeeping regulations.

There were no significant differences that pose a challenge to growth for LOBs concerning marketing, customers, employees, and competition. These responses indicate that many Latino business owners believed that these areas of potential concern were similar across generations. One possible explanation for the concurrence of GS surrounding these business challenges may be the linked fate of LOBs contextualized within the larger and shared socioeconomic reality faced by LOBs. This linked fate may be a product of the principle of replenished ethnicity (Jiménez 2010) whereby new Latino immigrant entrants restock Latino ethnic identity, forging a cultural convergence at this higher level of abstraction. Certainly, more research into business challenges across generations of Latino business owners is warranted.

Alternative to Business Ownership

Latino business owners were asked what they would choose if they were "offered a paid employment job that provides" them with their "current earnings and work conditions," provided that by accepting this position it would be costless to close their existing business or keep their LOB. More than 6 in 10 (60.4 percent) respondents chose to stay on with their LOB. Overall, this suggests that most Latino business owners are happy with their entrepreneurial decision. There was a significant difference in GS between those agreeing with the statement (8.26 percent) and those rejecting the statement (7.83 percent), whereas less acculturated Latino business owners were more interested in remaining in business than working for

TABLE 10.7. *Sources of Business Challenges and Mean Generation Score*

Source of Challenge, Growth in…	Not a Challenge		Small Challenge		Big Challenge		F	P	N
	Mean GS	% Response	Mean GS	% Response	Mean GS	% Response			
Finances	7.50	23.8	8.23	53.5	7.99	22.7	4.406	.013	604
Marketing	8.10	27.3	8.17	35.6	7.76	37.1	—	n/s	604
Customers	8.31	26.4	7.95	44.8	7.79	28.8	—	n/s	604
Employees	8.27	37.7	7.85	45.1	7.81	17.2	—	n/s	604
General economy	8.24	18.5	7.71	46.4	8.26	35.1	3.720	.025	604
Competition	7.75	22.7	7.95	45.8	8.25	31.5	—	n/s	604
Technology	7.82	31.0	8.47	46.3	7.30	22.7	11.530	.000	604
Political climate	8.56	37.4	7.87	33.3	7.43	29.3	11.400	.000	604
Accounting systems	8.29	42.3	7.82	44.5	7.68	13.2	3.131	.044	604

Source: SLEI Survey of U.S. Latino Business Owners 2016–2017.

Notes: n/s = not significant; analysis, comparison of means, ANOVA.

someone else.[16] Again, the concept of immigrant optimism may be at work where high-skill immigrants (Fernández-Reino 2016), relative to those remaining in sending countries, find entrepreneurship a valued career path.

The 2016 Presidential Election of Donald Trump

Because of the timing of the SLEI survey, LOBs were asked if they believed that the election of Trump as president of the United States would impact their business's prospects for growth, funding, and innovation. Those LOBs with significantly lower mean GSs believed that the election would have a negative impact for their business in regard to growth, funding, or innovation. And this group made up one-third to nearly half of all respondents (Table 10.8). This expected finding follows the vitriolic rhetoric of Trump as candidate and president with regard to immigrants and their contributions. Higher mean GS LOBs felt that the prospects for business growth, funding, and innovation would all improve under Trump. About one-third of Latino business owners who indicated that the presidency of Trump would have no impact for business growth and funding had significantly lower GSs. This finding may reflect an isolated view of businesses and presidential impact, immigrant optimism, or some yet unknown factor. Higher GS Latino business owners also responded that Trump would have no impact on innovation. The Trump presidency has proven to be anything but predictable. Future research as to the full impact of the Trump presidency on LOBs will be an interesting subject to examine over the course of time. This nascent political economy discussion also indicates the robustness of the GS measure for subjects beyond the environment of business.

TABLE 10.8 *President Donald Trump, LOB Prospects, and Generation Score*

	Business Growth		Funding		Innovation	
	GS	%	GS	%	GS	%
No	7.56	30.2	7.63	31.5	8.22	31.0
Yes, negatively	7.64	36.9	7.63	31.3	7.17	34.1
Yes, positively	8.81	32.9	8.62	37.2	8.61	34.9
F	17.124		11.845		20.479	
P	.000		.000		.000	
N	604		604		604	

Source: SLEI Survey of U.S. Latino Business Owners 2016–2017.

Note: Analysis, comparison of means, ANOVA.

CONCLUSION AND POLICY IMPLICATIONS

The health of the general U.S. economy depends in part on the health and success of LOBs. We find that as Latinos become more deeply acculturated into U.S. society as measured by GS, Latinos also become more involved in the entrepreneurial business landscape. Because over one-third of more than 56 million Latinos are relatively new immigrants to the United States, we expect that LOBs will continue enterprise startups at rates that far outpace (perhaps exponentially) the national average. Of particular interest are the LOBs at scale or the potential to scale (i.e., those LOBs with or within reach of $1 million in revenue), which includes a disproportionate share of immigrant entrepreneurs.

Based on the findings presented in this study, we know that new arrivals have a GS of zero, yet the average GS of LOBs is 8.0. As Latinos acculturate, more LOBs will be created; yet immigrants are also important contributors particularly at the higher end of the business revenue pipeline. Because of the magnitude of the Latino population, facilitating the success of LOBs is a critical public policy concern now and into the next couple of generations.

A clear majority of owners of Latino businesses prefer business ownership to a comparable wage or salary if given the choice. Hence, most Latino business owners are fundamentally entrepreneurial in outlook whereby they prefer self-employment, and most likely operationalize their LOB as an opportunity-oriented enterprise. Yet many LOBs are not counted in formal censuses, where a large number of businesses begin life in the informal economy, outside of the purview of government authority, oftentimes as necessity-driven enterprises with business operators with lower GSs (Pisani et al. 2017; Richardson and Pisani 2012).

We also note that this drive toward self-employment is happening beyond Spanish-language enclaves where English and the business returns to operating in English (with clients and employees) outweigh monolingualism in Spanish or even bilingualism (Spanish and English). This is somewhat paradoxical given that the largest-revenue LOBs are those with the lowest mean GS, suggesting that some of these high-revenue and low-GS firms are endowed with other attributes (e.g., greater initial funding and financial resources, higher human capital assets, English-language fluency) that spur business growth beyond what we find in this study. As Latinos acculturate, English-language ability often acquired in school becomes an asset that may translate into a future LOB. As such, schools provide an important language learning facility not only for greater civic participation but also for enhanced self-employment and business ownership opportunity.

Public policy may be explicitly directed toward LOBs with regard to financing. We find that a majority of LOBs do not solicit investments from formal banking institutions or from other capital providers such as microlenders, ventures capitalists, and angel investors. Particularly acute are a lack of access to business mentors and to online resources for lower-acculturated LOBs. In absence of formal access to capital, a majority of LOBs have solicited investments from family and friends. In order to better penetrate this segment of LOBs, more recognizable and actionable information offered in English and Spanish targeted to LOBs is recommended. Finally, soliciting firms are more likely headed by lower-acculturated business owners. While the Small Business Administration does offer its website in Spanish, accessing and acting upon government information may be problematic from the viewpoint of Latinos with mixed documented family members and the potential deportation risk associated with government interactions (Bean et al. 2015). This uneasiness may persist until comprehensive immigration reform legislation finally becomes law. This area continues to be a constraint for LOBs accessing funds to start and grow the business in an environment that views the Trump presidency with mixed results.

As this chapter only begins the exploration of acculturation and the success of LOB, future research may compare LOB success and acculturation by state and regional location (e.g., traditional and nontraditional receiving communities) and by a larger LOB sample that may permit more advanced multivariate statistical analyses. The role of citizenship and legal documentation, particularly mixed-family documentation, should also be explored. The GS does not uncover the documentation status of immigrants or distinguish between the immigrant age of arrival. While a potential limitation, the GS is not intended to consider documentation and may be refined by researchers with year of arrival data. Nevertheless, its simplicity and analytic robustness are its strengths.

Other areas fruitful for further acculturation research consideration include immigrant business ownership and enterprise scale or scalability, immigrant optimism, and the progression of informal to formal enterprises. Beyond patterns and connections presented in this chapter, further research with a larger representative LOB sample and tailored research questions may operationalize many of the chapter topics into formal hypotheses for testing. Fundamentally, this chapter has in many ways set the future stage for more formalized research analyses regarding LOBs and acculturation. This acculturation methodology modeled through the GS may also prove salient for other recent immigrant groups and business ownership such as Arab Americans.

NOTES

1. The Survey of Business Owners conducted in 2017, not currently available, will reveal the latest numbers of LOBs.
2. We use the terms acculturation and assimilation interchangeably in this chapter.
3. We use entrepreneurship, self-employment, and business owner interchangeably in this article, after Blanchflower and Oswald (1998).
4. For two recent examples, see Samaratunge, Barrett, and Rajapkse (2015) for Sri Lankan immigrant entrepreneurs in Australia and Knight (2015) for Polish immigrant entrepreneurs in the United Kingdom.
5. Following the Pew Hispanic Center (Lopez 2013), we use the terms Hispanic and Latino interchangeably.
6. To test whether the full SLEI sample and the SLEI spotlight survey sample were comparable for the GS of the respondent and parents, a comparison of means test and accompanying ANOVA was estimated. The full sample only asked birth location of the respondent and parents. The spotlight survey additionally asked the birth location of each grandparent. The two samples (weighted) were not significantly different along the GS for the respondent and parents, full sample mean = 4.52 (N = 3,865), spotlight sample mean = 4.42 (N = 616), F = 0.598, p = .439.
7. For example, the first author of this chapter has a GS of 11, where only one grandparent was foreign born (all others born in the United States). The second author has a GS of 6, where he was born in the United States and so was one parent, the others in the computation were foreign born (i.e., one parent and all grandparents).
8. Duncan et al. (2017) use the National Longitudinal Survey of Youth, 1997 (NSLY97), rounds 1-16, to study educational outcomes of Latinos between generations, conventionally constructed. The NSLY97 is a national sample of

a U.S. birth cohort from 1980-1984 that includes a representative sample of Hispanics. In rounds 10-13, the NSLY97 asks the birth location of parents and grandparents and when combined with earlier rounds of birth questions for respondents may provide a GS. The survey is somewhat skewed toward early arrivals or natural born citizens as all respondents had to be present in the United States by the ages of 12 to 16 as well as skewed to the birth cohort of 1980 to 1984. Nevertheless, a mean GS for Hispanics computed by the authors for the NSLY97 is 4.81 (with a standard deviation of 2.9, N = 1,851). This result in GS is a little higher than that calculated from the 2006 Latino National Survey reported in Table 10.2 and discussed above. To our knowledge, the NSLY97 and the 2006 are the only two nationally representative samples of Latinos where the GS may be calculated apart from the present LOB analysis.

9. Comparison of means ANOVA, F = 6.945, p = .009, N = 604.

10. This includes LOBs of Mexican heritage, Puerto Rican heritage, Cuban heritage, other Latin American heritage with GS of 8.15, 8.05, 7.39, and 7.81, respectively (comparison of means ANOVA, F = 1.911, p = .126, N = 604).

11. The GS for number of employees is as follows: zero, 8.77; 1 to 9, 8.12; 10 to 49, 7.22; 50-99, 8.11; 100 to 499, 7.30; 500 to 999, 6.48; and 1,000 or more, 6.84 (comparison of means ANOVA, F = 6.913, p = .000).

12. Cross-tabulation results indicate that LOB owners fluent in English conduct business with employees just in English 33.8 percent of the time, mostly English 25.7 percent of the time, equal amount of English and Spanish 25.7 percent of the time, mostly Spanish 7.4 percent of the time, just Spanish 0.0 percent of the time, and 4.9 percent of LOB owners reported no employees (Pearson Chi-square = 46.106, p = .001). Additional Cross-tabulation results indicate that LOB owners fluent in English conduct business with clients just in English 34.5 percent of the time, mostly English 30.9 percent of the time, equal amount of English and Spanish 21.6 percent of the time, mostly Spanish 12.3 percent of the time, just Spanish 0.0 percent of the time, and 0.8 percent of LOB owners reported no employees (Pearson Chi-square = 34.017, p = .026).

13. Cross-tabulation results indicate that LOB owners fluent in Spanish conduct business with employees just in English 16.3 percent of the time, mostly English 24.6 percent of the time, equal amount of English and Spanish 41.9 percent of the time, mostly Spanish 13.0 percent of the time, and just Spanish 0.0 percent of the time, and 4.3 percent do not have employees (Pearson Chi-square = 219.446, p = .000).

14. Cross-tabulation results indicate that LOB owners fluent in Spanish conduct business with clients just in English 15.3 percent of the time, mostly English 30.6 percent of the time, equal amount of English and Spanish 35.2 percent of the time, and mostly Spanish 18.9 percent of the time (Pearson Chi-square = 229.969, p = .000).

15. This result was significant at the .000 level, Pearson Chi-square = 37.416 (cross-tabulation).

16. Comparison of means ANOVA, F = 4.535, p = .034, N = 604.

REFERENCES

Aguilera, Michael B. 2009. "Ethnic Enclaves and the Earnings of Self-Employed Latinos." *Small Business Economics* 33(4):413–25.

Bean, Frank D., Susan K. Brown, and James D. Bachmeier. 2015. *Parents without Papers: The Progress and Pitfalls of Mexican American Integration.* New York: Russell Sage Foundation.

Blanchflower, Dwight G., and Andrew J. Oswald. 1998. "What Makes an Entrepreneur?" *Journal of Labor Economics* 16(1):26–60.

Borjas, George J., and Lawrence F. Katz. 2007. "The Evolution of the Mexican-Born Workforce in the United States." Pp. 13–55 in *Mexican Immigration to the United States*, edited by George J. Borjas. Chicago: University of Chicago Press.

Calo, Bea V. 1995. "Chicano Entrepreneurs in Rural California: An Empirical Analysis." PhD diss., University of California, Davis.

Curci, Roberto, and Robert Mackoy. 2010. "Immigrant Business Enterprises: A Classification Framework Conceptualization and Test." *Thunderbird International Business Review* 52(2):107–21.

Dávila, Alberto, and Marie T. Mora. 2013. *Hispanic Entrepreneurs in the 2000s: An Economic Profile and Policy Implications.* Stanford, CA: Stanford University Press.

Duncan, Brian, Jeffrey Groggor, Ana S. Leon, and Stephen J. Trejo. 2017. "The Generational Progress of Mexican Americans." NBER Working Paper No. 24067. http://www.nber.org/papers/w24067.

Escobar, Gabriel. 2006. "The Optimistic Immigrant." Pew Research Center. http://www.pewresearch.org/2006/05/30/the-optimistic-immigrant/.

Fairlie, Robert W., and Javier Miranda. 2017. "Taking the Leap: The Determinants of Entrepreneurs Hiring Their First Employee." *Journal of Economics & Management Strategy* 26(1):3–34.

Fernández-Reino, Mariña. 2016. "Immigrant Optimism or Anticipated Discrimination Explaining the First Educational Transition of Ethnic Minorities in England." *Research in Social Stratification and Mobility* 46(December):141–56.

Fraga, Luis, John A. Garcia, Rodney Hero, Michael Jones-Correa, Valerie Martinez-Ebers, and Gary M. Segura. 2012. *Latinos in the New Millennium: An Almanac of Opinion, Behavior, and Policy Preferences*. New York: Cambridge University Press.

Gershon, Sarah A., and Adrian D. Pantoja. 2014. "Pessimists, Optimists, and Skeptics: The Consequences of Transnational Ties for Latino Immigrant Naturalization." *Social Science Quarterly* 95(2):328–42.

Ilhan-Nas, Tulay, Kadar Sahin, and Zuhal Cilingir. 2011. "International Ethnic Entrepreneurship: Antecedents, Outcomes and Environmental Context." *International Business Review* 20(6):614–26.

Jiménez, Tomás R. 2010. *Replenished Ethnicity: Mexican Americans, Immigration, and Identity*. Berkeley: University of California Press.

Knight, Julie. 2015. "Migrant Employment in the Ethnic Economy: Why Do Some Migrants Become Ethnic Entrepreneurs and Others Co-Ethnic Workers?" *Journal of International Migration and Integration* 16(3):575–92.

Light, Ivan. 2005. "The Ethnic Economy." Pp. 403–25 in *The Handbook of Economic Sociology*, 2nd ed., edited by Neil J. Smesler and Richard Swedberg. New York: Russell Sage Foundation.

López, Gustavo, and Eileen Patten. 2015. "The Impact of Slowing Immigration: Foreign-Born Share Falls among 14 Largest U.S. Hispanic Groups." Pew Research Center, September 15. http://www.pewhispanic.org/files/2015/09 /2015-09-15_hispanic-origin-profiles-summary-report_FINAL.pdf.

Lopez, Mark H. 2013. "3: Hispanic Identity." Pew Research Center. https://www .pewresearch.org/hispanic/2013/10/22/3-hispanic-identity/.

Lopez, Mark H., Ana Gonzalez-Barrera, and Eileen Patton. 2013. "Closing the Digital Divide: Latinos and Technology Adoption." Pew Hispanic Center, March 7. http://assets.pewresearch.org/wp-content/uploads/sites/7/2013/03 /Latinos_Social_Media_and_Mobile_Tech_03-2013_final.pdf.

Malkin, Victoria. 2004. "'We Go to Get Ahead': Gender and Status in Two Mexican Migrant Communities." *Latin American Perspectives* 31(5):75–99.

Orozco, Marlene, Paul Oyer, and Jerry I. Porras. 2018. "2017 State of Latino Entrepreneurship Report." Stanford Latino Entrepreneurship Initiative, Graduate School of Business, Stanford University. https://www.gsb.stanford .edu/faculty-research/publications/state-latino-entrepreneurship-2017.

Pisani, Michael J. 2012. "Latino Informal Immigrant Entrepreneurs in South Texas: Opportunities and Challenges for Unauthorized New Venture Creation and Persistence." *American Journal of Business* 27(1):27–39.

Pisani, Michael J. 2013. "Cross-Border Consumption of Informal and Underground Goods: A Case Study of Alternative Consumerism in South Texas." *Social Science Quarterly* 94(1):242–62.

Pisani, Michael J. 2014. "Utilizing Informal Household Work Substitutes along the U.S.-Mexico Border: Evidence from South Texas." *Journal of Borderlands Studies* 29(3):303–17.

Pisani, Michael J., and Carlos Sepulveda. 2012. "Conceptualizing Household Consumption Informality in the South Texas Borderlands." *Perspectives on Global Development and Technology* 11(2):320–36.

Pisani, Michael J., and Chad Richardson. 2012. "Cross-Border Informal Entrepreneurs across the South Texas–Northern Mexico Boundary." *Entrepreneurship & Regional Development* 24(3–4):105–21.

Pisani, Michael J., Joseph M. Guzman, Chad Richardson, Carlos Sepulveda, and Lyonel Laulié. 2017. "Small Business Enterprises and Latino Entrepreneurship: An Enclave or Mainstream Activity in South Texas?" *Journal of International Entrepreneurship* 15(3):295–323.

Portes, Alejandro, and Rubén G. Rumbaut. 2014. *Immigrant America: A Portrait*. 4th ed. Oakland: University of California Press.

Portes, Alejandro, and William Haller. 2005. "The Informal Economy." Pp. 403–25 in *The Handbook of Economic Sociology*, 2nd ed., edited by Neil J. Smesler and Richard Swedberg. New York: Russell Sage Foundation.

Richardson, Chad, and Michael J. Pisani. 2012. *The Informal and Underground Economy of the South Texas Border*. Austin: University of Texas Press.

Richardson, Chad, and Michael J. Pisani. 2017. *Batos, Bolillos, Pochos and Pelados: Class and Culture on the South Texas Border*. Rev. ed. Austin: University of Texas Press.

Richardson, Chad, and Rosalva Resendiz. 2006. *On the Edge of the Law: Culture, Labor & Deviance on the South Texas Border*. Austin: University of Texas Press.

Rivers, Douglas, Jerry I. Porras, Natassia Rodriguez-Ott, and Phil Pompa. 2016. "State of Latino Entrepreneurship 2016." Stanford Latino Entrepreneurship Initiative, Graduate School of Business, Stanford University. https://www.gsb.stanford.edu/faculty-research/publications/state-latino-entrepreneurship-2016.

Rochín, Refugio I. 2013. "Rural Latinos: An Assessment of Evolving Conditions." Pp. 81–94 in *The Economic Status of the Hispanic Population: Selected Essays*, edited by Marie T. Mora and Alberto Dávila. Charlotte, NC: Information Age Publishing.

Rochín, Refugio I., Rogelio Saenz, Steve Hampton, and Bea Calo. 1998. "Colonias and Chicano/a Entrepreneurs in Rural California." Research Report No. 16, Julian Samora Research Institute, Michigan State University.

Samaratunge, Ramanie, Rowena Barrett, and Tissa Rajapkse. 2015. "Sri Lankan Entrepreneurs in Australia: Chance or Choice?" *Journal of Small Business and Enterprise Development* 22(4):782–96.

Shinnar, Rachel S., Michael B. Aguilera, and Thomas S. Lyons. 2011. "Co-Ethnic Markets: Financial Penalty or Opportunity." *International Business Review* 20(6):646–58.

Striffler, Steve. 2007. "Neither Here nor There: Mexican Immigrant Workers and the Search for Home." *American Ethnologist* 34(4):674–88.

Telles, Edward E., and Vilma Ortiz. 2008. *Generations of Exclusion: Mexican Americans, Assimilation, and Race.* New York: Russell Sage Foundation.

Vallejo, Jody A. 2012. *Barrios to Burbs: The Making of the Mexican American Middle Class.* Stanford, CA: Stanford University Press.

Verdaguer, María E. 2009. *Class, Ethnicity, Gender and Latino Entrepreneurship.* New York: Routledge.

Wang, Qingfang, and Wei Li. 2007. "Entrepreneurship, Ethnicity and Local Contexts: Hispanic Entrepreneurs in Three U.S. Southern Metropolitan Areas." *GeoJournal* 68(2–3):167–82.

Yang, Chulguen, Stephen M. Colarelli, Kyunghee Han, and Robert Page. 2011. "Start-Up and Hiring Practices of Immigrant Entrepreneurs: An Empirical Study from an Evolutionary Psychological Perspective." *International Business Review* 20(6):636–45.

Zarrugh, Laura H. 2007. "From Workers to Owners: Latino Entrepreneurs in Harrisonburg, Virginia." *Human Organization* 66(3):240–48.

Zhou, Min, and John R. Logan. 1989. "Returns on Human Capital in Ethnic Enclaves: New York City's Chinatown." *American Sociological Review* 54(5):809–20.

CHAPTER 11

The Business of Language: Latino Entrepreneurs, Language Use, and Firm Performance

Alberto Dávila, Michael J. Pisani, and Gerardo Miranda

INTRODUCTION

Whether a Hispanic ethnic enclave in South Texas or a Latino-owned[1] business (LOB) in Michigan, it is not unusual for customers and business owners to interact in Spanish, English, or some mixture of both. While geography and ethnic density may influence language interaction among LOBs and their clientele, the recent diffusion of Hispanics and Latino-owned enterprises throughout the United States does not limit potential language interaction.

The 2012 U.S. Survey of Business Owners (SBO) reports that 89.5 percent of Hispanic enterprises conduct business in English.[2] The same survey also notes that 58.2 percent of Hispanic enterprises conduct business in Spanish. As far as sales magnitude and business transaction language for LOBs, the SBO finds a similar pattern for business revenue matching transactions by language use (i.e., Spanish or English) and sales.[3] While the SBO does not report specifically on bilingualism, clearly many LOBs are able to transact business and make sales in both English and Spanish with customers. These figures also suggest that some LOBs transact business in a single language, primarily English or Spanish.[4]

Contextually, LOBs operating in economic environments where English and Spanish language use is random expand their customer reach if they are "able to respond rapidly and flexibly with multiple language options" (Alarcón et al. 2014:111). Not doing so may hurt or limit business opportunities. In high-context cultures (where implicit and nuanced communication may be as important or more prevalent than explicit communication [Hall, 1976]) such as that found in Hispanic populations and high client customer contact sectors such as health care and public services, those most flexible and able to respond quickly are bilinguals and bilingualism, which thus may be an important attribute within the labor market (Alarcón et al. 2014; Morando 2013). That said, in a social context, bilingualism might hinder business transaction through labor-market discrimination and could be associated with an adverse cultural trait by majority groups, as we note below.

Within these three language-transaction profiles—English only, Spanish only, and bilingual (Spanish and English)—in connection with business performance, our central research question is "Are bilingual Hispanic entrepreneurs at a relative advantage or disadvantage in the business sector?" Utilizing primarily a unique and recent data source from the Stanford Latino Entrepreneurship Initiative (SLEI), this chapter considers the relationship between the language(s) used by Hispanic entrepreneurs and their business outcomes. In particular, we study how proficiency in Spanish, English, and both (i.e., bilingual entrepreneurs) relate to firm profitability, firm size by number of employees, and business revenues.

In the following conceptual discussion, our intent is not to advocate for any of the conceptual arguments. Rather, we provide a literature review on salient issues and note that the association between bilingualism and entrepreneurial outcomes is not conceptually clear. Indeed, this conceptual discussion highlights the importance of using more advanced and robust empirical methods with more specific and inclusive data to disentangle conceptual issues between bilingualism and entrepreneurial outcomes. We next discuss the conceptualization of bilingualism as a benefit and then as a cost. For a discussion on the neutrality (i.e., neither a cost nor a benefit) of bilingualism, see Fry and Lowell (2003).

LITERATURE AND CONCEPTUAL ISSUES

Foundational to our study are works rooted in human capital theory, sociolinguistics, social network theory, and labor market discrimination, with some influences rooted in neoclassical and psychological perspectives. For example, human capital refers to the skill-based investment (e.g., education and training) in personal development. We note that labor market discrimination describes an environment where market actors utilize observable characteristics (e.g., race, ethnicity, gender) to create unequal treatment in market and interpersonal exchanges. We discuss these foundations within the framework of bilingualism as a potential benefit and/ or cost to bilingual individuals here.

Bilingualism as a Benefit

In particular, the study of language and business outcomes for LOBs can be studied within the conceptual framework of second-language acquisition in a variety of fields. As a human capital investment, for example, individuals or entrepreneurs with multiple language proficiencies will reap higher returns (i.e., incomes). In the case of Spanish, English, and the ability to speak both languages (bilingualism), human capital theory would expect that localized Spanish-speaking entrepreneurs would do relatively well in Spanish-speaking areas. The same expectation would hold for localized English-proficient speakers in areas with a large share of English speakers. Bilingual speakers would do well in both language environments (i.e., Spanish and English) with a mixed-language clientele market. Where the LOB market is national, the ability of the entrepreneur to operate within the predominant national language would reap higher returns. This scenario may posit an earnings ceiling for bilinguals whereby the need for second-language ability is less important at higher rungs of national business activity (Alarcón et al. 2014).

This human capital rationale is supported by a U.S. study of bilingual (English and Spanish) nurses in which wage premiums were associated with bilingualism (Kalist 2005). In general, bilingual nurses earned a 5.0 percent wage premium. In areas with a higher concentration of Hispanics in the overall population, bilingual nurses earned a 3.3 percent wage premium, the premium reduced in part by the availability of more Spanish speakers among staff and supply of nurses (Kalist 2005; Alarcón et al. 2014). Using U.S. 2000 census data comparing Hispanics who are bilingual (English and Spanish) against Hispanics who are monolingual English speakers, Cortina, de la Garza, and Pinto (2007) find a 2.7 percent wage premium for bilingualism. Morando (2013) in her qualitative study in Dalton, Georgia, found that second-generation Latinos were able to use their bilingual language abilities along with other cultural resources early in their careers to secure employment and advance professionally.

Hence, bilingual entrepreneurs would appear to have a human capital advantage over their monolingual counterparts. With a bilingual clientele, workers, and suppliers more readily accessible to them, bilingual LOBs would stand to reap relatively higher returns. These returns may be amplified in high cultural context and contact environments.

The social network theory provides an alternative view as to why different bilingual entrepreneurs may be better off. From the perspective of this theory, one could argue that bilingual entrepreneurs benefit over their monolingual counterparts owing to favorable or multicultural living environments and information that are broader in scope by virtue of being fluent in two languages. As Morando (2013) notes, being fluent in English and Spanish languages allows entrance into both English- and Spanish-speaking networks. Some literature has found that of benefits of bilingualism in relation to networks can be observed from an early age, as Mexican-origin youths were found to have larger information networks (Stanton-Salazar and Dornbush 1995).

In addition, having access to both English- and Spanish-speaking networks can be viewed as a benefit of bilingualism from the perspective of structural holes or gaps and brokerage (Burt 1992, 2004). According to Burt (2004), good ideas can emerge in the intersection of social worlds, as brokerage across structural holes can provide a wider vision of and connection between groups. In the case of Latino entrepreneurs, bilinguals could be considered the brokers between the Spanish- and English-speaking business environments; hence, bilinguals may increase the likelihood that good ideas emerge and market gaps are filled.

As such, an entrepreneur who can communicate effectively with the Spanish- and English-speaking populations would be expected to have access to networks in both populations, while one who is monolingual or speaks mostly one language would have limited access to language systems and networks that only converse in the entrepreneur's one language. For entrepreneurial purposes, bilinguals' wider network could include broader customer and supplier bases, employee pool, channels of funding, and visibility of ideas than would otherwise not be seen. Therefore, one would expect that bilingual entrepreneurs may have more information accessed through multiple networks by virtue of speaking two languages.

Furthermore, research suggests that a feedback loop exists in the sense that bilingualism may lead to an expanded network, and a bilingual network may also lead to increased bilingualism proficiency. This relation among bilingualism and social networks has been observed in the case of individuals whose second language was Basque (Cenoz and Valencia 1993) and Swedish (Wiklund 2002). Similarly, Smith (2002) finds that linguistic proficiency among migrants was relative to the proportion of majority-group members in the migrant's social networks. This might suggest that bilinguals benefit from bilingual networks in a couple of ways. Bilingual networks provide bilinguals with an expanded network for resource acquisition as well as by enhancing their linguistic proficiency in both languages; together these effects may spill over into other competencies, such as those related to productivity. A research insight from this perspective is that it might allow researchers to identify bilinguals who have an active bilingual social network. On the other hand, having high fluency in both languages as a bilingual individual without a concomitant bilingual social network would eventually yield a relatively lower proficiency in the language(s) lacking in the network.

Bilingualism as a Cost

The study of language and business outcomes, particularly for the case of Hispanic entrepreneurs, may also be investigated within the context of language as a variable that leads to labor market discrimination. To the extent that language "signals" ethnicity or place of origin, Spanish-speaking Hispanic entrepreneurs might be pushed into self-employment because of a scarcity of employment opportunities (Dávila and Mora 2013). Furthermore, severe discrimination and resource constraints may prompt a portion of self-employed Hispanics to opt out of the formal economy and into the gray economy (Light 2005; Pisani et al. 2017).

These ideas can be framed within the context of the concept of business language. Language can be seen as having an influence in trust and being the immediate carrier of culture (Zhang and Harzing 2016:776). Additionally, language can also smooth social interactions (Arrow 1974).

Cultural values have also been associated with business language in the literature (Hall 1960). Relationships are negotiated by linguistic styles in communication that are culturally learned and thus vary by culture (Tannen 1995a, 1995b). Linguistic styles may include tone of voice, use of pauses, and pacing (George, Jones, and Gonzalez 1998). In this literature, care is taken to note that shared language does not suggest error-free understanding, because cultural values manifested through communication styles can act as barriers to analyzing and decoding explicit and implicit messages (Henderson 2005). As such, language and cultural competencies may not always be perfectly aligned (Peltokorpi and Schneider 2009). This may be particularly evident when individuals do not fully speak the same language, even though these groups still understand their cultures completely (e.g., bicultural if not fully bilingual).

According to Hogg and Terry (2000), social identity theory predicts that individuals categorize themselves and others to establish and maintain self-esteem and reduce uncertainty (see also Abrams and Brown 1989; Brown 2000; Tajfel 1974). These social categorizations might lead to long-term bias and discriminatory behavior (Hsee 1996), leading to problems when a social comparison is used to make decisions regarding the success of others (Tenbrunsel et al. 2000). Lauring (2008) extends social identity theory by introducing language as an object that is negotiated to categorize people and create identities. Furthermore, in the sociolinguistics literature other contexts are used to relate business language to potential economic outcomes. In particular, the conceptualization of how an individual's language can be used is considered in positive or negative differentiations (Giles, Bourhis, and Taylor 1977; Giles and Johnson 1981), as is the idea that ethnic-language groups view language as a characteristic marker of identity (Giles and Byrnes 1982).

Moreover, net of language proficiency, we add the foregoing conceptual possibility that accent may be "distasteful" to some customers, suppliers, or employers and may stigmatize (Gluszek and Dovidio 2010) and adversely impact business outcomes and earnings (Dávila, Bohara, and Saenz 1993) or employment opportunities (Carlson and McHenry 2006). Following the discussion above in terms of the language of business, an accent may therefore be used as an insidious signal or false proxy for dishonesty (Lev-Ari and Keysar 2010) or legal status of an entrepreneur or employee (Dávila et al. 1993), which may negatively influence business outcomes to the extent that it might create paid-employment scarcity and be another source of push-type monopsonistic practices. While it is much more likely that the accent is noticeable when conducting business in English (Hosoda and Stone-Romero 2010), accents in Spanish for Hispanic entrepreneurs are also possible and may disrupt social interactions with native Spanish speakers (Richardson and Pisani 2017). (Within this neoclassical discrimination theory framework, bilingual Latino entrepreneurs may also face an economic bias from other tangible attributes such as appearance [i.e., skin color], ethnic name, and socioeconomic networks.) It should also be noted that language proficiency can be associated with the proportion of speakers in the social network (Cenoz and Valencia 1993; Wiklund 2002), and some research has shown that accent can be seen as an important part of a speaker's social identity that conveys a considerable amount of social information (Edwards 1999; Giles and Johnson 1981; Lippi-Green 1997).

With regard to some relevant empirical work related to accent and outcomes, Spanish-influenced accents have been found to yield lower-status ratings by American listeners (Bradac and Wisegarver 1984; Brennan and Brennan 1981a, 1981b; De la Zerda and Hopper 1979; Giles et al. 1995; Rey 1997; Ryan and Carranza 1975). In other studies, those with a Mexican accent have been perceived as less intelligent, honest, credible, and professional than the standard American accent (DeShields and de los Santos 2000). This may lead to negative biases, particularly for those associated with disadvantaged and low-prestige minority groups (Hosoda and Stone-Romero 2010).

Additionally, researchers note that accent can be a powerful out-group cue (Gluszek and Dovidio 2010; Lev-Ari and Keysar 2010) whereby non-native speakers are judged as being less credible than native speakers when reciting the same statement (Lev-Ari and Keysar 2010). Indeed, a nonnative accent can be a stronger negative cue than race in the United States (Kinzler et al. 2009) and can bring forth a negative stigma (Nguyen 1993; Ryan 1983; Wated and Sanchez 2006; Weyant 2007). For example, some work has shown that a Hispanic accent, particularly one that is combined with a Hispanic-sounding name, can lead to higher unfavorable judgments (Purkiss et al. 2006).

However, it is important to note that Latino-accented English can have an upside in some cases. Hopkins (2014) studied Latino-accented English in a controlled psychological experiment of a large nationally representative U.S. sample exclusive of Latinos. Hopkins sought to determine whether Latino-accented English positively, negatively, or neutrally impacted viewer perceptions of a video clip focused on immigration policy. His findings suggest a positive view of immigrant-accented English, perhaps indicating that accented English is a marker of a sincere effort (eliciting social trust) to assimilate through language.

SURVEY DATA, METHODOLOGY, AND SAMPLE SUMMARY STATISTICS

The primary data source utilized in this chapter for the exploration of analysis relating bilingualism and business outcomes is derived from the SLEI surveys of the fall of 2016 and spring of 2017. The nationally representative survey was conducted in two rounds, the first in the fall of 2016 and the second in the spring of 2017 (described in detail in Chapter 5, this volume). To correct for unevenness in survey collection, associated weights were calculated and included in the data set. In all, 4,787 Latino enterprises were surveyed in the fall, with an additional follow-up survey of 616 chosen from the original respondents. As language use was emphasized in the second round of surveys, we utilize respondent data from both rounds of surveys; hence, our results are limited to the number of respondents completing the second survey round (n=616).

Four language-use questions focus our study: (1) "In what language(s) do you conduct business with your employees?" (2) "In what language(s) do you conduct business with your clients or customers?" (3) "How fluent are you in English?" (4) "How fluent are you in Spanish?" The possible response categories for the first two questions are (a) just English; (b) mostly English, some Spanish; (c) half English, half Spanish; (d) mostly Spanish, some English; e) just Spanish; and (f) I don't have employees. The possible response categories for the fluency questions include (a) completely fluent, (b) advanced, (c) conversational, (d) basic, and (e) know a few words at most. Combining the fluency questions, we were able to construct a new variable for bilingualism (fluency in Spanish and English).

In our multivariate analyses, respondents who answered either "completely fluent" or "advanced" in both questions were considered to be bilinguals. Those who responded "completely fluent" or "advanced" for English fluency and "conversational," "basic," or "know a few words, at most" for Spanish fluency were considered to be English-dominant. Those who responded the opposite—"completely fluent" or "advanced" for Spanish fluency and "conversational," "basic," or "know a few words, at most" for English fluency—were considered Spanish-dominants. This operationalization of bilingualism was considered adequate, taking into consideration that these are self-reported responses. As such, individuals who report speaking both languages in complete fluency or report being advanced in both languages are likely to be individuals who use both languages. Similarly, individuals are likely to favor their dominant (i.e., advanced, completely fluent) language over a language for which they believe to have a conversational or basic skill, particularly in conducting business.

Furthermore, we conducted a robustness test to consider the different possibilities related to gradations in bilingualism. First, we tested a more exclusive definition that only considers those who were completely fluent in both languages. Then we tested a more inclusive definition that included "completely fluent," "advanced," and "conversational." In both cases, our results did not change in a meaningful way.

In addition, we used the variable representing the entrepreneurs' proportion of Hispanic clients in an effort to capture their immediate language environment in which they conduct business. While the SLEI data set provides information in regard to the businesses' zip codes and states, we believe that the proportion of Hispanic clientele is a more meaningful variable for the purpose of our research endeavor. That is, we seek to examine how the language of entrepreneurs impacts their business outcomes. Following our conceptual discussion, language can be a skill or resource but also a marker of identity. Thus, while knowing the language of entrepreneurs' clientele would be ideal, this is a limitation of the data set. However, the variable of Hispanic clientele proportions might hint at the view of language as a characteristic marker of identity by ethnic-language groups (Giles and Byrnes 1982).

Another limitation regarding the language variables in this data set is the question of what language was acquired first, as an English-dominant entrepreneur who acquired Spanish would probably culturally differ from a Spanish-dominant entrepreneur who acquired English. In an attempt to address this possibility, we control for immigration in our analyses, as immigrants are more likely to acquire English after Spanish, while natives are more likely to acquire Spanish after English or both languages simultaneously. While this may not be the best methodological alternative, it is the only one available in the current data set. Future surveys might ask entrepreneurs which language was acquired first. Along this vein, future surveys might also ask a question that captures the likelihood or extent to which bilinguals might code-switch between English and Spanish. Understanding the extent to which bilinguals switch between English and Spanish may contribute to the discussion on bilingualism being a cost or a benefit and whether bilinguals are able to mitigate potential costs and capitalize on potential benefits.

In addition to the language questions, we constructed three outcome measures focused on profits and scale, year: profits (reported for 2015), number of current employees (reported for fall 2016), and annual gross revenues (reported for 2015). The response categories for profits are (a) profits, (b) losses, and (c) breakeven. The categorical responses for number of employees are (a) zero, (b) 1 to 9, (c) 10 to 49, and (d) 50 or more. Finally, annual revenues are categorized as (a) under $10,000, (b) $10,000 to $49,999, (c) $50,000 to $99,999, (d) $100,000 to $499,999, and (e) $500,000 and more.

Table 11.1 provides the sample summary statistics for languages used to conduct business with employees (Panel A) and clients and customers (Panel B) and age, gender, immigrant, Hispanic country of origin, and education. Generally, older Latino entrepreneurs are more English-dominant with employees and customers than younger Latino entrepreneurs. This pattern is similar for Latina entrepreneurs vis-à-vis their male counterparts. Immigrants rely more on Spanish for communicating with employees and customers than do nonimmigrant Latino entrepreneurs; however, most entrepreneurs are English-proficient. Entrepreneurs of Puerto Rican heritage are the most English-dominant, though more than half of Mexican-origin and Cuban-origin entrepreneurs communicate with employees and customers in English. Education, segmented by those with and without a college degree, shows a similar pattern of English dominance in communicating with employees and customers.

Table 11.2 illustrates the sample summary statistics for language fluency (English, Spanish, and bilingual) and age, gender, immigrant, Hispanic country of origin, and education. Examining age, younger Latino business owners possess greater Spanish language facility; older Latino entrepreneurs are more fluent in English. Male or female, most Latino business owners are fluent in English, whereas male business owners have a higher proportion of Spanish-language fluency. As expected with immigration status, those Latino entrepreneurs born outside the United States have a relatively high level of Spanish-language fluency compared to nonimmigrant Latino entrepreneurs and vice versa for English-language fluency, although immigrant business owners do reveal a generally high level of English-language fluency. With regard to heritage, Cubans have retained a higher share of Spanish fluency and exhibit a lower relative level of English fluency in an environment where Latino business owners are generally well endowed with English-language competency. Education and

TABLE 11.1 Sample Summary Statistics: LOB Languages Used in Conducting Business with Employees and Clients

Languages Used to Conduct Business with...	Mean Age	Gender		Immigrant		Country of Origin (Latin America)				Education	
Panel A: Employees		Male (%)	Female (%)	Yes (%)	No (%)	Mexico (%)	Puerto Rico (%)	Cuba (%)	Other (%)	College Degree* (%)	Less Than College Degree (%)
Just English	45.9	30.5	42.9	17.9	43.4	35.3	46.8	28.6	33.5	35.2	38.8
Mostly English, some Spanish	43.6	23.5	24.4	14.7	27.1	20.5	23.4	14.3	33.0	19.6	29.5
Half English, half Spanish	37.5	32.8	22.8	48.7	20.4	34.3	16.2	31.0	23.9	31.7	22.5
Mostly Spanish, some English	36.9	9.9	4.6	14.7	4.9	8.8	11.7	7.1	2.3	11.0	2.7
Just Spanish	34.5	0.3	0.0	0.0	0.0	0.0	0.9	0.0	0.0	0.3	0.0
I don't have employees (clients)	41.1	3.0	5.3	3.8	4.3	1.1	0.9	19.0	7.4	2.3	6.6
Panel B: Clients or Customers		Male (%)	Female (%)	Yes (%)	No (%)	Mexico (%)	Puerto Rico (%)	Cuba (%)	Other (%)	College Degree* (%)	Less Than College Degree (%)
Just English	47.0	31.2	43.7	28.2	40.7	29.3	42.2	29.3	48.6	31.8	45.1
Mostly English, some Spanish	39.9	27.2	40.7	25.6	36.9	43.5	25.7	19.5	28.0	33.2	35.0
Half English, half Spanish	38.3	27.9	9.6	30.1	14.8	20.1	19.3	31.7	14.3	23.4	12.8
Mostly Spanish, some English	40.9	9.6	4.0	13.5	4.5	6.0	11.9	0.0	6.3	10.7	1.6
Just Spanish	22.0	1.0	0.0	0.0	0.7	1.1	0.0	0.0	0.0	0.9	0.0
I don't have employees (clients)	37.0	3.0	2.0	2.6	2.5	0.0	0.9	19.5	2.9	0.0	5.4

Source: SLEI Survey of U.S. Latino Business Owners 2016–2017 (weighted).

* College degree includes associate degree or higher.

TABLE 11.2 Sample Summary Statistics: LOB Language Fluency

Language Fluency	Gender			Immigrant		Country of Origin (Latin America)				Education	
	Mean Age	Male (%)	Female (%)	Yes (%)	No (%)	Mexico (%)	Puerto Rico (%)	Cuba (%)	Other (%)	College Degree* (%)	Less Than College Degree (%)
Panel A: English											
Completely fluent	42.3	88.7	90.4	71.2	96.0	89.0	95.4	73.2	89.8	87.2	93.0
Advanced	36.9	7.0	5.9	15.4	3.4	10.3	2.8	4.9	4.0	9.3	2.7
Conversational	47.6	4.0	3.6	13.5	0.4	0.7	0.9	22.0	6.3	3.2	4.3
Basic	31.8	0.3	0.0	0.0	0.2	0.0	0.9	0.0	0.0	0.3	0.0
Know a few words at best	34.0	0.0	0.0	0.0	0.0	0.0	0.0	0.0	0.0	0.0	0.0
Panel B: Spanish	Mean Age	Male (%)	Female (%)	Yes (%)	No (%)	Mexico (%)	Puerto Rico (%)	Cuba (%)	Other (%)	College Degree* (%)	Less Than College Degree (%)
Completely fluent	39.5	48.7	33.7	69.0	31.3	43.5	28.2	65.0	40.0	42.3	39.3
Advanced	38.3	12.7	16.2	14.8	14.5	15.5	12.7	10.0	14.3	19.4	7.8
Conversational	43.2	15.0	14.5	3.2	18.8	13.4	20.0	17.5	13.1	17.4	10.9
Basic	48.9	9.0	14.9	1.3	15.6	6.7	18.2	5.0	18.3	10.4	14.4
Know a few words at best	45.9	14.7	20.8	11.6	19.9	20.8	20.9	2.5	14.3	10.4	27.6
Panel C: Bilingual	Mean Age	Male (%)	Female (%)	Yes (%)	No (%)	Mexico (%)	Puerto Rico (%)	Cuba (%)	Other (%)	College Degree* (%)	Less Than College Degree (%)
Yes	38.9	41.5	24.8	45.2	33.1	35.5	26.4	42.9	31.3	67.9	34.5
No	43.8	58.5	75.2	54.8	66.9	64.5	73.6	57.1	68.8	32.1	65.5

Source: SLEI Survey of U.S. Latino Business Owners 2016–2017 (weighted).

* College degree includes associate degree or higher.

bilingualism show a stark contrast between those with a college degree and those without. Latino entrepreneurs with a college degree display extensive bilingualism.

Table 11.3 displays our three business outcome measures utilizing the same variables from Tables 11.1 and 11.2 (i.e., age, gender, immigrant, country of origin, and education). Table 11.3 is included for comparison purposes. Highlights from Table 11.3 include larger profits, number of employees, and revenues for men vis-à-vis women and weaker profits for Latino entrepreneurs of Puerto Rican heritage. Table 11.4 presents the business outcome measures of business profits (Panel A), number of employees (Panel B), and revenue (Panel C) in conjunction with language facility in English, Spanish, and both English and Spanish (bilingual). Table 11.4 highlights include basic Spanish-language facility, smaller group profits, and a larger breakeven group as compared to English and bilingual responses. In terms of the number of employees, most LOBs are small concerns. This is also true of business revenue, with bilinguals outperforming monolinguals.

RESULTS

Beyond descriptive statistics, we employ a set of multivariate analyses to better discern business outcomes for LOBs, noting language influences. As we noted in the conceptual issues section earlier, the relationship between bilingualism and business outcomes is ambiguous a priori. The first analysis considers profitability with two estimations—breakeven (through a probit) and profit, breakeven, and loss (through an ordered probit). The second analysis considers firm size utilizing revenue and number of employees (both through ordered probit estimations). In this analysis we considered the characteristics of the entrepreneur (i.e., language, age, gender, education, immigration, and ethnicity), the firm (i.e., firm age), clientele (i.e., proportion of Hispanic clientele), and industry.

Profitability

In our probit regression model, where breakeven for LOBs is the dependent variable (breakeven =1, otherwise = 0), we find the following independent variables significant: English-dominant (English-language dominance), firm age (firm maturity), female (gender of business owner), college (college

TABLE 11.3 *Sample Summary Statistics: LOB Profits, Number of Employees, and Revenues*

	Mean Age	Gender		Immigrant		Country of Origin (Latin America)				Education	
		Male (%)	Female (%)	Yes (%)	No (%)	Mexico (%)	Puerto Rico (%)	Cuba (%)	Other (%)	College Degree* (%)	Less Than College Degree (%)
Panel A: Profits											
Profit	41.2	82.7	69.2	80.9	74.0	84.0	55.5	95.1	71.0	74.3	77.9
Loss	48.1	5.0	9.3	5.1	8.1	3.5	10.9	4.9	11.4	8.4	5.8
Breakeven	42.3	12.3	21.5	14.0	17.9	12.4	33.6	0.0	17.6	17.3	16.3
Panel B: Number of Employees											
None	42.5	27.4	47.2	32.7	37.2	37.5	43.2	7.1	36.6	37.3	34.2
1 to 9	43.4	58.3	41.3	54.5	48.0	48.1	35.1	66.7	57.1	46.8	53.7
10 to 49	34.9	10.7	6.6	7.7	9.0	11.3	12.6	4.8	2.3	9.0	8.2
50 or more	40.1	6.3	5.0	5.1	5.8	3.2	9.0	21.4	4.0	6.9	3.9
Panel C: Revenues ($1,000s)											
Less than 10	41.5	28.2	20.8	24.4	24.6	19.8	19.1	41.0	31.8	26.9	21.4
10 to 49.9	43.2	31.9	55.4	50.0	41.7	43.1	52.7	17.9	43.8	40.5	48.2
50 to 99.9	41.1	13.3	8.3	7.7	11.8	10.2	10.0	7.7	13.1	9.2	12.8
100 to 499.9	41.7	21.3	12.2	12.8	17.6	20.5	16.4	25.6	9.1	17.3	15.6
500 or more	39.7	5.3	3.3	5.1	4.2	6.4	1.8	7.7	2.3	6.1	1.9

Source: SLEI Survey of U.S. Latino Business Owners 2016–2017 (weighted).

* College degree includes associate degree or higher.

TABLE 11.4 Sample Summary Statistics: LOB Profits, Number of Employees, and Revenue and Language Facility

	English (%)					Spanish (%)					Bilingual (%)	
Panel A: Profits	Completely Fluent	Advanced	Conversational	Basic	Few Words*	Completely Fluent	Advanced	Conversational	Basic	Few Words*	Yes	No
Profit	74.8	82.1	91.3	100.0	—	79.4	82.8	85.2	45.9	75.0	76.0	75.7
Loss	8.0	0.0	0.0	—	—	3.2	2.3	6.8	8.1	20.4	4.0	8.9
Breakeven	17.2	17.9	8.7	—	—	17.3	14.9	8.0	45.9	4.6	20.0	15.3
Panel B: Number of Employees	Completely Fluent	Advanced	Conversational	Basic	Few Words*	Completely Fluent	Advanced	Conversational	Basic	Few Words*	Yes	No
None	35.7	52.5	18.2	—	—	23.3	28.7	44.9	47.2	56.5	18.1	44.8
1 to 9	49.9	30.0	81.8	—	—	53.8	57.5	44.9	47.2	38.9	56.3	46.5
10 to 49	8.9	7.5	—	100.0	—	13.7	12.6	3.4	2.8	2.8	16.1	5.0
50 or more	5.5	10.0	—	—	—	9.2	1.1	6.7	2.8	1.9	9.5	3.7
Panel C: Revenues ($1,000s)	Completely Fluent	Advanced	Conversational	Basic	Few Words*	Completely Fluent	Advanced	Conversational	Basic	Few Words*	Yes	No
Less than 10	24.1	30.8	27.3	—	—	19.4	23.0	27.6	21.9	37.4	18.0	28.0
10 to 49.9	43.8	35.9	63.6	—	—	48.2	36.8	43.7	56.2	31.8	45.5	42.9
50 to 99.9	10.6	10.3	9.1	100.0	—	8.9	24.1	11.5	5.5	6.5	10.0	10.9
100 to 499.9	17.4	12.8	0.0	—	—	17.0	11.5	16.1	12.3	22.4	20.0	14.9
500 or more	4.1	10.3	0.0	—	—	6.5	4.6	1.1	4.1	1.9	6.5	3.2

Source: SLEI Survey of U.S. Latino Business Owners 2016–2017 (weighted).

* Know a few words at best.

education), and industry (business sector). Variables that reduce the likelihood of an LOB from at least breaking even include English-language dominance, female ownership, college education, and firm sectoral participation in financial and information services relative to the construction sector (Table 11.5). These relationships fall in line with expectations from a human capital framework.

TABLE 11.5 *Multivariate Analyses*

	Probit Dependent Variable: Breakeven	Ord. Probit Dependent Variable: Profit/BE/Loss	Ord. Probit Dependent Variable: Revenue	Ord. Probit Dependent Variable: Number of Employees
Bilingual	0.490	0.100	0.324	0.217
	(0.398)	(0.333)	(0.232)	(0.241)
English-dominant	−0.764**	−0.565	−0.176	−0.030
	(0.346)	(0.349)	(0.268)	(0.264)
Age	−0.051	0.085	−0.007	−0.125***
	(0.075)	(0.054)	(0.047)	(0.036)
Age sq.	0.160	−1.128*	0.00	1.176***
	(0.824)	(0.624)	(0.001)	(0.398)
Age firm	0.086**	0.083***	0.039**	0.042***
	(0.041)	(0.022)	(0.018)	(0.015)
Age firm sq.	−0.270	−1.296***	−0.531*	−0.446*
	(1.186)	(0.338)	(0.292)	(0.259)
Female	−0.831***	−0.741***	-0.048	−0.038
	(0.317)	(0.210)	(0.172)	(0.145)
College	−1.177***	−0.295	0.106	0.097
	(0.329)	(0.247)	(0.168)	(0.168)
Immigrant	0.154	0.618	−0.865**	−0.157
	(0.684)	(0.480)	(0.368)	(0.296)
Years in U.S.	0.003	−0.017	0.028**	0.008
	(0.021)	(0.016)	(0.013)	(0.009)
Puerto Rican	−0.263	−0.378	0.003	0.173
	(0.472)	(0.277)	(0.178)	(0.204)

(continued)

	Probit Dependent Variable: Breakeven	Ord. Probit Dependent Variable: Profit/BE/Loss	Ord. Probit Dependent Variable: Revenue	Ord. Probit Dependent Variable: Number of Employees
Cuban	0.095	0.561	–0.155	0.064
	(0.625)	(0.529)	(0.439)	(0.241)
Other Hisp.	–0.244	–0.369	–0.522**	-0.027
	(0.350)	(0.252)	(0.213)	(0.193)
Hisp. client < Half	–0.493	0.133	–0.034	0.358
	(0.493)	(0.366)	(0.265)	(0.281)
Hisp. client = Half	–0.149	0.527	–0.263	0.082
	(0.487)	(0.358)	(0.287)	(0.296)
Hisp. client > Half	–0.448	0.066	–0.354	0.470
	(0.629)	(0.434)	(0.318)	(0.323)
Hisp. client = All	0.501	–0.928*	–0.006	0.095
	(0.769)	(0.479)	(0.414)	(0.394)
Industry				
fire	–0.984*	–0.369	–0.648*	–0.087
	(0.539)	(0.505)	(0.358)	(0.269)
Leisure	0.117	0.101	–0.445*	–0.529*
	(0.637)	(0.426)	(0.248)	(0.281)
Manuf. trade	1.235**	0.005	–0.343	–0.242
	(0.549)	(0.329)	(0.271)	(0.217)
Other service	0.652	0.758**	–0.105	0.108
	(0.406)	(0.353)	(0.240)	(0.236)
Prof. bus. service	0.024	0.525	-0.360	–0.527**
	(0.412)	(0.364)	(0.25)	(0.213)
N	615	615	615	615
Wald Chi^2	43.96	76.52	33.35	46.56
Chi2 Significance	0.0036	0.00	0.0571	0.0017
Pseudo R^2	0.3988	0.2107	0.0504	0.0803

Notes: *p<.10, **p<.05, ***p<.01.

Age sq. & age firm sq. divided by 1,000.

Language variables reference: Spanish-Dominant.

Ethnicity reference: Mexican.

Industry reference: Construction.

Highlighting language, Latino business owners who are English-language dominant are less likely to achieve at least breakeven results. Bilingual LOBs appear to be more likely to at least breakeven, though this result is not significant. Increasing the likelihood of achieving breakeven results are firm age (length of time in business) and sectoral participation in manufacturing relative to the reference category of construction, consistent with expectations.

Results from our ordered probit model for the categories of profit (the base), breakeven, and loss indicate that the square of the business owners' age and the square of the age of the firm are both significant and negative. This suggests a nonlinear negative association to profits for older firms and older business owners. Additionally, female LOBs and those LOBs serving a primarily Hispanic clientele are less likely to record a profit as compared to their male counterparts and LOBs with a more diverse (and less Hispanic) client base. Enhancing the likelihood of achieving profits are firm age (not its square) and business operations in services as compared to construction-sector LOBs. Bilingual LOBs appear to be more likely to record a profit, though this result is not significant.

Firm Size: Revenue

Results from our ordered probit model for revenue (with the base from low to high) reveal a negative and significant association with the Latino business owner as an immigrant and other Hispanic (not of Cuban or Puerto Rican origin in reference to owners of Mexican origin). Also negative are the square of the age of the firm and LOBs operating with the financial, insurance, and leisure sectors relative to Latino-owned construction businesses. This indicates that immigrants and other Hispanics are more likely to possess higher-revenue LOBs. Additionally, there are higher nonlinear revenues for LOBs over time, and the financial-, insurance-, and leisure sector–oriented LOBs generate more revenue than construction-oriented LOBs. Conversely, firms closer in age to startup have smaller revenue, as do Latino business owners with fewer years in residence in the United States. These two variables of firm age and number of years in residence in the United States are significant and positive.

Again, while the control variables used in this analysis follow conventional expectations, the language variables have minimal impact on the results. Most important to our exploratory empirical work is the fact that bilingual LOBs appear to be more likely to possess lower revenue enterprises, but this result is not significant. The negative result, on its own, would hint at the possibility of bilingualism bearing more costs (as per those discussed earlier) than benefits; if so, these results would counter those used by the conventional wisdom assumed by empirical work relating bilingualism to labor market outcomes.

Firm Size: Number of Employees

Results from our ordered probit model for number of employees (with the base from none to high) indicate a negative and significant association with the age of the Latino business owner and LOBs operating in leisure and professional business services vis-à-vis construction. Hence, Latino business owners who are older are more likely to have more employees, as are firms connected to leisure and professional services. On the other hand, we find a significant and positive association between the number of years the firm has been in business and the square of the age of the business owner. This suggests that older firms have fewer employees and also suggests a nonlinear relationship vis-à-vis age of the business owner possessing fewer employees.

In this third measure of the relationship between bilingualism and business outcome success, our results are similar: Bilingual LOBs appear to higher fewer employees, controlling for potential confounding factors, but again, this result is not significant.

Funding

Informal structures may be applied to informal financing of formal LOBs. Bilingualism might be relevant in the decision to procure funding to run a firm for some of the conceptual reasons mentioned above. Utilizing the SLEI data in preliminary empirical work, we employed a binary logit regression to examine how likely Latino entrepreneurs were to acquire funds from informal sources (e.g., family, friends, angel investors) to fund business growth (results available from the authors). We note that we use a binary logit approach, as opposed to the probit one, in these exercises as a result of using different statistical software; as is commonly known, probit and logit results are fairly consistent and yield fairly similar inferences. The findings of this preliminary work suggest that bilingual entrepreneurs were less likely to acquire funds from informal sources than were English monolingual entrepreneurs. However, an interaction between language and proportion of Hispanic clientele reveals that as the share of Hispanic clients increases, so too does the likelihood of acquiring funding from informal sources for bilingual Latino entrepreneurs. In addition, we examined the sources that denied funds to Latino entrepreneurs. Results from a binary logit regression (again utilizing the SLEI data) suggest that traditional sources (e.g., local and national banks) were more likely to deny a loan to bilingual entrepreneurs than to their English monolingual counterparts (results available from the authors); we note that the proportion of Hispanic clientele did not yield any significant results in contrast to funded LOBs.

Together, these auxiliary results from the SLEI data might suggest that as bilingual entrepreneurs face more barriers in traditional funding—and not for lack of trying—they may optimize their search for alternative funding pathways by means of informal sources. Additionally, their search for informal sources might be dependent on and moderated by the proportion of Hispanics in the area.

DISCUSSION AND POLICY IMPLICATIONS

From the results presented in this chapter, it would appear that bilingualism might have a complex impact on business outcomes beyond the simple notion that bilingualism expands opportunities for entrepreneurs. Adding to this complexity is this thought: it might also be important to consider differences among bilinguals—that is, native English speakers who later acquired Spanish versus native Spanish speakers who later acquired English. In the results presented above, bilinguals are compared against Spanish-dominants. In this case, it appears that no statistically significant results exist. However, when the regressions are run with the English-dominants as the base or reference group, it appears that bilingualism is positively and significantly associated with breaking even, being profitable, and having higher business revenues (see the endnote for coefficient values; full results available from the authors).[5] Thus, it seems that bilingualism results in a significant advantage over being English-dominant but does not result in a significant advantage over being Spanish-dominant. This might indicate that English-dominants can increase their revenue by acquiring Spanish, but these effects are not present for Spanish-dominants acquiring English. However, we note that some limitations of the current data set are its small number of Spanish-dominant respondents and the inability to tell which language was acquired first in bilingual respondents.

Thus, we caution the reader to take this into consideration when interpreting these results.

Moreover, other differences may exist in how business outcomes are reached. For example, it is possible that bilingualism has an indirect influence on business outcomes via industry selection and employee and customer pools. Therefore, while the language of entrepreneurs may not show a strong direct influence on their business outcomes, the means by which business outcomes are achieved may be influenced by their language, as suggested by the contrasting literature on bilingualism as a cost and a benefit. Thus, we invite future research to examine variables that may play a role in between the language of entrepreneurs and their business outcomes.

Our results provide at least two possible considerations, as reported above and in the main text of our results, when using contrasting referents for language (bilingualism and English-dominant). Comparing the business success of bilingual Hispanic entrepreneurs relative to those who are monolingual suggests few differences among these groups, although they hint at potential negative outcomes for bilingualism among Hispanic entrepreneurs. And it is bilingualism that is the primary focus of this chapter. If the negative outcomes were statistically significant, then a policy recommendation would be to enforce stricter antidiscrimination laws to promote bilingual entrepreneurship. This type of policy recommendation would be premature in that it would ignore some theoretical possibilities and would require a fuller and richer empirical analysis. The other consideration is that bilingual LOBs as compared to English-dominant LOBs perform well in both revenue size and profitability, though a focus on English-dominant LOBs beyond the primary scope of this chapter may be a topic for future research.

Consider that one interpretation for these results is that the language groups are and have labor-market experiences that are homogenous. This former finding and view, however, might be overly simplistic. The sample summary statistics used earlier to investigate the underlying socioeconomic characteristics dispel this notion, as reported. Despite the seemingly equal business success outcomes, the assessment that these are necessarily the same would require more analysis. In particular, we have already noted that the cost of bilingualism and the potential return of this human capital investment should be considered; the evidence for its value is mixed, as nurses earn a wage premium though tempered in heavily populated Hispanic areas (Kalist 2005) as contrasted by no market value at all (Fry and Lowell 2003).

To this observation we can add that it takes more effort to be bilingual than to be monolingual. Portes and his colleagues note the higher cost of bilingual education and that "strong nativist pressures toward mono-lingualism" often lead to immigrant language extinction in two to three generations (Portes and Schauffler 1994). Thus, some immigrants may be bilingual by nature, but natives (i.e., second generation and beyond) are bilingual if they purposefully put in the extra language acquisition effort. Therefore, individuals who choose to develop their skill in a second language probably see intrinsic (e.g., pride in heritage, extended network) and extrinsic (e.g., enhanced employment opportunities) rewards in doing so. Furthermore, the extrinsic reward is likely to be in the form of income (i.e., wage premiums or self-employment revenue), given that the larger social environment seems to prefer English; thus, a reward would not be expected in relation to other factors such as family/friends (the case may be different in ethnic enclaves). Bilingual Hispanic entrepreneurs might be those individuals who follow conventional wisdom and develop a skill in a second language in hopes of a positive return. Bilingual entrepreneurs might then seek this reward across employment and self-employment sectors, ultimately ending in the sector that offers that reward or the highest reward.

According to the theory of compensating wage differentials as inter-preted by modern labor economics (see, e.g., Ehrenberg and Smith 2017) in the form of the Hedonic model, individuals choose among an array of occupations to work in that provide differing compensation packages and risk. Occupational risk may cover a variety of outcomes, such as risk of business closure or injury on the job. This theory proposes that individuals have different preferences for risk and compensation and that to reduce risk, firms must incur costs. It follows that what could be taken to be compensation differences among groups could simply reflect differences in preferences for risk. Likewise, an observation, such as what we have in this chapter that bilingual and monolingual Hispanic entrepreneurs have a comparable business success, might be masking actual compensation differences among these groups.

We took an initial step in exploring this possibility by considering a series of logistic regressions using the SLEI data set (see our point above on probit vs. logistic regression). In these regressions we regressed firm revenue on bilingualism and a host of other control variables. Each regression used a dependent variable representing different cutoff points in revenue. For example, 1 = $100k or more, 0 = $99k or less; 1 = $500k or more, 0 = $499k or less; and 1 = $1M or more, 0 = $999k or less. In these regressions we find that bilingualism has a positive significant association with cutoff points of "$500k or more" and "$1 million or more." In lower cutoff points, bilingualism was negatively related and not statistically significant. While this by no means represents a robust empirical test of the theory of compensating wage differentials as applied to bilingual Hispanic entrepreneurs, we believe that it hints at a fruitful path for future research to consider with more robust analyses.

Although our analysis here is somewhat exploratory and a theoretical and empirical pursuit of this possibility goes beyond the purview of this chapter, we also consider the potential differences in informal sector activity between bilingual and monolingual Hispanic entrepreneurs. That is, bilingual entrepreneurs might pursue riskier business ventures with higher business rewards, as the hedonic model suggests.

Pisani et al. (2017) in their empirical study of small LOBs in heavily Hispanic South Texas reported the following business language-use patterns: 29.1 percent used mostly English, 59.0 percent used mostly Spanish, and 11.9 percent used an even mix of Spanish and English. When undocumented immigration status was introduced with LOBs that by default operate off the books or informally, the language of business was predominately Spanish, 87.2 percent of the time, or some mixture of Spanish and English, 11.4 percent of the time. The confluence of undocumented status and informality in South Texas is particularly salient for full-time business owners and workers, as immigration status necessitates business operations that fly under the radar of government authority because nearly all undocumented South Texas residents are native Spanish speakers (Richardson and Pisani 2012). Undocumented informal LOBs using a mix of Spanish and English reported above may represent arrival in the United States at a young age when English-language ability may have been acquired in grade school.

Nonetheless, informal businesses are composed of entrepreneurs of many different immigration statuses, and the fully documented in South Texas tend to cherry-pick those informal economic activities that produce the highest marginal returns as supplemental income to regular formal employment, such as a warehouse worker moonlighting as a gardener (Pisani and Yoskowitz 2006). This is in contrast to formal LOBs who reported using English, Spanish, and both English and Spanish in the conduct of business

33.3 percent, 54.5 percent, and 12.2 percent of the time, respectively. Business formality dispenses with the need to hide from government authority and broadens the client base beyond a local network that provides social protection for informal activities, hence tempering the need to operate nearly exclusively in Spanish and incorporating more of both languages in business transactions. As expected, Pisani et al. (2017) report that business language use evolves from immigrant LOBs (or first generation) to later LOB generations, from Spanish to mixed Spanish and English and eventually to English.

In South Texas, language use may be contrasted with necessity-driven enterprises, often initiated as a means to earn survival income, and opportunity-driven enterprises to fill market niches and gaps. Pisani et al. (2017) reported that necessity-driven LOBs function most often in Spanish (62.8 percent) while opportunity-driven LOBs function mostly in English (63.4 percent). For those business owners using both Spanish and English in business operations, they were spread nearly evenly and not significantly differentiated across necessity-driven businesses (10.1 percent of all necessity-driven businesses) and opportunity-driven businesses (14.4 percent of all opportunity-driven businesses). While monolingualism divides necessity-driven versus opportunity-driven enterprises, this is not so for LOBs operating in the dual Spanish and English environment, where the results are mixed. Pisani et al. (2017) also note that household income connected to business language usage was higher for enterprises conducting transactions in English (47.6 percent earning more than $40,000 annually) than for those operating in Spanish (12.7 percent earning more than $40,000 annually) or a mix of Spanish and English (29.6 percent earning more than $40,000 annually). Together these findings suggest that there may be a ceiling to returns and operational benefits to multiple language ability across various variables connected to business informality (e.g., immigration status, necessity- and opportunity-driven enterprises) in bilingual environments such as South Texas, but more research is needed to more fully understand the returns to informal LOB bilingualism across the United States.

CONCLUSION

At the essence of our market system is the scarcity of our resources and the need to make the best out of them through efficiencies and productivity.

Thus, as a society we are in a constant quest to make our scarce resources the best we can make them. For example, labor is improved through education, health, and longevity, while capital can be enhanced with technology. Similarly, Hispanic entrepreneurs are a scarce resource that needs to be utilized efficiently. We note in this chapter that Hispanic entrepreneurs are a population that is becoming more prominent in the United States, evidenced by the more than 3 million Hispanic-owned businesses in the United States and the nearly $500 billion in revenue that they generate, as reported in the 2012 SBO. As such, a society must recognize populations that are becoming more prominent and ask how we can make them better at what they do.

Consider the following: If we find that bilingual entrepreneurs have an advantage because of human capital skills, then no policy is needed. On the other hand, if we find that there is bias explaining unsuccessful outcomes from this group, the neoclassical perspective would suggest that this type of bias would be short-lived (because institutions would have to pay for this bias and as a result would be driven out of business in a competitive-market process). However, if unsuccessful outcomes are due to the negative effects of business language resulting from how institutions require them to conduct business, public policy could be used to solve this type of structural problem.

It would also be fruitful for future research to consider differences among bilingual speakers, as the experience of the bilingual whose first language is Spanish and second language is English can be different from the bilingual whose first language is English and second language is Spanish. A third category of simultaneous language acquisition of both Spanish and English, or naturally developed bilinguals, deserves further consideration. Olney (2017) and Phillipson (2004) note this distinction, arguing that although an individual can acquire and become fluent in an additional language, native speakers of the language tend to retain a meaningful advantage. Furthermore, phenotype might be an additional factor that adds to the complexity of the relationship between language and entrepreneurial outcomes. For example, consider studies that have found phenotype to have an effect in the labor market (Bohara and Davila 1992; Telles and Murguia 1990). As such, we suggest that future research collect richer data on the different languages and characteristics of Hispanic entrepreneurs as well as their employees and clientele.

In addition, we note that the informal economy is often the harbinger of business activity. Famously, Apple began informally in a garage in California's Bay Area; Nike was born informally in a bedroom in a Portland, Oregon, suburb. It is thus no surprise that many businesses begin life informally, as it is the first rung in the stepladder toward formality where the climb up is realized through business growth and public awareness (Richardson and Pisani 2012). Informal beginnings, then, are not anathema to business development—oftentimes informality is just the first baby step on the pathway toward business success. Because of the many institutional and nativist barriers faced by Latinos, there may be a much higher incidence of informal origins for LOBs. Bilingual Latinos may be best positioned to navigate between institutional and nativist barriers precisely because they are be able to understand the institutional and cultural dimensions of formal and informal marketplaces. If so, public policy should support bilingual Latino entrepreneurs particularly in the early to middle stages of business development, as the U.S. business environment relies more heavily on the contributions of Latinos to advance national economic growth and prosperity. Further exploration and research are warranted to untangle these questions.

NOTES

1. We use the terms "Hispanic" and "Latino" interchangeably throughout this chapter.
2. These data were retrieved from the SBO "Characteristics of Businesses: 2012 Tables" available at www.census.gov.
3. The SBO reports that 96.7 percent of LOBs sales are transacted in English, while 60.1 percent of sales are transacted in Spanish.
4. The SBO also reports language transactions for LOBs in a conglomeration of African languages, Arabic, Chinese, French, French Creole, German, Hindi/Urdu, Italian, Japanese, Korean, Polish, Portuguese, Russian, Tagalog, and Vietnamese. Only business conducted in Portuguese rises to 1.0 percent of business interactions.
5. When using English-dominants as the base group, bilingualism is significantly related to breakeven (1.254*** [0.369]), profitability (0.665** [0.275]), and business revenues (0.500** [0.236]) but is not significantly related to number of employees (0.247 [0.189]).

REFERENCES

Abrams, Dominic, and Rupert Brown. 1989. "Self-Consciousness and Social Identity: Self-Regulation as a Group member." *Social Psychology Quarterly* 52:311–18.

Alarcón, Amado, Antonio de Paolo, Josiah Heyman, and María C. Morales. 2014. "The Occupational Location of Spanish-English Bilinguals in the New Information Economy: Health and Criminal Justice Sectors in the US Borderlands with Mexico." Pp. 110–37 in *The Bilingual Advantage: Language, Literacy and the US Labor Market*, edited by Rebecca M. Callahan and Patricia C. Gándara. Bristol, UK: Multilingual Matters.

Arrow, Kenneth J. 1974. *The Limits to Organizations*. New York: Norton.

Bohara, Alok K., and Alberto Davila. 1992. "A Reassessment of the Phenotypic Discrimination and Income Differences among Mexican Americans." *Social Science Quarterly* 73(1):114–19.

Bradac, James J., and Randall Wisegarver. 1984. "Ascribed Status, Lexical Diversity, and Accent: Determinants of Perceived Status, Solidarity, and Control of Speech Style." *Journal of Language and Social Psychology* 3:239–55.

Brennan, Eileen M., and John S. Brennan. 1981a. "Accent Scaling and Language Attitudes: Reaction to Mexican American English Speech." *Language and Speech* 24:207–21.

Brennan, Eileen, M., and John S. Brennan. 1981b. "Measurements of Accent and Attitude toward Mexican American Speech." *Journal of Psycholinguistic Research* 10:487–501.

Brown, Rupert. 2000. "Social Identity Theory: Past Achievements, Current Problems and Future Challenges." *European Journal of Social Psychology* 30:745–78.

Burt, Ronald, S. 1982. *Structural Holes*. Cambridge, MA: Harvard University Press.

Burt, Ronald, S. 2004. "Structural Holes and Good Ideas." *American Journal of Sociology* 110(2):349–99.

Carlson, Holly K., and Monica A. McHenry. 2006. "Effect of Accent and Dialect on Employability." *Journal of Employment Counseling* 43(2):70–83.

Cenoz, Jasone, and Jose F. Valencia. 1993. "Ethnolinguistic Vitality, Social Networks and Motivation in Second Language Acquisition: Some Data from the Basque Country." *Language, Culture, and Curriculum* 6(2):113–27.

Cortina, Jerónimo, Rodolfo O. de la Garza, and Pablo M. Pinto. 2007. "*No Entiendo*: The Effects of Bilingualism on Hispanic Earnings." Working Paper

2007-03, Institute for Social and Economic Research and Policy, Columbia University, New York.

Dávila, Alberto, Alok K. Bohara, and Rogelio Saenz. 1993. "Accent Penalties and the Earnings of Mexican Americans." *Social Science Quarterly* 74(4):902–16.

Dávila, Alberto, and Marie T. Mora. 2013. *Hispanic Entrepreneurs in the 2000s: An Economic Profile and Policy Implications.* Stanford, CA: Stanford University Press.

De la Zerda, Nancy, and Robert Hopper. 1979. "Employment Interviewers' Reactions to Mexican-American Speech." *Communication Monographs* 46:126–34.

DeShields, Oscar W., and Gilberto de los Santos. 2000. "Salesperson's Accent as a Globalization Issue." *Thunderbird International Business Review* 42(1):29–46.

Edwards, John. 1999. "Refining Our Understanding of Language Attitudes." *Journal of Language and Social Psychology* 18(1):101–10.

Ehrenberg, Ronald G., and Robert S. Smith. 2017. *Modern Labor Economics: Theory and Public Policy.* New York: Routledge.

Fry, Richard, and B. Lindsay Lowell. 2003. "The Value of Bilingualism in the U.S. Labor Market." *Industrial and Labor Relations Review* 57(1):128–40.

George, Jennifer M., Gareth R. Jones, and Jorge A. Gonzalez. 1998. "The Role of Affect in Cross-Cultural Negotiations." *Journal of International Business Studies* (29):749–72.

Giles, Howard, and Jane L. Byrnes. 1982. "An Intergroup Approach to Second Language Acquisition." *Journal of Multilingual and Multicultural Development* 3(1):17–41.

Giles, Howard, and P. Johnson. 1981. "The Role of Language in Ethnic Group Relations." Pp. 199–243 in *Intergroup Behavior*, edited by John C. Turner and Howard Giles. Oxford, UK: Blackwell.

Giles, Howard, Angie Williams, Diane M. Mackie, and Francine Rosselli. 1995. "Reactions to Anglo- and Hispanic-American–Accented Speakers: Affect, Identity, Persuasion, and the English-only Controversy." *Language and Communication* 15:107–20.

Giles, Howard, R. Y. Bourhis, and D. M. Taylor. 1977. "Towards a Theory of Language in Ethnic Group Relations." Pp. 307–48 in *Language, Ethnicity, and Intergroup Relations*, edited by Howard Giles. London, UK: Academic Press.

Gluszek, Agata, and John F. Dovidio. 2010. "The Way *They* Speak: A Social Psychological Perspective on the Stigma of Nonnative Accents in Communication." *Personality and Social Psychology Review* 14(2):214–37.

Hall, Edward T. 1960. "The Silent Language in Overseas Business." *Harvard Business Review* 38(2):87–96.

Hall, Edward T. 1976. *Beyond Culture*. New York: Anchor Books.

Henderson, Jane K. 2005. "Language Diversity in International Management Teams." *International Studies of Management and Organization* 35(1):66–82.

Hsee, Christopher K. 1996. "Elastic Justification: How Unjustifiable Factors Influence Judgements." *Organizational Behavior and Human Decision Processes* 66(1):122–30.

Hogg, Michael A., and Deborah J. Terry. 2000. "Social Identity and Self-Categorization Processes in Organizational Contexts." *Academy of Management Review* 25:121–40.

Hopkins, Daniel J. 2014. "The Upside of Accents: Language, Inter-Group Difference, and Attitudes toward Immigration." *British Journal of Political Science* 45(3):531–57.

Hosoda, Megumi, and Eugene Stone-Romero. 2010. "The Effects of Foreign Accents on Employment-Related Decisions." *Journal of Managerial Psychology* 25(2):113–32.

Kalist, David. 2005. "Registered Nurses and the Value of Bilingualism." *Industrial and Labor Relations Review* 59(1):101–18.

Kinzler, Katherin D., Kristin Shutts, Jasmine DeJesus, and Elizabeth S. Spelke. 2009. "Accent Trumps Race in Guiding Children's Social Preferences." *Social Cognition* 27:623–34.

Lauring, Jakob. 2008. "Rethinking Social Identity Theory in International Encounters: Language Use as a Negotiated Object for Identity Making." *International Journal of Cross Cultural Management* 8(3):343–61.

Lev-Ari, Shiri, and Boaz Keysar. 2010. "Why Don't We Believe Non-Native Speakers? The Influence of Accent on Credibility." *Journal of Experimental Social Psychology* 46(6):1093–96.

Light, Ivan. 2005. "The Ethnic Economy." Pp. 403–25 in *Handbook of Economic Sociology*, edited by Neil J. Smesler and Richard Swedberg. New York: Russell Sage Foundation.

Lippi-Green, Rosina. 1997. *English with Accents: Language, Ideology, and Discrimination in the United States*. New York: Routledge.

Morando, Sarah J. 2013. "Paths to Mobility: The Mexican Second Generation at Work in a New Destination." *Sociological Quarterly* 54(3):367–98.

Nguyen, Beatrice B.-D. 1993. "Accent Discrimination and the Test of Spoken English: A Call for an Objective Assessment of the Comprehensibility of Nonnative Speakers." *California Law Review* 81:1325–61.

Olney, William W. 2017. "English Proficiency and Labor Market Performance: Evidence from the Economics Profession." *Economic Inquiry* 55(1):202–22.

Peltokorpi, Vesa, and Schneider, S. C. 2009. "Communicating across Cultures: The Interaction of Cultural and Language Proficiency." *Proceedings of the 2009 International Workshop on Intercultural Collaboration*: 289–92.

Phillipson, Robert. 2004. *English-Only Europe? Challenging Language Policy*. New York: Routledge.

Pisani, Michael J., and David W. Yoskowitz. 2006. "Opportunity Knocks: Entrepreneurship, Informality and Home Gardening in South Texas." *Journal of Borderlands Studies* 21(2):59–76.

Pisani, Michael J., Joseph M. Guzman, Chad Richardson, Carlos Sepulveda, and Lyonel Laulié. 2017. "Small Business Enterprises and Latino Entrepreneurship: An Enclave or Mainstream Activity in South Texas?" *Journal of International Entrepreneurship* 15(3):295–323.

Portes, Alejandro, and Richard Schauffler. 1994. "Language and the Second Generation: Bilingualism Yesterday and Today." *International Migration Review* 28:640–41.

Purkiss, Sharon L. S., Pamela L. Perrewe, Treena L. Gillespie, Bronston T. Mayes, and Gerald R. Ferris. 2006. "Implicit Sources of Bias in Employment Interview Judgments and Decisions." *Organizational Behavior and Human Decision Processes* 101(2):152–67.

Rey, A. 1977. "Accents and Employability: Language Attitudes." *Language Sciences* 47:7–12.

Richardson, Chad, and Michael J. Pisani. 2012. *The Informal and Underground Economy of the South Texas Border*. Austin: University of Texas Press.

Richardson, Chad, and Michael J. Pisani. 2017. *Batos, Bolillos, Pochos, and Pelados: Class and Culture on the South Texas Border*. Austin: University of Texas Press.

Ryan, Ellen B. 1983. "Social Psychological Mechanisms Underlying Native Speaker Evaluations of Nonnative Speech." *Studies in Second Language Acquisition* 5:148–59.

Ryan, Ellen B., and M. A. Carranza. 1975. "Evaluations of Middle-Class and Lower-Class Speakers of Standard American and German-Accented English." *Journal of Language and Social Psychology* 1:51–61.

Smith, Robert C. 2002. "Gender, Ethnicity, and Race in School and Work Outcomes of Second-Generation Mexican Americans." Pp. 110–25 in *Latinos: Remaking America*, edited by M. M. Suarez-Orozco and M. M. Paez. Berkeley: University of California Press.

Stanton-Salazar, Ricardo D., and Sanford M. Dornbush. 1995. "Social Capital and the Reproduction of Inequality: Information Networks among Mexican-Origin High School Students." *Sociology of Education* 68:116–35.

Tajfel, Henri. 1974. "Social Identity and Intergroup Behaviour." *Social Science Information* 13:65–93.

Tannen, Deborah. 1995a. *Talking from 9 to 5*. New York: Avon Books.

Tannen, Deborah. 1995b. "The Power of Talk: Who Gets Heard and Why." *Harvard Business Review* 74 (September–October):138–48.

Telles, Edward E., and Edward Murguia. 1990. "Phenotypic Discrimination and Income Differences among Mexican Americans." *Social Science Quarterly* 71:682–96.

Tenbrunsel, Anne E., Kimberly A. Wade-Benzoni, David M. Messick, and Max H. Bazerman. 2000. "Understanding the Influence of Environmental Standards on Judgements and Choices." *Academy of Management Journal* 43(5):854–67.

Wated, Guillermo, and Juan I. Sanchez. 2006. "The Role of Accent as a Work Stressor on Attitudinal and Health-Related Work Outcomes." *International Journal of Stress Management* 13:329–50.

Weyant, James M. 2007. "Perspective Taking as a Means of Reducing Negative Stereotyping of Individuals Who Speak English as a Second Language." *Journal of Applied Social Psychology* 37:703–16.

Wiklund, Ingrid. 2002. "Social Networks from a Sociolinguistic Perspective: The Relationship Between Characteristics of the Social Networks of Bilingual Adolescents and Their Language Proficiency." *International Journal of the Sociology of Language* 153:53–92.

Zhang, Ling E., and Anne-Wil Harzing. 2016. "From Dilemmatic Struggle to Legitimized Indifference: Expatriates' Host Country Language Learning and Its Impact on the Expatriate-HCE Relationship." *Journal of World Business* 51:774–86.

CHAPTER 12

How Can Entrepreneurship Serve as a Pathway to Reduce Income Inequality among Hispanic Women?

Ruth E. Zambrana, Leticia C. Lara, Bea Stotzer, and Kathleen Stewart

INTRODUCTION

Income inequality plays a determining role in the living standards of families, as it diminishes financial security and oftentimes closes the economic opportunity structure. Self-employment, or entrepreneurship, has traditionally been studied as a pathway for upward mobility among ethnic groups and immigrants who view it as a strategy for increasing their financial security and a chance to provide a better life for their children. Latinos/Hispanics (hereafter these labels are used interchangeably), who are projected to comprise more than a quarter of the population by 2060 (Colby and Ortman 2014), have historically been engaged in street and market vending in major urban areas or cityscapes (Morales 2009a, 2009b). Recent data show that Latinas are now starting businesses at one of the highest rates, and as of 2014 Latina-owned businesses had increased to over 1 million businesses nationally. Latinas own 44.5 percent of all Latino-owned firms (Bernstein 2016; Orozco, Oyer, and Porras 2018; Dávila, Mora, and Zeitlin 2014). Although Hispanic businesses are on the upswing, limited data are available on important questions such as who are Latina entrepreneurs, what are their lived experiences, and what do these new economic developments signify for Latino women's income equality, individual/family upward class mobility, and community well-being? Drawing on U.S. government survey data, other survey sources, empirical studies, and reports such as the Stanford State of Latino Entrepreneurship Research Report 2018 and Pew Research Center reports, we have recast the data within the economic and social trajectory of U.S. relationships with Mexican-origin and immigrant populations and interrogated it to assess the meaning of business ownership growth for the social and economic mobility of Mexican-origin women and their families (Telles and Ortiz 2008; Valdez 2011; Verdaguer 2009; Agius Vallejo and Canizales 2016). To add to the body of work on Mexican-origin entrepreneurs, this chapter presents the results of a descriptive study to explore the drivers of entrepreneurial activity and the patterns of resources used to grow the businesses of entrepreneurs in the Los Angeles area. The data provide a snapshot of these entrepreneurs and their particular perspectives embedded in place, gender, race, and ethnicity. Finding answers to questions such as who is included in the upswing and who is benefiting provide important guidance for inclusion and policy initiatives to reduce income inequality and provide equity in opportunity across the nativity, ethnic, class, gender, and immigration continuum.

DEMOGRAPHIC FACTORS: GENDER, RACE, ETHNICITY, AND INCOME INEQUALITY

The following section provides a brief overview of gender differences in earnings and indicators of income inequality. Gender, income, and wealth gaps are well documented. For 90 percent of women, wages have stagnated since 2003 (Mishel, Bivens, Gould, and Shierholz 2012). Figure 12.1 displays data on the wage gap in median annual earnings in 2012. The gap of male to female earnings is highest among Hispanic and black women. Wage inequality is associated with multiple labor market factors including low-wage jobs, seasonal work, discrimination, residence in communities of limited opportunity, limited access to fringe benefits in the labor sector, and limited wealth (savings and assets) (Shapiro 2017). The wage gap applies to both pay and quality of employment. In 2011, over 55 percent of women were poverty-level wage workers, and in 2010, 40.7 percent of female-headed families with children lived in poverty (Mishel et al. 2012).

Gender differences are present in business ownership. Latinos represent 12 percent of total U.S. self-owned business firms (Dávila et al. 2014). Between 2007 and 2012, Latino women business ownership grew by 87 percent, and "although the growth rate in the number of Latina-owned firms remains healthy, they tend to be smaller than male owned

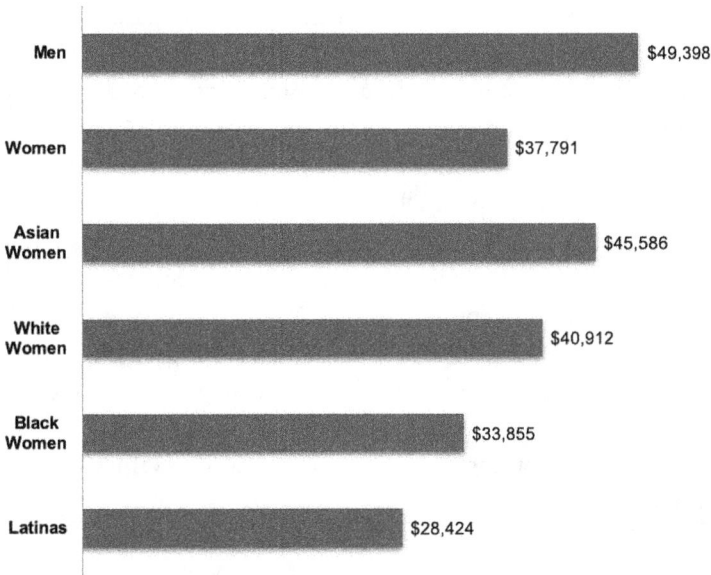

Figure 12.1 The wage gap: median annual earnings, 2012. (Source: *The State of Working America, 12th Edition,* 2012: Key Numbers from the Economic Policy Institute.)

firms" (Orozco et al. 2018:11; see also Melgoza and Palomarez 2015). Although growth in minority-owned and women-owned businesses is flourishing (Chang and Lui 2010; Orozco et al. 2018), Latina business owners are more likely to have lower incomes, work in the service sector, have lower English fluency rates; they are also less likely to be married, have less business experience, and are often younger. Yet they are equally or more educated (college graduates) than their male counterparts (Zuiker et al. 2003; Ryan and Bauman 2016). Additionally, the mean income for self-employed Latino women is 16 percent of the mean income of self-employed Latino men. The growing rate of businesses owned by women of color (it is unclear who this category includes) suggests that there is strong potential for women of color to build wealth through entrepreneurial activity (Chang and Lui 2010).

Although Hispanic women overall (namely Mexican-origin, Salvadoran, and Puerto Rican) have less education, income, and wealth compared to other racial/ethnic women, high rates of business ownership are reported. These economic and demographic data are critical in contextualizing the meaning of current trends for Hispanic women (by ethnic subgroup and nativity) and their families. Answers to questions regarding where the new capital is coming from, who has access to it, and how these developments will inform the future economic progress of Latinas require inquiry. New data can provide deep insight into ways to strengthen the pathways of business formation and open new industry sectors to reduce the income inequality gap for all Hispanic women.

Staggering upward numbers do not provide a comprehensive picture of earnings and impact on income inequality. A recent article by Valletta (2017) discusses several reports on Hispanic women entrepreneurs: "While minority owned business drive all the growth, they disproportionately have less gross receipts, which means that their ability to generate new jobs is not being exercised. The issue trickles down to Latino women who lag behind their full potential earning 36 cents to the dollar in revenues versus their female counterparts."

These data partially inform why the poverty rate and income gaps have remained relatively stable for over four decades. The Hispanic poverty rate in 1980 was 21.4 percent, and in 2010 it had increased slightly to 22.1 percent. The income inequality gap between Hispanics and whites has persisted over the past four decades. Hispanic median household income ($34,000) was 67 percent that of whites in 1970, and by 2014 it was 61 percent of white household income. Conversely, in 1970 Hispanic household income was about 20 percent higher than that of blacks, but that gap has narrowed over the past two decades. The median adjusted income for households headed by Hispanics in 2014 was about the same as that of households headed by blacks, $43,300 (Pew Research Center 2016), demonstrating significant racial/ethnic gaps in household income over five decades (see Figure 12.2).

Income inequality increases if wealth is taken into account (Keister and Moller 2000). Median Latino and black family wealth levels are about 90 percent lower than median white family wealth. The median white family wealth was $130,102 in 1989 and $134,008 in 2013, adjusting for inflation, and $64,165 and $91,440 for Asian families, compared to Latino and black families where the medians were $9,229 (1989) and $13,900 (2013) and $7,736 (1989) and $11,184 (2013), respectively (Boshara, Emmons, and Noeth 2015). The average black or Latino family owns no stock and is nearly twice as likely as white families to have zero or negative net worth. Figure 12.3 displays the percentage of families with no wealth. Close to 20 percent (18.6 percent) of white families, 33.9 percent of black

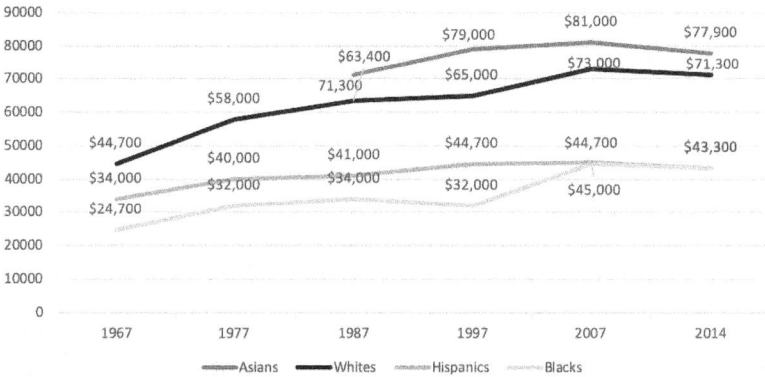

Figure 12.2 Racial gaps in household income persist, mean adjusted household income. (Source: Pew Research Center tabulation of the 1964–2015 Current Population Survey Annual Social and Economic Supplement.)

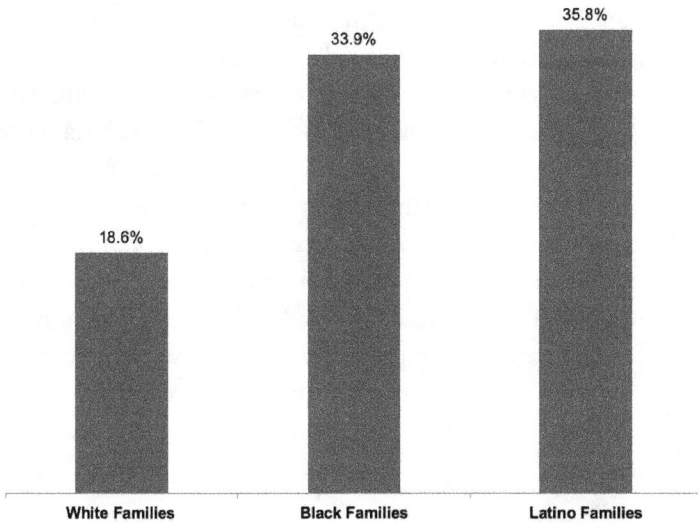

Figure 12.3 Percent of families with no wealth or with debts exceeding their assets. (Source: *The State of Working America, 12th Edition*, 2012: Key Numbers from the Economic Policy Institute.)

families, and 35.8 percent of Latino families have no wealth or have debts exceeding their assets.

The Great Recession had a startling adverse impact on median family wealth for all demographic groups, but nonwhite families were especially hard hit. Figure 12.4 displays the devastating impact on median

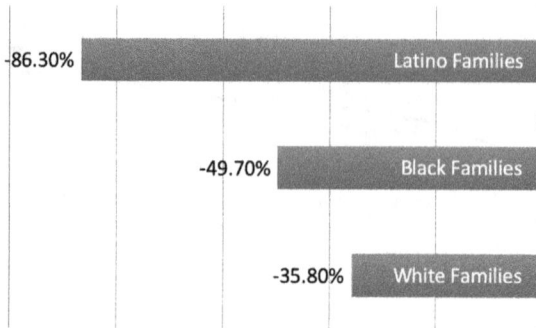

Figure 12.4 Impact of great recession on family wealth percent decrease in median family wealth, 2007 to 2010. (Source: *The State of Working America, 12th Edition*, 2012: Key Numbers from the Economic Policy Institute.)

family wealth among racial/ethnic groups in the United States, particularly Latinos. From 2007 to 2010, the median family wealth for whites was reduced by 35.8 percent, while the median family wealth for blacks plummeted by 49.7 percent and for Latino families by 86.3 percent. Another significant asset is homeownership rates, which in 2011 were 44.9 percent for black families, 46.9 percent for Latino families, and 73.8 percent for white families (Mishel et al. 2012). The impact of the economic recession on wealth and assets among Latinos by nativity, immigration status, race/ethnicity, and gender is unknown. For Latino women who are socially and economically disadvantaged, especially Mexican-origin groups, the question if how entrepreneurship can serve as a pathway to reduce income inequality is pivotal. Can business formation decrease household income gaps, increase assets and wealth, and economically strengthen families and communities?

BUSINESS FORMATION: IMMIGRATION, RACE, ETHNICITY, GENDER, AND EDUCATION

Higher business formation rates may be driven by three major factors: necessity of lower-skilled and professional workers having trouble securing employment or seeking new and/or alternative options, increased number of women with children seeking more flexible employment opportunities, and increased immigration among predominantly educated, upper middle-class

Subgroup

Hispanic 14
26
Dominican 18
10
Puerto Rican 18
34
Total 12
28
Central America — Guatemalan 8
9
Nicaraguan 22
32
Salvadoran 9
32
South American — Chilean 36
33
Ecuadorian 21
30
Venezuelan 53
36
Other Hispanic 18

Percent: 0   20   40   60   80   100

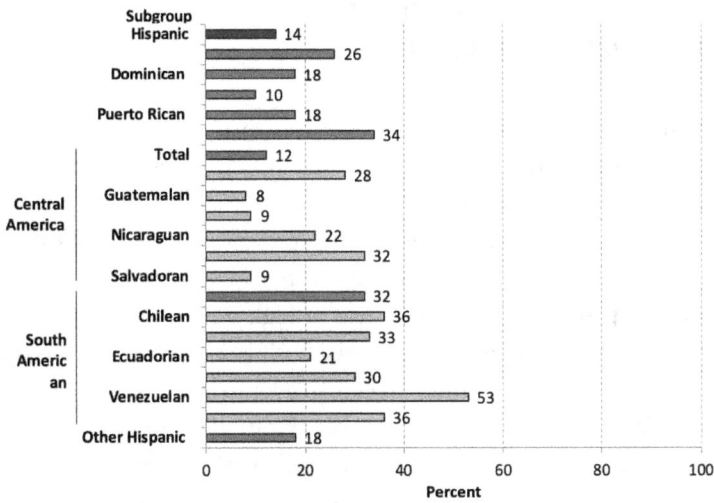

Figure 12.5 Percentage of adults age 25 and older with a bachelor's or higher degree, by selected Hispanic subgroups: 2014. (Source: Pew Research Center Tabulation of the 1964–2015 Current Population Survey Annual Social and Economic Supplement.)

Latin American populations. In 2010, about one-third of all Hispanics in the United States were noncitizens (Mattingly and Pedroza 2015), and the majority of non-Mexican Hispanics had higher education rates than the Mexican American population. Figure 12.5 displays levels of education by Hispanic country of origin. Women's educational levels reflect similar patterns of educational attainment to men's by country of origin. Immigrants from Cuba, Spain, and South American countries such as Colombia, Venezuela, and Peru have 25–35 percent college graduation rates, which is almost three times the rate of Mexican college graduates (10 percent) and almost twice as high as the rate for Puerto Ricans (18 percent). Increases in Latino entrepreneurship coincide with high levels of immigration, particularly from South America (1990–2000). Data show that college-educated immigrants are most likely to be entrepreneurs. Millennials (the children of immigrants) are also developing businesses at a higher rate, which suggests family transfer of wealth, an important area of future inquiry (Orozco et al. 2018). In contrast, black and Hispanic women have lower levels of education and higher rates of unemployment and are more likely to be the financial head of household compared to white or Asian women, which may account for the surge in self-employment (Zambrana 2011; Vega 2015).

CAN ENTREPRENEURSHIP REDUCE
HISTORIC INCOME INEQUALITY?

To explore in depth the factors that contribute to a "sudden opening" of the economic opportunity structure for Latino women, this section examines regional and immigration patterns and institutional and structural barriers to accessing the resources to assist with startup, growth, and sustainable business opportunities. The growth of Latino entrepreneurship varies by region and immigration patterns. Geographic areas of high immigrant concentrations present with higher rates of Latino-owned businesses. The top four states are New York, 3.1 percent; Florida (Miami), 2.1 percent; Texas, 2.4 percent; and California (Los Angeles), 2.1 percent. From 2012 to 2015, the fastest growing regions were in the Western North Central and East North Central divisions. The Pacific census division continues to be the largest division, with a projected 22 percent increase (Melgoza and Palomarez 2015). The Latin American immigration flow over the last three decades has bolstered the Hispanic economic, social, and racial diversity (Zambrana 2011). From 2000 to 2010, the rate of self-employment among Latino immigrants, predominantly from Mexico, grew by 2 percentage points and played a key role in this growth. High years of immigrant flows contributed to immigrant business owners now being more than twice as likely as native-born Latinos to start businesses (Dávila et al. 2014). The key question is why the sudden interest in the immigrant surge in businesses? Historically, Mexican immigration has been a large and important employment migration stream, but Mexican-origin women-owned business development was not part of the discourse.

Although there has been an emphasis on women business-owner success in recent decades, it has predominantly focused on majority culture women and has overshadowed the barriers that Latino women generally and low-income Latino women in particular experience in their efforts to create a pathway to income equality. For many low-income Latino women, entrepreneurship activities have subsisted in informal economy sectors, and the barriers confronted have included structural forms of discrimination that have impeded access to financial capital and resources from mainstream institutions combined with family obligations, economic constraints, and a limited external social network.

Obstacles that Latina business owners confront, such as family responsibilities, social normative expectations, and available personal capital, differ from those of their male counterparts. Business startup decisions of Latina entrepreneurs are positively affected by family social support that enables them to be better prepared, such as engaging in research, planning, and other activities needed for starting a business (Chang et al. 2009). One study of Mexican American female entrepreneurs in Los Angeles found that in the absence of supportive relationships, three elements contributed to successful business endeavors: prior business experience, interpersonal and familial dynamics, and labor market experiences (Morales 2009b). However, Latina entrepreneurs had fewer contacts and met with contacts less often than non-Latino business owners and relied on family and friends more than other business owners and associations for business-related information (Ortiz-Walters et al. 2015). In effect, the merging of individual drive, determination and persistence, strong familial and institutional supports, financial capital, and business experience or access to business experiences represent the building blocks of successfully navigating business development and growth to secure income equality and financial stability (Morales 2009a; Verdaguer 2009).

In summary, traditional labor markets, discriminatory practices, and low human and financial capital among predominantly native-born Mexican, Puerto Rican, and immigrant women have served as barriers to self-employment activity. Yet the impact of the Great Recession, the mass exodus of predominantly highly educated racialized white immigrants from Latin America from 1980 to 2000, and the current political climate laid a strong foundation for Latino business growth. Latinas, similar to non-Hispanic white women, have developed nontraditional work options to exercise flexibility to support family roles and professional autonomy. However, the data show that Latinas fall at or near the bottom of the economic and social capital indicators with differences by race, class, nativity and ethnic background, which reduces their access to resources as entrepreneurs. For Latina entrepreneurs compared to their non-Hispanic white counterparts, their businesses tend to remain small and generate fewer scaled firms, do not scale up over time, and are more likely to encounter institutional barriers (Robles and Cordero-Guzman 2007; Orozco et al. 2018:18–20).

INSTITUTIONAL BARRIERS TO ENTREPRENEURSHIP

Significant barriers to entrepreneurial success are observed among Latinas in the United States. These include limited credit history, a potential shortage of role models, underpreparedness, language difficulties (for some), and difficulty accessing bank loans and federal small business financing

(Dávila et al. 2014; Orozco et al. 2018:19). Moreover, educational attainment rates and socioeconomic status, individual or family wealth, customer demographics, age of enterprise, age of owner, and especially access to financial capital have been identified as significant variables in explaining Latino self-employment rates and business ownership success (Robles and Cordero-Guzman 2007). Low educational attainment, while being a driving force in creating the push into self-employment, may at the same time be contributing to the marginal existence of many Latino small businesses. The lack of financial resources for operation and expansion purposes contributes to the blocked business stage growth. For young disadvantaged Latino males, self-employment produces higher earnings than wage work, yet these results do not hold true for young disadvantaged Latino females (Fairlie 2004; Robles and Cordero-Guzman 2007).

Despite the growth in women-owned businesses, Latinas remain underrepresented among business owners. Unmarried Hispanic women are particularly less likely to own business assets; only 1 percent of single Hispanic women own business assets, compared to 4 percent of single black women and 8 percent of single white women. However, while overall rates may be low, the growth rate of businesses owned by Latino women is significant, which suggests that there is strong potential for women to build wealth for themselves and improve income equality as well as financial assets and social mobility through entrepreneurship. Yet, Latino women as successful entrepreneurs is an understudied area of inquiry.

Based on existing scholarship, we develop three central claims: (1) a rapidly increasing number of Latinas are pursuing economic opportunities by becoming business owners; (2) although Latina entrepreneurship has the potential to improve the lives of Latinas and their families, in its current forms Latina entrepreneurship is available to few, blocks doors to many, and continues to reproduce inequality; and (3) an in-depth analyses of the demographic characteristics and community material conditions of successful entrepreneurs and those who are not can provide a useful road map to identify how policy makers can bolster Latina-owned businesses to increase income equality and narrow the wealth gap.

METHODS

The study employed a mixed methods design using interviews and surveys.[1] Three major questions guided the study: (1) What motivations and attitudes guided decision making among Mexican American entrepreneurs to develop their own business? (2) What economic behaviors did Mexican American entrepreneurs use to launch their businesses? (3) What strategies were most helpful to Mexican American entrepreneurs in growing their businesses?

Sample Criteria and Selection

Five criteria for sample selection were (a) females, (b) Mexican origin, (c) foreign or U.S.-born, (d) business ownership for a minimum of five years, and (e) residence and business ownership in the Los Angeles area. Participants were identified through personal networks. Two of the coauthors (Lara and Stotzer) had access to local women's business networks in Los Angeles and generated a list of 20 potential participants (business owners who met the study criteria) between October 2016 and April 2017. All referrals were contacted to explore interest and willingness to participate. Of the 20 women contacted, 13 agreed to participate (65 percent engagement rate). Ten of the 13 women who agreed to participate completed the interview. During the course of planning and delivering interviews, 3 women withdrew (23 percent attrition rate) and proffered the following reasons for withdrawal: 1 reported a death in the family and no longer felt emotionally available to participate, and 2 participants reported limited time availability due to demanding workloads.

Instruments and Procedures

Participants completed a 51-item survey and an interview schedule protocol consisting of 24 semistructured questions. Survey items obtained demographic data on participants and partner (e.g., age, ethnic group identification, education, marital status, number of children) as well as household assets including savings, home ownership, sources of financing for business, other employment, number and type of businesses, business networks, use of technology and health status. For this chapter, survey items are used to describe respondents (see Table 12.1). Interview questions were adapted from several sources: (1) a prior entrepreneurial study conducted in Texas (Valdez 2011), (2) survey items from the U.S. Census Bureau Survey of Business Owners, and (3) other national and state surveys. The interview questions were designed to supplement the survey data by eliciting rich narratives on motivations for launching the business and resources and strategies used to grow the business (see the box for examples of questions). In addition, participants were invited to comment on any experience that would assist us in understanding the process of becoming Latina entrepreneurs.

Examples of Interview Questions

- Why did you decide to go into business for yourself?
- How did you start your business?
- Who works with you in your business?
- What types of resources have helped you grow your business?
- Where have you been able to get additional money to keep the business going?
- Who or what has been most helpful in helping you grow your business?
- What banking products or services would be most helpful to continue growing your business?
- Looking back over the last six months, who are the people in your life that you talk to regarding business matters that are important to you?

Standardized procedures were used in all interviews. First, participants were provided with a computer tablet to respond to 51 web-based survey items. The interviewer was available onsite to provide technical support to the participants if questions arose in completing the electronic survey and/or using the computer tablet device. A trained bilingual/bicultural Mexican American interviewer conducted interviews primarily in English, either at respondents' home (n=6) or place of business (n=3) or in a community setting (n=1). The respondents selected their preference of interview location that aligned with personal schedules. Interviews obtained experiential (lived-experience) information. Interviewees were encouraged to share their experiences of developing and sustaining a business. Face-to-face interviews averaged 45 minutes, and the survey completion averaged 22 minutes with a total average interview time of 67 minutes.

Five of the 10 respondents rescheduled the interview at least once due to interference with work, illness, family activities, vacation, or holidays. A $50 cash compensation was given to participants upon completion of the interview. Research protocol was reviewed and approved by Institutional Review Board committee at the University of Maryland.

Limitations

Data are limited by sample self-selection, small sample size, and potential selection biases of participants, as all were known to two of the authors. Respondents may have avoided disclosing personal, financial, or familial information that they perceived to be confidential. Respondents who self-selected to participate in the study could have individual characteristics of self-starter and strong prior business experience, which limits generalizability. Nonetheless, respondents sharing their narrative as entrepreneurs inform the body of knowledge on their business ownership trajectory, dreams, and aspirations and shed light on the experiences of a Hispanic subethnic population, Mexican American women.

Data Analyses

Survey data were collected using Qualtrics, a qualitative software program used by social science researchers. For survey data, descriptive frequencies were run on sociodemographics, family, and business characteristics. All qualitative interview data were recorded and transcribed by a bilingual/bicultural research firm and initially coded and analyzed by a Los Angeles–based research associate. Data were analyzed separately, and each transcript was read by two qualitatively trained sociologists and a research associate. Consensus was reached on major themes by three coders.

RESULTS

Table 12.1 displays sample demographic and business characteristics of study respondents. Respondents ranged in age from 42 to 57 years with a mean age of 51.5 years.[2] The majority (80 percent) were U.S.-born and 20 percent were born in Mexico, but all were U.S. citizens and spoke English and Spanish equally. The majority (60 percent) had a BA/BS college degree, 20 percent earned a technical degree, and another 20 percent were high school graduates. Regarding marital status, half of the respondents were divorced, 30 percent were married, and 20 percent had never married. The majority were homeowners (70 percent) and had 1–2 children (70 percent). Among married respondents, husbands were employed full-time.

In regard to business characteristics of the sample, six respondents were first-time business owners and six were aware of minority-owned business programs. The business sectors varied from food to sales, with the majority

TABLE 12.1 *Demographic and Business Characteristics of Study Respondents (N=10)*

Demographic	(%)	Business Characteristics	(n)
Mean Age	51.1 years (42–57 age range)	First time business ownership	6
Nativity		Awareness of minority-owned business programs	6
U.S.-born	80%	Type of Business	
Born in Mexico	20%	Food	1
U.S. citizenship	100%	Construction	1
Languages spoken (English and Spanish equally)	100%	Sales	1
		Service: Beauty salon, cleaning	5
Education		Other: Commercial real estate, interior design	2
BA/BS college degree	60%	Did you seek business information?	7
Technical degree	20%	Did you apply for a small business loan from any source?	1
High school graduate	20%	Total gross business revenues	
Marital Status		• <$40,000	2
Divorced	50%	• $41,000–$80,000	3
Married	30%	• $80,000+	5
Never married	20%	Percent of Hispanic Customers	
Homeowners	70%	• All/most	2
		• Some/few	8

in some form of service (n=5). When study respondents were asked "Did you apply for a small business loan from any source?" nine respondents reported no, although the majority sought business information (n=7). More respondents reported using their personal savings rather than obtaining a loan. However, all respondents reported seeking advice from other businesspeople. The majority reported that they served some/few Hispanic customers, and half (n=5) reported total gross business revenue of $80,000 or more. In comparison, 30 percent of Hispanic households who identify themselves as small business owners earn more than $100,000 per year compared to 23 percent of all U.S. households (Melgoza and Palomarez 2015).

MEXICAN AMERICAN WOMEN ENTREPRENEURS: NARRATIVES OF LIVED EXPERIENCE

The interview data yielded several themes that provide rich insights into motivating factors associated with business startups. Three principal themes emerged: desire for flexibility in family and professional schedules, the use of personal financial resources due to fear of debt and perceived institutional barriers, and the importance of social networks and mentors in business growth.

Motivation: Flexibility in Multiple Roles

The first theme revolved around multiple family role responsibilities. Respondents report that the primary motivation to start their businesses was based on a combination of factors including wanting or needing the flexibility to raise their children and spend time with their families, the number and ages of their children, and the misalignment of work schedules. One participant with a 4-year-old son who left her job after 15 years explained that her employer wanted her to work every weekend. The new schedule no longer worked for her family. At the time her husband was working and traveling, so she had to take care of her young son. Another woman explained her childcare situation: "I have two sons. One of my sons was born with special needs. I realized that my son would need added support, so I wanted to make myself available to care for him." Another woman described her work life before becoming self-employed: "I had to turn down work because it meant that I would have to travel more and I would need to be away from my son. I wanted to be there for my son." In addition, respondents welcomed the increased flexibility and freedom as new business owners in order to participate in family and personal interests. For example, one respondent described a sense of privilege about being able to leave work when her son was ill or when she wanted to attend her son's Little League games.

Flexibility and freedom also allowed women to engage in philanthropic and volunteer work that aligned with their personal values and business practices. All respondents expressed a shared value for community involvement. They provided examples of giving and promoting the welfare of others through money, time, and sharing knowledge and products, which included sponsoring Little League and school programs and serving on boards of community organizations, schools, local business chambers, and rotary clubs. They also provided free or low-cost products to help the community or individuals who needed support.

Their sense of responsibility also extended to their employees and customers. For example, an owner acknowledged that as a woman, she has insight and the added benefit of understanding the women who worked for her: "I understand. I am more flexible at work with my female employees, who have children. I allow them to leave work when their child is sick or if they need to address some parenting issue. I know and understand what it takes to be a parent and having to work." For many respondents, self-employment provided the elusive family-work integration that many women strive for but rarely attain.

Personal Finances: Fear of Debt and Institutional Barriers

A common sentiment among the participants was their aversion to borrowing money from financial institutions for starting, maintaining, and growing their business to circumvent financial debt. Respondents reported that they invested their own assets such as savings, work income, or credit charged to personal credit card accounts when starting their small businesses and valued their decision to not borrow money from banks. They expressed feeling a sense of pride in starting their business without having borrowed money from a bank.

Participants' decision to not explore bank loans when starting or operating their small business was influenced by the following internal and external factors: (1) limited or no awareness of the type of bank loans available for small businesses, (2) an inability to obtain a loan due to rejection from a bank, (3) avoiding debt because they had internalized personal values (socialization) from parents about borrowing money, and (4) viewing personal savings as a viable and accessible financial resource to start and manage their businesses.

Respondents also reported negative experiences and hearsay regarding banking policies, which discouraged them from approaching banking institutions. One woman stated that "I am not a person who turns to banks to grow my business. I guess my personal philosophy is that banks ask too much of small business owners, so I never looked into that." Another stated that

My bank turned down my loan application three times. I am not sure where the five-year rule comes from. When I got my first line of credit with the bank, it was after five years. It wasn't a loan; it was a line of credit for $10,000 that served as an overdraft protection. I honestly feel it was the mark of the five years for getting a loan that helped. They wanted to see the last 2–3 years of taxes. I also didn't approach Small Business Administration back then because I didn't even know they existed.

For many of the respondents, knowledge of available resources was sorely lacking and resistance to the use of financial institutions was prevalent. Participants attributed their resistance to the idea that banks ask too much, which is likely associated with discriminatory exclusionary practices that are masked by time-consuming bureaucratic processes. This possibility is also reified by the fact that as noted above, a participant was given a loan five years into her business. In other words, oftentimes Latino subgroups need to prove themselves first or work twice or three times as hard as other groups in order to obtain resources.

These data show a strong reliance on personal savings to launch a business and confirm prior findings of institutional barriers, discrimination, and lack of prior experiences with government institutions such as the Small Business Administration (Orozco et al. 2018:18–20; Robles and Cordero-Guzman 2007; Morales 2009b). However, respondents were able to identify strategies and resources that they found very helpful in building and sustaining their businesses.

Networks and Mentors Are Important

All respondents sought advice from other business owners. They also reported that access to membership in local chambers of commerce and professional associations provided them with learning opportunities for acquiring business-related training, meeting new people, and fostering relationships with other business owners. Developing professional relationships and networks within and outside their market sector provided both personal and professional support. These relationships with small business owners offered opportunities to share ideas and seek consultations from other business owners and also help generate potential clients. Access to business-oriented people with similar passions for operating a small business helped them remain inspired in their entrepreneurial journey. Listening to other business owners share the challenges and successes of being an entrepreneur created a sense of personal validation for the women's business experiences. Additionally, women worked to network and connect with professionals at meetings who served as future consultants and mentors. One respondent described her involvement:

> I look up to other business professionals that have the same type of business. I would come to group type sessions to discuss business matters. Again, here's where the Chamber of Commerce and Rotary Club helps and comes in. Rotary club business groups have lots of retired people. They have a good head on their shoulders and lots of wisdom. This is the type of business circle of family that helps you in highs and lows.

Access to mentors and role models is critically important in any field but perhaps more so in the field of entrepreneurship, where contemporary markets are flooded with global capital and digital and Internet pathways that have become major marketing outlets. Mentors provide not only knowledge but also equally important strategies and alternative options to redirect business opportunities and identify potential partners, other mentors, and/or organizations. In addition, mentors can inspire and encourage staying power in the face of challenges. Moreover, in the absence of familial support, mentors, power brokers, and professional brokers can provide needed business acumen and access to different types of resources.

Discussion

These data unveil a high level of motivation and grit among Mexican-origin female entrepreneurs to be successful. Our results confirm prior findings reported for Peruvian and Salvadoran women (Verdaguer 2009). Studies have documented that socioeconomic status as measured by education level (socioeconomic status) matters significantly and is often associated with family business succession and middle-class status. As observed by Valdez, "specifically middle-class privilege allows some Latino/as to perceive enterprise as an opportunity for job satisfaction rather than an alternative to job dissatisfaction" (Valdez 2011:50). Our study narratives illustrate that fear of debt, less knowledge of existing resources, discrimination, and barriers of access to institutional resources were prevalent. Verdaguer (2009:120) found that more women than men "explained that self-employment was often a response to harsh discrimination and exploitative working conditions." Yet prior scholarship confirms that Latinas, like other women, seek autonomy and flexibility not only for managing work and family roles but also for engagement in volunteer activities and community uplift. These data inform a growing body of knowledge on women entrepreneurs and emphasize the links between individual, institutional, and community development factors (Morales 2009a; Robles and Cordero-Guzman 2007).

To calibrate our study findings with a Latina entrepreneur sample, we compared differences and similarities with the Stanford Latino Entrepreneur Initiative (SLEI) Survey of U.S. Latino Business, the largest study of Latina entrepreneurs (n=270). The areas of comparison include motivations to start a business and initial sources of funding. The primary responses for SLEI respondents on motivation were "always wanted my own business" and "wanted to earn a greater income" versus study respondents who reported "need for family role flexibility." Regarding initial sources of funding, 69 percent of study respondents relied on personal savings versus 39 percent of SLEI participants. Multiple sources of funding were reported by SLEI respondents: 70.5 percent rely on family and friends, 33.9 percent on credit cards, 19.2 percent on venture capital, 15.9 percent on loans, and 15.5 percent on inheritance. These differences in startup funds suggest that immigrants from Latin America who have high levels of human and financial capital account for a significant number of the Latino surge in entrepreneurship. Among study respondents, only 20 percent were immigrants, while the Annual Survey of Entrepreneurs data report that 52.4 percent of Hispanic business owners were not born in the United States (Dávila et al. 2014; Mattingly and Pedroza 2015). As argued eloquently by Verdaguer (2009), intersectional coconstituted identities of race, ethnicity, class, and nativity matter in the immigrant integration process and access to the opportunity structure. We argue that self-employment and entrepreneurship represent important opportunities for native-born Mexican American, Puerto Rican, and other disadvantaged Latinos to open pathways out of poverty, increase income equality, and accelerate upward social mobility if institutional barriers are decreased and financial and social capital resources are increased.

Entrepreneurship among Hispanics as a group has primarily focused on growth of small business owners, number of firms, number of employees, and market performance. A closer look at the spectrum of small business startups by women is needed to inform new lines of inquiry regarding divergent entrepreneurial pathways. Future research is important for exploring definitions of success, social mobility, and income equality accounting for the intersectional identities measured by multiple demographic indicators of immigrant versus native-born status, race and ethnic subgroup, access to financial resources, level of education, and motivation for engaging in entrepreneurship. Exploring why earning gaps persist, finding the metrics of success, and uncovering how to improve the financial outcomes, economic mobility, and income and wage equality of Latino women entrepreneurs is critical for improving individual and family economic well-being and guiding future research directions.

Scholars have proffered divergent viewpoints on the role of entrepreneurship for Latinos and its ability to provide sufficient economic rewards to decrease income inequality. Some scholars have argued that entrepreneurship no longer remains a traditional mobility ladder for Latinos as it has for Asian immigrants and their descendants (Raijman and Tienda 2000; Sanders and Nee 1996). Other scholars point to the growing number and the broadening spectrum of Latino-owned businesses and argue that an incomplete picture has been painted of Latino entrepreneurs by class, race, and ethnic subgroup (Valdez 2011; Verdaguer 2009; Agius Vallejo and Canizales 2016). These scholars have produced scholarship to document differences and suggest innovative research directions and ethnic- and class-specific policy interventions to improve the business acumen and negotiating strategies of Latina entrepreneurs so they can successfully interface with institutional power structures.

While there may be similarities in the experiences of Latino subgroups, the aggregate grouping of "Hispanic" or "Latino" may inappropriately mask the intragroup differences in human and financial capital resources of Latino small business startups (Robles and Cordero-Guzman 2007; Verdaguer 2009). The stark differences among Latino communities by race, ancestry, ethnicity, education, and socioeconomic status (class), combined with unique immigrant and disadvantaged intergenerational experiences (Telles and Ortiz 2008), are important features driving the Latino entrepreneurial landscape (for a discussion of the historical conditions that differentiate Cuban and Mexican immigrant entrepreneurship, see Chapter 2 in this volume). For instance, significant differences exist between exporting patterns of Latino firms when assessing intragroup comparisons (Robles and Cordero-Guzman 2007). Mexican immigrants experienced the largest growth in entrepreneurship rates. While just 6.3 percent of that population was self-employed in 1990, 10.6 percent of the population was employed by 2012 (Dávila et al. 2014). In 2012, more than one in seven Cuban immigrants were entrepreneurs (Dávila et al. 2014). Thus, a pan-ethnic Hispanic/Latino group aggregation disallows critical inquiry regarding what subgroups have initiated businesses, what their most urgent needs are, and who they serve in terms of resources, what range of opportunities are covered (e.g., home cottage industries, market industries, small businesses including consultants), what role race and the color line play in business growth, and how we can use this opportunity as a way to reduce income inequality.

CONCLUSION

More recent economic and political shifts have reinvigorated the entrepreneurship discourse due to a trend of disinvestment since the 1980s in U.S. labor markets. Disinvestments in national economic stability and sustainable employment practices include outsourcing of U.S. manufacturing and production of goods to foreign countries and an exploding global movement of human and financial capital. These economic events have had a particularly hard impact on low-wage workers and have diminished the employment infrastructure. For example, the increase in professional immigrant visas and global civil unrest has encouraged significant numbers of elite immigrant groups to migrate to the United States, and they are the most likely to become entrepreneurs due to higher levels of education, prior experience, and access to financial and social capital. Future studies, policy, and practice must address the economic, social, and place needs of both immigrant and native-born communities, with particular attention to the income inequality gaps by gender, race, and class and their impact on Latinas in low-resourced and low-opportunity communities.

Future research can be enhanced in two ways: by applying geospatial analysis that tracks changes in economic and financial institutional indicators in low-, middle-, and high-income communities and the collection of specific demographic data. For example, SLEI data show that while Latino firms are located all over the United States, 75 percent are in majority non-Latino neighborhoods serving mostly non-Latino customers. Data and observations suggest a white color line among Hispanic entrepreneurs that contributes to serving a predominantly non-Hispanic white customer base. Place is important in understanding processes of business growth. Geospatial techniques can reveal place-based differences and trends that otherwise are often undetected, such as the degree to which nearness or distance of financial institutions plays a role in facilitating new business growth, possibly affording one community an opportunity that another community does not have. Geospatial methods can detect clusters, or hot spots, of business activity to map business development and resource changes in communities, such as an increase in the number of census tracts or blocks over time that correspond to self-employment. Tools to monitor longitudinal changes and identify where Latina entrepreneurs thrive in terms of place and business customer base can initiate inquiry to answer new questions: Does racialization matter in serving a white versus non-white customer base? Does the intersection by race/indigeneity, education, and business sector predict customer base? Do more racialized Latinos cater to a Latino customer base, for example, Dominican hair salons? How are service sectors distributed by geographic place: urban, rural, or suburban by state?

Future data collection must be more rigorous in its ability to describe demographic characteristics of entrepreneurs and place. Generalizations of Hispanic business growth are informed by aggregate data such as college-educated immigrants. Use of aggregate data continues to mask the high levels of income inequality, class stratification, and institutional discrimination experienced by predominantly low-income native-born Mexican American and Puerto Rican women and racialized and economically disadvantaged immigrant entrepreneurs. Demographic data can pinpoint ethnic group patterns and communities in need of resources and technical financial assistance to ensure community-driven interventions so as to create resource-healthy communities of opportunity.

The dynamic growth of Latina-owned businesses may transform the economic and political landscape in the United States in the years ahead (Melgoza and Palomarez 2015). Yet attention must be focused on financial capital startups and the expansion needs of experienced corporate and business-trained Latino/a entrepreneurs who oftentimes confront potential tax policy barriers (Morales 2012). In response to these barriers, programs need to be developed to inform banks and Small Business Administration agents about how to strengthen or create relationships with Latinos where they are nonexistent. Banks can partner with community stakeholders to create innovative programming that aligns with the financial business needs of the population. A targeted focus for developing practices and policies that destigmatize Latinos as high risk and increase relationships and trust are imperative for supporting the economic growth of Latina entrepreneurs. Other strategies include partnerships between less experienced and more experienced Latina entrepreneurs in a mentoring model. Community-based organizations can offer basic financial resource and entrepreneurial support services. Most imperative are initiatives to inform financial institutions about how to improve access to fair banking loan practices and banking products. Institutional change is an important first step in creating self-employment mechanisms for entrepreneurial growth so as to increase income equality and social mobility. U.S. financial institutions are the first world drivers that can promote a long-term boom in Latina entrepreneurial success and increase income equity and wealth among all Latinas and their families.

ACKNOWLEDGMENTS

We gratefully acknowledge the grant award from JP Morgan Chase Foundation Grant #21269289 (2015–2017) to New Economics for Women, Bea Stotzer (principal investigator) and Ruth E. Zambrana (coprincipal investigator and study director). We also thank Wendy Hall for the preparation of this manuscript and the thoughtful and insightful comments of reviewers.

NOTES

1. Additionally, 4 of the 10 women provided recommendations for strengthening survey tools and future research themes on the topic.
2. Five of the 10 participants shared additional personal reflections that they believed influenced their experience as Latina entrepreneurs, such as family, children, culture, power, leadership, value of mentors, and gender.

REFERENCES

Agius Vallejo, Jody, and Stephanie L. Canizales. 2016. "Latino/a Professionals as Entrepreneurs: How Race, Class, and Gender Shape Entrepreneurial Incorporation." *Ethnic and Racial Studies* 39(9):1637–56.

Bernstein, Robert. 2016. "Hispanic-Owned Businesses on the Upswing." U.S. Census Bureau. https://www.census.gov/newsroom/blogs/random-samplings /2016/12/hispanic-owned_busin.html.

Boshara, Ray, William R. Emmons, and Bryan J. Noeth. 2015. "The Demographics of Wealth-How Age, Education and Race Separate Thrivers from Strugglers in Today's Economy—Essay No. 1: Race, Ethnicity and Wealth." *Demographics of Wealth* (1):1–24.

Chang, Erick P., Esra Memili, James J. Chrisman, Franz W. Kellermanns, and Jess H. Chua. 2009. "Family Social Capital, Venture Preparedness, and Start-Up Decisions: A Study of Hispanic Entrepreneurs in New England." *Family Business Review* 22(3):279–92.

Chang, Marik L., and Meizhu Lui. 2010. *Lifting as We Climb: Women of Color, Wealth, and America's Future.* Oakland, CA: Insight Center for Community Economic Development.

Colby, Sandra L., and Jennifer M. Ortman. 2014. "Projections of the Size and Composition of the U.S. Population: 2014 to 2060." Current Population Reports, P25-1143. U.S. Census Bureau, Washington, DC.

Dávila, Alberto, Marie T. Mora, and Angela Marek Zeitlin. 2014. "Better Business: How Hispanic Entrepreneurs Are Beating Expectations and Bolstering the US Economy." Washington, DC: The Partnership for a New American Economy.

Keister, Lisa A., and Stephanie Moller. 2000. "Wealth Inequality in the United States." *Annual Review of Sociology* 26(1):63–81.

Mattingly, Marybeth J., and Juan M. Pedroza. 2015. "Why Isn't the Hispanic Poverty Rate Rising?" *Pathways: Magazine on Poverty, Inequality and Social Policy* (Spring):9–12.

Melgoza, Cesar, and Javier Palomarez. 2015. "Hispanics Businesses and Entrepreneurs Drive Growth in the New Economy." 3rd annual report. Geoscape. http://bit.ly/2btWM5a.

Mishel, Lawrence, Josh Bivens, Elise Gould, and Heidi Shierholz. 2012. *The State of Working America, 12th Edition.* Ithaca, NY: Cornell University Press.

Morales, Alfonso. 2009a. "Public Markets as Community Development Tools." *Journal of Planning Education and Research* 28(4):426–40.

Morales, Alfonso. 2009b. "A Woman's Place Is on the Street: Purposes and Problems of Mexican American Women Entrepreneurs." Pp. 99–125 in *An American Story: Mexican American Entrepreneurship and Wealth Creation*, edited by John S. Butler, Alfonso Morales, and David L. Torres. West Lafayette, IN: Purdue University Press.

Morales, Alfonso. 2012. "Understanding and Interpreting Tax Compliance Strategies among Street Vendors." Pp. 83–106 in *The Ethics of Tax Evasion.* New York: Springer.

Orozco, Marlene, Paul Oyer, and Jerry I. Porras. 2018. *2017 State of Latino Entrepreneurship*. Stanford Latino Report. Stanford, CA: Stanford Graduate School of Business.

Ortiz-Walters, Rowena, Monica C. Gavino, and Denise Williams. 2015. "Social Networks of Latino and Latina Entrepreneurs and Their Impact on Venture Performance." *Academy of Entrepreneurship Journal* 21(1):58.

Pew Research Center. 2016. *On Views of Race and Inequality, Blacks and Whites Are Worlds Apart*. http://assets.pewresearch.org/wp-content/uploads/sites/3/2016/06/ST_2016.06.27_Race-Inequality-Final.pdf.

Raijman, Rebeca, and Marta Tienda. 2000. "Immigrants' Pathways to Business Ownership: A Comparative Ethnic Perspective." *International Migration Review* 34(3):682–706.

Ryan, Camille L., and Kurt Bauman. 2016. "Educational Attainment in the United States: 2015; Population Characteristics Report: Current Population Reports. U.S. Census Bureau. https://www.census.gov/content/dam/Census/library/publications/2016/demo/p20-578.pdf.

Robles, Barbara J., and Hector Cordero-Guzman. 2007. "Latino Self-Employment and Entrepreneurship in the United States: An Overview of the Literature and Data Sources." *Annals of the American Academy of Political and Social Science* 613(1):18–31.

Sanders, Jimy M., and Victor Nee. 1996. "Immigrant Self-Employment: The Family as Social Capital and the Value of Human Capital. *American Sociological Review* 61(2):231–49.

Shapiro, Thomas M. 2017. *Toxic Inequality: How America's Wealth Gap Destroys Mobility, Deepens the Racial Divide, and Threatens Our Future*. New York: Basic Books.

State of Latino Entrepreneurship 2018. Research Report. Stanford School of Business, Stanford Graduate School of Business. In collaboration with the Latino Business Action Network.

Telles, Edward E. and Vilma Ortiz. 2008. *Generations of Exclusion: Mexican-Americans, Assimilation, and Race*. New York: Russell Sage Foundation.

Valdez, Zulema. 2011. *The New Entrepreneurs: How Race, Class, and Gender Shape American Enterprise*. Stanford, CA: Stanford University Press.

Valleta, Lili Gil. 2017. "Latina Entrepreneurs Elevate Minority Business Issues during Meeting with President Trump." Huffington Post, March 27. https://www.huffingtonpost.com/entry/latina-entrepreneurs-elevate-issues-and-opportunities_us_58d9744be4b0e6062d922ff0.

Vega. Tanzina. 2015. "U.S. Sees Big Spike in Black and Hispanic Women Entrepreneurs." CNN, August 18. http://money.cnn.com/2015/08/19/smallbusiness/minority-women-entrepreneur/index.html.

Verdaguer, Maria Eugenia. 2009. "Gender and Resource Mobilization Strategies." Pp 116–45 in *Class, Ethnicity, Gender and Latino Entrepreneurship*. New York: Routledge.

Zambrana, Ruth Enid. 2011. "Girlhood to Womanhood." Pp. 89–114 in *Latinos in American Society*. New York: Cornell University Press.

Zuiker, Virginia Solis, Mary Jo Katras, Catherine P. Montalto, and Patricia D. Olson. 2003. "Hispanic Self-Employment: Does Gender Matter?" *Hispanic Journal of Behavioral Sciences* 25(1):73–94.

PART IV

PRACTICE AND POLICY

SLEI-Education Scaling Program: A Business Program of "National Economic Imperative"

Marlene Orozco

INTRODUCTION

Small businesses and entrepreneurship have long been the driver of the U.S. economy. While the rate of business starts has been declining in the United States (Decker et al. 2014; Morelix, Hwang, and Tareque 2017), minority-owned firms and particularly Latino-owned businesses have the greatest growth of new businesses (Orozco, Oyer, and Porras 2017; Rivers et al. 2016). The growth rate of Latino-owned business outpaces that of all other demographic groups. With the growing Latino population alongside its youthful makeup, there is great potential for Latino entrepreneurs to turn around the long-term decline of entrepreneurial dynamism in the United States. However, these Latino-owned firms tend to be smaller than their non-Latino counterparts. In 2012, we expected an additional $1.38 trillion to be added to the U.S. gross domestic product if the opportunity gap facing Latino firms relative to their non-Latino counterparts were closed (Rivers et al. 2015)—that is, if the average Latino business generated annual sales equal to the average non-Latino-owned business. In today's dollars, that is about $70 billion more, or $1.47 trillion.

Alongside this growth, the discourse around Latino-owned firms has shifted over time. Beyond moral or social obligations, programs are framing the support of Latino-owned entrepreneurs and firms as a national economic imperative given their growing presence, upward trends, and significant contributions to the economy. As a primary policy recommendation for strengthening the growth of Latino-owned firms, there is a call to create and fund education and training programs that are culturally competent and convenient and target growth-oriented entrepreneurs of color (Alvarez 2017; Klein 2017). While government at all levels and nonprofits provide training and technical assistance to new entrepreneurs, fewer focus specifically on firms poised for growth, or scaled firms. Scaled firms in this context are defined as firms generating at least $1 million in annual revenue. Moreover, small business programs for nascent entrepreneurs are often structured around short interventions or specific outputs, such as one-day workshops for incorporating a business or creating a business, marketing, or financial plan. These programs often lack specialized components that go beyond the educational training to provide ongoing and culturally specific support to Latino entrepreneurs as they navigate the growth process.

Heeding the call for culturally competent, high-capacity, and convenient programming, the Stanford Latino Entrepreneurship Initiative (SLEI)–Education Scaling program, in collaboration with the Latino Business Action (LBAN), focuses on Latino business owners with poised-for-growth firms. This immersive program provides owners the education, enhanced networks, and personal mentorship and a better understanding in accessing capital resources to scale their business, create jobs, and build a stronger economy. The seven-week program kicks off at Stanford University, where entrepreneurs take courses with world-renowned professors, participate in live case studies, network with each other, and learn more about the online course. The custom course is based on curriculum developed by two Stanford professors, Huggy Rao and Bob Sutton, adopted to meet the unique challenges that Latino entrepreneurs might face in scaling their business. The course, titled "Scaling Up Your Venture," speaks directly to the scaling issue that the SLEI-Research program (see Chapter 5 in this volume) highlights as key to the success of Latino-owned businesses. At the culmination of the program, participants return to Stanford for a closing program that includes seminars from highly successful Latino entrepreneurs, meeting with several capital providers, and a certification ceremony with participants' families.

The program has over 500 alumni from more than 30 states and Puerto Rico who collectively generate over $1.9 billion in annual gross revenue. This chapter provides a detailed look at the experiences of program participants through 30 qualitative in-depth interviews. In particular, it seeks to understand how poised-for-growth Latino entrepreneurs navigate their growth process. The chapter concludes with a larger discussion on the efforts of SLEI-Ed alumni in their communities as they elevate the Latino business ecosystem and reshape the national discourse of Latino entrepreneurship.

BACKGROUND

On the whole, the implications of strengthening the growth of Latino-owned firms on both upward mobility and the creation of community wealth has largely been understudied. It is not until recently that Latino-specific and general minority business programs have begun this work through their respective program evaluations. The early literature on ethnic economies considered a series of push and pull factors that shape ethnic business development—that is, the reasons why ethnic communities engage in entrepreneurship. These factors include market conditions, government policies, ethnic social networks, and resource mobilization (Waldinger, Aldrich, and Ward 1990). These early studies also highlighted the importance of ethnic concentration, or the enclave, but often only to the extent that it impacts the economic outcomes of employees instead of the business owners themselves (Portes and Jensen 1992; for more on the enclave see Chapter 9 in this volume). I conceive of recent Latino entrepreneurship in three simultaneous and overlapping time periods. These time periods provide the context in which Latino entrepreneurship is discussed at a national level and simultaneously influences research and programmatic agendas.

Proliferation of Latino Enclaves (1980–1994)

Early research on Latino entrepreneurship as a means of social mobility began with sociologist Alejandro Portes and colleagues as they considered the outcomes of Cuban immigrants in Miami. They found the capacity of ethnic enclaves to provide immigrants with a path for upward mobility. The single best predictor of self-employment was employment by another Cuban three years earlier (Portes and Zhou 1993; Wilson and Portes 1980). Since the 1980s, researchers have analyzed the entrepreneurial activity of

Cubans in Miami given their clustered concentration. During the Mariel boatlift in 1980, the influx of Cuban refugees increased the Miami labor force by 7 percent and a saw a 20 percent increase in the Cuban working population (Card 1990). During this period and throughout other immigrant influxes, one of the chief discourses of nativists and immigrant policy makers alike is the extent to which immigrants depress labor market opportunities of the less-skilled natives.

The natural experiment of the Mariel Boatlift demonstrated the capacity of cities to both absorb the growth in the supply of labor and provide new market opportunities for the growing population. However, one must consider the larger sociopolitical context that underlines the structural opportunities and challenges for Latino entrepreneurs, such as market conditions and access to ownership through government policies (Waldinger et al. 1990; Waldinger, Chishti, and Editors 1997). Given the refugee status of this group of Cuban immigrants, there was a tacit acceptance unlike that of undocumented immigrants (namely, those from Mexico and Central American countries) who are perceived as perpetually foreign (for more on the historical circumstances of Cuban entrepreneurs compared to other Latino groups, see Chapter 2 in this volume).

Beyond Miami, the limited but budding literature on Latino-owned businesses has considered entrepreneurship in other Latino enclaves such as in Los Angeles (Vallejo 2012), New York, Chicago (Raijman and Tienda 2000), and Houston (Valdez 2011). Through a circular pattern, dense Latino populations yield emergent Latino entrepreneurism and vice versa. However, Latino-owned businesses have also existed outside of dense Latino metro areas and are forming new gateways of entrepreneurship (see Chapter 5 in this volume for a map of Latino-owned businesses). Still, Latino entrepreneurship has historically been considered a localized phenomenon limited to a few central cities in the United States. When the North American Free Trade Agreement (NAFTA) went into effect in 1994, it eliminated duties and quantitative restrictions with Mexico. This agreement opened up opportunities for bilingual and bicultural U.S. Latinos. Additionally, it was Latino border entrepreneurs and their business organizations that proved to be largely instrumental in getting NAFTA nearly unanimously supported by the Texas congressional delegation (Korzeniewicz and Smith 1996). Ultimately, this expanded Latino business reach beyond the enclave and localized communities and into international markets.

Professionalization of Latinos (1978–2014)

With the opening up of higher education through policies such as Affirmative Action and the legacy of the 1960s, a significantly larger number of Latinos attended and graduated from college than ever before, giving rise to the professionalization of Latinos. According to Pew Research, in 2014, 35 percent of Latinos ages 18 to 24 were enrolled in a two- or four-year college, up from 22 percent in 1993. This 13 percentage point increase amounted to 2.3 million Latino college students in 2014 (Krogstad 2016). SLEI research finds that Latino entrepreneurs tend to be more highly educated than the Latino general population. In 2017, more than twice the number of Latino business owners held at least a four-year college degree (37 percent) compared to the Latino general population (16 percent). Thus, the increasing opportunities of higher education among Latinos has coincided with the increase in Latino entrepreneurship more broadly. Beyond formal education, there has also been a rise in entrepreneurial training targeting minority business owners with long-standing programming coming from the federal government through the Minority Small Business and Capital Ownership Development Program, commonly known as the 8(a) Program.

Given statutory backing in 1978, the 8(a) Program resulted in a merger of two distinct types of federal programs: those seeking to assist small business in general and those seeking to assist racial and ethnic minorities (Congressional Research Service 2019). Federal programs for racial and ethnic minorities began developing around the same time as those for small business, but there was no explicit overlap until the 8(a). The 8(a) Program provides training, technical assistance, and government contracting opportunities to participating small business owners whom are "socially and economically disadvantaged"[1] and demonstrate "potential for success" (Congressional Research Service 2019:1). In fiscal year 2016, 8(a) firms were awarded more than $27 billion in federal contracts. While the number of Latino firms served by 8(a) is not publicly available, there was a growing decline in the number of firms certified from 2010 to 2015 at the same time that the overall number of Latino firms in the United States was rising. Furthermore, in 2015 SLEI found that among Latino business owners, 22 percent had never heard of the Small Business Administration (SBA), 51 percent hard never heard of small business investment companies, and 56 percent had never heard of the Small Business Innovation Research program, three of the largest and most-well known government funding programs for small businesses (Rivers et al. 2015). SLEI finds underwhelming government usage among Latino-owned businesses, as Latino firms have the lowest rates of business loans from federal, state, or local government and government-guaranteed business loans from a financial institution. Furthermore, nine times the number of Latino firms would like government loans than currently have them, representing the largest funding gap among all desired funding types (Orozco et al. 2017).

Still, the structuring of the 8(a) Program through the resulting amendment to the Small Business Act captures the shifting discourse of Latino entrepreneurship. The law indicates "that the opportunity for full participation in our free enterprise system by socially and economically disadvantaged persons is essential if we are to obtain social and economic equality for such persons and improve the functioning of our national economy" (Small Business Investment Act 1958). Recent congresses have had particular interest in the program given the role of minority-owned businesses in job creation. Even Donald Trump, a vocal proponent against immigration (although SLEI finds that Latino immigrants disproportionately have successful scaled firms relative to native-born Latinos) proclaimed October 22 through October 28, 2017, "National Minority Enterprise Development Week" to recognize the contributions of minority-owned businesses to the economy.

Latino Entrepreneurship as a National Economic Imperative (2013–Present)

The most recent period of Latino entrepreneurship is categorized as one that elevates the rhetoric to national economic imperative. In 2013, Professor Jerry Porras of the Stanford Graduate School of Business and a group of Latino MBA alumni came together to form a nonprofit 501(c)3 organization, the Latino Business Action Network (LBAN), focused on making America stronger through LBAN-funded Latino research and education impact programs at Stanford University. LBAN's mission is to "strengthen the United States by empowering leaders to grow substantial firms that create jobs, develop leaders, and a spawn a new generation of companies." It is through the collaboration with LBAN that the SLEI-Ed program develops the growth-capacity of Latino entrepreneurs. LBAN embodies the shift in discourse of Latino entrepreneurship as one of national importance.

This national discourse was similarly elevated through the Aspen Institute Forum on Latino Business Growth in the spring of 2017. The

Aspen Institute Latinos and Society Program convened 27 experts and practitioners to address and devise solutions regarding the growth barriers of Latino-owned firms (Alvarez 2017). The calls for action included bolstering the availability of business training and education programs given the "dearth of business resources meeting the developmental needs of Latino business owners whose businesses are ready for continued growth and scale" (Alvarez 2017:18). Table 13.1 compares programs that support small poised-for-growth (i.e., scaling) companies with potential for job creation. While certainly not exhaustive, as there are other localized Latino programs not listed here, the table captures prominent programs with a national reach that specifically target minority, Latino, or other historically underserved entrepreneurs (e.g., those from low-income communities). Most of these programs teach related topics that support entrepreneurs through the growth process. However, a smaller subset, including the SLEI-Ed program, have specialized components that address the ongoing needs of Latino entrepreneurs. The remainder of the chapter explores the growth experiences of SLEI-Ed alumni both in their experiences with the program and as they reflect on past and future challenges and opportunities.

METHODS AND DATA

The present study uses a qualitative approach to highlight the ways in which Latino entrepreneurs navigate their growth process.[2] The SLEI-Ed program recruits poised-for-growth[3] business owners to apply and participate in an executive education program that runs twice a year. For each cohort, a group of 70–80 business owners are selected from upwards of 240 applicants to participate in a seven-week online course geared at scaling a business. The specialized components of the program include weekly mentorship[4] meetings, tailor-made webinars, and a capital provider speed-pitching session, among others. Currently there are over 500 alumni of the program. I selected a randomized stratified subset to interview, sampling for range across industries, gender, and geographic location, resulting in 30 cases. Among baseline business questions, respondents self-identify on the application as having Hispanic or Latino background, as this program specifically targets the growth of Latino-owned businesses. While some business owners are located in the local San Francisco Bay Area, the program recruits participants from a national database and networks.

TABLE 13.1 National Latino/Minority Entrepreneurship Scaling Programs

Program	Structure and Length	Eligibility and Requirements	Latino / Minority Focus	Curriculum and Topics	Specialized Components	Cost	Location
SBAs Emerging Leaders Program	7-month program Classroom learning + out of class preparation	At least $400,000 annual revenue At least 3 years in business At least 1 employee, other than self	55% minority-owned 16% Latino (2015)	StreetWise 'MBA™ Strategic Growth Action Plan Financing and Access to Capital Government Contracting	Mentoring	Free	51 cities, SBA District Offices
Interise's StreetWise 'MBA™	Licenses program to partners who deliver through their own locally branded programs	Partner specific	42% minority-owned 36% low-to-moderate income community (2016)	Curriculum by Interise Strategy Financial analysis Accessing capital Marketing Sales strategy Talent Contracting Growth plan	Live cases	Partner specific	80+ locations

Program	Format	Eligibility	Demographics	Curriculum	Additional Services	Cost	Location
Goldman Sachs 10,000 Small Businesses	12-week program	At least $150,000 annual revenue At least 2 years in business At least 4 employees, including the owner	No data on racial/ethnic makeup of participants	Curriculum by Babson College Growth plan Financial analysis Leadership Talent Marketing Legal Operations	Mentoring Networking events Business support clinics	Free	33 sites across U.S. and UK 100 local and national partners
Tuck Executive Education at Dartmouth—Minority Business Programs	1-week program Residential program	At least $300,000 in annual revenue 3–5 years of ownership management experience	100% minority-focused No Latino-specific data available	Curriculum by Tuck Executive Education Accounting and Cash Flow Strategy Operations Leadership Capital	None	$4,900	Dartmouth University, Hanover, NH

(*continued*)

TABLE 13.1 *(Continued)*

Program	Structure and Length	Eligibility and Requirements	Latino / Minority Focus	Curriculum and Topics	Specialized Components	Cost	Location
Minority Business Executive Program (MPEP) at University of Washington Foster School of Business	1-week program Residential program	At least $300,000 in annual revenue	100% minority-focused No Latino-specific data available	Curriculum by Foster Executive Education Finance and accounting Negotiations Strategy Marketing Leadership Supply chain management	None	$4,250	University of Washington, Seattle, WA
Stanford Latino Entrepreneurship Initiative–Education Scaling Program	7-week program On-campus sessions 2 weekends + online	At least $1 million in annual revenue or have raised at least $500,000 of external funding	100% Latino-focused	Curriculum by Stanford GSB Executive Education Strategy Financial analysis Accessing capital Operations Marketing Sales strategy Talent Contracting Pitch deck	Mentoring Live cases Design thinking Session with over 50 capital providers Regional alumni networking events	$1,000	Stanford Graduate School of Business, Stanford, CA

Table 13.2 presents descriptive statistics of the interview sample. While Latina business owners are driving much of the overall growth in Latino-owned businesses (Davila and Mora 2013), they make up 30 percent of scaled Latino-owned businesses. Latinas are oversampled in this study and represent 38 percent of those interviewed. Moreover, 70 percent of the respondents are married, and nearly half (47 percent) are married to a white partner. This is important to note, as intermarriage marks a traditional assimilation benchmark. Socioeconomic status is another assimilation benchmark captured here through homeownership (74 percent). Given the success of their businesses, all respondents report currently being part of a self-described middle-class or higher-class status. Their childhood backgrounds, however, include greater variation, with a little less than half (43 percent) coming from low-income/working-class or lower middle-class backgrounds. As previous studies on entrepreneurs have noted, it is important to consider class backgrounds in our interpretation of results, as this tends to color entrepreneurial outcomes (Valdez 2011).

Immigrant-owned businesses represent nearly half of all Latino-owned businesses and 46 percent of this sample. As Figure 13.1 shows, there is a fair spread in the geographic location of respondent's businesses from Manassas, Virginia, to Salinas, California. Finally, it is important to note that 58 percent of the sample reports a family history of entrepreneurship, with parents and siblings currently or previously owning businesses and 54 percent of the business owners having had or currently having family members working for them including spouses, children, and siblings. As an example, one business owner has five of his eight siblings and a son working for his software company. Another business owner employs his mother, father, father-in-law, and four other close relatives in his wholesale company. One entrepreneur describes this prevalence by saying "we're very *familia*." While early conceptualizations considered the training functions of ethnic economies for coethnic employees (Raijman and Tienda 2000), there is the potential training function of highly specialized businesses for subsequent family members.

The pool of interview subjects seemingly captures elements of sample bias in that these business owners may systematically differ from non-applicants to the program. However, since the goal of this study is to consider how Latino business owners with a proven business track record strategize their growth process, the sample yields an upward look into activities undertaken by these business owners. Furthermore, a nonrandom

TABLE 13.2 *Descriptive Statistics of Latino Business Owner Respondents*

Descriptive	Percent/Avg.
Gender	
Female	38%
Male	62%
Age	42
Married	70%
Partner race	
White	47%
Hispanic	53%
Family history of entrepreneurship	58%
Family work in business	54%
Education (4 years+)	74%
Ancestry	
Mexican	35%
Cuban	9%
Puerto Rican	4%
Central America	17%
South American	26%
Spanish	9%
Mixed Race	30%
Native-Born	54%
Homeownership	74%
Childhood class	
Low-income/working class	30%
Lower middle class	13%
Middle class	40%
Upper middle class	17%
Industry	
Technology/software	26%
Professional, scientific, and technical services	40%
Educational services	14%
Real estate	4%
Transportation	4%
Waste management	4%
Manufacturing	8%
Years in business	9

Source: SLEI-Ed interview respondents.

Note: N = 30. Central American includes Guatemalan, Honduran, and Nicaraguan.

South American includes Argentinian, Colombian, Peruvian, Venezuelan, and Brazilian.

Figure 13.1 Business location of respondents. (Source: SLEI-Ed interview participants.)

sample is preferred in that the program itself serves as an instance of high network connectivity as people hear about the program through chambers of commerce (both Hispanic and general), business contacts, email list-servs, social media ads, and personal referrals. Thus, participants of this program are presented as "unique cases" (Small 2009). Interviews occur in person wherever possible for those located in the San Francisco Bay Area, otherwise via videoconference or phone, and last on average 60 minutes.

I begin each interview with a specified set of questions asked of all participants including detailed histories of how they came to start the business, their family life and community growing up, the communities they live in now and are involved with, and their business development. From there, I follow up on their responses to trace new themes as each interview progresses. Each respondent completed a follow-up demographic survey for any information not gleaned in the interview or previous program surveys. The interview protocol slightly shifted over time as new themes emerged inductively. This iterative process allows future interviews to adapt to insights gained from previous interviews (Glaser and Strauss 1967). All business owners and their businesses are presented under pseudonyms to protect anonymity.

In the summer of 2017, SLEI conducted its first annual alumni survey of cohorts one through three, with data 18 months after cohort one completed the program, 12 months since program completion for cohort two, and 6 months for cohort three. Taken together, the alumni survey had a 78 percent response rate. Some of these findings are presented here.

FINDINGS

The research questions of this study are twofold. First, how do poised-for-growth Latino entrepreneurs navigate their growth process? Second, what are SLEI-Ed alumni doing in their communities to elevate the Latino business ecosystem and reshape the national discourse of Latino entrepreneurship? SLEI-Ed entrepreneurs recount their experiences in navigating their growth process in two ways: (1) through their varied financial experiences and (2) training experiences in the 8(a) Program, through SLEI-Ed, or both. Among the Latinas in this sample, about half have done both programs, and a smaller subset of Latino males have engaged in both programs.

Financing: An Essential Growth Factor

Access to capital remains a prominent challenge for Latino business owners (see Chapter 5). External sources of financing such as bank and government loans, venture capital, and angel investing are critical in helping a business scale. SLEI-Ed entrepreneurs describe the ways in which they navigate the process. Not unlike national trends, 78 percent of SLEI-Ed alumni started their companies by self-financing, while only 22 percent had investors. Among those who requested funds from friends or family to start their business, they reflect on being "fortunate" or having "personal angels." Others recount serendipitous exchanges in their friendship network that led to their funding. When successful, these entrepreneurs describe their funding experience as "very unique," as they understand the importance of varied networks in securing funding. Edward, cofounder of a health care technology firm, describes his attempts at tapping into his personal network: "As family goes, mine and my partners, it's kind of exhausted. We had a few friends, cousins, and sort of not the closest family, but folks that we knew that were actually open to investment. We went through a few of those rounds, but my list of contacts wasn't very long that had that kind of capital. I should have explored my friend list deeper [Laughter]."

Research on the minority middle class often cites close ties to poorer coethnics (Vallejo 2012), which disadvantages entrepreneurs who, like Edward, may quickly exhaust the resources of their personal network. In other cases, the personal network of the kind needed to finance entrepreneurial endeavors may not exist, and the entrepreneur is instead seen as the provider in the network.

At their growth stage, many SLEI-Ed entrepreneurs recount less than positive experiences with banks. Miguel, cofounder and COO of a product development firm, describes his first experience with the bank as "really bad." They had marked him as a "high-risk company" and did not want to give him a credit line:

> The funny thing was that we actually wanted a credit line taken and backed by a CD or a money market account that we were going to drop money into. We were telling the bank, "We're going to buy a $20,000.00 CD, and I just want you to open me a line of credit against those $20,000.00, so you have that money there. Let's start the relationship." And they actually told us, "No, we cannot do that." That was the first one. The second time we went

to the bank, they kind of said, "Okay, but I am not going to lend you all the money that you're depositing, even in the CD. If you deposit $20,000.00, then I'm just going to give you a $10,000.00 credit line. And you have to sign this document where you basically say that you are personally liable for any business you do with the bank from now on." So we did not sign that year. A long time afterwards, we kept saving enough money so that we built kind of our own credit line.

Here, Miguel describes a bank that is unwilling to work with his particular requests. SLEI-Ed entrepreneurs often recount a sense of anxiety in trying to work with banks, particularly when they must be personally liable, as Miguel describes. In some cases, entrepreneurs such as Francis, president and founder of a design firm, have put up multiple mortgages on their personal home to personally secure the loans. Others refuse to secure funding through personal collateral and instead have to get creative in their search. Even when the banking relationship has been established, the sense of anxiety does not always dissipate. Francis describes his relationship with the banks: "I feel like I'm at their mercy all the time. So in spite of the fact that they've seemingly been reasonable, I'm always concerned that it's going to dry up and they're going to yank me." Francis describes a perpetual power imbalance with banks. However, some entrepreneurs are finding success with local banks and community funds. On the national survey, SLEI finds higher usage rates among local banks compared to national banks. Lori is one example of this. She describes going to national banks, but "no one would loan to me." She then went to a community loan fund. She made her case with them in a matter-of-fact way: "I told this bank, I said, 'Look, we're going to be doing a million. . . . We are exponentially growing and we are going to be one of the most influential businesses in this county. I want a bank we can have a relationship with.' She said, 'Okay.' They wrote us this loan and they were really good and they came back to me and said, 'What else can we do for you?'"

As evidenced by both Lori's retelling of her community fund experience and Miguel's bank experience, entrepreneurs describe wanting to have a relationship with banks. Beyond a transactional exchange, Latino entrepreneurs seek a humanizing experience so that lenders can hear out their situation and work with them flexibly. Karla captures this desire to be known by the lender beyond the paperwork that they see.

Karla, president of an industrial company, was seeking about $240,000 to buy her first industrial machinery. Karla describes what it took for her to finally secure funding:

> It was a strong push from my end but getting a loan was tough. Even the last bank that ended up saying "yes" they initially called me to say "no." They called to say, "sorry and thanks for all your effort but we're going to have to bow out." I was pretty pregnant at the time and frustrated. I was taking the call at the doctor's office and I had to take the call outside. I told them, "You don't understand our tenacity. You don't understand our drive. You don't know us. All you have is a bunch of paperwork that I sent you and I understand that you don't want to lend us money but I'm going to keep going. Somebody's going to lend us that money and were going to pay our loans back. We're good risk and I'm going to prove that to whoever believes in me. I'm going to make sure that you're aware of it and that you should have taken a risk on us. You could have made a lot of money on us but that's fine. Thanks for your time and I appreciate it." And then I hung up the phone. The broker called me and apologized and I told him "I'm just pretty tired of getting no's all the time." And then I went into my doctor's office. When I came out, I had a voicemail from the broker saying the bank had called him and changed his mind. I was like I have everything to gain and nothing to lose. I'm just going to scream at these people and I did.

Karla's experience captures the resilience that Latino entrepreneurs have to embody, often working past multiple "no's" and searching until someone is willing to take a chance on them. Furthermore, Karla's insistence on the bank getting to know her personally—her tenacity, her drive—points to an unintended consequence of the advent of the credit score. Banks assess risk based on the "bunch of paperwork" they receive and then make snapshot, quantitative judgments of loan-worthy or -risky business ventures. Before credit scoring, lenders assessed applicants on qualitative measures, such as payment history and other reputation-based characteristics. Latinos whose families span multiple generations in the United States may stand to benefit from these small-town arrangements. However, newly arriving immigrants are disadvantaged all around, lacking U.S. credit histories and any reputation-based measures unless they come into an enclave where their families from the sending country are known.

Moreover, the funding experiences of Latinas slightly converge from that of the Latino male entrepreneurs. In the 2017 *State of Latino Entrepreneurship* research report, SLEI reports Latino-owned firms growing in number at rapid rate but Latina entrepreneurs face a funding ceiling, as they perceive of themselves as being "less qualified" to receive funding from financial institutions compared to their male counterparts, even when holding firm size constant (Orozco et al. 2017). We see some of this among Latina SLEI-Ed entrepreneurs. For instance, Margarita, owner of a growing bakery, describes putting together "a fantastic binder, beautiful with all the information and I presented to the bank and everyone told me, 'no, no, no, no.'" Later she would go on to present the same binder to the SBA loan office. As she describes, "I introduced myself, I brought in my product. Of course, I didn't qualify for anything." Given her previous experiences with banks, Margarita may have decided to settle for one store. While she was persistent in her funding efforts and eventually secured loan funding, it is possible that other Latinas continue to perceive of themselves as less qualified and self-impose barriers to scale in addition to the externally imposed barriers. Previous research has shown a similar gendered perception of qualification among women who think they are not qualified to run for office, even when having comparable educational, occupational, and professional success relative to men (Lawless 2015). As an additional example, Daniela, a SLEI-Ed entrepreneur with extensive financial background, describes fund-raising as "not my best talent," although she has successfully raised two rounds of a few million dollars.

There are distinctions in mind-set between how Latinas at the unscaled and scaled business levels operate.[5] As depicted in Chapter 12, unscaled Latina-owned firms feel a sense of pride in starting their business with personal savings and not borrowing money from banks. Still, external financing remains an essential growth factor. Even when scaling, a different mind-set creeps in—gendered perceptions of qualifications—when seeking funding. Latinas may realize the need for additional funding to continue on a path toward scalability but may doubt that they have what it takes for such funding. That is, for some Latinas, they must first feel sufficiently confident in their level of success and qualifications in order to pursue funding, counting themselves out of the funding pipeline.

However, some Latinas are setting forth efforts to combat the gendered perceptions of others. For example, Tina, a serial entrepreneur who previously owned a chain of gas stations, pinpointed a gendered hindrance to her business development when securing funding:

> I don't think Hispanic hindered me as much but I think being female more. When I first opened the gas station business and was going after the first loan, and maybe it was perception on our part but we put my husband out there first because he's an Anglo guy and I thought that it might be easier for people to give us loans or support the business. Behind the scenes I was the one doing the schmoozing and the venture capital solicitation, but in front of the bankers we'd put my husband just in case.

Tina highlights the importance of understanding the experiences of Latino entrepreneurs navigating their business growth through an intersectional lens. In particular, many of the SLEI-Ed Latinas discuss the salience of their gender identities in their respective industries.

It should be noted that some Latino entrepreneurs, even at the scaled level, do not desire external sources of funding. Jorge, owner of a software company, describes:

> Our experience is a bit different in the entrepreneurship arena in the sense that we are a bootstrap company and we don't aim to raise equity in any sense. We have very successfully grown with our customers' money and that's probably a different approach to growth and to financing, but it's definitely the most stable and the most realistic, in my opinion. The path is very complex because we have to be very, very scrappy with our expenses and to have a very good controlling system on expenses, but it has already brought us many benefits in regards to the internal control of our company. We don't have VCs behind us making us change everything but we have complete control of our company and that has really paid off for the future.

Jorge brings forward the idea of internal control. In the 2015 Survey of U.S. Latino Business Owners, SLEI found that although half of respondents believe they could grow faster if they had additional capital,

67 percent are concerned about losing control of their business (Rivers et al. 2015). However, this company is in a unique position, as it is utilizing internal business to fund business growth, a source of funding that has an 8 percentage point funding gap. In the 2017 Survey of U.S. Latino Business Owners, SLEI finds that 16 percent of Latino firms are leveraging business revenue but that 24 percent would like to access business revenue to fund their business growth. That is, many Latino-owned businesses are not in position to leverage business revenue for growth. Overall, financing proved to be a challenging experience for all entrepreneurs. They navigate this largely through persistence, resilience, and finding the right type of capital. This includes local community banks, equipment financing, loan sharks, and bootstrapping, or self-financing.

Growth through the SBA's 8(a) and Procurement

Related to fund-raising, government contracting is a way in which businesses can secure high-dollar contracts with a fixed term. Given the high volume of government spending on set-aside and sole-source contracting, about $27 billion in 2016, SLEI-Ed entrepreneurs are readily familiar with the 8(a) Program. Among the SLEI-Ed Latinas interviewed for this study, half of them reveal a successful completion or near completion of the 8(a) Program or SBA loan engagement. However, Latino firms in the United States have the lowest number of government-backed loans, and nine times the number of firms report that they would like to have them. This represents the largest funding gap among specific funding types for Latinos. Thus, there is still much work to be done at the government level in terms of engaging a wider range of Latino business owners.

Although government support of minority businesses exists with the 8(a) Program, Latino entrepreneurs are quick to point out that it is their distinctive qualities that led them to their success. As Martha notes, "Being Latina gives me that passion and drive. Latinos are entrepreneurs. We do whatever it takes to make a living. I think being Latina has actually helped me, and SBA or not, I still would be climbing the ladder . . . maybe just not as fast." For Martha, it is the qualities she attributes with being Latina that have fueled her passion and success, above and beyond the support she received from the SBA.

Similarly, Vanessa, president of a professional services company, describes her own initiative that led to her success with the 8(a) Program: "It's important to know that simply by having the certification will not automatically deliver contracts to your door. It took us 4 years to get our first contract, and over the course of the remaining five years, we won several sole-source and competitive 8(a) contracts. When used wisely, this program can be extremely successful and help businesses gain a competitive advantage."

Others have not been as successful with the SBA. Andres, a software business owner, attempted to participate in the 8(a) Program but found the requirements too cumbersome, as the SBA wanted "a business plan, our financials, our projected financials. They wanted stuff that was forwarding looking that we didn't have access to at all." Andres also indicated that he would get calls from people saying they would help him fill out the application, but they requested $10,000. Eventually Andres hired someone, and they built a business plan; however, this was when the 2007–2008 economic recession hit. Juan thought "Great, I have a beautiful business plan, we're going to make a lot of money but no one was investing anything, anywhere. So I got a pretty business plan still, but we didn't have access to funding." While some business interventions focus on the creation of a business or a financial plan, these stories prove that Latinos need support beyond the creation of these materials, especially as it relates to expanding access to funding. Through the SLEI-Ed program, entrepreneurs meet with capital providers of all types as they expand their understanding of what type of capital exists while simultaneously networking with the gatekeepers.

Growth through the SLEI-Ed Program

Overall, alumni recount highly positive responses to their experiences in the program evaluation surveys, in interviews and on the alumni survey. Since exiting the program, businesses are recounting 20–60 percent growth in size (expanding to additional states and adding more employees) and revenue. On the whole, SLEI-Ed alumni are using diversified sources of external funding at higher rates than the general Latino business-owner population. Moreover, since completing the program, 61 percent of alumni report creating new products or diversifying their existing products.

Among cohorts 1–3, the alumni survey revealed that 89 percent of participants have had contact with each other since the program ended. As a motto of the program, "do business with each other and get business for each other," 57 percent of alumni report doing business with each other or other Latino-owned firms, and 38 percent reported getting business for each other. Other important measures of educational program success are student completion and satisfaction rates, including participant recommendation of the program to others. SLEI-Ed entrepreneurs have a 99 percent completion rate, one of the highest among all of Stanford's executive education programs. Furthermore, 98 percent indicate that they would recommend the program to others. In fact, over one-third of new participants come directly from referrals of previous participants. Among the lessons learned are the following:

> "SLEI-Ed started with a module on business valuation. This was very helpful to help me think about the sale of the company. After SLEI-Ed things crystallized and I was able to sell the company to another, much larger player in the industry."

> "Now my mindset is to scale. To develop the right people and procedures to scale my business. The only reason to start a business is to scale it, end of story."

> "I constantly try to utilize what I learned through the SLEI-Ed program. One example is being eager to find 'broken windows.' I encourage our team members to do so and look at this as a positive. This way we can take steps to fix them and it is an easy way to be 'better today than you were yesterday' and to be 'better tomorrow than you are today.'"

> "We have used the "broken windows" tools to fix interoffice procedures on quality control. We have also utilized the tools learned from SLEI-Ed when hiring new employees."

> "In many business situations, I have been able to use business terminology that I learned at SLEI-Ed, which help to make my business conversations more relevant. Such as: presenting my product line to a potential distributor."

Finally, alumni are encouraged by the possibility of future collaboration through structured alumni events. To date, several regional alumni gatherings have organically convened.

COMMUNITY AND SOCIETAL IMPACT

There is great potential for SLEI-Ed alumni to build the "Latino commonwealth" that one SLEI-Ed entrepreneur envisions. This entrepreneur captures the sentiment of a group of Latino entrepreneurs who see their work as having a larger purpose. Through commitment, passion, and fervent activity, Latino entrepreneurs are engaging with their communities. Some SLEI-Ed alumni stand as models for incorporating "community" as a core value of their business. While many alumni recount their community involvement through their participation on boards, there is much intentionality behind their involvement.

Alexis, an immigrant from Central America, owns a successful transnational software company. He explicitly builds in community involvement as a core value into his company. Alexis emphasizes the importance of building community: "Community involvement is a huge thing for us in Latin America, especially in Guatemala and in Colombia as well. Part of our contract that's supported by human resources comes with a clause that community service is a must. There are options for how they can help. They can either donate materials, computers, or make time to go teach teachers how to use the computers with the kids."

When asked why community service is a must for him, Alexis recounts that "our childhood was a bit challenging because the opportunities were not there. We look at these kids and try to help them in any way we can to not have them go through that." Robert has also made community an explicit part of his businesses core values. When asked why, he states,

It's important to give back to the community that you're a part of. We see our communities as the actual physical geographical community but we also think of all of our clients as part of our community, our vendors, as well as our colleagues within [our business]. Even some of our competitors are part of the community. We really like to share our successes and failures with everybody. It's how we get in touch with the human element.

The human element desired with community involvement parallels the approach that Latino entrepreneurs take in financing their business with their desire to establish relationships. As Latinos represent a collectivist culture, this influence can take shape in their business, as in the case with Alexis and Robert.

For some, while community lives in their company's core values, others describe an evolutionary experience. Tina describes her community involvement as a three-tiered progression. First, when she and her husband owned gas stations, her community involvement on boards was largely industry-related. That is, through trade associations, her goal was to stay on top of the latest industry-specific content and use this network for education and resources. When she converted to business brokerage, the next tier of involvement was related to growing her network. She sat on a lot of small business boards as she was looking for clients. Now as the president of a business organization, Tina is "looking more for influence." She describes this influence as needing to be "on the right boards and in the right seat so that I'm representing [the region] or women business leaders or Latinos or whatever my particular hat is on that board so that our voice is heard." Similarly, David is very purposeful about his involvement on boards. While he has been a part of many, as a rule he always joins the fund-raising and financing committees. He reasons that "if you want to ever effect change you have to be able to financially direct the change and understand how the money is going to be spent and then you have to go out and raise the dollars for it."

Yet, for some this notion of community came a time when they were reflecting on their larger purpose. Lucas finds himself at a crossroads. Much of his community involvement has been with middle school– to high school–age children. At one point, he started a nonprofit to support students as early as fifth grade complete community service. The revenue generated was then used for scholarships. When reflecting on why he has been actively involved, he asserts that "it's natural. It's almost like breathing to me. I don't think twice about helping somebody if I can." As he reflects on his current involvement and his next big project, he says that "I took a little time away. Maybe my business took my time away but I had to regroup. I had to find a purpose of why am I doing this? Am I doing this so people can see me on stage? Am I doing this so people can see me in the community? What is the real purpose of me doing it?"

In this line of reflection, Lucas holds his involvement to a high standard. He wants to make sure that the activities he engages in are purposeful and have a long-lasting impact rather than serve as self-promotion. He is now working with the local high school to support a business program among the vocationally tracked students.

Across the board, SLEI-Ed alumni are actively involved in their communities and recounted their experiences starting nonprofits, performing pro bono work, serving on boards, or working with students in a variety of ways. Among the couple of entrepreneurs who were taking the time to focus on their family members (such as by providing them internships at their business or donating their travel miles) and had little time to go beyond their immediate family, they shared aspirations about extending their involvement in the future. James, who runs a double bottom-line company, captures the tension in growing his business but also staying true to his mission:

> When it comes to doing my philanthropic work, I'm in a place right now where it's easier for me to just give money than it is for me to get directly involved but I want my play to be more volunteering. Now, we do practice what we preach at my company to at least once a month go volunteer for a local organization. It's a great team building opportunity and it allows me to grow that part of my soul. As more of my company stabilizes, I want to be able to do more of that you know, get your hands dirty work in the future.

James details how he came to develop his philanthropic perspective. He comes from two very generous parents, and even though they grew up in a mobile home, they would give whatever little change they had at church or donate their clothes to families in Mexico around Christmastime. It was this upbringing that taught him "giving makes you happy. Giving heals your soul." James ultimately translated these early life lessons into a company that is now transforming the work environment and is serving a double bottom-line: profit and positive social impact.

CONCLUSION

The discourse around Latino entrepreneurship has been elevated to a national level, and SLEI-Ed entrepreneurs are helping carry this movement forward. While the early literature on ethnic economies focused on businesses in ethnic enclaves and confined business reach to a localized nature, we are seeing greater engagement with the pairing of Latino businesses as they relate to the larger U.S. economy. As an example, JP Morgan Chase recently published a piece in *The Atlantic* with the headline "Latino Entrepreneurs May Be the U.S. Economy's Best Bet." The article highlights success stories, including that of Ana Bermudez, a SLEI-Ed alumna and the founder of TAGit. Other headlines from Forbes and CNBC capture the new discourse: "Economic Growth's New Driver: It's All about Latino Entrepreneurs" and "Latinos: The Force behind Small-Business Growth in America." This national attention can work to bring awareness to the growth issues that Latino entrepreneurs face. Highlighted in this chapter are the experiences of entrepreneurs in accessing capital, both their failed attempts and successes. I also highlight the importance of business education and training programs.

More specifically, this chapter focuses on the experiences of Latino entrepreneurs who are successfully scaling their companies. Future studies can consider an interrelated group of stakeholders advancing a Latino commonwealth from the business owners' perspective including the suppliers, customers, and social institutions. In particular, the strategic ways in which this network works together to advance a positive narrative should be examined. For example, in the early work on black enterprise, DuBois (1899) found that black clientele make black businesses successful. Similarly, the social processes that inform the consumer habits of the Latino population that specifically engage with Latino business owners, within and beyond the enclave, can help us understand the success of a new generation of Latino-owned businesses (see Chapter 9 for a discussion on social network utilization and enclaves). Externally, there are other stakeholders such as media and government that can converge (or diverge) from the Latino business-owner narrative.

Moreover, this chapter explored the relationship that Latino entrepreneurs have with their communities. Large bodies of work have considered collective responsibility as a presumed cultural value, particularly as one that shapes the identity of members in the African American community (McAdoo 1997; DuBois 1903) and as a preference for cooperative behavior (Allen and Bagozzi 2001). Similarly, Vallejo and Lee (2009) find that among upwardly mobile professionals, Mexican Americans experience an obligation to "give back" to their family, especially if they experience rapid social and economic mobility. However, we knew little about whether

Latino entrepreneurs felt a similar sense of obligation to their communities, as they define it. We find that while some Latino entrepreneurs specifically channel their efforts back into their racial and ethnic community, many more are contributing to larger definitions of community—their intersecting identities (i.e., regional, gender, ethnic), physical communities, and youth, among others. In doing so, Latino entrepreneurs demonstrate the ways in which supporting their efforts in turn contributes to a stronger national economy but also stronger U.S. communities.

NOTES

1. According the Small Business Act, "socially disadvantaged" individuals are those who have been "subjected to racial or ethnic prejudice or cultural bias because of their identity as a member of a group without regard to their individual qualities." Included in congressional findings, black Americans, Hispanic Americans, Native Americans, and other minorities are socially disadvantaged. In 1989, the law defined "economically disadvantaged" as "individuals who have a net worth of less than $250,000, excluding ownership in the 8(a) firm and equity in his or her primary residence."

2. The author notes that the scaling-up strategies set forth in this chapter were most salient to the entrepreneurs in the sample. There is a potentially larger set of strategies, including entrepreneurs' narratives, market research, business intelligence inputs, and novel collaborative forms, among others, not addressed here.

3. As minimum requirements for the program, applicants must have businesses with at least $1 million in gross annual revenue and three years of business existence. Startup businesses must have secured at least $500,000 in external funds.

4. Mentors are selected through a rigorous screening process to meet minimum qualifications of executive management experience, business success, and/or successful investing. Mentors need not come from a Latino background.

5. Interview respondents from Chapter 12 represent smaller scaled businesses (see Table 12.1 in that chapter for detailed business characteristics), with the highest revenue bracket representing $80,000 in annual revenue. Respondents in this chapter represent scaled firms, or those generating at least $1 million in annual revenue, representing the top 3 percent of Latino- and Latina-owned firms. Both sets of respondents could be considered

"networked" or participating in formal business organizations based on sampling procedures. This characteristic has been found to positively correlate to growth measures.

REFERENCES

Allen, Richard, and Richard Bagozzi. 2001. "Consequences of the Black Sense of Self." *Journal of Black Psychology* 27:3–28.

Alvarez, Sarah. 2017. *Unleashing Latino-Owned Business Potential: A Report of the Aspen Institute Forum on Latino Business Growth.* Aspen, CO: Aspen Institute.

Card, David. 1990. "The Impact of the Mariel Boatlift on the Miami Labor Market." *Industrial and Labor Relations Review* 43(2):245–57.

Congressional Research Service. 2019. *SBA's "8(a) Program": Overview, History, and Current Issues.* Congressional Research Service Report R44844. https://fas.org/sgp/crs/misc/R44844.pdf.

Dávila, Alberto, and Marie T. Mora. 2013. *Hispanic Entrepreneurs in the 2000s: An Economic Profile and Policy Implications.* Stanford, CA: Stanford University Press.

Decker, Ryan, John Haltiwanger, Ron Jarmin, and Javier Miranda. 2014. "The Role of Entrepreneurship in US Job Creation and Economic Dynamism." *Journal of Economic Perspectives* 28(3):3–24.

DuBois, W. E. B. 1899 [1971]. *The Negro in Business: Report of a Social Study Made under the Direction of Atlanta University, Together with the Proceedings of the Fourth Conference for the Study of the Negro Problems, Held at Atlanta University, May 30-31, 1899.* New York: AMS Press.

DuBois, W. E. B. 1903. *The Souls of Black Folk.* Chicago: A. C. McClurg.

Glaser, Barney G., and Anselm L. Strauss. 1967. *The Discovery of Grounded Theory: Strategies for Qualitative Research,* Vol. 1. Piscataway, NJ: Transaction Publishers.

Klein, Joyce A. 2017. *Bridging the Divide: How Business Ownership Can Help Close the Racial Wealth Gap.* Aspen, CO: FIELD at the Aspen Institute.

Korzeniewicz, Roberto Patricio, and William C. Smith. 1996. *Latin America In the World-Economy.* Westport, CT: Praeger.

Krogstad, Jens Manuel. 2016. "5 Facts about Latinos and Education." Pew Research Center. http://www.pewresearch.org/fact-tank/2016/07/28/5-facts-about-latinos-and-education/.

Lawless, Jennifer L. 2015. "Female Candidates and Legislators." *Annual Reviews Political Science* 18:349–66.

McAdoo, John L. 1997. "The Roles of African American Fathers in the Socialization of Their Children." Pp. 183–97 in *Black Families*, edited by H. P. McAdoo. Thousand Oaks, CA: Sage.

Morelix, Arnobio, Victor Hwang, and Inara S. Tareque. 2017. *Zero Barriers: Three Mega Trends Shaping the Future of Entrepreneurship*. Kansas City, MO: Ewing Marion Kauffman Foundation.

Orozco, Marlene, Paul Oyer, and Jerry Porras. 2017. *State of Latino Entreprenuership 2017*. Stanford, CA: Stanford Latino Entrepreneurship Initiative, Stanford University.

Portes, Alejandro, and Leif Jensen. 1992. "Disproving the Enclave Hypothesis: Reply." *American Sociological Review* 57(3):418–20.

Portes, Alejandro, and Min Zhou. 1993. "The New Second Generation: Segmented Assimilation and Its Variants." *Annals of the American Academy of Political and Social Sciences* 530:74–96.

Raijman, Rebeca, and Marta Tienda. 2000. "Training Functions of Ethnic Economies: Mexican Entrepreneurs in Chicago." *Sociological Perspectives.* 44(3): 439–56.

Rivers, Doug, Jerry Porras, Natassia Rodriguez Ott, Phil Pompa, and Tiq Chapa. 2016. *State of Latino Entrepreneurship 2016*. Stanford, CA: Stanford Latino Entrepreneurship Initiative, Stanford University.

Rivers, Douglas, Remy Arteaga, Tiq Chapa, and Jessica Salinas. 2015. *State of Latino Entrepreneurship: Research Report 2015*. Stanford, CA: Stanford Latino Entrepreneurship Initiative, Stanford University.

Small Business Investment Act. 1958. Public Law 85-699; 72 Stat. 689 codified as amended through P.L. 115-371.

Small, M. L. 2009. "'How Many Cases Do I Need?': Skirting Common Pitfalls in Pursuit of Scientfic Fieldwork." *Ethnography* 10(1):5–38.

Valdez, Zulema. 2011. *The New Entreprenuers: How Race, Class and Gender Shape American Enterprise*. Stanford, CA: Stanford University Press.

Vallejo, Jody Agius. 2012. *Barrios to Burbs: The Making of the Mexican American Middle Class*. Stanford, CA: Stanford Unviersity Press.

Vallejo, Jody Agius, and Jennifer Lee. 2009. "Brown Picket Fences: The Immigrant Narrative and 'Giving Back' among the Mexican-Origin Middle Class." *Ethnicities* 9(1):5–31.

Waldinger, Roger, Howard Aldrich, and Robin Ward. 1990. *Ethnic Entreprenuers Immigrant Business in Industrial Societies*. Newbury Park, CA: Sage Publications.

Waldinger, Roger, Muzaffar Chishti, and Editors. 1997. "Immigrant Entrepreneurs." *Research Perspectives on Migration* 1(2):1–16.

Wilson, Kenneth, and Alejandro Portes. 1980. "Immigrant Enclaves: An Analysis of the Labor Market Experiences of Cubans in Miami Author." *American Journal of Sociology* 86(2):295–319.

CHAPTER 14

The G.R.E.A.T. Gacela Theory: Increasing Capital and Conditions for Success for High-Potential Latino Entrepreneurs Capable of Transforming Our Economy and Our Country

Monika Mantilla

INTRODUCTION

One of the most significant economic opportunities in America today is tapping into the Latino marketplace and harnessing the intellectual and entrepreneurial strength of the Hispanic[1] community. The Hispanic community is a growing and increasingly relevant emerging domestic market. Emerging domestic markets are markets dominated by ethnically diverse businesses and/or customers in the United States that tend to be underserved and overlooked but have vast potential for economic development. According to Nielsen (2015), multicultural markets are expected to become the numerical majority by 2044, and 21 of the top 25 most populated counties in the United States are already more than 50 percent multicultural. As aspiring entrepreneurs, Latinos currently show more interest than non-Latinos in initiating business startups (Bates, Bradford, and Seamans 2018). Hispanic business owners alone could add more than an estimated $1.4 trillion to economic output if properly supported and unleashed (Rivers et al. 2017).

Traditionally, research on access to capital for minority- and women-owned businesses has generally focused on debt financing and direct commercial borrowing. Capital sources come from for-profit financial institutions and not-for-profits, including community development financial institutions (Robb 2013; Van Auken and Horton 1994). As such, our society does not appear to be daring greatly to seize opportunities or lay the code to fix the pervasive problem of the lack of capital in historically underserved communities, this despite their high business growth and potential. However, market opportunity and innovations in technology and the development of the digital economy have ushered in new players and stakeholders. There are new hope and paradigms in the debt and equity financing space. This includes new funds, investment teams, institutions that connect highly skilled entrepreneurs with capital and corporate access, and digital solutions such as capital platforms enabled by capital providers, online lending, and crowd funding. Furthermore, developing economies report novel ways of approaching equity financing, or venture capital funding, in emerging markets (Drover et al. 2017).

This chapter explores the various types of capital (both debt and equity) and ecosystem support that might provide a wider avenue of opportunity for high-potential Latino entrepreneurs. This is especially so for Latino-owned businesses (LOBs) that have crossed the $1 million in revenue threshold and can scale way beyond that initial milestone. Additionally, I offer a few perspective-expanding ideas for key stakeholders to see themselves as drivers of change. Finally, the chapter concludes with policy recommendations in the form of a call to action, which can be equally applicable to small- and medium-size businesses. This is a book about LOBs, but I must emphasize that the lessons and suggestions I outline in this chapter are applicable to high-potential entrepreneurs in a variety of multicultural or other underserved markets, such as the African American–, Asian American–, and women-owned businesses and markets. After describing and segmenting the LOB universe, I specifically focus on funding for LOBs with high potential to scale, what I label "G.R.E.A.T.[2] Gacelas," those "too big/too little" Latino entrepreneurs and small business owners with high growth potential and annual revenues between $1 million and $20 million.

The purpose of capital can vary. At Small Business Community Capital II (SBCC), we developed a model for capital with five broad categories, which we refer to as "G.R.E.A.T." strategies. I utilize this framework and apply it to the highest growth potential segment of LOBs. The G stands for *g*rowth of the company's core business, the R for *r*efinancing to take advantage of their record of success, the E for *e*xpanding into new product/service offerings or geographic markets, the A for *a*cquisition of a competitor or supply chain partner, and the T for *t*ransitioning ownership to the next generation or a new management team. Each of these G.R.E.A.T. strategies presents its own set of challenges and opportunities for any entrepreneur including the Latino entrepreneur, and all typically require funding and strategic resources to execute correctly. Therefore, a crucial part of enabling their growth is addressing their funding challenges.

Throughout the chapter, I include several mini case studies of LOBs to provide insights into success factors and the role of capital in their entrepreneurial journey from the perspective of both providers and receivers of capital. I must emphasize that these mini case studies are not unknown entities; they are friends, colleagues, and partners whose relationships represent the kinds of networks vital to continued growth and success in the Latino community. In my experience, producing ecosystems of value creation provides one of the most reliable paths to success in the private equity and venture capital world—and our Latino community is no different.

Some LOB mini case studies are past $20 million in revenue, which illustrates the point that this segment deserves focus and learning about their scaling experience and indeed provides valuable insight. I explore new promising prototypes of funding and support that can be matched to G.R.E.A.T. Gacelas—LOBs at different growth trajectories. Some of these novel prototypes are similar to consumer-oriented investor circles or investment clubs but have a business-oriented and scalability investment dynamic.

INVESTMENT ECOSYSTEMS/VEHICLES

The investment ecosystems/vehicles I propose provide different capital access and strategic resources to minority- and women-owned small businesses. These businesses are in fact the new majority of high-potential enterprises at different stages of development (e.g., from $1 million to $5 million or $5 million to $20 million in revenue).

A few initiatives are currently being incubated around this collaborative concept, in which capital, industry and management expertise and corporate access can be harnessed to improve outcomes. One of the first models of this kind is a small business investment company (SBIC) impact private equity fund, the first Latina-run SBIC fund that I have had the honor and pleasure to cocreate and lead. The investment vehicle brings together public and private institutional investors, private investors, corporations, and ecosystem participants in coordination to:

(a) Harness the power of collaboration at a significant scale, including a new paradigm supplier diversity analytical and execution model;

(b) Target above-market returns;

(c) Achieve significant corporate supply chain improvements;

(d) Invest in low- and moderate-income areas and with minority business and women entrepreneur;

(e) Enable high-quality jobs creation; and

(f) Institutionalize powerful value creation and investment processes.

This particular investing dynamic contributes to sustaining and scaling the Latino entrepreneur pipeline. It also focuses on developing an investment environment that promotes sustainability, scalability, active and collaborative ecosystems (including shared strategic resources), and long-run growth and societal transformation. Currently, I am working on supporting the creation of similar models focused on capital gaps with high potential. This includes such groups as firms with $250,000 to $1 million in earnings before interest, tax, depreciation, and amortization and minority women-owned enterprises in technology. Further along, we envision other investment vehicles based on specific capital structure needs (equity, debt, and mezzanine[3]), regions (North, South, East, West, and Midwest), industry focus, and specific pockets of value creation. The common recipe is finding valuable entrepreneurs and backing them to expand or acquire companies, helping them gain access to scalable markets and valuable ecosystems and providing the right capital structure at the right times.

G.R.E.A.T. GACELAS: A KEY ACTOR OF THE LOB UNIVERSE

According to the 2012 U.S. Census Bureau Survey of Business Owners (SBO), the average LOB had annual sales receipts of $143,271. But the story of more than 3 million LOBs cannot be captured in a single number. Fully 94 percent of LOBs are enterprises with less than $250,000 in annual sales, often referred to as mom-and-pop shops; these firms are a vast and vital part of our community, but they are not the focus of this chapter. LOBs with annual sales from $1 million to $20 million and with

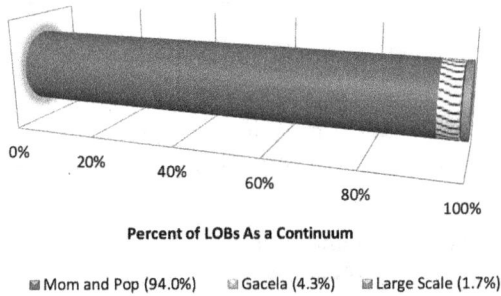

Figure 14.1 Latino-owned business type. (Source: U.S. Census Bureau, Survey of Business Owners, 2012.)

the potential to scale but are often bypassed by traditional funding sources are the focus of this chapter (Figure 14.1).

These are what I described above as G.R.E.A.T. Gacelas—too little/too big high-potential businesses with sales ranging from $1 million to $20 million. They are considered too big by many entry-level funding sources and too small for mature or more traditional funding sources. In essence, these firms are disconnected to capital markets (see Box 14.1).

BOX 14.1
Cidrines

Mari Cidre is President and CEO of Cidrines (founded in 1978), the leading maker of breads and pastries in Puerto Rico. At present, Cidrines is quickly expanding into the mainland U.S. market and its products can be found in supermarkets (i.e., Walmart, Kroger, Winn-Dixie, Fiesta, and soon in CVS) and warehouse clubs (i.e., Sam's Club) in Florida, New York, the mid-Atlantic, and Texas. Cidre notes that the act of securing capital led to the advantage of accessing instrumental business networks previously unavailable. Access to capital has helped Cidrines update its manufacturing footprint and expand in a capital-intensive sector. More importantly, the strong relationship that Cidrines built with its capital provider has proved invaluable in developing networks to increase business opportunities, make steady progress in modernizing a family business, and refocus company leadership on strategic planning. Cidre believes that her strong relationship with her capital provider allows her to be clearer in thought and direction, more transparent in communication and information flow, and more proactive in anticipating project and other company needs.

Business knowledge and education do matter, though. Cidre possesses over 20 years of professional corporate management experience in multinational enterprises including a number of years as a CFO as well as an educational foundation in finance (MBA) and accounting (BA). This background allows Cidre to seamlessly navigate various business networks and successfully bridge corporate and family business environments. Her advice to entrepreneurs seeking to raise capital is "jump in, don't be afraid, be proud of your business" and "just do it." Cidre advises entrepreneurs to be "professional, make the effort, take the time, be dedicated, disciplined, and focused." For Latino/as, she adds that one should position oneself in both worlds (Hispanic and mainstream America) and "play by the rules established by the market." Cidre suggests that Latino/as should not forgo Latino culture but should also embrace the larger culture and incorporate the best of both in order to gain entry to and succeed in the larger American marketplace.

Source: Interview with company officials, winter 2017–2018.

But just because businesses of this size share the same problem—access to capital—does not mean they share the same solutions. LOBs with $1 million in annual revenue have far different needs than those with $5 million, which in turn have different needs than those with $20 million. Industry, margins, team expertise, and track record as well as geography are all variables that shape the different needs and capital availability.

Beyond the mom-and-pop shops, the 2012 SBO found that 142,751 (4.3 percent) of LOBs fell in the $250,000 to $1 million group, with the remaining 54,817 (1.7 percent) having sales over $1 million. Among this group, annual sales averaged $5.8 million, suggesting a wide dispersion of sales data and that a substantial portion of LOBs over $1 million in sales fall into the $1 million to $20 million sales range.

To update and refine our view of this $1 million-plus group, we turn to the 2016 Stanford Latino Entrepreneurship Initiative (SLEI) Survey of U.S. Latino Business Owners. Out of a sample of 4,787 LOB's, SLEI found that in the intervening four years, this share of businesses grew to make up 2.7 percent of LOBs:

- 2.3 percent had sales between $1 million and $2 million;
- 0.3 percent had sales between $2 million and $5 million; and
- 0.1 percent had sales over $5 million.

LOBs with $1 million to $20 million in sales are an important link in the conduit to the creation of firms generating sales over and above $20 million and the perfect breeding grounds to find G.R.E.A.T. Gacelas.

Furthermore, this G.R.E.A.T. Gacelas segment has extraordinary potential to transform the Hispanic community, substantially accelerating economic development in terms of wealth creation and quality jobs creation. This very small yet very high-potential group has been systematically disregarded as capital (both debt and equity), and ecosystem solutions remain inadequately provided. Many large financial institutions, perhaps following a Community Reinvestment Act guideline, continue to focus on companies of less than $1 million in revenue, leaving the highest-potential group with the highest economic mobility potential, without the right nurturing and resources.

In the teams that I lead and in my personal and professional endeavors, I have dedicated the last eight years of professional investment focus to this segment, and it is my intent to continue doing so in the years ahead. I urge others to find the business owners in this segment, allocate resources to nurture them, and help them become an engine of societal transformation.

The SBO categorization of LOBs—from mom-and-pop businesses, the too big/too little enterprises, and large-scale businesses—can also be seen as a pipeline toward creating and growing G.R.E.A.T. Gacelas and ultimately large-scale Latino-owned firms. Figure 14.2 displays the percentage of firms in the $250,000 and over categories using the SBO data. Going forward, we need further research to better understand firms in the $1 million to $20 million in revenue segment, which are unfortunately lumped into a single category for much research. Within these enterprises, there are many hidden G.R.E.A.T. Gacelas—companies with great potential to scale quickly, or the gazelles (thus our translation for "Gacelas").

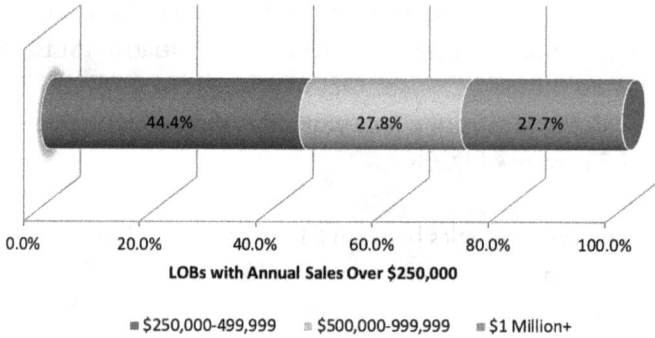

Figure 14.2 LOB's "Latent *Gacelas*" and beyond. (Source: U.S. Census Bureau, Survey of Business Owners, 2012.)

They are critical to the success of the U.S. economy. Their capacity for rapid growth makes them a crucial part of any efforts to close that $1.4 trillion gap between the size and scale of LOBs as compared to U.S. businesses in general (Alvarez 2017). But in order to realize their growth potential, these businesses often require capital.

More directly, a significant obstacle to realizing these businesses' potential growth and output is the lack of capital and ecosystem/strategic resources. This failure stems from structural gaps that have not been addressed in an organized, comprehensive manner. The following section explores potential solutions from a practical perspective, identifying the various types of capital sources (allocators, enablers, and conveners) that might provide a wider avenue of funding opportunity for sustaining Latino entrepreneurs at the takeoff, bridging, and growth stages of the business life cycle.

LOB FUNDING CHALLENGES

Foundations, private money, corporations, banks, and institutional investors have a phenomenal and game-changing opportunity to look at the enormous societal transformation potential that building an effective marketplace for these G.R.E.A.T. Gacelas will reap for our society. The support and creation of expert capital allocators and enablers will help build the foundation for a better society and economic system. Current charitable dollars can turn into impact dollars that have a phenomenal multiplier and societal lifting effect. A successful entrepreneur at the right scale is a seed for magnificent societal progress, as these entrepreneurs create jobs, income stability, educational opportunities, and innovation platforms. They become role model figures and access health care and well-being resources for their families, their employees and respective families, and the communities in which they work and live. But today, otherwise viable entrepreneurs frequently find themselves alone and constrained of capital and key resources, unable to maximize the human potential for them and others.[4]

In particular, an extensive body of research shows that minority-owned businesses in the United States, including Latino-owned enterprises, face truncated access to debt and equity capital and higher finance costs (Bates and Robb 2013) and are underserved and at times discriminated against in the capital marketplace (Bates et al. 2018; Dávila and Mora 2013; Jackson and Bates 2013; Robb 2013). Very importantly, societal transformation and enablement opportunities are clear, yet many foundations and nonprofits have yet to focus and deploy their valuable resources to the maturity and enablement of this market. Compounding the problem, minorities (Lerner et al. 2017; Mollick and Robb 2016) and Latinos (Mantilla Garcia 2003; Paglia and Robinson 2016; Robb 2013) are even more underrepresented in the fund management sector. Nonetheless, there is growing momentum and research suggesting that targeted funding to minority and LOBs reap above-market returns (Jackson and Bates 2013). This above-market premium may seem counterintuitive at first, but an underserved market suggests inefficiencies, an opening or gap in the marketplace in which first movers can take advantage. The persistence of this funding gap suggests that above-market returns are available to capital providers into the foreseeable future.

It stands to reason that funding sources that are more diverse at the management level (e.g., ethnicity, gender) are more likely to be more open to funding diverse businesses. Paglia and Robinson (2016) indicate just this in their study of SBICs, where they find that "racially diverse SBICs make more investments in minority-led and minority-owned" enterprises and invest more in low- and moderate-income communities. And while relatively small in number, Latino-owned or heavily represented financial service providers are beginning to emerge, particularly in the new millennium (Altura Capital Group and New American Alliance 2010) (see Box 14.2). Further, the democratizing role of crowd funding and digital financial solutions may also benefit Gacelas and allow them to break the institutional barriers of more traditional funding sources, especially in greatly overlooked sectors such as the arts (Mollick and Robb 2016).

BOX 14.2
Varadero Capital

Fernando Guerrero is managing partner and chief investment officer for Varadero Capital, an alternative investment firm located in New York City with capital resources greater than $1 billion. While a capital resource for others, Varadero Capital successfully began its own initial capitalization during 2009 at the height of the Great Recession, an achievement in its own right. While the financial markets were in turmoil in 2009, Varadero Capital navigated the challenging economic conditions, secured seed capital as an investment startup from a European financial institution, and negotiated for access to other capital resources. Guerrero suggests that entrepreneurs generally and Hispanic entrepreneurs specifically who are seeking to raise capital "nurture and maintain relationships; build a reputation for high integrity and fair dealing; look for win/win arrangements, especially for early/seed capital; and always put your investors ahead of all other interests." He also suggests that entrepreneurs get moving. "Getting started is essential even if the initial capital arrangement is suboptimal given that the journey is unpredictable and the opportunity cost associated with delays can be very meaningful."

Source: Interview with company officials, winter 2017–2018.

I envision a model in which public, private, and nonprofit sectors work together toward the creation of collaborative ecosystems of value creation in which high-potential and highly qualified entrepreneurs can be provided with the tools (experiences, capital, and strategic resources) to maximize their growth potential. But when capital and business-building support remain unavailable, this generates a vicious cycle of suboptimal job creation, reduced economic output, unharnessed human potential, and a weaker nation as a whole. The fascinating and exciting news is that capital sources, capital enablers, and capital conveners (public, private, and non-profit), are in a position to collectively change the current course of capital access and set a new trajectory of prosperity and innovation through efficient flow of capital and strategic resources targeted to LOBs.

WHAT WE CAN DO

To effectively address the divide in capital and resources for LOBs, it is important to address the complexity of its nature and that solutions vary significantly depending on size, growth potential, historical and expected financial performance, industry, and stakeholder environment. Table 14.1 below outlines an initial road map that takes into consideration different "architectural" realities and solutions and the engagement of different stakeholders depending on size of companies, the industries they belong to, and the type of capital they need.

The following 10 recommendations/proposals are intended as a guiding framework to fill in the gaps in the existing landscape and forge connections between relevant stakeholders, enabling LOBs greater access to capital and incentives for those who would provide it:

1. Learn from middle-market efficiencies: create a Latino financial infrastructure and collaborate with existing capital providers targeting LOBs.
2. Create clusters of innovation and cross-nurturing for LOBs.
3. Invite the socially responsible and impact-investing community as well as foundations, endowments, and family offices to work with the Latino community and invest in LOBs.
4. Entice corporate America with "new" (Latino) markets and a new supplier diversity philosophy.
5. Invite financial regulators and financial institutions to develop new channels of capital and innovation through the Community Reinvestment Act.
6. Harness institutional investors to build a robust emerging manager category.
7. Continue to leverage the role of the SBA and other government offices.
8. Develop a strong base of Hispanic depository institutions.
9. Address the financial awareness and financial planning needs of the Latino population.

TABLE 14.1 *Building a Capital Road Map and Guide for Architectural Gap Assessment*

Architecture (Capital Sources; Conveners, Enablers)	Company Size (Annual Revenues)	Industry	Capital Facilitators
Government leaders and legislators: Public policies and legislation at the federal, state & local levels.	$0–$50K	Largest activity vs. largest priority	**Debt:** SBICs, Banks
Investment policies	$50–$250K		Community banks, Other lenders, CDFIs
Institutional investors, corporations, endowments and foundations, family offices, financial institutions	$250K–$1 million	Mature vs. growing	**Equity** Private investors, SBICs
Insurance companies	$1–$5 million	High margin vs. low margin	Family offices, Private equity funds, CDFIs
Chambers and industry associations/platforms	$5 –$20 million	High barriers vs. low barriers	**Mezzanine** SBICs, Banks
Data/research/academic resources	$20–$100 million	Clusters:	Other private lenders, CDFIs
	$100 million+	• Consumer	
		• Manufacturing	
		• Health/wellness	
		• Corporate Services	
		• Other services	
		• Food & Beverage	
		• Technology	
		• Education	
		• Leisure	
		• Construction/real estate	
		• Finance	
		• Other	

10. Strengthen initiatives that train entrepreneurs to scale and strengthen business and capital ecosystems and are committed to action-oriented research

1. Learn from Middle Market Efficiencies: Create a Latino Financial Infrastructure and Collaborate with Existing Capital Providers Targeting LOBs

The development of capital middle markets in the United States has proven essential for small and midsize business growth. Through our work, alongside a network of collaborators, we are in the midst of creating a financial infrastructure of capital providers and capital intermediaries for different market segments throughout the financial continuum. In conjunction with this effort, there should be active collaboration with existing capital providers (financial and nonfinancial) who want to serve the LOB market and allocate dollars and strategic resources to it.

Capital providers can come in many forms: large-, mid-, and small-size banks as well as community banks, insurance companies, family offices, endowments and foundations, community development entities, including community development financial institutions, pension funds, credit unions, private equity funds (including venture, SBICs, growth and buyout), debt funds (including mezzanines), and other financial and credit institutions. Capital providers usually work closely with capital intermediaries, advisers, and investment bankers that package, market, and facilitate transactions.

Regardless of their shape and size, all capital providers have a role to play in creating a stable economy that expands capital access and generate market and above-market returns. Throughout the financial continuum, different types of capital providers may be appropriate depending on firm size, industry, and other characteristics (see Box 14.3).

In essence, what is needed is "fit for purpose" financing whereby the appropriate financial tools and resources are fashioned for the LOB at its current (and potential) stage of development (Drover et al. 2017). This is part of a larger and holistic goal of building and filling a pipeline of LOBs throughout the revenue continuum. With a robust pipeline of LOBs, a sufficient and meaningful number of high-potential, scalable, and sustainable enterprises can then be targeted for accelerated attention and financing. This is especially so in the G.R.E.A.T. Gacela category.

BOX 14.3
BXM Holdings

Roberto Herencia is President and CEO of BXM Holdings, located in Chicago; he has held this position since BXM's founding in 2010. BXM is an investor and sponsor of a community bank fund—in essence, an investment fund with a focus on community banks. Herencia has extensive experience, more than 30 years, in the financial/banking sector. Raised in Puerto Rico, he took his first banking job after graduating from Georgetown University with a degree in finance, working for First Chicago in the early 1980s including 4 years abroad in Mexico and Brazil (Yerak 2012). Since his start at First Chicago, Herencia has held many positions of financial leadership including chairman of the Board of Byline Bancorp (holding company for Byline Bank, Chicago), chairman of the board of FirstBankCorp (holding company for First Bank, Puerto Rico), member of the board of directors of the Overseas Private Investment Corporation (U.S. government), and member of the board of directors of Banner Bank (western United States).

With about $350 million raised within the firm, BXM Holdings was able to take controlling positions in a portfolio of community banks. Herencia states that he was able to access capital for BXM Holdings based on his "track record as a [bank] operator, CEO of community banks, and [his] strong personal relationships [with investors] built over the years." Along his career path, he earned his MBA in finance from Northwestern University. Even so, Herencia continues, "it was never a straight line, failing at times to secure equity due to timing or poor market conditions"; with even greater resources "we could have invested in more banks." He advises entrepreneurs seeking to raise capital to have an "investment thesis" and "understand and know who will operate the business in which you are investing." Finally, Herencia cautions, this work "is a fulltime job!"

Source: Interview with company officials, winter 2017–2018.

2. Create Clusters of Innovation and Cross-Nurturing for LOBs

As much as the right capital, the right business supporters, and the right public policies are needed, all change begins with us. Our Latino community must continue the process of developing high-caliber purposeful business organizations fueled by a commitment to excel, constantly learn and improve, and create bridges with other LOBs, industry collaborators, and their communities (see Box 14.4). Scalable LOBs must strive to continuously strengthen and expand their capabilities including the provision of the highest quality of goods and services to the marketplace, generate improved and solid profit margins, and possess the right capital structure. Fully developed networks of not just LOBs but also Latino-focused researchers, nonprofits, educators, mentors, and advisers in related fields can enable this pursuit. They may do so by providing a venue for sharing industry information, discovering opportunities for collaboration, and making practical experience and advice more easily accessible. These clusters of value creation will allow LOBs and the Hispanic community as a whole to learn, grow, and thrive.

BOX 14.4
Hector Hoyos

A serial entrepreneur, Hector Hoyos has successfully raised over $500 million in capital for his technology companies. Yet, difficulty in accessing capital (through debt and equity capital acquisition strategies) may have cost him and his companies' opportunities to scale into the billions of dollars. Hoyos notes that "the first time [acquiring capital] is the hardest because you have no track record and you have to sacrifice substantial ownership and control in many ways. The second one is much less [difficult]. If the third one comes after two successes, you can write and demand your own terms." Particularly challenging for Hoyos was geographical discrimination in the pursuit of capital; he and his technology security companies are based in Puerto Rico. Hoyos argues that "great tech comes from anywhere. You have a collection of dedicated people with great minds that are of a kindred spirit." But capital providers were skeptical of investing in tech from Puerto Rico, which was seen as being off the beaten path. Overcoming this bias was the result of building a track record of success through an "innovative vision in disruptive yet effective and much-needed technology solutions and products." In offering advice to other Hispanic entrepreneurs seeking to raise capital, Hoyos suggests that they "focus on a vision to achieve one thing and line up the best professionals around you" in pursuit of achieving that vision. From his many years of experience in accessing capital and leading businesses, he notes that "there are many people with great ideas. There are *very few* people with great ideas that can properly execute them into reality. Great visionaries are the ones who can execute [successfully]. The money will always chase after the great visionaries that can execute." Finally, "you, the entrepreneur, become the real asset, and people will pay your price in the beginning and in the end."

Source: Interview with company officials, winter 2017–2018. Hoyos also successfully started and sold Eyelock and Veridium.

Latino youths remain the Latino community's best asset. They are the promise of tomorrow. Organizations that promote, train, and connect young professional talent in STEM and business careers through leadership, cultural, educational, and workforce programs, such as the Hispanic Heritage Foundation, must continue to be supported to ensure they can expand the capacity for proven models (see Box 14.5).

BOX 14.5
Jordi Muñoz

Jordi Muñoz is in the business of making drones. In 2007, a 20-year-old Muñoz immigrated to the United States from Tijuana, Mexico. In his free time, he tinkered with odds and ends to make drone prototypes. He blogged about his progress and within two years had teamed up with Chris Anderson, then editor of the technology magazine *Wired,* to launch a business manufacturing drones for the consumer marketplace. Muñoz became the chief technology officer, inventing and making drones, and Anderson focused on the business component.

The company, 3D Robotics, quickly took flight securing $5 million in venture capital in 2012, $30 million more in 2013, and another $64 million in 2015; in all, 3D Robotics was able to access more than $100 million in total venture capital funds. Anderson's connection to the technology world facilitated the company's access to financing. At its height in early 2015, 3D Robotics employed 350 people in the San Francisco Bay Area, Austin, San Diego, and Tijuana (where manufacturing was located); had sales of more than $10 million annually; and was valued at more than $360 million. As quickly as the company rose as a leader in the U.S. drone marketplace, it quickly succumbed to competition from Chinese manufacturers in mid-2015 and 2016. Nevertheless, this Latino-cofounded company was able to raise $100 million as a primary early mover in the consumer drone landscape. Like many entrepreneurs, Muñoz moved on and now leads mRobotics as he seeks to regain traction in the drone and consumer robotics field.

Source: This account relies on the accounts provided by Mac (2016), Morris (2015), and Shontell (2014).

3. Invite the Socially Responsible and Impact-Investing Community as Well as Foundations, Endowments, and Family Offices to Work with the Latino Community and Invest in LOBs

Socially responsible and impact- and mission-driven investors have an invaluable opportunity to focus on LOBs as huge enablers for societal transformation. Endowments, foundations, family offices, impact investors, large banks, and other institutional investors can and should enable the consolidation and creation of investment ecosystems/vehicles, which are capital sources and ecosystems for small women-owned and minority-owned businesses. The SBA SBIC program is an important source of capital that should be accessed by funds seeking to serve these markets and LOBs. One of the areas with more noticeable capital gaps is the early-stage and small-size firms with up to $20 million in annual revenue. These enterprises tend to find limited or suboptimal capital solutions. Some non-profits and community development financial institutions will provide small capital amounts that usually do not exceed $500,000 and frequently are in the $25,000–$50,000 range. Yet, these firms need equity and debt financing, usually ranging from $1 million to $20 million, to achieve their business potential (see Box 14.6).

BOX 14.6
Nation Waste, Inc.

Maria Rios is President and CEO of Nation Waste, Inc., a waste disposal company with headquarters in Houston and operations in the greater Houston and Austin areas. Rios is no ordinary entrepreneur; she landed in *Fortune* magazine's list of most powerful women in the United States in 2013 (Sellers 2013). Her journey began in El Salvador, where she grew up in the midst of civil unrest, war, and violence. Her parents moved the family to Houston in 1980, when Rios was 13. All at once, she transitioned into a new culture, language, and the Texas school system. Along the way, she helped her mother and family earn money cleaning office buildings and eventually worked for a waste management firm, where during three years she learned the operation from the ground up (Flick 2015). By the end of 1997, Rios had earned her degree in business from the University of Houston and had begun her own waste management enterprise.

The role of external debt financing in the growth of Nation Waste, Inc., was indispensable, as the acquisition of a single commercial truck for their business costs upwards of $300,000. In all, Nation Waste has accessed over $20 million in external financing that permitted "investment in equipment, innovation, and technology" as well as business diversification (e.g., portable toilets, recycling, corporate partnerships), according to Rios. Besides persistence and tenacity, key elements to raising capital for Rios and Nation Waste were fourfold: "(a) building credit form the beginning;

(b) developing business relationships with bankers (before the need for loan assistance); (c) establishing credibility and a good reputation with many stakeholders, including the public; and (d) evolving a business plan into a growth plan."

Rios's advice to entrepreneurs seeking capital is "build relationships and explore new capital relationships for the present and the future; develop a transparent, accurate, and growth-minded business plan; don't overpromise or underdeliver; be proactive; and be distinct [differentiated] from others." She reflects that had she had earlier and easier access to capital, she would have diversified her operations earlier, noting that "once I realized the leverage and power of capital, I was more inclined to execute [and take action]." Another lesson learned was "how to digest all my financials and understand the significance of accurate financial projections." Finally, Rios strives to be a lifelong learner, seeking out new educational opportunities and skills for continuous improvement of her company and herself.

Source: Interview with company officials, winter 2017–2018.

4. Entice Corporate America with "New" (Latino) Markets and a New Supplier Diversity Philosophy

The Latino business community needs to continue to invite corporate America to collaborate. There is a highly qualified group of business leaders who can join boards of directors or leadership, become strategic partners or advisers, and provide valuable insights about our market opportunities and how to seize them. Additionally, these business leaders can work in collaboration with CEOs and treasury departments, particularly with their supplier diversity and procurement leadership groups. Teaming up with Hispanic business owners can bring corporate America market intelligence, supply chain solutions, and access to and affinity from increasingly vital Latino markets. This invitation departs from the old supplier diversity model (of finding a specific vendor for a specific job to fulfill a specific quota to check a diversity box) and moves to a proactive demonstration of corporate values and responsibility that recognizes the supply chain and market value, insight, and experience that these suppliers can and should provide. It goes beyond a onetime contract to the creation of partnerships and joint business models whereby the best products, talent, capital, and strategic focus are harnessed, creating new markets and new opportunities for all participants (see Box 14.7).

BOX 14.7
Santana Group & Forma Automotive LLC

Building on her 20 years of industry experience in workforce management, where she excelled in creating value for enterprises in the United States and Mexico, Rosa Santana began her extraordinary entrepreneurial journey founding Integrated Human Capital (IHC) in 2002, with offices in Texas and Mexico. IHC continued Santana's involvement in the human resource staffing sector. At IHC's startup, she applied and earned MBE (minority business enterprise) and WBE (woman business enterprise) certifications, which provided access to mentors and business networks and information. Through MBE, Santana learned that Toyota was building a manufacturing plant in San Antonio and was seeking local companies for potential partnerships.

Santana took action. "In no time, I made myself local in San Antonio and opened a small office there. That same year, I attended my first Toyota Opportunity Exchange in Cincinnati, Ohio, which is where I had my first opportunity to do business with Toyota by providing human capital solutions to an onsite supplier. Over the next 12 years, I continued to develop relationships with Toyota's other suppliers and eventually became the staffing agency of choice for 18 of the 21 onsite suppliers. I continued to grow my business elsewhere, joining forces with competitors and clients to deliver solutions to business challenges."

In 2009, Santana expanded her business portfolio (the Santana Group) through joint ventures to include Diversa, a managed service company, and Oveana, a contact center and business process outsourcing company. A few years later, a new opportunity presented itself to her. "Then when I least expected it, I was told about a potential opportunity to supply Toyota directly. Several of their supplier diversity staff and leaders became my internal champions and recommended me for a direct supplier opportunity."

From this opportunity, Forma Automotive LLC was established in 2014 under Santana's leadership. Santana became the first Hispanic woman-owned direct Tier 1 supplier to Toyota, noting that "we started production in August of 2015, and today we build 500 Tacoma truck beds per day. Partnering with Toyota and their suppliers has been instrumental in helping me grow my business, create jobs and put people to work, and impact the community in ways that would never have been possible otherwise. Likewise, Toyota gained a loyal, hardworking partner who has become an integral part of their San Antonio manufacturing operations."

Source: Interview with company officials, winter 2017–2018.

5. Invite Financial Regulators and Financial Institutions to Develop New Channels of Capital and Innovation through the Community Reinvestment Act

The Community Reinvestment Act is intended to encourage depository institutions to help meet the credit needs of the communities in which they operate, including low- and moderate-income neighborhoods, consistent with safe and sound operations. Institutions that can receive Community Reinvestment Act credit are encouraged to invest in vehicles that provide capital and technical resources to low- and moderate-income communities and LOBs. Historically, Community Reinvestment Act efforts have focused on real estate investments (low-income housing) and supported nonprofits and community development financial institutions. The percentage of dollars invested in small businesses remains small. Large banks that have supported SBIC investments usually gravitate to the larger, more mature ticket vehicles. Nonprofits and community development entities (corporations and partnerships that are intermediary vehicles for the provision of loans, investments, or financial counseling in low-income communities) serve an important part of the financial continuum, but they have not typically played a role in achieving capital support for the size of companies studied in this chapter ($1 million to $20 million in revenue).

Investors are invited to consider opportunities to finance the creation or expansion of Latino financial institutions (e.g., funds, banks); this is an important step for our community to adequately serve its own needs and participate in the development of its own solutions. Hispanics with banking and fund management expertise should find ways to create partnerships that will provide them the capital to build or acquire financial institutions. Private equity and debt funds that focus on this goal would greatly benefit from the support of depository institutions that can in turn benefit from economic, strategic, and marketing gains as they create affinity, connectivity, and knowledge of Latino markets to offer their products and services. In sharp contrast, many large banks have shied away from these types of investments (frequently bringing up size or years in business as limitations). The creation of concrete incentives for achieving certain target allocations of capital to these funds will in turn help low- and moderate-income communities and Latino-owned small businesses through various growth stages, which would be extremely beneficial to the Hispanic economy and to overall job creation in our country.

I frequently label this important area of work as becoming "architects of our own solutions" so we can integrate and collaborate with other market participants.

6. Harness Institutional Investors to Build a Robust Emerging Manager Category

Many institutional investors have created emerging manager programs to invest with small, diverse investment management firms. These programs harness the alpha generation opportunity of small and entrepreneurial investment management firms. Yet the market today has a vast cadre of underutilized Latino investment talent that has gone relatively untapped by institutional investors. New mentoring and training models are needed to cultivate career sustainability for emerging managers that can deliver high-caliber institutional products, career growth, and personal network expansion. This can be achieved by highlighting the performance case of emerging manager programs, including the economic, social, and transformational value they bring to the investment management industry, and developing models that provide the conditions for sustainability, scalability, and success.

Beyond the U.S. market, the nature of capital is truly global; hence, there is a need to foster the development of global working groups and working relationships with global institutional investors. The Pan-Hispanic world (i.e., Latin America, the Caribbean, and Spain) is a natural fit where investment opportunities and value creation models can be harnessed. However, institutional investment policies and asset allocation guidelines often create "buckets" that act as a deterrent and de-incentivize these Pan-Hispanic or Pan-American strategies. These artificial barriers must be revaluated to allow for new value creation models to emerge.

7. Leverage the Role of the SBA and Other Government Offices

The U.S. government is the largest single buyer of goods and services in the country, yet access to government contracts by small businesses is difficult, given numerous market research and market access obstacles. These obstacles lead many Latino small businesses to shy away from these opportunities. LOBs should be encouraged to participate in government contracting (procurement), and a transparent facilitation mechanism should be adopted to make this a reality. A simple rule that requires large asset managers or service providers in other industries to include small and minority firms in a percent of their contract fulfillment would provide fertile territory for growth. Too frequently, waivers are granted or this rule is not exercised, arguing absence of capable service providers.

In addition, I believe that the lending and investing programs of the SBA have played a pivotal role in the financing of small businesses and the creation of capital providers (including SBIC funds). We should continue to find systematic ways to ensure that LBOs know about SBA programs and are in a position to effectively access and utilize them. Our national and local chambers of commerce can play an important connector and mediating role.

8. Develop a Strong Base of Hispanic Depository Institutions

The active support from policy makers such as the Federal Reserve, the U.S. Treasury, the National Credit Union Administration, the Federal Deposit Insurance Corporation, and the Office of the Comptroller of the Currency, should be solicited to jointly reverse the trend of the declining number of minority depository institutions, banks owned by minorities (e.g., Hispanics), all of which are frequently serving minority and Hispanic communities. Minority depository institutions play a very important role in providing effective solutions for the underbanked and the unbanked populations. Mobile solutions and other access and education solutions should be implemented to provide Latino communities with the banking services they require.

9. Address the Financial Awareness and Financial Planning Needs of the Latino Population

Latino communities are markets thirsty for information about and opportunities for financial resources that will allow them to ensure a brighter financial future for their families. The Latino community welcomes innovative thinking from insurance companies and financial institutions that are committed to addressing their financial needs, including building Hispanic financial capacity and working side by side with Hispanic service providers to create win-win solutions.

I see the idea of investing with Latino values in mind gaining more and more traction every day. LOBs and Latinos generally ask their financial advisers to bring them sound investment strategies that consider Hispanic values and desires for a better society within a framework that provides satisfactory economic returns, a moderate risk profile, and a tax knowledge plan to ensure business asset protection and credits.

10. Strengthen Initiatives That Train Entrepreneurs to Scale and Strengthen Business and Capital Ecosystems and Are Committed to Action-Oriented Research

Initiatives such as the SLEI/LBAN training program are invaluable mechanisms for identifying and supporting high-potential business owners (i.e., G.R.E.A.T. Gacelas). These platforms generate valuable support ecosystems and connectivity with mentors, capital providers, educators, and corporations. Embedded in this program is a capital webinar, which I have the joy of teaching, where participants are exposed to key concepts regarding capital. This allows them to situate themselves in the capital continuum and create a preparation and execution plan for seeking the optimal capital resources for growth. There is also a capital matching session within the program. Future research initiatives should include gaining a better understanding of capital gaps and solutions to bridging these gaps.

CONCLUSION AND A CALL TO ACTION

I conclude this chapter with an aim to introduce and briefly describe work fronts, or areas of potential collaboration. Each one of them represents an opportunity for additional research and practice as well as an opportunity to enlist new champions for change.

A lack of capital creates significant market inefficiencies including suboptimal job creation, suboptimal economic output, latent market failures, and unrealized human potential. For societies and its members to prosper, capital must be available. Capitalism can only function when hardworking, smart, and savvy entrepreneurs find a way to achieve their dreams and find the proper resources to bring to market and expand novel products and services that make societies better. Without capital, innovation and progress stall. It is possible to chart a new course of prosperity and innovation through the efficient flow of capital.

Such innovations may originate from many corners. For example, Latino capital sources continue to expand and have the potential to be cultural and economic conduits for nurturing and growing the LOB family and community (Moreno 2017).[5] However, we cannot rely solely on these emerging entities to make the comprehensive changes we wish to see in the Hispanic business landscape. We need solutions from the key stakeholders of today. One such group is capital enablers and conveners—people and organizations that cultivate and create conditions for change. Examples of actions that resource allocators can make include the creation of foundations, legislative changes, investment policies, a policy around small and minority business participation, and investment summits focused on impact and diversity. Legislators, policy makers, fiduciaries, and board members can all lead the drive toward positive change.

Key metrics of success should include:

1. Significant increase in capital flowing to LOBs especially G.R.E.A.T. Gacelas, including angel, debt, equity, mezzanine, and bridge financing (which can come from private, strategic, or financial investors).
2. Accelerated connectivity and ecosystem building among high-potential LOBs/G.R.E.A.T. Gacelas, which can also create additional capital sources as successful entrepreneurs and advisers (lawyers, accountants, management consultants) enable smaller and synergistic players to emerge.
3. The creation of a reinvigorated multisector common agenda across the federal government (e.g., U.S. Treasury, SBA, the Department of Commerce, the Federal Reserve, the National Credit Union Administration, the Office of the Comptroller of the Currency, the Federal Deposit Insurance Corporation, the

Consumer Financial Protection Bureau, the Pension Benefit Guarantee Corporation, legislators, and so on) with corporate CEOs and members of corporate boards; directors and board members of endowments and foundations as well as of trade associations, chambers and councils; and corporate treasurers and chief investment officers who focus on expanding capital and strategic opportunities for LOBs.

4. Increase in research and associated metrics to benchmark and track progress while gaining a more in-depth systematic understanding of the Gacelas population and their pursuit of G.R.E.A.T. scaling strategies.

5. The establishment of working groups to continuously listen to the voice of LOBs across a variety of industries—especially those historically challenging to penetrate, such as investment management and value-added goods and services—to implement programs that address their most significant obstacles and provide them with a clear opportunity to scale and compete in the marketplace.

Latino entrepreneurs can take actions to continue to improve their game. As a valuable tool, we recommend that our entrepreneurs ask themselves these questions: Is my company a G.R.E.A.T. company? Which of these strategies provides the clearest path to realizing my company's potential, and where am I on my path toward executing that strategy? Whether pursuing growth, recapitalization, expansion, acquisition or transition, do I have a clear understanding of the capital and strategic resources my company requires?

Another valuable tool is to study the paths to success charted by the business owners who came before them. To that end, Table 14.2 summarizes many of the common threads introduced in the mini case studies throughout the chapter's boxes. Common threads include networking, relationship building, persistence (never give up), performance, and foundational knowledge, all within the market arena. These elements apply to any entrepreneur but were particularly common to all LOBs interviewed.

As a practitioner in the financial management industry, I have crisscrossed the country working with institutional investors, financial institutions, and business owners, talking to stakeholders and actively participating in the creation of policy, investment vehicles, and supplier

TABLE 14.2 *LOB Financial Success: Common Themes from the Mini Case Study Experiences*

Theme	Description
Networking	Utilizing professional networks, both mainstream and Latino, in accessing funding and strategic resources.
Relationships/ Ecosystem/ Collaboration/ Win-Win Mentality	Building and maintaining relationships on foundations of trust, fair dealing, win-win arrangements, and mentorship. Bridging and effectively navigating cultural differences between Latinos and the general U.S. business culture in establishing meaningful cross-cultural relationships. Ability to tap and connect to mainstream ecosystems/markets.
Never Give Up	Valuing and modeling persistence, perseverance, hard work, and tenacity in business.
Performance	Executing business plans, creating success, and understanding the financials.
Foundations	Building successful businesses on the foundations of adequate preparation: higher education, work experience, and Latino cultural heritage.
Marketplace	Finding a market niche or disruption opportunity in the market and pursuing it.
Bottom Line	With success and a proven track record come greater opportunities.

diversity/supply chain solutions. I have seen firsthand the need for a new paradigm, a new burst of "daring G.R.E.A.T.ly" solutions, an integrated and bold initiative, and a comprehensive road map that charts the way to Latino prosperity and progress when it comes to the utilization and harnessing of diverse investment talent and diverse entrepreneurs. Key stakeholders include the private sector (corporations, financial institutions, and institutional investors), the public sector (federal, state, and local as well as public pension funds and financial regulators), and nonprofits (endowments and foundations).

As with any societal transformation, it is imperative that we continue to raise awareness among private, corporate, and nonprofit leaders across America. Any of the 10 recommendations/proposals above can be paths that leaders can further explore, champion, and expand upon through research, financial resources, capital solutions, grants, programs, and support. Providing opportunity for capable Latino business owners eager to succeed, on an individual or a programmatic basis, can bring a positive and compelling transformational opportunity for our society and our country.

I dream of a day when human potential is maximized and societal transformation can occur through entrepreneurial success. They key word is "increased multisector collaboration." You can contribute something toward this dream by assisting or capitalizing an entrepreneur, giving him/her sound advice, sharing this chapter and book with someone you think can be an agent of change, leading public policies or legislation that improve opportunities and access to capital and strategic resources, providing LOBs with business opportunities, studying hard to one day become a successful entrepreneur or a capital provider, rethinking supplier diversity, funding a bank or a fund, opening your networks, creating or supporting programs, and developing research. Let's continue to build our future and dare G.R.E.A.T.ly together!

ACKNOWLEDGMENTS

This chapter was written with collaboration from Michael J. Pisani. The author also appreciates the encouragement and helpful comments on an earlier version of this chapter from Dr. Barbara Robles and Stanford Business School Emeritus Professor Jerry Porras.

NOTES

The author is a managing partner of the private equity impact fund SBCC with 27 years of management and investment experience. She has been a strong advocate of building financial capacity and effective ecosystems in minority (now majority) business communities. She sits on the boards of the Latino Business Action Network, the Hispanic Heritage Foundation, and the United States Hispanic Chamber of Commerce USHCC, where she chairs the Capital Committee.

1. In this chapter the terms "Hispanic" and "Latino" are used interchangeably.
2. A term utilized and coined by the private equity impact fund SBCC to represent the different capital and strategic trajectories of businesses, further described in the chapter.
3. Mezzanine financing is a hybrid of debt and equity with warrants/ownership rights to the lender.

4. Funding is a significant challenge and central to this chapter. While Latino entrepreneurs face a variety of other challenges as detailed in previous chapters, funding obstacles are the focus of this chapter.

5. At the consumer level, the e-platform emoneypool (www.emoneypool .com) unites small online savings and loan communities similar to rotating savings and credit association to pool resources up to $5,000 per person. Conceptually, this association is but a small-scale version of the work that *madrina* groups may engage.

REFERENCES

Altura Capital Group and New American Alliance. 2010. "American Latinos in Financial Services: A Study of Emerging Financial Service Providers." New American Alliance.

Alvarez, Sarah, ed. 2017. "Unleashing Latino-Owned Business Potential: A Report of the Aspen Institute Forum on Latino Business Growth." The Aspen Institute Latinos & Society Program, Washington, DC.

Bates, Timothy, and Alicia Robb. 2013. "Greater Access to Capital Is Needed to Unleash the Local Economic Development Potential of Minority-Owned Businesses." *Economic Development Quarterly* 27(3):250–59.

Bates, Timothy, William D. Bradford, and Robert Seamans. 2018. "Minority Entrepreneurship in Twenty-First Century America." *Small Business Economics* 50:415–27.

Dávila, Alberto, and Marie T. Mora. 2013. *Hispanic Entrepreneurs in the 2000s: An Economic Profile and Policy Implications*. Stanford, CA: Stanford University Press.

Drover, Will, Lowell Busenitz, Sharon Matusik, David Townsend, Aaron Anglin, and Gary Dushnitsky. 2017. "A Review and Road Map of Entrepreneurial Equity Financing Research: Venture Capital, Corporate Venture Capital, Angel Investment, Crowdfunding, and Accelerators." *Journal of Management* 43(6):1820–53.

Flick, Lauren. 2015. "Blue Collar Millionaires: The $30M Empire Built on Trash." CNBC, July 22.

Jackson, William E., III, and Timothy Bates. 2013. "The Viability of the Minority-Oriented Venture Capital Industry: Implications for Diversifying Investment Strategies." U.S. Small Business Administration.

Lerner, Josh, Ann Leamon, Meagan Madden, and Jake Ledbetter. 2017. "Diverse Asset Management Project Firm Assessment: Final Report." Bella Research Group.

Mac, Ryan. 2016. "Behind the Crash of 3D Robotics, North America's Most Promising Drone Company." *Forbes*, October 5.

Mantilla Garcia, Monika. 2003. "American Latinos in Financial Services: Phase I, White Paper." New American Alliance.

Mollick, Ethan, and Alicia Robb. 2016. "Democratizing Innovation and Capital Access: The Role of Crowdfunding." *California Management Review* 58(2):72–87.

Moreno, Robyn. 2017. "Money Madrinas: 12 Latinas Who Invest in Other Women." *Latina*, May 18.

Morris, Regan. 2015. "The Mexican Immigrant Who Set Up a Global Drone Firm." BBC News, February 23.

Nielsen. 2015. "The Multicultural Edge: Rising Super Consumers." Diverse Intelligence Series. The Nielsen Company. https://www.nielsen.com/wp-content/uploads/sites/3/2019/04/the-multicultural-edge-rising-super-consumers-march-2015.pdf.

Paglia, John, and David T. Robinson. 2016. "Measuring the Representation of Women and Minorities in the SBIC Program." U.S. Small Business Administration.

Rivers, Douglas, Jerry Porras, Natassia Rodriguez-Ott, and Eutiquio Chapa. 2017. *State of Latino Entrepreneurship 2016.* Stanford, CA: Stanford Latino Entrepreneurship Initiative/Latino Business Action Network, Stanford Graduate School of Business.

Robb, Alicia. 2013. "Access to Capital Among Young Firms, Minority-Owned Firms, Women-Owned Firms, and High-Tech Firms." U.S. Small Business Administration.

Sellers, Patricia. 2013. "Meet the New Fortune MPW Entrepreneurs." *Fortune Magazine*, September 10.

Shontell, Alyson. 2014. "A Hot-Shot Magazine Editor and a Tijuana Teenager Met Online and Made $5 Million Building Drones." Business Insider, December 12.

Van Auken, Howard E., and Hayward Horton. 1994. "Financing Patterns of Minority-Owned Small Business." *Journal of Small Business Strategy* 5(2):31–44.

Yerak, Becky. 2012. "A Big Wheel in the Banking Community: Born in Puerto Rico, Roberto Herencia Has Found a Home Here." *Chicago Tribune*, September 24.

A New National Economic Imperative

Marlene Orozco, Alfonso Morales,
Michael J. Pisani, and Jerry I. Porras

This volume has been the result of a desire by the Stanford Latino Entrepreneurship Initiative (SLEI)—a Latino Business Action Network (LBAN)/Stanford collaboration—to bring together a multidisciplinary group of scholars drawn from all over the country. The main focus of this group is the creation of a vibrant research community dedicated to generating knowledge about Latino entrepreneurship in the United States as well as expanding its impact by attracting others to join in the effort to create a substantial body of research literature on this topic. This volume is the first output of this nascent community. More will be said about the process of creating this group in later sections.

Advancing an integrative program that at the same time is accommodative of disciplinary assumptions, policy prescriptions, and educational opportunities would be a substantial feat, yet it is the goal we set for ourselves in producing this volume. Central to an integrative research program is a need to unite the existing projects and individual programs advanced by a variety of scholars doing research in this field. We make no pretensions that all scholars will coalesce under our banner; however, we do believe that at a minimum, many scholars can take advantage of the SLEI-Research program by leveraging its national reports (see Orozco, Oyer, and Porras 2017), informing its data collection process, accessing databases created by SLEI, and advancing research projects. To date, the SLEI-Research program has proven to be supportive of graduate students as well as providing training opportunities and publication possibilities for faculty of many disciplines and interests.

This volume represents an initial appreciation for the ongoing work of individual scholars united in the service of greater understanding of Latino entrepreneurship. However, our vision does not stop there. We see how scholarly studies can help inform public policy, we see how scholarship can support and improve the education of Latino entrepreneurs and of society more generally, and we believe that a better understanding of Latino entrepreneurship is supportive of our society and economy, inclusive of existing and new perspectives and purposes.

While we do believe that scholarship can inform public purposes, we also acknowledge that our principal role is science—that is, science in the public service arena grounded in firm and robust methodologies and clear theory. In what follows, we review new questions that this book has helped raise and new products from ongoing discussions from our meeting in March 2018. We hope that the following discussion motivates new research, catalyzes new relationships, and helps identify new research opportunities.

RESEARCH QUESTIONS

One important class of entrepreneurial behavior that we feel is important to investigate is that associated with *supply chain and procurement relationships*. Such relationships lie within the invisible infrastructure of entrepreneurship. We need a clear understanding of how Latino entrepreneurs participate, both as suppliers and purchasers, in supply chains at the local, national, and international levels. We should point out that within the international realm, the *Latino business global footprint* has yet to be studied.

An important corollary of this question would be research to learn how it is Latino entrepreneurs seek and create *mutually beneficial relationships*. One important working hypothesis is that Latino entrepreneurs are competing within an industry but developing interindustry supply chains and partnerships. Here we think we have an important advantage to share, as we are in the process of developing panel data to help uncover supplier relationships over time.

Financing remains a vast and underexplored topic. While it is clear that ethnic entrepreneurs often lack access to formal financing, new research is finding otherwise. Furthermore, Latino businesses are producing financial institutions, such as banks, as well as investment funds. The scope and impact of these latter efforts needs to be better understood.

Human resource questions loom large. We know that Latinos are an attractive workforce in agriculture, industry, and a host of other fields. We know that Latinos have formed or joined a variety of professional associations and organizations enhanced by social media platforms aside from chambers of commerce. We need a strong sense of how these professional organizations funnel resources to nascent entrepreneurs or become entrepreneurial themselves. A firmer understanding of the breadth of trajectories into entrepreneurship is still very important, as is whether or not and how Latinos exploit a variety of government programs, local, state, or federal.

Considerations of future research can explore whether and how Latinos engage in *serial entrepreneurship* by connecting multiple firms under one business model and self-consciously exiting from one ownership model and obtaining a different model. In short, we would not be surprised that Latinos are engaged in the same experiments that other entrepreneurs embrace. However, we also expect different trajectories to similar outcomes shaped by the legacies of discrimination and immigration as well as by experimentation born of different resources and relationships.

We believe that entrepreneurship is as important as classical scholars conceived, but it also takes importance from its broad connections to *other intellectual problems* that social scientists typically tackle. These include research questions of acculturation and assimilation, economic contribution, informality, language-use patterns, regional economic analysis, and questions related to gender and how women navigate household, professional, and other relationships on their way to entrepreneurship.

Like most entrepreneurial ventures, Latino entrepreneurs establish businesses in hopes of profitability and wealth creation. However, in the course of producing economic contributions (job creation, investment, etc.), Latino entrepreneurs are also engaged in many kinds of *noneconomic activities* such as service on boards, volunteering their time, and engaging in nonprofit work. Many Latinos are seeking to contribute to the improvement of the social environment and making important noneconomic contributions to society at large. In doing so, these entrepreneurs are helping to reconstruct stereotypes and establish the expectations we should all have of each other in improving our society. Important research questions here include whether or not and how much Latino entrepreneurs'

noneconomic activities and interests mirror those of the majority population. Are Latinos adopting the same memberships on boards and engaging
in similar philanthropy? If so, does this constitute assimilation, or is it a
form of a minority culture of mobility (Neckerman, Carter, and Lee 1999)?
Further, business and entrepreneurship are changing, so what does it mean
to assimilate? Family concerns are not absent from the literature of non-
Latino business, so is there more in common here than scholars or policy
makers might assume?

THE SLEI INFUSION

Beginning in 2016 at Stanford Graduate School of Business, SLEI sponsored meetings of scholars focused on Latino business, entrepreneurs,
and wealth creation. These were scholars who had previously published
many important books and articles in the field. Among those previously
published titles there are two related books—*An American Story: Mexican
American Entrepreneurship and Wealth Creation* (2009), edited by John
Butler, Alfonso Morales (of this volume), and David Torres, and *Hispanic
Entrepreneurs in the 2000s: An Economic Profile and Policy Implications*
(2013), by Alberto Dávila and Marie Mora (also of this volume). The
Butler et al. was the first of its kind focusing specifically on Mexican
Americans and was well received for the variety of research methods as
well as the variety of topics the authors considered. The Dávila and Mora
volume was targeted to economists and academics and considered the
variety of Hispanic groups.

Our volume is similar to these two in that its authors consider a variety
of topical questions, yet it is distinct in that we also bring an important
examination of historical processes. This allows the reader to maintain a
historical perspective instead of being limited by our contemporary situation. Furthermore, our volume utilizes the unique SLEI data set that
supports a comprehensive understanding of business success and what that
means across Latino subgroups, between rural and urban settings, and
with respect to sociohistorical contexts. Other contributors of this book
have been prolific in the field of minority self-employment (Fairlie 2011;
Fairlie and Robb 2008), Mexican American professionals and entrepreneurs (Agius Vallejo 2012), agricultural and informal economies (Pisani
2012; Pisani et al. 2017; Pisani and Guzman 2016; Richardson and Pisani,

2012), language patterns and Latino self-employment (Dávila and Mora 2000), Latina entrepreneurship (Robles 2002), public markets and Latinos (Morales 2009), and the intersection of race, class, and gender in entrepreneurship (Valdez 2011). Finally, the process through which this book was developed is fairly unique. Rarely have a group of scholars on Latino issues been gathered together over a two-year period to discuss the content of their work, relate that work to each other, and produce a book. Most importantly, the scholars represented here had the opportunity to think beyond their individual research programs to create a more integrated approach to their work.

In our 2017 meeting, three of the editors of this volume agreed to advance an effort at a more integrated approach to scholarship that could have application to society, reinforce the efforts of LBAN, and make a substantial contribution to knowledge. A more difficult task for notoriously individualistic researchers is hard to imagine. However, again with the exceptional support of the SLEI and LBAN, they made the effort, thankfully supported by a fourth editor (Orozco).

The 2018 meeting of the group included a visioning session to chart the future efforts, scholarly and otherwise, of SLEI and in relationship to LBAN. We decided to foster the individual spirit that characterizes the scholarly life but also to continue our meetings and seek joint opportunities to publish, build policy, and welcome other interested parties to the different parts of our effort. Collectively, we created a vision for the future of SLEI research.

The goal of SLEI research is to understand the state of Latino entrepreneurship by analyzing data and shaping research in this field. By leveraging large data sets and collecting unique national data, SLEI synthesizes trends and reports them out to wide audiences including business leaders, policy makers, academics, media, and capital providers. SLEI engages academic scholars through annual convenings to mobilize a larger network of interdisciplinary scholarship and increase the visibility of our research and impact regionally. It hopes to be the nucleus for an ever-expanding number of scholars researching Latino entrepreneurship and for developing and growing the literature in this field.

This work would not be possible without the national survey that SLEI administers with the fiscal support of LBAN. The SLEI Survey of U.S. Latino Business Owners is a nationally representative cross-sectional survey that has been fielded annually since 2015. SLEI hopes to construct a nationally representative panel of Latino entrepreneurs in order to obtain year-over-year data about the changes within individual businesses. To date, SLEI has created a longitudinal panel of the participants of the SLEI–Education Scaling program, and although it is not representative of the average Latino entrepreneur, it does allow for a deeper exploration of the persistent growth challenges of scaled firms (i.e., firms generating at least $1 million in annual revenue or more).

In order to reach a vast array of Latino entrepreneurs across firm sizes, industries, geographies, and other defining characteristics, SLEI welcomes the efforts of strategically collaborating institutions in disseminating the survey to their membership and networks. SLEI is thankful to the work of Hispanic chambers of commerce such as the Chicago, Tucson, Houston, and Austin chambers. They have encouraged their members to take the survey as an expression of their shared desire for data and informed decision making. Additionally, SLEI is augmenting efforts to collaborate with other research institutions and nonprofit organizations. As one example, the Latino Community Fund in Georgia is working with faculty from Georgia universities and a statewide steering committee to provide input on the national survey instrument that addresses local needs. In this way, local leaders are forming regional arms to inform questions and collect data that can in turn be compared to other regions and national trends. Furthermore, these local efforts allow for on-the-ground outreach and local canvasing that can reach smaller and unincorporated businesses.

In light of these growing nationwide efforts to realize the many economic and noneconomic benefits of Latino entrepreneurship, the authors wish to remind readers that our specific focus on Latino entrepreneurship is urgent now for many of the same reasons scholars fostered the "scientific" study of business 100 years ago. Latino entrepreneurs are integrating newcomers into society through employment and integrating themselves into local, national, and international business networks. However, Latino business is not simply organized by and focused on Latinos, nor does it only use or produce Latino-related goods and services or serve only Latino customers, and Latino businesses are not located only in primarily Latino neighborhoods. Instead, Latino businesses are integrated into the mainstream of our economy and are leading the creation of a new mainstream for our country.

For Latinos and for business in general, the economy cannot be separated from society. The ongoing demographic changes we are witnessing will continue to produce innovation among entrepreneurs along with social, economic, and political shifts. We will be among those following these developments and even fostering them. We hope that the scholarship in this volume and the attitude we take as professionals help transform the perception of participation in the economy by Latinos from subjects of charity to actors with objectives and capacities to be successful and impactful in a variety of economic activities in service to society.

REFERENCES

Agius Vallejo, Jody. 2012. *Barrios to Burbs: The Making of the Mexican American Middle Class*. Stanford, CA: Stanford University Press.

Butler, John S., Alfonso Morales, and David L. Torres, eds. 2009. *An American Story: Mexican American Entrepreneurship and Wealth Creation*. West Lafayette, IN: Purdue University Press.

Dávila, Alberto, and Marie T. Mora. 2000. "English Skills, Earnings, and the Occupational Sorting of Mexican American along the US-Mexico Border." *International Migration Review* 34(1):133–57.

Dávila, Alberto, and Marie T. Mora. 2013. *Hispanic Entrepreneurs in the 2000s: An Economic Profile and Policy Implications*. Stanford, CA: Stanford University Press.

Fairlie, Robert. 2011. "Kauffman Index of Entrepreneurial Activity, 1996–2010." Kansas City: E. M. Kauffman Foundation.

Fairlie, Robert, and Alicia Robb. 2008. *Race and Entrepreneurial Success*. Cambridge: MIT Press.

Morales, Alfonso. 2009. "Public Markets as Community Development Tools." *Journal of Planning Education and Research* 28(4):426–40.

Neckerman, Kathryn, Jennifer Lee, and Prudence Carter. 1999. "Segmented Assimilation and Minority Cultures of Mobility." *Ethnic and Racial Studies* 22:945–65.

Orozco, Marlene, Paul Oyer, and Jerry Porras. 2017. *State of Latino Entrepreneurship 2017*. Stanford, CA: Stanford Latino Entrepreneurship Initiative, Stanford Graduate School of Business.

Pisani, Michael J. 2012. "Latino Informal Immigrant Entrepreneurs in South Texas: Opportunities and Challenges for Unauthorized New Venture Creation and Persistence." *American Journal of Business* 27(1):27–39.

Pisani, Michael J., and Joseph M. Guzman. 2016. "The Exceptional One Percent: US Farmworker and Business Owner." *Journal of Agriculture, Food Systems, and Community Development* 6(2):225–42.

Pisani, Michael J., Joseph M. Guzman, Chad Richardson, Carlos Sepulveda, and Lyonel Laulié. 2017. "Small Business Enterprises and Latino Entrepreneurship: An Enclave or Mainstream Activity in South Texas?" *Journal of International Entrepreneurship* 15(3):295–323.

Richardson, Chad, and Michael J. Pisani. 2012. *The Informal and Underground Economy of the South Texas Border*. Austin: University of Texas Press.

Robles, Bárbara J. 2002. "Latina Microenterprise and the U.S.-Mexico Border." *Estey Centre Journal of International Law and Trade Policy* 3(2):307–27.

Valdez, Zulema. 2011. *The New Entrepreneurs: How Race, Class, and Gender Shape American Enterprise*. Stanford, CA: Stanford University Press.

About the Contributors

Jody Agius Vallejo is an associate professor of sociology and American studies and ethnicity at the University of Southern California.

Geraldo L. Cadava is an associate professor of history at Northwestern University.

Cristina E. Cruz is a professor of sociology at Ana G. Mendez University–Dallas Area Campus.

Alberto Dávila is the dean of the Donald L. Harrison College of Business and Computing at Southeast Missouri State University.

Elsie L. Echeverri-Carroll is the senior research scientist at the University of Texas at Austin.

Robert W. Fairlie is a professor of economics at the University of California, Santa Cruz.

Joseph M. Guzman is the director of the Alliance Economic Policy Institute in the W. A. Franke College of Business at Northern Arizona University.

Leticia C. Lara is an adjunct professor of Chicana/o studies in the sociology and social work departments at California State University, Northridge.

Edna Ledesma is an assistant professor of planning and landscape architecture at the University of Wisconsin–Madison.

Monika Mantilla is president and CEO of Altura Capital Group.

Linda M. Matthews is the associate dean of undergraduate studies at the University of Texas Rio Grande Valley.

Gerardo A. Miranda is a PhD candidate in the school of business at the University of Texas Rio Grande Valley.

Marie T. Mora is Associate Provost for Academic Affairs and Professor of Economics at the University of Missouri–St. Louis.

Alfonso Morales is a professor of planning and landscape architecture at the University of Wisconsin–Madison.

Marlene Orozco is a PhD candidate in sociology and is the SLEI lead research analyst at Stanford University.

Paul Oyer is the Mary and Rankine Van Anda Entrepreneurial Professor, a professor of economics, and the SLEI faculty codirector at Stanford University.

Iliana Perez is the director of research and entrepreneurship at Immigrants Rising.

Michael J. Pisani is a professor of international business at Central Michigan University.

Jerry I. Porras is the Lane Professor of Organizational Behavior and Change, Emeritus, and the SLEI faculty codirector.

Barbara Robles is the principal economist of the Board of Governors of the Federal Reserve System.

John Sargent is a professor of international business and entrepreneurship at the University of Texas Rio Grande Valley.

Kathleen Stewart is the director of the Center for Geospatial Information Science and an associate professor in the department of geographical sciences at the University of Maryland.

Bea Stotzer is the CEO of NEW Capital.

Zulema Valdez is a professor of sociology at the University of California, Merced.

Ruth E. Zambrana is a professor of women's studies; the director at the Consortium on Race, Gender, and Ethnicity; and an ADVANCE fellow at the University of Maryland.

Index

www.ingramcontent.com/pod-product-compliance
Lightning Source LLC
Chambersburg PA
CBHW061001220326
41599CB00023B/3788